WARNING: CLIMBING IS A SPORT WHERE YOU MAY BE SERIOUSLY INJURED OR DIE.
READ THIS BEFORE YOU USE THIS BOOK.

This guidebook is a compilation of unverified information gathered from many different climbers. The author cannot assure the accuracy of any of the information in this book, including the topos and route descriptions, the difficulty ratings, and the protection ratings. These may be incorrect or misleading and it is impossible for any one author to climb all the routes to confirm the information about each route. Also, ratings of climbing difficulty and danger are always subjective and depend on the physical characteristics (for example, height), experience, technical ability, confidence and physical fitness of the climber who supplied the rating. Additionally, climbers who achieve first ascents sometimes underrate the difficulty or danger of the climbing route out of fear of being ridiculed if a climb is later down-rated by subsequent ascents. Therefore, be warned that you must exercise your own judgment on where a climbing route goes, its difficulty and your ability to safely protect yourself from the risks of rock climbing. Examples of some of these risks are: falling due to technical difficulty or due to natural hazards such as holds breaking, falling rock, climbing equipment dropped by other climbers, hazards of weather and lightning, your own equipment failure, and failure of fixed protection.

You should not depend on any information gleaned from this book for your personal safety; your safety depends on your own good judgment, based on experience and a realistic assessment of your climbing ability. If you have any doubt as to your ability to safely climb a route described in this book, do not attempt it.

The following are some ways to make your use of this book safer:

1. **CONSULTATION:** You should consult with other climbers about the difficulty and danger of a particular climb prior to attempting it. Most local climbers are glad to give advice on routes in their area and we suggest that you contact locals to confirm ratings and safety of particular routes and to obtain first-hand information about a route chosen from this book.

2. **INSTRUCTION:** Most climbing areas have local climbing instructors and guides available. We recommend that you engage an instructor or guide to learn safety techniques and to become familiar with the routes and hazards of the areas described in this book. Even after you are proficient in climbing safely, occasional use of a guide is a safe way to raise your climbing standard and learn advanced techniques.

3. **FIXED PROTECTION:** Many of the routes in this book use bolts and pitons which are permanently placed in the rock. Because of variances in the manner of placement, weathering, metal fatigue, the quality of the metal used, and many other factors, these fixed protection pieces should always be considered suspect and should always be backed up by equipment that you place yourself. Never depend for your safety on a single piece of fixed protection because you never can tell whether it will hold weight.

Be aware of the following specific potential hazards which could arise in using this book:

1. **MISDESCRIPTIONS OF ROUTES:** If you climb a route and you have a doubt as to where the route may go, you should not go on unless you are sure that you can go that way safely. Route descriptions and topos in this book may be inaccurate or misleading.

2. **INCORRECT DIFFICULTY RATING:** A route may, in fact be more difficult than the rating indicates. Do not be lulled into a false sense of security by the difficulty rating.

3. **INCORRECT PROTECTION RATING:** If you climb a route and you are unable to arrange adequate protection from the risk of falling through the use of fixed pitons or bolts and by placing your own protection devices, do not assume that there is adequate protection available higher just because the route protection rating indicates the route is not an "X" or an "R" rating. Every route is potentially an "X" (a fall may be deadly), due to the inherent hazards of climbing, including, for example, failure of fixed protection, your own equipment's failure, or improper use of climbing equipment.

THERE ARE NO WARRANTIES, WHETHER EXPRESS OR IMPLIED, THAT THIS GUIDEBOOK IS ACCURATE OR THAT THE INFORMATION CONTAINED IN IT IS RELIABLE. THERE ARE NO WARRANTIES OF FITNESS FOR A PARTICULAR PURPOSE OR THAT THIS GUIDE IS MERCHANTABLE. YOUR USE OF THIS BOOK INDICATES YOUR ASSUMPTION OF THE RISK THAT IT MAY CONTAIN ERRORS AND IS AN ACKNOWLEDGMENT OF YOUR OWN SOLE RESPONSIBILITY FOR YOUR CLIMBING SAFETY.

This book is for my dad.
He shared his love of the Oregon Cascades,
and gave me the freedom to follow my own path.

ACKNOWLEDGMENTS

I BEGAN THIS PROJECT in 1988, filled with optimism that I'd crank out the finished product within a few months. During these years, the Berlin Wall fell, and the Soviet Union crumbled, but my Smith Rock guide still wasn't finished. After four years of telling everyone my guidebook would be out "next spring," I'm surprised anyone still listened.

At first, I assumed that I'd done all the research during my seventeen years of exploring every nook and cranny of the Smith Rock region. Putting it down on paper seemed only a minor diversion. This "minor diversion" turned into the biggest project I'd ever embarked on. If I'd tried to write this book alone, relying totally on my limited knowledge, I never could have done justice to the area. Fortunately, dozens of climbers came to my aid – because of them this book is finally complete.

I've been especially fortunate to have Bruce Adams take most of the photos for this guide. Bruce's work adds greatly to the quality of the book. Jim Ramsey offered his insights into the early history of the region, and Kevin Pogue steered me through the geology section. I also relied heavily on the state park information that Ranger Doug Crispin kindly provided.

Several climbers carefully read the text, offering helpful comments and spotting errors I'd glanced over dozens of times. I'd especially like to thank the following individuals, who went out of their way to help me: Chuck Buzzard, Tom Egan, Jeff Frizzell and Jeff Thomas.

I've had help from so many others that it's impossible to thank everyone. Those who made valuable contributions include Jim Anglin, Mike Barbitta, Kent Benesch, Dan Carlson, Mark Cartier, Jim Davis, Eric Freden, Chris Grover, Tom Heins, Bob McGown, Sean Olmstead, Tim Olson, Mike Pajunas, Doug Phillips, Mike Puddy, John Reed, John Rich, Brooke Sandahl, Mike Steele and Mike Volk. I apologize to anyone I've overlooked – hopefully seeing your comment used in the book will serve as a thank you.

A special thanks goes to George Meyers, who weathered my early procrastinations with an amazing display of patience; his efforts brought the book to life. Finally, I give thanks to my wife, JoAnn. More than anyone else, she encouraged me when I got frustrated with the immensity of the task.

For the last few years, I've spent every free moment working on this guide, living only for the day I finished it. It's funny, but now that I'm finally done, I'm reluctant to let it go. Smith Rock is such an ever-changing place that the moment the ink dries, this guide will be out of date. I've tried to include first ascents up to the last possible minute, but already a few climbs have missed the deadline, and couldn't be included. These include **Five-Gallon Buckets** (5.8), left of **Light on the Path**, and **J.T.'s Route** (5.10b), left of **Fred on Air**. Of course, tomorrow's new route won't be included anywhere in the book, but that's what future editions are for. To help make that next edition better, please send any corrections or new route information to me, in care of Chockstone Press.

Climber's Guide

to

Smith Rock

Climber's Guide

—— to ——

Smith Rock

Alan Watts

Chockstone Press
Evergreen, Colorado

Cover photo: Russell Erickson on Chain Reaction, 5.12, by Greg Epperson.

ISBN 0-934641-18-8

Published and Distributed by:
Chockstone Press, Inc.
Post Office Box 3505
Evergreen, CO 80439

PREFACE

THIS GUIDEBOOK CAPS my seventeen years of impassioned involvement with Smith Rock. I've seen Smith evolve from the neighborhood crag to an international hot spot, and throughout the years my fascination has never wavered. I've spent some of the best moments of my life scrambling on those colorful walls towering above the Crooked River. In writing this guide, I hope to give something back to the area that continues to give me so much.

Since the last guidebook came out in 1983, Smith climbing changed dramatically. With hundreds of new routes, and skyrocketing popularity, the demand for a new climbing guide grew each year. To fill the void, a series of topo guides hit the market. The first, error-ridden efforts were by non-locals, who drew upon their limited Smith experience to earn a quick buck. These guides confused everyone, until Dan Carlson stepped in with the first of his annual series of *Smith Rock Route Finders*. His guides were much more accurate and fulfilled a need, but he intentionally limited the scope to only the best-known climbs.

An area with Smith's diversity and popularity deserved a complete guide, so I started working on this book in the summer of 1988. Two years of half-hearted efforts, interspersed with long binges of climbing, only scratched the surface of the project. Finally getting serious, I hung-up my La Sportivas and began the final push in September of 1990. Twenty months later, I emerged from my office, bleary-eyed and overweight, but with the finished product in hand.

Anyone who climbs at Smith Rock knows it deserves special treatment, and I've done my best to do justice to the area. I've decided against including only selected climbs, favoring a complete guide for two reasons. First, only a complete listing conveys the history of the area: What was a breakthrough route 20 years ago might be forgotten today. Second, climbers tend to congregate in the same place, waiting in line for the most popular climbs while ignoring little-known routes around the corner. I hope this guide will alleviate, rather than add to the overcrowding problem, as climbers explore new areas.

By nature, a climbing guide isn't a book you'll read breathlessly from cover to cover. Route descriptions make painfully dry reading, but I've tried to add a little spice here and there. In covering the climbs, I've combined the strong points of both topo and text guides. A topo or photo provides essential information that words could never convey, but they give no insight into the subtle nuances and history that make each route unique. Therefore, I've used text to complement the visual aids. I've also included extended essays on Smith Rock history and ethics. Through it all, I hope you'll gain some insight into why Smith commands such a hold on everyone climbing here.

My involvement with Smith Rock goes back as far as I can remember. Raised just 20 miles north in the small town of Madras, Smith started as nothing more than a Sunday picnic area to me. My dad did some exploring in the late 50s and early 60s and his love for climbing passed over to me at an early age. When I first climbed at Smith in 1975, the area had scores of routes, and a 40-year history. I eagerly entered the scene, yet only followed the path of others.

By the early 80s, totally enthralled with Smith, I quit school and devoted myself to developing whatever potential the crags held. I had plenty of ambition, and coincidentally I arrived at the right time, with the right bag of tricks. It took several years (though it seemed like overnight) before the park was transformed into a destination area. With Smith plastered across magazine covers around the world, debates raged about the ethics of our local crag. Understandably, the whole atmosphere of the place changed dramatically.

There are times when I truly miss the old days, when a few of us had the park to ourselves. We'd place bets on when – or if – anybody would ever come here, as we picked one plum after another. Now and then, I'll find myself out there totally alone, and I'll recall the righteous devotion that characterized my younger years growing up at Smith. But, fortunately, times change. Change is good for climbing, and essential for the development of any discipline. The future for Smith Rock holds many mysteries, as the hard routes of today become warm-ups tomorrow, and the climbs of the 80s fade into memories. Yet despite what the future brings, I feel fortunate that I was part of that era of Smith history. I simply could not imagine my life without my exploits on those crumbly walls and dusty trails.

Alan Watts
April 2, 1992

TABLE OF CONTENTS

Smith Rock's main climbing area.

INTRODUCTION

WITHIN A FEW MONTHS during 1986, an unknown climbing area with the undistinguished name of Smith Rock rose like a rocket to the top of the U.S. climbing scene. Almost overnight, these Central Oregon crags became a major destination for climbers throughout the world. The techniques used to develop Smith Rock had considerable influence on the birth of sport climbing in this country, and fueled the ethical debates of the era. Today, Smith remains at the forefront, and many consider it the best sport climbing area in the country.

Despite all the attention, few climbers appreciate the diversity of Smith Rock. Best known are the dozens of climbs at the upper end of the spectrum – despite recent developments elsewhere, no area in the country boasts as large a selection of difficult routes. But Smith offers more than steep, tendon straining lines. Balancing the scales are dozens of moderate routes, making Smith an excellent place to learn how to climb. While the famous routes of the Dihedrals and Morning Glory Wall attract most of the attention, the climbing experience goes much deeper for those willing to leave the mainstream. A collection of modern and traditional routes – on two distinctly different rock types – awaits anyone willing to do a little hiking.

The biggest surprise for many first-time visitors is Smith's unique beauty. The Crooked River lazily winds its way through the canyon, cutting a path through the multi-colored cliffs and spires – below a typically blue sky. To the west, the snow-capped volcanoes of the Cascade Range rise on the horizon, above the flat checkerboard of irrigated plains. Popular for decades with hikers, birdwatchers, and photographers, the scenic beauty alone makes Smith worth visiting.

While Smith Rock would surely grace postcards and calendars even if no one climbed here, it's the brilliant routes that gave the area worldwide recognition. For the climber, Smith is a paradise. While the traditionalist will find many naturally protected routes, the convenience and gymnastic appeal of the bolted sport climbs attract most of the visitors. A dry, moderate climate adds to the allure, making climbing feasible year round. Most of the climbing in the region lies within the boundaries of Smith Rock State Park. A full-time ranger oversees this 623-acre playground, living here year-round. Unlike many other areas in the country, the relationship between the climbers and the owners is one of cooperation rather than conflict. The State Parks of Oregon protect the scenic beauty and wildlife, but they have no intentions of curtailing the use of Smith Rock to climbers. As activity surged during the 80s, the park service chose not to regulate the sport. Instead, they planned a way to accommodate the increasing number of visitors. This situation is rare in the United States, as stringent rules burden many other climbing areas. If the climbing community continues to manage the development of Smith Rock wisely, this progressive policy should remain intact.

Aside from its liberal attitude toward climbing, the park service maintains an excellent system of trails, and recently opened a new campground, complete with hot showers. The consideration the park service gives climbers greatly adds to the Smith Rock experience. All visitors should return the favor by cooperating with the rangers.

HOW TO GET THERE

Located in the high desert of Central Oregon, Smith Rock State Park sits two miles east of Highway
97 near Terrebonne. To the south are the larger communities of Redmond and Bend. Oregon's major
cities of Portland, Eugene and Salem are two-and-a-half hours west, beyond the Cascade mountains.

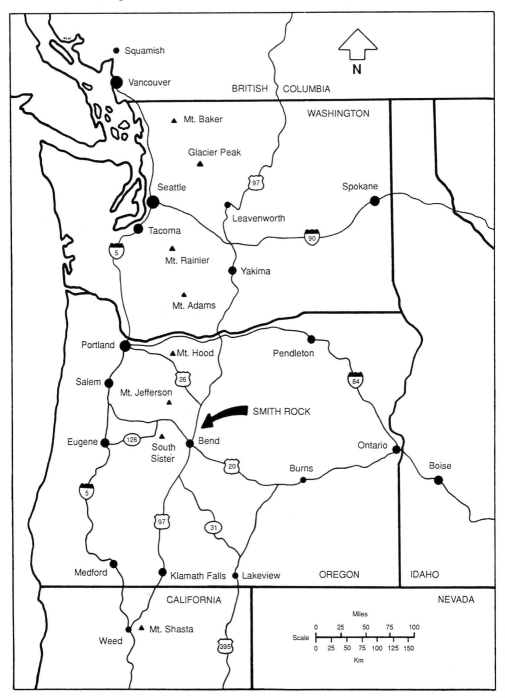

Since any state road map shows Smith Rock, you'll have no problem finding your way here. I've given approximate driving times from several U.S. climbing areas below:

Lake Tahoe	8 hours
City of Rocks	9 hours
Yosemite	11 hours
Squamish	11 hours
American Fork	12 hours
Joshua Tree	20 hours
Boulder	20 hours
Hueco Tanks	35 hours

Once in Terrebonne, signs mark the turns on the final three miles of the journey. If you're arriving by bus, Greyhound operates daily service into the area. The nearest terminal is in Redmond, but you can ask the driver to stop in Terrebonne. With luck, you can hitch a ride into the park – otherwise, expect a 45-minute hike to the campground.

If you're traveling by air, fly to the pint-sized Redmond Municipal Airport, which is 10 miles south of Smith Rock. United Express provides service from San Francisco and Portland, while Horizon Air serves the region from Portland and Seattle. Typically, you can fly into Redmond for the same fare as a trip to Portland. Avis, Hertz and Budget rental cars serve the airport if you want to rent a vehicle.

TOPOGRAPHY

The Smith Rock region lies along the western edge of Oregon's high desert, near the geographic center of the state. To the east are the foothills of the Ochoco Mountains, and the endless desert of eastern Oregon. To the west, sparsely-vegetated plains rise gently to the forests and mountains of the Cascade Range. These snow-capped volcanoes stand prominently on the horizon, separating the region from the heavily-populated western part of the state. From north to south, you can see Mt. Hood (11,239 feet), Mt. Jefferson (10,497 feet), Three-Fingered Jack (7,841 feet), Mt. Washington (7,749 feet), Black Butte (6,436 feet), North Sister (10,094 feet), Middle Sister (10,054 feet), South Sister (10,385 feet), Broken Top (9,175 feet) and Mt. Bachelor (9,065 feet). The Smith Rock region sits along the southwest base of a series of rounded buttes. The highest of these peaks is Gray Butte (5,108 feet), rising four miles northeast of the parking area. To the east of the campground (2,850 feet), the highest point of the obvious, road-scarred hillside stands at 4,230 feet. Lined with juniper trees, ponderosa pine and sagebrush, the aptly-named Crooked River cuts a tortuous path through the steep scree slopes and towering cliffs of tuff. The river originates 60 miles to the east in the Ochoco Mountains and eventually joins the Deschutes River on its path to the Columbia River and the Pacific Ocean.

CLIMBING

To say that Smith Rock became a worldwide destination because of the quality of the rock would be wrong. Amazingly, Smith rose to such prominence despite the rock quality, not because of it. Except for a few sections of perfect stone, the tuff is soft and often crumbly. Paradoxically, these walls offer a remarkable collection of the best sport routes in America. Most climbs contained some loose rock and required cleaning before the first ascent. Fortunately, once thoroughly scrubbed, the rock almost magically transforms into high-quality stone. Still, even after thousands of ascents, seemingly solid holds occasionally will snap. Because of this, soloing at Smith is an extremely dangerous pursuit. After all, holds break no matter how good you are. Although there are routes up to 600 feet high, the most popular lines are one pitch long. The Smith sport climber considers a long route anything you can't lower off of with a single rope.

The basalt of the Gorge adds to the diversity of Smith climbing. Apart from its volcanic origin, the basalt is about as far removed from the tuff as possible. When you step into the Gorge, you'll feel you've left Smith, and arrived at a completely different area. The columnar basalt offers jam cracks, stemming corners, and gorgeous arêtes on flawless rock. As with the tuff, the basalt hosts both bolted sport routes and traditional lines.

Because of the relative isolation of Smith Rock, the climbing scene developed slowly. Little more than 100,000 people live within a 100-mile radius of the park, so few climbers grew up nearby. While the seclusion slowed the early development, it helped build a tight-knit scene. Eventually, the standards in the park boomed, owing to the fact that the regulations and red tape strangling other areas never plagued Smith Rock. Today, Central Oregon supports a strong climbing community, based mainly in Bend.

CLIMATE

Despite the common portrayal of Oregon as a drenched rain forest, Smith Rock sits in the midst of a semi-arid desert. The region enjoys mostly sunny days throughout the year, and the four distinct seasons bring refreshingly different weather patterns. The volcanoes of the Cascade range provide a natural barrier against the onslaught of storms from the Pacific. While rain soaks western Oregon, little moisture falls on the east side of the mountains. Central Oregon averages less than nine inches of rain per year, so you'll rarely get washed out here. As the legend goes, it never rains at Smith Rock.

While rain rarely spoils a visit, the temperature extremes might. The summertime highs sometimes hit 100 degrees, while the mercury can dip below zero during the winter. The best time to visit Smith Rock is the spring and fall, with April, May and October having the most consistently good weather. While highly erratic, February and March typically make better months for extreme redpoint attempts. The shorter fall season begins in mid-September, and ends abruptly by the end of November.

I've compiled a month-by-month chart showing the 30-year averages of aspects of Redmond weather, so you'll get an idea of what to expect when you arrive. Average high temperatures in the canyon are at least five degrees warmer than Redmond, and the extremes vary 20 degrees from the averages.

	HIGH	LOW	PRECIP.	SNOW
JANUARY	42.4	21.4	1.05 inches	6.6 inches
FEBRUARY	47.3	25.0	.74 inches	3.4 inches
MARCH	53.9	27.3	.54 inches	1.3 inches
APRIL	62.4	31.1	.52 inches	.7 inches
MAY	69.1	36.9	.95 inches	trace
JUNE	74.7	42.1	1.07 inches	trace
JULY	85.0	46.5	.33 inches	none
AUGUST	82.8	44.5	.25 inches	none
SEPTEMBER	76.4	39.7	.46 inches	none
OCTOBER	65.3	33.8	.69 inches	.2 inches
NOVEMBER	52.0	27.8	.85 inches	1 inch
DECEMBER	44.9	25.2	1.05 inches	3.2 inches
YEAR TOTAL	63.0	33.4	8.50 inches	16.4 inches

Despite the extremes of the seasons, climbers visit Smith Rock every month of the year. If you're lucky, you'll find acceptable conditions during the off-season. Typically, for instance, the hottest months of the summer have very low humidity, and you can find shade throughout the day. The winter makes a poorer choice as the days are short and the nights cold. Even in the best winter conditions, you can climb for only five hours during the middle of the day. Still, anyone living nearby relishes the clear days so common in the winter, since the sun bakes any south-facing crag.

Welcome to Smith Rock.   Photo: Alan Watts

CAMPING

Until recently, Smith lacked a convenient campground. This changed in the summer of 1991, when the park service opened a walk-in camping area south of the old bivouac site. A 50-car parking area, and well-maintained showers and sanitary facilities greatly improved the camping situation. The $2 charge per person each night includes unlimited use of the showers.

The entrance to the camping area is left off Crooked River Drive about 100 yards beyond Rockhard. After signing in at the self-registration booth, and checking the bulletin board for current regulations, you can find a campsite in the trees. Anyone sleeping in a vehicle will likely get booted, since the park service doesn't allow this. A state park rule limits your stay to two weeks, but is enforced only to get rid of troublemakers. With good behavior, you can stay for months at a time, but the campground is a very poor choice if you're into cranking music for a redpoint celebration. Your party will aggravate relations with nearby residents, give climbers a bad name and get you kicked out of the camping area – all in the same evening.

A carefully-constructed trail leads directly into the canyon from the camping area, passing behind Rope De Dope Rock then circling to the bridge below Picnic Lunch Wall. Within the next several years, a planned second bridge near the Phoenix Area will shorten the approach to the most popular crags.

GEOLOGY

The best-known and most popular climbing at Smith takes place on the multi-colored cliffs and spires of tuff. The Smith Rock tuff is one of several volcanic rock types comprising the Gray Butte Complex. The tuff originated in early Miocene time, between 17 to 19 million years ago, when gaseous, silica-rich magma found its way to the surface somewhere near today's park. Relieved of the pressure of overlying rocks, the gas trapped within the magma expanded, producing explosive eruptions that shattered the magma into small fragments. Erupted into the air, the fragments of molten rock solidified into volcanic ash and formed incandescent clouds. The hot ash and rock fragments from the explosions accumulated as thick deposits near the site of the eruptions. Silica-rich magma later intruded the tuff deposits, feeding additional explosive eruptions. These intrusions cooled to form the shattered rhyolite dikes that make up Shiprock and portions of the Smith Rock group. As the tuff cooled, shrinkage and lithification produced parallel sets of joints that have weathered to form the crack systems in the Dihedrals and other areas. Over time, chemical reactions slowly altered the Smith Rock tuffs, converting the original glassy volcanic ash into the clay minerals that make up the rock today.

Much of the tuff at Smith Rock contains angular fragments of rhyolite or pumice called xenoliths. Incorporated into the tuff during the explosive eruptions, the xenoliths consist of stray fragments of older rocks. Typically finer-grained and less altered than the tuff, they weather less readily. This differential weathering causes them to jut out, producing the knobby face climbs so popular at Smith Rock. The pockets, called vesicles, are the remnants of bubbles of trapped gas that accumulated in the tuff immediately after its eruption. They range from bathtub-sized buckets to one finger pockets.

The quality of Smith Rock tuff for climbing varies dramatically throughout the park. The darker rock generally is more solid due to a greater concentration of cementing mineral oxides in the outer layers. The process that forms this tough outer crust, called case hardening, distinguishes the best of the rock from the softer junk. The red-brown color is primarily the result of the oxidation of iron.

The other rock type of interest to climbers is the basalt of the Gorge. Erupted 1.2 million years ago from the Newberry volcano south of Bend, highly-fluid lava flowed down the valley of the ancestral Crooked River. This basalt flow filled the canyon between the Smith Rock tuff and the 4.5-million-year-old Deschutes Formation basalt. The Crooked River then slowly eroded the Newberry basalts, producing the present-day canyon. As is typical of many basalt climbing areas, the routes generally follow vertical columnar cooling joints.

ENVIRONMENTAL IMPACT

The delicate environment of Smith contrasts with the rugged majesty of the cliffs. Its popularity during the last few years has taken its toll on the park, but fortunately Smith remains relatively unspoiled. The park service places a top priority on protecting the environment, and most climbers and visitors treat the area with respect. Everyone who climbs at Smith puts a strain on the environment, whether they leave behind chalk marks, slings, or boot rubber. Yet it takes only common sense, and a small amount of effort, to preserve the natural beauty and wildlife.

Considering the heavy traffic, Smith is surprisingly litter-free. Most of the junk thrown on the trails by tourists gets picked up by the first climber to come along. Still, most of us are guilty from time to time. Climbers who wouldn't think of leaving behind their Gatorade bottles and Powerbar wrappers sometimes throw wads of tape, and snuff out their cigarette butts in the dirt.

A growing problem over the past few years has been the lack of any sanitary facilities in the main climbing area. Two chemical toilets sit in the trees just before the bridge, but when the urge strikes, a ten minute dash back to the toilets is out of the question. The most secluded boulders in the main area reek of human waste, and toilet paper litters the hillside. Fortunately, the park service plans to install a toilet below the Dihedrals, and this should lessen the severity of the problem. Meanwhile, this predicament will only worsen.

The hillsides above the river are extremely fragile and easily destroyed by erosion. Nothing detracts more from the beauty of Smith than trail-scarred hillsides. Since the park service constructed a series of staircased trails, many areas are in better shape than they were a decade ago. Please stay on the established trails whenever possible, and resist the temptation to barrel straight down to the river.

Wildlife is a non-renewable resource that must be protected. Smith supports a wide variety of animal life, including mule deer, muskrats, cottontail rabbits and porcupines. You'll even see downed trees along the river with the telltale tooth-marks of the beaver population. The reptiles in the area include sagebrush lizards, bull snakes, and a few rattlesnakes. For bird watchers, Smith is among the best places in Central Oregon: Canadian geese and great blue herons make their homes near the water. Golden and bald eagles, prairie falcons and red-tailed hawks nest on the cliffs high above the river.

The park prohibits climbing near active nesting sites a few months each year, and during those times, you'll need to avoid nearby routes. Adult birds scare easily, putting their eggs and newly-hatched offspring in danger of death from hypothermia. There are active nests on the northwest face of the Smith Rock Group, near the Red Ryder Buttress and the Brain Salad Surgery gully. The Federal Eagle Act of 1978 sets these standards, so you'll get in a heap of trouble if you don't respect the rules. Ensuring nesting success for Smith's birds of prey is a major management goal of the park service. If we threaten their existence by plundering nests, we'll place the future of Smith climbing in jeopardy. For a list of closed areas, refer to the campground bulletin board or talk with the ranger.

Private land surrounds much of Smith Rock State Park, and many people make their homes nearby. Please respect their right to privacy by staying off their land, and keeping down the noise. An impromptu rock concert in the parking lot during the 70s damaged relations between climbers and locals for years. Several residents resent Smith's popularity and the associated mob scenes in the parking lot. The locals have a valid complaint when boisterous, drunken climbers wander into their backyards.

The park service has no regulations governing bolting, first ascents and other climbing activities. Instead they leave these decisions to the consensus opinions of local climbers. For a detailed discussion on the impact of climbing at Smith Rock, see the section on ethics.

GUIDE SERVICE

The Smith Rock Climbing School offers year-round instruction, and guided ascents. The office sits hidden in the trees behind the day-use parking lots, with a sign marking the entrance off Crooked River Drive. The school offers classes March through November, for all levels of climbers. They place an emphasis on small groups, with the instruction tailored to meet the needs of the students. For a brochure, write or call: Smith Rock Climbing School, P.O. Box 955, Terrebonne, OR 97754 (503) 548-0749

CLIMBING STORES

For 25 years, the rustic **Rockhard** store (formerly **Juniper Junction**) has greeted anyone visiting the park. For convenience, Rockhard can't be beat – it's just a quarter-mile from the parking lot. The storefront features Kate's Saloon – a movie set from a John Wayne and Katherine Hepburn movie filmed locally in the early 70s. Originally a gift/ice cream shop, Rockhard started selling climbing gear when the sport boomed. Today, they offer a full selection, along with their world-famous huckleberry ice cream.

Terrebonne's **Redpoint Climbers Supply** is the most complete climbing store in the area. They stock every piece of climbing gear you'll ever need, including the La Sportiva shoes so necessary for Smith's hardest routes. The owner, Dan Carlson, maintains a notebook to keep track of new routes and report bad bolts, loose blocks, and other dangers.

Although more of a nordic ski shop, the small **Tri Mountain Sports** store in downtown Bend also sells a limited selection of climbing gear. Throughout the seventies, they were the only place in Central Oregon to buy equipment. It also stocks a full selection of clothing, boots, packs and mountaineering gear.

EMERGENCY INFORMATION

In case of a medical emergency, dial 911 from the pay phone at Juniper Junction, or stop at the ranger headquarters immediately to the south. The nearest hospital is the Central Oregon District Hospital (548-8131) in Redmond. They have an emergency room doctor on staff 24 hours a day.

OTHER ACTIVITIES AT SMITH

Smith Rock offers alternatives for the outdoor athlete other than climbing. Mountain biking, whitewater rafting, hiking and fishing are all popular.

Mountain biking grows in popularity every year at Smith. State parks officials have a shaky view on the future of the sport, so it's best to avoid the most heavily-populated regions. The best rides climb up and over the Burma Road. Beyond are miles of back roads that make excellent mountain bike excursions.

During high-water conditions, the Crooked River provides a challenge for the expert kayaker and whitewater rafter. Unfortunately, chemicals from farmers fields pollute the enticing waters of the Crooked River. You'd be wise to resist temptation and not swim here – especially if you have any open wounds. The river supports a measly fish population, so you'd be better off looking into some of Central Oregon's better fishing spots. Hunting is illegal – if you're caught, your next vacation stop will be the local jail.

Smith also makes a wonderful place to go hiking. A loop trail starts at the bridge and winds downstream along the Crooked River before cutting uphill beyond Monkey Face. The trail continues to the top of Staender Ridge, then heads back down to join the river trail. A shorter hike follows a path up Misery Ridge, ending with an excellent view of Monkey Face and the Cascade peaks to the west.

OTHER PLACES OF INTEREST IN CENTRAL OREGON

Central Oregon ranks among the top recreational areas in the country. The lure of the nearby Cascade mountains, the Deschutes National Forest and the Deschutes River are largely responsible for the incredible growth of the region in the past few years. If you're tired of rock climbing, you might want to spend a rest day taking in some of Central Oregon's beautiful scenery.

The Mt. Bachelor ski area, 20 miles west of Bend, dominates the local economy. Acclaimed for its ideal climate, clear dry air and abundant powder, Bachelor attracts hundreds of thousands of skiers each year. The ski season typically begins in November and can run into July. The 3,200 vertical feet of diversified terrain suits skiers of all abilities. Nine chairlifts cover the slopes, with the summit chair rising to the top of the 9,065-foot volcano. You can ride the summit lift throughout the summer to get an effortless view of the spectacular Central Oregon country. Mt. Bachelor and the surrounding area also offer outstanding nordic skiing. Since Bend revolves around the skiing industry, there's no shortage of information about where to go.

To escape the heat of Smith in midsummer, you might want to climb a Cascade volcano. The easiest routes vary from long hikes to moderate rock-and-snow climbs. The rock quality typically makes the tuff of Smith seem as solid as Yosemite granite, but the mountains are stunningly beautiful and a great way to cool off. If you're looking for more of a challenge, there are dozens of routes of varying difficulties. Mt. Washington, in particular, offers some long climbs on tolerable rock. Jeff Thomas' *Oregon High,* found in local climbing shops, provides all the information you'll need.

Water sports are another popular summertime activity in Central Oregon. The rapids of the Deschutes River offer excellent whitewater rafting. The best locations are upstream from Bend, and down river below Warm Springs, north of Madras. Several local guide services cater to the sport. Renowned for its world-class windsurfing, the Columbia River Gorge stretches between Oregon and Washington just two hours to the north. Nearer to Smith, Haystack Reservoir (twelve miles north on Highway 97) and Elk Lake (30 miles outside Bend on the Cascades Lake Highway) are good board-sailing spots when the wind blows.

SURROUNDING TOWNS

The Smith Rock campground makes a fine place to sleep, but most climbers eventually grow tired of hanging out in the dirt and venture out to sample the amenities of Central Oregon. Within thirty miles are the towns of Bend, Redmond, Terrebonne, Sisters, Madras and Prineville. Apart from

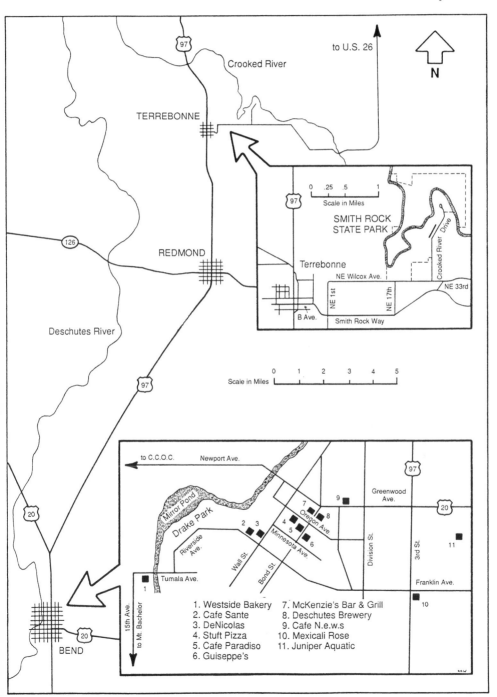

1. Westside Bakery   7. McKenzie's Bar & Grill
2. Cafe Sante   8. Deschutes Brewery
3. DeNicolas   9. Cafe N.e.w.s
4. Stuft Pizza   10. Mexicali Rose
5. Cafe Paradiso   11. Juniper Aquatic
6. Guiseppe's

recreation, the main industries of these communities are farming and forest products. Climbers visiting the area rarely travel into Sisters, Madras and Prineville, as larger towns are nearer the park. In this section, I'll briefly describe the highlights of the three nearest towns. I've listed a few of my favorite eating places, and other restaurants popular with local climbers. The following code will keep those on a budget from getting in over their heads:

$	Under $5 per person
$$	$5 to $10 per person
$$$	Over $10 per person

For all the information you'd ever want about the region, drop by the Central Oregon Welcome Center along Highway 97 on the north side of Bend, or write for free information:

Bend Chamber of Commerce   Redmond Chamber of Commerce
63085 N Highway 97   427 S.W. 7th Street
Bend, OR 97701   Redmond, OR 97756
(503) 382-3221   (503) 923-5191

TERREBONNE

This wide spot in the road is the gateway to Smith Rock. Home to 400 people, Terrebonne has flourished during the past few years, reaping the economic benefits of its proximity to Smith. There isn't much here, but if you're content with the basics, you'll find everything you need. Since it's just three miles from the campground, you typically can bum a ride to buy groceries.

LODGING

You'll find no overnight lodging in Terrebonne, so if you're tired of roughing it, you'll need to continue six miles further into Redmond.

RESTAURANTS

La Siesta $/$$ As a time-honored tradition with Smith climbers, be sure to sample this Mexican restaurant at least once during your stay. The support of climbers financed a recent move into a new, much-larger building. Reasonably priced, the selection of breakfasts and dinners are surprisingly tasty.

The Sun Spot $ This fast-food joint sits on the same lot as the original Ferguson's Market. You won't want to eat here if you're diet conscious, but they've got ice cream, decent breakfasts and good burgers.

NIGHT SPOTS

Terrebonne Jacks sits near Ferguson's Market. This genuine western tavern attracts scores of cowboys every weekend. Although the patrons should be used to it by now, you might want to think twice before venturing in wearing your hot pink lycra.

MISCELLANEOUS

Terrebonne revolves around **Ferguson's Market**. The new location at the north end of town doesn't match the small-town charm of the original, but it offers a full selection of groceries and snacks. Nearby are the **Terrebonne Post Office**, a **True Value Hardware Store** and **Redpoint Climbers Supply**.

REDMOND

Redmond, population 7,875, rests along Highway 97 six miles south of Terrebonne. With its full selection of motels, stores, restaurants and other facilities, Redmond is the best place to stock up on food and eat out when you don't want to travel into Bend. It's also the transportation center of Central Oregon with the Redmond Municipal Airport, and the nearest bus depot to Smith.

LODGING

Since Redmond is only a 10-minute drive from Smith, it's the best place to stay if you want to sleep in a bed instead of a tent. There are a dozen choices here, and you can count on spending an average of $45 per night for the typical room. At the low end of the scale, you can get a room with a double bed at **The Hub** on the north end of town, for $30 per night. They offer weekly rates at $175. At the other end of the spectrum, a room at the **Inn at Eagle Crest** costs $85 per night.

RESTAURANTS

While Redmond contains a more complete selection than Terrebonne, it lacks many high-quality restaurants. Still, it's close enough to Smith that most climbers come here when they want to eat out. You'll find the usual assortment of generic chains like **McDonalds, Burger King, Dairy Queen, Pizza Hut** and a **Subway** sandwich shop. The following choices are also popular with climbers. You can walk into any of these restaurants after a day of climbing without feeling out of place.

Sno-Cap Drive In $ Renowned for its massive burgers and locally-made ice cream, this fast food joint north of town is popular with binging climbers not concerned about clogging their arteries. Only a true glutton can down the Sno-Cap's infamous Power Pak in one sitting.

Golden Corral $/$$ This legendary place at the south end of town has stuffed thousands of climbers over the past decade. An all-you-can-eat menu features a massive salad bar, potato bar and ice cream bar, among other offerings. Most climbers get burnt out on the gluttony sessions, but others come back night after night to repeat the gorging ritual.

Chan's Restaurant $$ The best Chinese restaurant in town is on the south side of Redmond. Chan's serves a huge selection of entrees cooked in different styles, including Szechuan, Mandarin and Cantonese.

NIGHT SPOTS

Redmond is largely a western town, and all too often the bar-goers are rednecks living only for a good drunk every weekend. Eccentric climbers with wild hair, odd clothes and dangling earrings would be well-advised to travel into Bend to avoid getting the shit kicked out of them.

MISCELLANEOUS

Redmond offers the nearest banks, library, laundromat, hospital and movie theater to Smith Rock. A trip to the Cascade Swim Center near the Redmond High School provides a good break during a hot spell. This indoor pool, complete with jacuzzi and sauna, costs only $2 per visit. Nearby are the community tennis courts, and across town on the road to the airport sprawls an 18-hole public golf course.

BEND

As the recreational and economic hub of Central Oregon, Bend ranks among the fastest growing cities in the Northwest. Resting in the shadows of the Cascade mountains, 25 miles south of Smith, Bend makes the best choice when taking a day off from the rocks to sample the local color. Centered along the Deschutes River, the town stretches between the semi-arid desert to the east and the forests to the west. Since the community relies heavily on tourism, there are plenty of restaurants, motels, stores and parks. Despite a paucity of cultural opportunities, a young, athletic population makes Bend the most progressive town in the region.

LODGING

Bend offers a complete selection of motels, resorts and bed & breakfasts, although most non-camping climbers stay in Redmond to shorten the daily drive. Still, if the time you spend after a day on the rocks is as important as the climbing itself, you might want to stay here.

RESTAURANTS

You'll find dozens of dining choices in Bend, varying from the usual collection of forgettable chains to some delectable, high-priced cuisine. The following restaurants are among my favorites. They're casual and popular with the climbing crowd.

The Westside Bakery $ An extremely popular early-morning hang for Bend's climbers, the Westside features scrumptious breakfasts, lunches and pastries in a relaxed atmosphere.

DeNicola's $/$$ This small Italian food joint in downtown Bend has excellent pizza – sold by the slice. It's a popular lunch spot for many of Central Oregon's climbing types.

Cafe N.E.W.S. $/$$ A fashionable place for the young crowd, Cafe N.E.W.S. features food from the north, east, west, and south. You'll find savory, healthful food on one end of the spectrum, and decadently delicious desserts on the other. After eating, you can burn some calories with a game of ping pong.

Stuft Pizza $/$$ You'll find the best pizza in town at Stuft Pizza. The hand-thrown Sicilian-style pizza and other tasty offerings usually pack the place. Unfortunately, they don't deliver to the Smith Rock campground.

Cafe Sante $/$$ This small breakfast-and-lunch spot offers healthful food that appeals to climbers who care about what they eat. The creatively prepared selections are both good for you and undeniably scrumptious.

Giuseppe's Ristorante $$/$$$ For the best Italian food in Central Oregon, visit Giuseppe's. Hand-rolled fresh pasta, an extensive wine list and intimate atmosphere make it a good choice when you want to celebrate. You'll likely have to wait if you don't have a reservation (389-8899).

Mexicali Rose $$ An area favorite, Mexicali Rose sits at the intersection of Highway 97 and Franklin Street. Besides offering the best Mexican food in town, they stock a full bar featuring thirst-quenching margaritas.

NIGHT SPOTS

Central Oregon has a shortage of quality night life, and Bend is no exception. Still, as the largest town in the area, it offers more than Redmond or Terrebonne. You won't find much diversity in the music here, as the bars rarely book anything but country, rock and roll and the occasional blues band. The following places are popular with local climbers:

Deschutes Brewery & Public House Extremely trendy, the Brewery makes three varieties of traditional ale at their location on Bond Street. As a bonus, they serve excellent food. A band plays to a full house every Friday and Saturday night. The Brewery is smoke-free, so you won't have to choke on cigarette smoke.

McKenzie's Bar & Grill The Ore House located across the street from the Brewery, also packs them in every weekend. Food is served here as well as a fully-stocked bar – if beer alone won't quench your thirst. Dancing to live music is offered every Thursday, Friday and Saturday nights.

Cafe Paradiso This yuppie hang-out appeals to Bend's intellectual crowd. You can come here and play checkers or chess, or read their selection of magazines. They don't serve any real food, but they've got excellent desserts and espresso, along with a selection of wine and imported beers.

GYMS

While Bend has a good selection of gyms, there's a curious lack of artificial climbing walls. After all, Bend is home to three of the country's major wall manufacturers (Entre Prises USA, Metolius and Vertical Concepts). The best choice for a climber's workout is **Central Oregon Community College.** Open to the public for a few hours in the evening, their facility contains a complete weight room and a small climbing wall. To check on the current schedule, call 385-5514.

If C.O.C.C. isn't open, you can train at the **Juniper Aquatic and Fitness Center.** They've got a small weight room, indoor and outdoor pool, sauna, jacuzzi and tennis courts. The tennis courts are free, but the pool and weight room cost $2 per person. There are other gyms in town, including the **Central Oregon Athletic Center** and **The Body Shop,** that charge a single use fee from $5 to $6.

HISTORY

BRIMMING WITH BREAKTHROUGH ascents, influential changes, and colorful individuals, Smith Rock has a long and vibrant history. While the dozens of extreme routes might attract most of the attention, Smith's development began decades before anyone heard of sport climbing. From the earliest days of bold scrambles on crumbling pinnacles, Smith slowly evolved to the bolted test pieces of today. Along the way, each generation learned from those who came before, adding their unique touches, then passing the torch to others. The role Smith played in U.S. climbing would have been far less significant if these pioneers hadn't laid the foundations.

I feel that many climbers don't understand that the easy cracks they scoff at today gave rise to the overhanging faces that now capture their attention. But these relics were stepping stones, every bit as significant when first climbed as the hardest lines are today. A detailed history of Smith Rock would make a fine book in its own right. Unfortunately, I'm forced to touch briefly on only the best and most influential climbs. I've tried not to turn this section into a tiresome chronology of first ascents. To me, the people, attitudes, and ethics that shaped Smith climbing are far more fascinating.

Being a part of Smith history has given me a first-hand perspective on the growth of the area, but it also handicaps me. It's hard to stand outside my involvement and look at it without a strong bias. On one hand, I don't want to dwell on my role, and on the other, I can't completely ignore it. I've tried to tread this precarious line between egoism and humility carefully, but I've inevitably wavered from side to side.

Patrick Edlinger on White Wedding (5.13d/14a).   Photo: Brooke Sandahl

PRE-CLIMBING HISTORY

Thousands of years before the drilling of Smith's first bolt, Indian tribes passed through the region, camping and hunting along the banks of the Crooked River. Archaeologists believe that Native Americans came to Central Oregon more than 13,000 years ago. The arrowheads of Smith's earliest visitors are sometimes found on the hillsides above the river. The first white men who came through the region were trappers with the Hudson Bay Company, led by Peter Skeen Ogden, in 1825. They followed the Deschutes and Crooked Rivers upstream, fording the river a few miles upstream from today's park.

The origin of the Smith Rock name is subject more to local legend than fact. The most colorful story credits the name as a memorial to a soldier who was part of an army detachment sent to check on Indian problems. As the saga goes, soldier Smith only aggravated matters, and the angry Indians chased him to the top of a spire. Rather than meeting his fate at the hands of the fuming natives, he leapt to his death. Most likely, this oft-told tale was invented by someone searching for a lively explanation for Smith Rock's mundane name.

In reality, Smith Rock was named after Linn County Sheriff John Smith, who was later appointed the Indian agent at Warm Springs. A group of five explorers, travelling over the Santiam Pass in 1867, made a trip to what is now the Prineville area. They chronicled their journey in the *Albany State's Right Democrat*, and in describing Smith Rock, stated it was named for John Smith.

For the next several decades, Smith Rock was merely a local landmark for settlers who arrived in the late 1800s, and founded nearby towns. Coping with the hardships of settling new land, these pioneers had little reason to explore Smith Rock. But early in the century, a farmer homesteaded in the canyon. He built a house on the flat ground at the base of the Monument, and raised vegetables irrigated by canals cut from the Crooked River. He eventually gave up the idea, since the ground was so porous most of the water didn't make it to his sun-scorched crop. The road he built still cuts across the hillside below the turnaround, and the remnants of his home are nestled in the pines.

Shattering the quiet history of Smith Rock during the 1940s was a massive engineering project run by the U.S. Bureau of Reclamation. To serve the Madras/Culver region to the north, an irrigation canal was cut through the Smith Rock area. Workers tunneled directly through the hillside under Staender Ridge, and again through Indian Ridge. They also built an impressive bridge and siphon system to carry the water across the Gorge. A huge pumping station, just upstream from the basalt crags, drew excess water out of the Crooked River, forcing it uphill to the canal. The most visible by-product of the irrigation project is a switchbacked road cutting across the hillside north of the Marsupial Crags. Engineers nicknamed it the Burma Road, after the winding path linking Burma and China.

THE EARLY YEARS – 1935 TO 1959

The earliest climbers began exploring Smith Rock before World War II. The first recorded ascent occurred in 1935, when Johnny Bissell scaled the prominent Squaw Rock. Members of the WyEast Climbers, a group of progressive young mountaineers from the Portland area, visited Smith in May, 1936. We know nothing about what they climbed, but they surely scaled spires later attributed to others. A decade passed before anyone else chronicled their ascents. In 1946, Ross Petrie and Dave Pearson hiked into the canyon and climbed "anything with a summit," coming away with the first ascents of Shiprock, Independence Tower and Staender Summit. Petrie returned three years later with Dave Wagstaff and Bill Van Atta, scaling the bulbous pillar of the Poplar (5.7). In these early years, there were no local climbers – those visiting Smith drove over the mountains from the Willamette Valley. Understandably, the top climbers of the era turned their attention more to the Cascade peaks rather than the tuff of Smith.

This changed in the mid-fifties, as the first Smith Rock specialists entered the scene. Vivian and Gil Staender began visiting in 1955, climbing many spires on the ridge that today bears their name.

They pioneered Bette's Needles, Flattop, Rotten Crack, and new lines on nearby pinnacles. Unlike others, who visited Smith only out of curiosity, the Staenders focused their attention here. At the same time, Jim and Jerry Ramsey began exploring the area. Living nearby in Madras, the Ramsey brothers were Smith's first local climbers. With a variety of partners, including Alan Green and my dad, Jack Watts, they pioneered several moderate but dangerous routes to the top of the spires. While some of the pinnacles may have received earlier unrecorded ascents, the Staenders and Ramseys had the most impact on the future of Smith Rock. Through their efforts, the area became known to climbers throughout the state.

Although the number of routes increased manyfold during the fifties, there were no advancements in free climbing standards. This wasn't really a reflection on the caliber of the climbers, but instead a consequence of the prevailing attitude. Back then, all that mattered was the summit – there was no emphasis placed on pushing free-climbing levels. If getting to the top meant using an occasional aid move, shoulder stand, or scaling sordid rock – that was fine. The grades they gave their routes indicated more the degree of danger than the pure difficulty of the moves. If a route protected easily, it might receive a class 3 rating, even if it was really 5.6.

The activity in the 50s was focused in other places than today's popular areas. Climbers usually would approach the area along the canal, parking at the Burma Road. Understandably, the pinnacles of Staender Ridge and other nearby crags saw most of the attention. Since today's popular areas required a much longer approach, they received little attention.

THE SIXTIES

After years of only scattered activity, the sixties saw Smith's first "new route boom." But the start of the decade was significant for several reasons apart from first ascents. In 1960, the Oregon State Highway Department's park division created Smith Rock State Park. They built the picnic and sanitary facilities still in use today. The new park attracted people to the area that never before knew it existed. Soon after, Jim and Jerry Ramsey along with Vivian Staender, gathered together the loose ends in *A Climbers Guide to the Smith Rocks,* the first guidebook to the area. Impossible to find today, this classic guide appeared in the 1962 Mazama Annual, and first brought attention to Smith climbing. It likely had more to do with the rapid growth in the early 60s than anything else.

Fittingly, the decade began with the first ascent of Monkey Face, by Dave Bohn, Jim Fraser and Vivian Staender on January 1, 1960. Spread over several wintery days, this ascent made a big ripple among the few local climbers. Even though they drilled aid bolts the entire way, the **Pioneer Route** still broke new ground. It marked the beginning of the aid climbing era that dominated Smith for more than a decade.

While Monkey Face stole most of the attention, the most impressive effort occurred quietly the next year, as Jim Ramsey made the first free ascent of The Awl. His ascent was a visionary accomplishment in that it broke with the summit-only tradition of the time. After climbing the spire on aid, Ramsey felt that the first pitch, a short, inside corner, would go free. He left a pin in place and went for it, wearing canvas deck shoes with gummy rubber soles. "Going for the top as fast as I could," Ramsey risked hitting the ground before pulling onto a ledge above the crux. Curiously, since he never publicized his achievement, it remained unknown for two decades. In 1961, Smith climbers measured success only by whether they reached the top of a spire – the fact that Ramsey did The Awl free didn't matter. He considered it more of a stunt than a climbing achievement of any importance. At 5.10c, this short pitch easily was the hardest free route in Oregon. Despite the rapid growth in free climbing near the end of the decade, the Awl would remain the Smith standard for nearly 10 years.

The peak-bagging era began winding down in the mid-sixties after the first ascents of the Christian Brothers. With the pinnacles climbed, the climbers searched for more difficult routes. The best efforts were long aid ascents on Monkey Face, each far eclipsing the standard of the original line.

The most remarkable climb was **Bohn Street/West Face Cave,** by Dave Jensen and Bob Martin in 1963. They followed an incipient seam left of the original route, relying on ratty A4 pins instead of bolts. Their bold accomplishment drove the final nail in the coffin of Smith's bolt-ladder era. No longer would a line of aid bolts be a viable means of reaching a summit.

By the middle of the decade, climbers initiated changes that would alter the nature of the game. In search of new routes, they began shifting the arena from the spires surrounding the Burma Road to today's crags, which lie further downstream. Here, they found better quality rock but few summit towers. Forsaking the prize of standing atop a pinnacle, the first wall climbs came into vogue. The earliest of these non-summit routes were **Rattlesnake Chimney** (5.6) and **Western Chimney** (5.5) in 1963, by George Cummings. Technically, these routes weren't advances by any stretch of the imagination, but they heralded things to come. Another route that paved new ground was the first ascent of **Sky Ridge** in 1968 by Jensen and Cummings. Before **Sky Ridge,** everyone pioneered new lines starting from the ground and climbing to the top, placing protection along the way. This first changed when Jensen and Cummings hiked up the backside to the top of **Sky Ridge,** and pre-placed protection bolts on rappel. Their deed was an example of someone thinking about what would work best, unencumbered by restrictive traditions. Although their tactic didn't catch on for over a decade, they unwittingly stumbled upon the roots of Smith sport climbing.

In the early sixties, Jim Ramsey taught an intermediate climbing class at Smith, and immediately saw potential in a skinny, knicker-clad kid. Soon this youngster, Kim Schmitz, was at the top of Smith climbing. An all-round climber, Schmitz matched Ramsey's effort on The Awl, led the impressive **East Face** of Monkey Face, and pioneered a handful of other routes. His influence would have been far greater if he hadn't left Oregon for the greener pastures of Yosemite. Next came the exploits of Tom and Bob Bauman. The Baumans earned a reputation in their teens by pioneering terrifying routes on the miserable rock of the Oregon Cascades. For them, the Smith tuff must have seemed like iron. Many of their better efforts were on other Oregon crags, but they left their mark on Smith as well. Bob soloed first ascents not far off the top level of the day, including **Cinnamon Slab** (5.6) and **Parking Lot Crack** (5.8). Tom climbed the **West Face Variation, Peking,** and **Lion's Jaw** (all 5.8), and pushed the level of Smith aid climbing. His ascent of Picnic Lunch Wall in 1969 with Kim Schmitz was the crowning jewel of the Smith big-wall era.

By the end of the decade, the free-climbing standard at Smith hadn't increased at all since Ramsey's ascent of the Awl. The grades had consolidated greatly during these years, but nothing else approached 5.10. Since the free-climbing game still wasn't well-established, the best lines were multi-pitch routes mixing free and aid moves. Still, changes were brewing as the new decade drew near. With free ascents of **Amphetamine Grip** (5.7), **Spiderman** (5.7), **King Kong** (5.9) and **Godzilla** (5.8), Danny Gates and Steve Strauch spearheaded the shift toward free climbing.

THE SEVENTIES

Smith Rock free climbing eventually came of age during the 70s, but at the start of the decade, aid still dominated the sport. Tom Rogers led the way, nailing several future free routes, including **Pack Animal, Sunshine Dihedral, Wartley's Revenge** and **Trezlar.** His ascents of **Last Gasp** (5.9) and **As You Like It** (5.10b) showed that he was capable of high standard free climbs, but he never exploited his talents.

Smith's first free climbing specialist was Del Young, who quickly blew away the existing standards. A thin crack wizard, Young pioneered **Delirium Tremens** (5.10a), **Sunjammer** (5.10b) and **Theseus** (5.10c). His best effort was **Minotaur** (5.10d), a short finger crack on the Student Wall basalt. Not far off the U.S. standards at the time, this was Smith's first 5.11, even though sticky rubber eventually dropped the grade a notch.

Wayne Arrington on the first ascent of Hand Job (5.10a), 1973.   Photo: Tom Rogers

While the basalt offered the hardest free routes, development accelerated on the tuff as well. The driving force was Dean Fry. With a penchant for pushing unprotected climbing on bad rock, the tuff suited Fry just fine. Over two years, Dean pioneered 30 routes, including some of the most difficult and serious lines at Smith. Among his most influential climbs were **New Testament** and **Zebra** (both 5.10a) and **Moonshine Dihedral** (5.9). His bold lead of **Methusula's Column** (5.10a) was visionary – it was the first bolted face route in the Dihedrals. Tragically, his promising career ended in October of 1973. After mastering **Karate Crack** and the **Peapod Cave** (Smith's first two-pitch 5.10), Fry died in a car accident on his way home to Corvallis. If he had lived, he would have rewritten the history of Smith climbing. A memorial plaque to Dean rests at the hiking bridge spanning the Crooked River.

While Fry dominated climbing on the tuff, Wayne Arrington made his mark on the basalt. The Student Wall had drawn attention since the 50s, but Arrington was the first to realize the potential of the columnar basalt. After returning from a harrowing stint as a helicopter pilot in Vietnam, Arrington arrived at Smith highly motivated and seemingly fearless. Climbing mainly in the Gorge, he pioneered over 30 routes, including **Hand Job** (5.10a), **Taxdor** and **Titus** (unprotected 5.9 offwidths). Unfortunately, Arrington never kept track of his ascents. But, his climbs inspired others to push Gorge standards. The most impressive effort occurred in 1975, when Paul Landrum and Ken Currens doubled the number of hard Gorge routes in a single week. Their ascents of **Morning Star** (5.10c), **Prometheus** and **Wildfire** (both 5.10b) brought the Gorge to the top of Smith free climbing.

Despite the climbing exploits of Dean Fry, Wayne Arrington and others, Smith Rock might still be a backwater area if not for the efforts of Jeff Thomas. During a prolific period in the mid-to-late seventies, Thomas dominated Smith climbing like none before him; his name became synonymous with Oregon free climbing. Young's ascent of **Minotaur** aside, Jeff firmly established the 5.11 grade at Smith Rock. He had considerable influence on the impressionable youngsters of the era (including myself), as he pushed free climbing levels with a calm nonchalance. Built more like a lumberjack than a free climber, Thomas' flawless footwork and iron will pulled him through where stronger climbers failed. As a wide-eyed 19-year-old, I vividly remember belaying Jeff on **No Brain, No Pain,** a viciously overhanging hand crack. At the crux, he slotted a critical nut, then moved down to rest before clipping it. After psyching, he went for the top, concentrating so fully on the moves he forgot to clip in. Jeff didn't notice his mistake until it was too late to reverse the moves – horrified, I envisioned my hero doing the pancake. Upon discovering his plight, Jeff glanced down and muttered, with a tinge of delight in his voice, "Oh-oh, I'm in trouble now." As I prepared to catch the whipper to end all whippers, Jeff serenely stormed the rest of the pitch without placing another piece.

Thomas first made his mark on Smith climbing in 1972 with his ascent of **Unfinished Symphony,** a multi-pitch aid route. It was free climbing though, that secured his place in Smith history. For the next seven years Thomas pioneered a steady stream of new routes, first breaking through with **Brain Salad Surgery** (5.11a). His best year was 1977, when he freed **Shoes of the Fisherman** (5.11b), the third pitch of the **S.W. Corner** (5.11a) and **Lion's Chair** (5.11a). The next year, he added **Wartley's Revenge** (5.11b) and **I Almost Died** (5.11a) to his tick list.

With dozens of first ascents under his belt, Thomas redefined Smith Rock climbing, and his style became the accepted ethic of the day. Traditionally oriented, Jeff disdained rappel-placed bolts, and drilled only from the ground up. On his hardest routes, he worked out the moves after hanging – a practice later called hangdogging. His style of rehearsing moves before a redpoint ascent became the area standard. Thomas capped his career with two guidebooks to the area. His second book, *Oregon Rock,* came out in 1983, and was the last complete Smith guide until now.

Despite the efforts of Thomas, Smith standards remained far below the rest of the U.S. When Tony Yaniro's **Grand Illusion** (5.13b) became the world standard in 1979, Smith's hardest route was eight grades behind. Smith free climbing had fully developed in the 18 years following the first free ascent of the Awl, but the top level rose just three notches. This soon changed with remarkable speed.

Bridging the gap between Thomas' climbs and the sport routes of the eighties was Chris Jones, a rare talent from Eugene. He arrived on the scene in 1978, the same year he miraculously survived a 150-foot ground fall in Yosemite. Spooked by his near-death experience, he preferred bouldering, and only rarely led climbs. Jones somehow combined an innate clumsiness (he could never manage a forward roll in his college gymnastics class), with a huge amount of raw strength to tear apart Smith standards. When told by his eighth-grade P.E. teacher that anyone who could crank a one arm pull-up would get an A for the class, Jones stood in line with everyone else. He'd never tried one before, but he stunned his instructor by collecting on the bet. Once he started his meticulously structured training regime, he matured into one of the most powerful boulderers in the world.

Jones was the mentor of three young climbers who entered the University of Oregon in 1978. Two were from Madras - myself and Bill Ramsey, the son of the Smith pioneer. A driven individual with the physique of a body builder, Ramsey possessed legendary toughness on the rock. While rooming together in our freshman year, he built tolerance for painful cracks by pouring salt on his open wounds. The third climber, Alan Lester, spiced up the scene. High on drive, but low on natural talent, Lester would eventually transform himself into one of the best climbers in the country. Locked in a competitive struggle under the wings of Jones, we converted the once-listless Columns (a basalt toproping spot in downtown Eugene) into Oregon's most fiercely competitive area. By the end of the decade, the standards at this pint-sized crag far exceeded anything at Smith. These silly trick routes eventually would have a profound impact on Smith climbing. Far ahead of the rest of us, Jones was the first to transfer his basalt expertise to the tuff of Smith Rock. Not surprisingly, he dominated the scene in 1979.

In April of 1979, Jones teamed with Bill Ramsey and nabbed the highly-coveted first free ascent of Monkey Face. Their spectacular route, called **Monkey Space,** featured two pitches of 5.11. Later that year, Jones toproped **Sunshine Dihedral** free, and bumped Smith standards to 5.11d with his redpoint of **Rising Expectations.** While impressive, these routes paled in comparison to Jones' exploits on the boulders. He spent the summer living in Bend, devoting every free moment to training and bouldering. He pumped gas, survived on a nauseating collection of nutrition-free junk food, and quietly demolished the technical standards at Smith. Wearing his trademark cords and tattered, long-sleeved tailored dress shirt – even on the hottest days – Jones managed a remarkable series of extreme boulder problems. His best efforts, including **Tator Tots Direct** and the **Jones Exit** to the Cave, were so much harder than anything else few climbers could grasp the level. His boulder problems inspired his three disciples, and provided a training ground for extreme moves. By the start of 1980, all that remained was moving his standards from the boulders to the steep faces.

THE EIGHTIES

As the 80s began, the prevailing attitude was that the golden age of Smith Rock climbing was over. Only a few classic cracks remained, and the only other options were seemingly impossible faces. Undaunted, I dropped out of school in 1980, moving back home to live with my tolerant parents. Like everyone else, I figured the steep faces weren't possible, so I set my sights on climbing every remaining crack.

To pioneer my routes, I rappeled from the top, removing loose rock and pre-placing bolts. This went against the ground-up tradition of the day, but since Thomas was no longer active, there wasn't anyone to slap my hand. My decision to break with tradition wasn't a visionary act by any stretch of the imagination. Instead, it seemed like a sneaky way of putting up more routes. I never cared for the misery of starting up first ascents on Smith tuff from the ground, snapping holds and pulling off blocks along the way. Eliminating the dangers beforehand only seemed logical. By combining this top-down style with the already established hangdogging ethic, the setting was right for some real breakthroughs.

Unfortunately, for a couple years I wasn't good enough to make these advances. Still, I kept struggling through the unaesthetic cracks, coming away with the occasional classic. During the next five years, I fully devoted myself to Smith climbing, eventually discovering the potential of the vertical faces and improving enough to climb them. Through these years, bouldering held much of my attention, since finding mid-week climbing partners was almost impossible. Although there was a group of Smith regulars, there were few full-time climbers. Still, I'd be flexing my ego if I said I was solely responsible for the prolific development of the era. A rapidly improving Alan Lester kept the scene competitive in the early years, with **Class Dismissed** (5.12a), and a free ascent of the **North Face** of Monkey Face (5.11d). Kent Benesch, Chuck Buzzard, Jim Anglin, Tom Blust, Chris Grover and Brooke Sandahl also made significant contributions.

Looking back over the dozens of routes pioneered in the early to mid-80s, there were a few that really helped Smith climbing move forward. In 1980, I first rappeled a steep wall in the Dihedrals, surprised to find big holds that weren't visible from the ground. Although little more than a quick dash between cracks, **Karot Tots** (5.11b) was a predecessor of the future. Unconvinced that the Dihedrals held promise, I spent the next two years climbing increasingly disgusting cracks, eventually bumping the standards to 5.12b/c with **Midnight Snack.** By now, the crack-climbing era was dead-ending quickly, so I turned to the blank faces of the Dihedrals out of desperation for something new.

I'd rappeled an especially appealing face right of **Tator Tots** as early as 1981, but at the time the holds seemed far too small. Disappointed, I wrote in my journal that this face was "very solid B2 with no rests, and as far as I'm concerned that's impossible!" I optimistically checked the line again the next year, and this time it looked feasible. After attempts spread over seven days, I finally succeeded on **Watts Tots** (5.12b) in early 1983.

Encouraged by my success, I decided to blow off a good climbing day and check out the tempting arête left of **Moonshine.** Astonished, I discovered a big jug at the lip of the roof, and quickly bolted the line. No one was more surprised than myself when I succeeded on **Chain Reaction** (5.12c) a month later. Now almost everything seemed possible, and we were off to the races. Over the next two years, the standards progressed rapidly. Soon came **Split Image** (5.12d), **Double Stain** and **Darkness at Noon** (5.13a). My best ascent during these years came in August 1985, when I freed the entire **East Face** of Monkey Face. I'd succeeded on the individual pitches the year before, but a hanging belay at 85 feet had allowed a complete recovery. I became obsessed with eliminating this point of aid, and launched into a barrage of attempts to free the route in one long pitch. I practiced by doing toprope laps on the 5.12c lower section until I could climb the approach without the hint of a pump. Still, it took several days of effort before I succeeded on the flaring pin scars and awkwardly leaning edges of the final bulge. For 14 months, the **East Face** (5.13c/d) was the hardest free climb in North America.

Throughout the boom years of the early to mid-80s, our climbing style was essentially the same as practiced today. After cleaning and bolting on rappel, we'd carefully rehearse the moves before our redpoint ascents. There were only two differences. First, we'd never leave quickdraws in place between attempts. Even if we tried a route several times in a day, we'd pull the draws after each go, for some silly reason. The other difference was our sparse use of bolts. Whenever possible, we'd use natural protection, drilling holes only when we couldn't wiggle in R.P.s or Friends. Ethically, we had no aversion to bolts, but hand drilling four inch holes was a trauma. Back then, we only fantasized about power drills.

The Smith scene was far different in 1985 than it is today. While most of the Dihedral's routes were already there, almost none of the climbers were. Smith was a locals-only area – rarely would out-of-state visitors come through. The local climbers were a tight-knit bunch – always competitive, but never viciously so. We'd climb new routes, boulder and fool around like a bunch of school kids on summer vacation. There was a certain naivete and charm to the old days, before Smith Rock became famous. As the standards of the area grew, the excitement level rose, as we realized our efforts were paying off. We always dreamed that the world would someday discover Smith Rock, but for years it never happened.

Our isolation during these years was a vital part of Smith's evolution. Since the climbing grapevine wasn't nearly as developed as it is now, we'd scour magazines for trivia on other areas. We worked hard trying to catch up with everyone else, never realizing that we really weren't behind at all. The European ethics evolving at the same time had no influence during these years – we didn't know how Europeans climbed. Our sport climbing convictions only grew stronger when we learned how closely the European style matched ours.

Slowly, the word got out about the quality of Smith Rock. Jonny Woodward, Geoff Weigand and Kim Carrigan visited Smith in 1985 and tore through the classic lines. They nabbed many second ascents, including Woodward's flash of a runout horror called the **Heinous Cling** (5.12c). Their influence led to our briefly abandoning redpoints, settling for yo-yos instead. Oddly, the event that increased the exposure of Smith Rock wasn't any particular ascent, but the visit of an Austrian photographer. Visiting Smith on a whim to check out photo opportunities, Heinz Zak was thrilled by what he saw. His brilliant pictures appeared in almost every climbing magazine, bringing the area to the attention of the world. The locals-only days disappeared forever.

My single-minded approach to climbing eventually backfired. I started 1985 by climbing 126 consecutive days at Smith Rock, never realizing that I might hurt myself in the long run. After day 80, my fingers started to ache, and my power tapered off, but since I'd set a goal of climbing every day that year, I foolishly kept with it. Eventually, overuse injuries forced an extended layoff, and I went back to finish school, much to the delight of Mom and Dad. While the number of climbers visiting Smith increased ten-fold in 1986, the new route pace almost slowed to a halt. If not for a visit by two French climbers, the year might have been a complete bust. Instead, it ranked among the most memorable in Smith history.

Jean Baptiste Tribout and Jean Marc Troussier were already famous in France, but they arrived at Smith almost unknown in the States. In five weeks, they blew the place apart, repeating most of the hardest routes, and climbing six new lines. Easily the most impressive effort was Tribout's ascent of the left wall of Sunshine Dihedral. I'd attempted this outrageous line on toprope two years earlier, but wasn't close to linking the moves. Jaws dropped, and eyes opened wide when Tribout succeeded after ten hard-fought days. As the first 5.14 in the U.S., **To Bolt or Not to Be** (5.14a) far exceeded the grade of any other route in the country.

Tribout's ascent had a major impact on climbing, not just at Smith, but throughout the U.S. His ascent validated the tactics used locally for years, and forced climbers to take a serious look at the restrictive ethics of their local areas. The most driven climbers in the U.S. wanted desperately to catch up to the Europeans, and they realized that only by playing the same game could they hope to. Bolters and bolt choppers clashed, debates raged, tempers flared and fists flew. In the end, sport climbing was left standing throughout the country.

Jerry Moffat on the third ascent of To Bolt or Not To Be (5.14a).   Photo: Cathy Beloeil

Adding more fuel to the fire set by **To Bolt or Not to Be** was the introduction of the power drill. A few days after the French left Smith Rock, Chris Grover acquired a Bosch Bulldog (a cordless hammer drill) and carried it into the canyon for the first time. Grover, described in a 1986 *Outside* article as Smith's "guardian troll" began climbing locally in the seventies and was my main climbing partner for many years. As the long-time resident expert, and coach to countless young climbers, Grover is among the most colorful characters in Smith history. Puffing on his trademark Camel, he forever changed Smith Rock when he drilled the first bolt of **Churning in the Wake**. The main obstacle to preparing new routes – the 45 minutes of hand drilling per bolt – was no more.

Dozens of new routes fell the next two years, spurred by the ease of the power drill. The development of the Churning Buttress moved the emphasis away from the Dihedrals. Shortly after Sean Olmstead led **Churning in the Wake** (5.13a), nearby lines such as **Kings of Rap** (5.12d), **Oxygen** (5.13a/b) and **Vicious Fish** (5.13c/d) became highly-regarded testpieces. Yet despite the new route frenzy, Tribout's level remained unmatched until Scott Franklin arrived on the scene from the Gunks. Powerfully built, tempestuous and undeniably gifted, Franklin repeated **To Bolt or Not to Be** in late 1987. A few months later, he added his own creation – **Scarface** (5.14a). Franklin proved not just to Smith locals, but all Americans, that it was possible to compete with the Europeans. With Scott leading the way, 1988 was a banner year for Smith climbing. Many difficult routes fell, including **White Wedding** (5.13d/14a), in an encore performance by Tribout. English legend Jerry Moffatt capped the year by climbing the triple crown – **To Bolt, Scarface** and **White Wedding** – in a one-month visit.

Smith ethics became more refined during these years, influenced heavily by the Europeans. After Tribout's 1986 visit, the yo-yo ethic fortunately died quickly, and we returned to pulling the rope after each go. We also abandoned our practice of carrying the gear on each attempt, leaving behind fixed quickdraws. The ease of power drilling accelerated the use of bolts. Gone forever were the days of protecting first ascents with shaky R.P.s between widely-spaced bolts. Not surprisingly, no one grumbled.

The most dramatic decade in Smith history finished slowly in 1989, with few extreme first ascents. Despite further consolidation at all levels, no one broke through to a higher grade. Tom Egan and Jeff Frizzell provided much of the firepower, pioneering dozens of basalt lines in the Upper Gorge. Brooke Sandahl added new routes on the tuff, discovering a jungle gym called **Easy's Playhouse**. But among many top climbers, a shift in emphasis took a major toll on the new route pace. The effect of organized competitions slowly changed the sport throughout the world. On-sight standards went through the roof while ultimate difficulty levels remained on a plateau. Lynn Hill's ascent of **Taco Chips** (5.12d), Tribout's efforts on **Slit Your Wrist**, **Time's Up** and **Aggro Monkey** (all 5.13b), and Jim Karn's ascent of **Power** (5.13b) were the most influential on-sights of the late 80s.

THE NINETIES AND BEYOND

The last two years have seen no shortage of new routes at Smith. Easier climbs blossomed everywhere, as climbers turned their attention to untouched walls. Fewer upper level routes fell, but **Bum Rush the Show** (5.13b), **The Product** (5.13a), **Big Tuna** (5.13b/c) and **Villain** (5.13d) proved that the art of the extreme first ascent was far from dead. Unfortunately, the hardest ascents split the amicable scene. Tribout made enemies during encore visits with his ascents of **Scene of the Crime** (5.13b) and **Bad Man** (5.13d/14a). Because Smith first ascents require such unusual amounts of preparation, the person doing the work traditionally has the rights to the route.

In a throw back to the mid-seventies, most of the recent new route activity was centered in the unheralded Upper Gorge. Frizzell and Egan led the way, pioneering more than 50 routes between them. Today, the Upper Gorge offers more routes 5.12 or harder than either the Dihedrals or Morning Glory Wall, though it receives relatively little attention.

The trend toward training and on-sight leads – in favor of pushing technical difficulty – changed Smith Rock climbing. For many youngsters, the goal no longer is pioneering the hardest routes, but winning the World Cup. Anyone training for competitions ignores multi-day projects, opting for on-sight attempts and marathon training days. This is a perfectly legitimate direction for free climbing to go, since increased on-sight levels are every bit as impressive, perhaps more so, than pushing toward 5.15. Still, it suggests that ultimate difficulty advancements at Smith may be slow in coming.

Epitomizing the new emphasis on using Smith as a gymnasium was Jim Karn. As the recently-crowned king of American free climbing, Karn routinely tore through the hardest routes, on-sighting **Bum Rush the Show** (5.13b), and sometimes cranking multiple 5.13s and 5.14s in a day. Obviously, Karn could push Smith's top level higher if he wished, but he leads a new generation with other interests.

Hopefully, the pursuit of new routes will continue to play a major role in the future of Smith Rock. But with dozens of extreme lines to tempt them, most climbers ignore the hassles of first ascents, instead indulging in the sheer fun of repeating established lines. As a consequence, with the exception of the basalt, the new route pace at Smith has recently slowed to a crawl. Smith will forever be popular even if nothing new happens, but only with new routes will Smith standards stay competitive with the rest of the world.

The best example of what's possible at Smith Rock occurred shortly before this book went to press. In April of 1992, **To Bolt or Not To Be's** five-and-a-half year reign at the top of Smith standards ended. J.B. Tribout again was the man of the hour, as he succeeded on **Just Do It**, on the east wall of Monkey Face. This breathtaking route resisted attempts by some of the world's best climbers, including Scott Franklin and Didier Raboutou. At 5.14c, it easily eclipsed the level of America's hardest routes, solidifying Smith's position at the top of the sport. But while this overhanging wall was clearly a landmark ascent, it's only the beginning of the future at Smith Rock.

But a new route free-for-all won't ensure a good future for Smith Rock. Today, with seemingly limitless options, it's hard to fathom that we'll eventually run out of new routes. But some year in the future, climbers will succeed on the final first ascent, and Smith will become a showcase for what was done in the past. It's crucially important that climbers don't hasten the inevitable by chiseling tomorrow's 5.15s down to 5.12c. Regrettably, this has happened and could sentence Smith climbing to a premature death. The future rests squarely on the shoulders of climbers only now entering the sport. They'll choose the direction that Smith will take in the years to come. As the responsibility shifts from generation to generation, I only hope climbers will treat Smith Rock with the same respect as those who came before them.

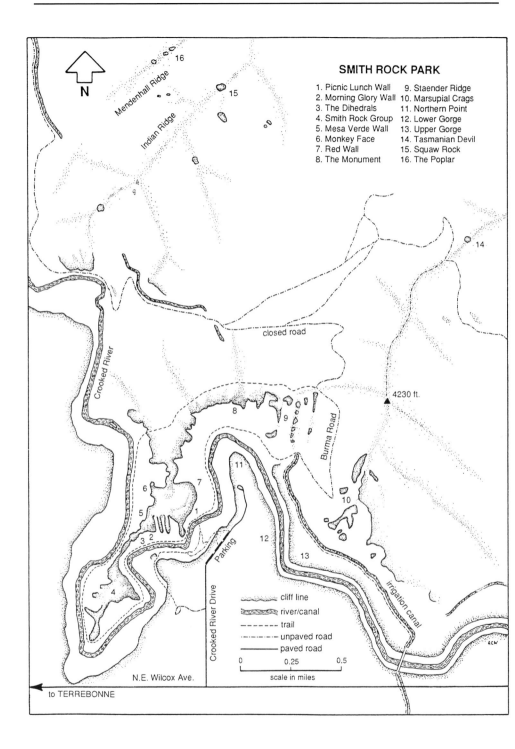

SMITH ROCK PARK

1. Picnic Lunch Wall   9. Staender Ridge
2. Morning Glory Wall   10. Marsupial Crags
3. The Dihedrals   11. Northern Point
4. Smith Rock Group   12. Lower Gorge
5. Mesa Verde Wall   13. Upper Gorge
6. Monkey Face   14. Tasmanian Devil
7. Red Wall   15. Squaw Rock
8. The Monument   16. The Poplar

SMITH CLIMBING ETHICS

SMITH ROCK BECAME well-known in the midst of the most hotly-contested debate in the history of U.S. climbing. Differing radically from the norm at the time, Smith ethics garnered national attention and roused the U.S. scene. Old-school climbers felt Smith lacked traditional values, and saw the area as a digression in the advancement of the sport. Yet, if it's true that imitation is the sincerest form of flattery, then local eithics eventually won out. As the first sport climbing area in the country, Smith opened the door to what is now the fast-growing segment of the sport.

By nature, ethical discussions will rub some climbers the wrong way. Already, I've surely tweaked those with opposing views. Only if everyone shared the same views would we have a controversy-free sport. Aside from putting the climbing magazines out of business, this idealistic scenario would retard growth. Only the work of creative individuals, employing a variety of tactics, keeps climbing vibrant and ever-changing. A single ethic would stifle this vital creativity. We'd have a hopelessly one-dimensional sport if the entire country mirrored Yosemite – or for that matter, Smith Rock. Without question, the tactics employed at Smith work well here, as the soft rock favors the local approach. But these ethics might be totally unacceptable elsewhere. The rock type, tradition and the majority voice of each area's climbers should dictate local ethics – not what outsiders preach.

For this reason, I'm not trying to convince others that Smith ethics are the only way. They might make sense in your area, and they might not. I'll simply highlight what local climbers practice and attempt to explain why. To understand Smith ethics, it helps to be familiar with the history of the local climbing style. For a better understanding of this evolutionary process, please refer to the history section.

Those who feel Smith lacks traditional values are both right and wrong. We don't share the ground-up ethic considered traditional in many places, but most of these areas had little direct influence on the local scene. The seclusion of Smith allowed us to use imagination, not imitation, to build suitable ethics for the crumbly walls of tuff. In the process, we stumbled upon the roots of sport climbing – as did others throughout the country. Without condemnation from peers, we built quickly upon Smith's unique tradition. By the time we discovered how much our tactics differed from the norm, we believed so much in what we were doing that more restrictive ethics seemed preposterous.

Despite any differences, old school climbers are as welcome here as sport climbers. If the thought of hangdogging leaves you ill, you can visit Smith and practice your beliefs without attack. You can establish new routes from the ground up, drilling boldly by hand, and no one will ever chop your route. Only if you feel it's your evangelical mission to save Smith from the "sins" of sport climbing, will you be frowned on.

While the Smith climbing community allows more latitude than many other areas, there are limitations. Free-for-all ethics make no more sense at Smith than they do anywhere else. Since certain practices jeopardize the future of the area, I'll do some moralizing myself. I realize I'm treading on precarious ground as I attempt to define the hazy line between what's right and wrong, but hey – it's my book.

FIRST ASCENT CONSIDERATIONS

First ascents at Smith Rock present some unusual challenges. Only rarely can you create a quality route by merely rappeling and drilling bolts. The crumbly volcanic tuff always requires some degree of cleaning – no one appreciates a filthy route with holds snapping off and loose blocks perched to tumble. New routes should add to the quality of Smith climbing – not detract from it. We prepare new routes almost exclusively on rappel (or more precisely, on jumars). Because of the importance of cleaning, the top-down approach makes a lot more sense at Smith than starting from the ground. If you come here and pioneer a line from the ground up, you won't offend anyone, but you'll score no more points than rappel bolters. Like any route, your ascent will only be criticized if you leave it filthy.

In extreme cases, the preparation of a new route may take several days of work. Because of this, climbers pioneering new lines at Smith have the right to the eventual first free ascent. This goes for climbs of all levels, whether 5.7 or 5.14. When climbers don't respect one's right to complete a project, it takes away much of the motivation for doing new routes. Why bother to go to all the work if pirates are waiting to reap the benefits from your efforts? After enough time passes, attempting climbers typically open their unfinished routes to the masses, but as long as you're engaged in active pursuit, it should remain yours to finish.

USING BOLTS ON FIRST ASCENTS

Bolts protect nearly all the new routes done at Smith in recent years. The use of bolts grew steadily throughout the 80s, and today they're the norm. The earliest sport climbs at Smith often used a few pieces of natural gear between widely-spaced bolts. The biggest reason for the early reluctance to drill was more logistical than ethical. When hand drilling, we used bolts sparingly simply because they were such a chore to place. The power drill instantly changed this. Suddenly, it took 30 seconds to bore a hole that once took 45 minutes. With the power drill came the end of mixed protection at Smith. Today, almost all new routes use bolts exclusively, ignoring any natural protection. Many local climbers haven't brought any gear other than quickdraws into the park for years.

The convenience of the drill understandably creates some problems. When each bolt hole took an hour to drill, we'd take great care to place them in the proper location. Otherwise, we'd have to spend another hour relocating it. With power, climbers often set bolts haphazardly in hard-to-clip places. You should think carefully about where to drill each bolt on a new route. Fortunately, the most-commonly used anchors aren't permanent and are easily removed. If you realize after the fact that you blew it, be sure to relocate any ill-placed bolts, and fill the old bolt holes.

When placing bolts at Smith, please use only hangers that match the color of the rock. These are available through Metolius, and greatly decrease the visual impact of the sport. They cost a little more, but the park service loves them. Also, never leave rappel webbing behind – you should equip all anchors with the Metolius Rap Hanger.

CHIPPING

Anyone putting up new routes in a soft-rock area knows how fine a line separates cleaning from chipping. Often, you can brush away the worst of the tuff with a toothbrush. If you leave a Smith route totally in its natural state, you'll wind up with a dirt pile that only detracts from the area. We try to make the best of what we've got here, and to do that we must clean new routes.

I'm not in any way endorsing chipping at Smith. I'm merely trying to establish that what constitutes sculpting is unclear. Some pontificating climbers (who almost never visit Smith) decry the local cleaning practice, equating it with hacking holds. If you define chipping as the removal of any rock, then 99% of Smith routes would qualify, as we pull loose stone off almost every line. But the chisel and power drill are never standard cleaning tools.

Yes, there are chipped routes – by anyone's standards – at Smith Rock. But these lines are fortunately scarce. The chipping and drilling of holds at Smith Rock is not an acceptable practice. It never has been, and hopefully never will be. If you feel that the route you're working on needs a chipped (not just cleaned) hold, then maybe you aren't the right person to do the first ascent.

GLUING

Often controversial, but blown way out of proportion, is the practice of reinforcing crucial holds and dangerous flakes with epoxy. Most of the more difficult lines at Smith have a few glued holds. We consider this not only acceptable, but a necessary part of pioneering quality routes on substandard rock. Epoxy should be used sparingly, as it's easy to make a big mess, but if properly done no one will even notice. When properly used, epoxy has less visual impact than a single bolt.

PLASTIC HOLDS

Plastic holds are not an acceptable means of establishing new routes. A few experimental plastic climbs already litter an isolated crag at Smith, but any additional artificial holds will be removed. The plastic routes are undeniably fun, as they make possible impossible roofs, but a proliferation of these lines could ruin Smith and close the place for climbers.

OTHER ETHICAL CONSIDERATIONS:

FIXED GEAR

Besides permanently fixed bolts and rappel anchors, sport climbers leave their projects equipped with quickdraws. These aren't permanent, but on the most popular routes they might as well be. As soon as one climber removes their draws, another replaces them. When you climb a route equipped with quickdraws, please leave them behind. They belong to someone actively working on the route. Quickdraw thievery is much less of a problem here than many other places, since Smith locals deal harshly with the criminals.

Since new route preparation often takes several days, climbers will leave behind a fixed rope. Like quickdraws, these ropes aren't booty, and belong to those preparing the new lines. There has been a problem with ropes getting stolen for many years, so never leave your line within reach of the ground. Unfortunately, climbers sometimes get bored with their new route prospects, leaving ropes behind to rot. Anyone fixing a line must be responsible for removing the rope, as abandoned ropes seem to tweak the park service more than anything else.

HANGDOGGING

As a necessary part of succeeding on the hardest lines, hangdogging is the standard practice at Smith. More respected than working out the moves off the rope is an on-sight lead, but there's no reason to restrict yourself unless you want to. Every route at Smith could be done without dogging, but this seems a trivial contrivance to the sport climber. Someone could eventually climb every route wearing Air Jordans as well, but why bother? At Smith, hangdogging is the tradition – not merely a rebellious deviation. Still, if you want to lower off each time you fall, that's perfectly okay. It is, after all, a personal choice affecting no one else.

REDPOINTING

Long before we had a name for it, redpointing was the style used on almost every Smith route. Climbers would carry their entire rack, and place all the gear and quickdraws on each attempt. This strict tradition eased in the second half of the 80s, and today we call any no-fall lead a redpoint ascent, regardless of whether quickdraws are in place. This welcomed change allowed climbers to focus on movement, rather than fumbling with gear. While this tactic only slightly lowers the difficulty of a bolted line, it slashes the grade of many naturally-protected climbs. Part of the original difficulty of these routes was possessing the stamina to place the gear and keep going. Still, only the old timers (or on-sight climbers) will ever start up the hardest of these lines with a rack full of gear.

TOPROPING

If you prefer staying away from the sharp end of the rope, toproping makes a perfectly acceptable way to climb. A redpoint lead is far more respected, but many climbers use a toprope to work out the moves before leading. A toprope ascent also can help in deciding where to place easy-to-clip bolts on a new route. The practice of wiring every move on toprope, then placing widely-spaced bolts, makes little sense. If you'd like to put up a truly bold climb, don't bother with the toprope, and take the whips like everyone else will have to do.

RETRO-BOLTING

Most older Smith Rock routes contained fewer bolts than the lines of today. A trend to modernize these routes, called retro-bolting, continues to sweep the area. If the individual who pioneered a run-out nightmare wants to open his route to the masses, then retro-bolting is fine. It becomes a more difficult call when we start bolting old lines done by others without their permission. I feel that we shouldn't modify any route that was historically significant when first climbed. Bolting these routes defaces a part of Smith history, and lessens the diversity of the area. All new routes in the future will be fully bolted, so it makes sense to preserve those few that aren't. If the current trend continues (and it probably will) routes like **Lion's Chair, Wartley's Revenge** and the **East Face** of Monkey Face eventually will end up bolted – along with every other climb in the park. Hopefully, this misfortune will never occur.

CLIMBING ETIQUETTE

With so many climbers crammed in a small area, we need to be mindful of those around us. On busy days, the most popular routes receive almost non-stop traffic. No one has the right to monopolize a route all day long. If you're spending a day trying to link a route, make room for others between your attempts. Most distressing are marathon toprope sessions. It's frustrating when you can't lead your project because 20 people are waiting in line to toprope it. Those wanting to redpoint a route typically have priority over toproping climbers.

After dozens of ascents, climbs can get hopelessly gummed with chalk. Anytime you're working on a route, bring a toothbrush along and scrub away any excess chalk you've left behind. This might seem like a petty matter, but an unbrushed, chalk-caked hold might be the difference between success and failure for the next guy.

HOW TO USE THIS BOOK

I'VE DIVIDED the nearly 1,000 Smith Rock routes into 14 chapters, packed with historical tidbits and details about each crag. Using a combination of topos, photos and text, I hope climbers can make satisfying route selections. Set in a sparsely vegetated semi-desert, Smith climbs are easy to find, since trees and overgrowth seldom block the view. You can refer to the map at the start of every section to find where each crag lies in relation to others.

Sometimes I've used jargon that might escape beginners, or anyone who hasn't kept current with the ever-changing climbing lingo. Rather than trying to explain each term, I'm assuming the reader is familiar with the vocabulary. This isn't a how-to-climb manual; I'd recommend buying one, especially if arête, redpoint and undercling aren't familiar terms. There are several excellent introductory books on the market, but I strongly suggest that beginners seek qualified instruction as well. This will speed your development and teach you life-saving safety techniques.

RATINGS

I've included ratings on all the climbs, which are defined as follows:

DIFFICULTY GRADES

This guide uses the well-understood Yosemite Decimal System, with routes 5.10 and harder sub-divided into a, b, c and d grades. Often, a route doesn't fit conveniently into a single grade, but instead of using a more practical three-tiered system (e.g. 5.10-, 5.10, 5.10+), I've stuck with the popular letter grades. When there isn't a consensus, I'll sometimes use a split rating (e.g. 5.12b/c).

The difficulty of a route may vary tremendously from person to person. Someone tall might glide through a reachy crux, only to flail on the rock-over move that shorter climbers cruise. To further complicate matters, a rating might change over time. Smith routes sometimes become more difficult as sharp-cut edges wear rounded and key holds snap off. On the other hand, some climbs are easier today, since the over-zealous brushing of chalk slowly widens pockets. And anyone willing to date themselves fondly remembers what sticky rubber did to the grading scale.

The decimal grade indicates the difficulty of linking a pitch on a redpoint ascent; only rarely will it reveal the rating of the hardest move. A relentless route with lots of 5.12 moves might rate 5.13, even though there weren't any 5.13 sections. Only in the rare case of a one-move climb – with an easy approach, and finish – will the rating of the hardest single move equal the grade of the route.

In theory, the Yosemite Decimal System should be totally open-ended, but we don't always use it that way. There has always been a stigma against breaking through to a higher grade. This inevitably leads to downgrading, and compresses a scale designed to expand. The problem with downgrading routes at the upper end of the spectrum is that we then must go down the scale, dropping every climb to keep things consistent. Today's 5.13a shouldn't be 5.12c tomorrow simply because we're reluctant to move to the next grade. I've decided to keep the hardest lines where they are for now, to avoid tampering with everything else. Over time, when a broader-based consensus develops, these routes may move up or down the scale without affecting the grade of other climbs.

SERIOUSNESS GRADES

To distinguish difficulty from danger, I've employed the familiar R and X system. At Smith Rock, the decimal and seriousness grades are totally independent. Therefore, a 40-foot runout on

5.10a will receive the same decimal grade as the identical route with bolts five feet apart. The difference will be reflected only in the R and X grades, used as follows:

R You could take long falls here, and maybe even hurt yourself. An R might suggest widely-spaced bolts, or just enough lousy protection to keep you off the ground.

X These routes have very long fall potential, often risking a grounder. Consider yourself lucky if you plummet off an X without getting seriously injured. Dangerously loose climbs also might receive an X, even if they protect well.

QUALITY GRADES

I've used a zero-through-four-star system in this guide. Like the decimal grade, the number of stars a route receives might change with time. Several bolted lines earned only a single star when first climbed, but they've since become three-star routes after hundreds of ascents brushed them clean. I've used the quality grades as follows:

No Stars Horrible – These routes aren't worth doing, unless you enjoy putrid rock and unaesthetic climbing.

★ Below Average – These climbs always contain some poor rock or unpleasant moves, but they might please undiscriminating climbers.

★★ Average – I've given more Smith routes this quality grade than any other. They are all worth doing, but lack the excellent rock or superior moves found on better climbs.

★★★ Above Average – This rating includes climbs with average moves on flawless rock and those with brilliant climbing on imperfect rock. They are all highly recommended.

★★★★ Classic – These lines are the cream-of-the-crop at Smith. To qualify as a classic, a route must have excellent moves, solid rock, and preferably a superb position.

EQUIPMENT

Smith contains a mixture of fully-bolted and traditionally-protected routes. The following designations will tell you when to bring more than a rack of quickdraws.

Gear – This means you'll need to carry some protection devices. I've listed the size of the biggest piece of gear required, and in some cases suggested exactly what to bring. While non-camming, low-tech devices suffice for the easier routes, I'm assuming you'll carry state-of-the-art gear for the harder lines. If you don't, the difficulty and seriousness grades might go up radically.

Bolts – These routes are bolted sport climbs; unless otherwise indicated, you'll need nothing but quickdraws.

Aid rack – This designation denotes aid climbs requiring both a rack of pins and the usual hodgepodge of aid gizmos.

No gear – Although sometimes led, these climbs lack any protection options. Bring a spotter instead of a belayer.

TR – These routes are purely toprope problems.

Projects – The 60-or-so projects at Smith haven't seen an all-free ascent at the time of this writing. By the time you read these lines, several will already be free climbs. Projects are in varying stages of readiness – some may have seen only toprope efforts, while others will be totally equipped, and on the verge of going free. I've always made an estimate of the finished grade, but these are merely shots in the dark. I've used a minus/plus system (e.g. 5.12–, 5.12, 5.12+) followed by a question mark for any project where the grade is in question. Star grades and equipment notes are reserved for completed routes.

TOPOS

Since topos provide information that a photo or text couldn't easily convey, I've used them to portray many of Smith's sport climbs. The typical topo includes information on equipment, cliff features, climbing type, anchors and number of bolts. Despite good intentions, I've inevitably made errors. Especially suspect are the number of bolts on each route; if you rely totally on the sketches, you'll curse my name when you run out of quickdraws at the next-to-last bolt.

The grades of each pitch aren't haphazardly placed on the topos: instead, they show the location of the crux. On more difficult routes, I've sometimes made estimates of the levels of individual sections. Since grading short segments of a ptich is far more prone to error than placing a number on the entire climb, I've usually deviated from the a/b/c/d grades to a less specific system of minuses and pluses (e.g. 5.12–, 5.12 or 5.12+). The neighboring key will help you decipher the topos.

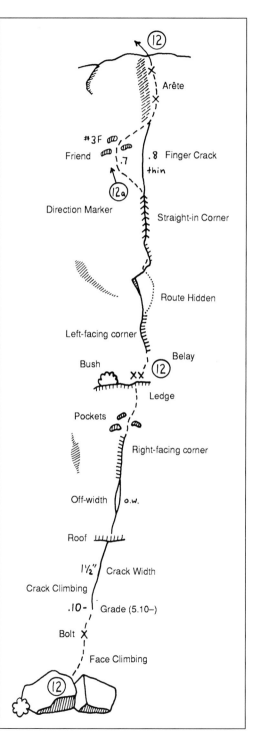

SAFETY CONSIDERATIONS

Smith's reliance on fixed gear gives unwary climbers a false sense of security. Most of the fixed pieces are reliable, but you shouldn't place blind trust in any bolt or pin. Inadequate hardware, or poor placements can turn bolts into a powder keg. As a rule, never rely on a single piece of fixed gear in a potentially fatal situation.

Never put much faith in any fixed pin on Smith tuff. Some placements remain solid for decades, but most loosen within a few months. I've pulled out dozens of so-called fixed pins with my fingers, sometimes in hair-raising situations. Pitons are far more reliable in the solid basalt of the Gorge, but even here, they fall out from time to time. Fortunately, fixed pins are a dying-breed at Smith – no one places them anymore.

Most bolts at Smith Rock are excellent, since every sport climb features three-eighths inch or half inch bolts. The most commonly used anchor today is the full-sleeved, half-inch by three and three-quarters inch Rawl Bolt. These test at nearly ten thousand pounds, and work well in the soft tuff. A variety of weaker, but still adequate bolts protect most routes from the 70s and 80s. Fortunately, only the most ancient routes sport quarter-inch bolts. You should never trust these dangerous relics on Smith tuff – or anywhere else, for that matter. Even the best bolts sometimes loosen, but a crank with a wrench usually tightens them. Eventually though, every bolt wears out and needs replacement. If you come across a bolt that seems unsafe, please document it in a notebook kept at Redpoint Climbers Supply. Eventually, some Good Samaritan will come along and replace it.

The anchors on most Smith sport routes are good, but you'll need to watch for worn rappel rings. The flimsy SMC rings wear especially quickly, so never trust just one of these. No one uses these hollow artifacts anymore, but even today's heavy-duty links eventually wear thin. To preserve the rings, refrain from lowering through them on extended toprope sessions; instead, use your own biners. Few climbers at Smith wear hard hats. Natural stonefall is rare, but there's enough loose rock to justify wearing a helmet for the safety-conscious climber. On many low-quality, multi-pitch routes, hard hats are essential, as the leader inevitably rains rock onto his/her helpless belayer.

Photo: Bruce Adams

This view of the main climbing area shows, from right to left,
Morning Glory Wall, Fourth Horseman, The Dihedrals and The Christian Brothers.

SUGGESTED ROUTES

I've listed several recommended routes for each grade. These are among the best in the area, and make good choices for anyone on a quick visit. The easier routes (below 5.5) aren't nearly as good as the more difficult lines, and they usually protect sparsely.

1st	Misery Ridge Trail, River Trail
2nd	Aggro Gully, Monument Gully
3rd	Little Three Fingered Jack, Koala Rock
4th	The Monument (North Ridge), Asterisk Pass, The Wombat
5.0	The Mole (North Ramp Variation), The Platform
5.1	Gunsight Rock, Squaw Rock (Spiral)
5.2	Limestone Chimney, Arrowpoint (Northwest Corner)
5.3	Flattop (South Buttress), Tasmanian Devil
5.4	Round River, Direct Northwest Crack
5.5	Bowling Alley, Lollypop League, Brogan Spire (south buttress), Western Chimney
5.6	Cinnamon Slab, Easy Reader, Super Slab, Moscow
5.7	Lichen it, Spiderman, Bunny Face, Dancer, In Harm's Way
5.8	Jete, Ginger Snap, White Satin, Out of Harm's Way
5.9	Revelations, Moonshine, Sunset Slab, Sundown
5.10a	Zion, Karate Crack, Phoenix, Cruel Sister, Cosmos
5.10b	Gumby, Barbecue the Pope, Badfinger, Blood Clot
5.10c	Kunza Korner, Last Chance, Morning Star, Calamity Jam
5.10d	Explosive Energy Child, Reason to Be, Moon's of Pluto
5.11a	Blue Light Special, E Type Jag, On the Road, Zebra Direct
5.11b	Toxic, Vomit Launch, Karot Tots, Monkey Space
5.11c	License to Bolt, Natural Art, Moondance, Drilling Zona
5.11d	Ring of Fire, Rising Expectations, Hieroglyphics
5.12a	Heinous Cling (lower part), Power Dive, Dreamin', Mojomatic
5.12b	Latest Rage, Watts Tots, Boy Prophet, Shark Infested Waters
5.12c	Da Kine Corner, Last Waltz, Chain Reaction, The Urge
5.12d	Kings of Rap, Taco Chips, Peruvian Skies, Split Image
5.13a	Churning in the Wake, Darkness at Noon, The Product
5.13b	Aggro Monkey, Scene of the Crime, Waste Case
5.13c	White Heat, Rude Boys, Big Tuna, Just Do It (lower part)
5.13d	Vicious Fish, Villain, Jam Master J
5.14a	Scar Face, To Bolt or Not to Be, Bad Man
5.14c	Just Do It

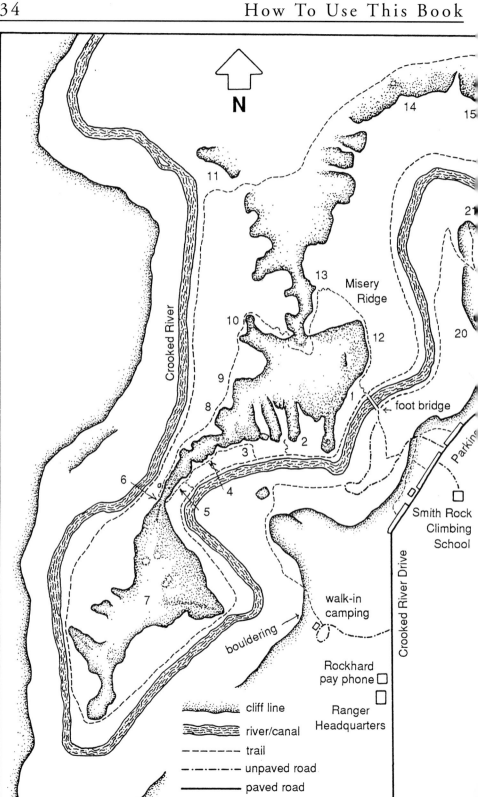

N

Crooked River

14

15

11

13   Misery
      Ridge

21

10   12

9   1   foot bridge

8

2   20

3

6   4

5

7   Smith Rock
                     Climbing
                     School

Parking

walk-in
camping

Crooked River Drive

bouldering

Rockhard
pay phone

Ranger
Headquarters

············· cliff line

〰〰〰 river/canal

- - - - - trail

-·-·-·- unpaved road

―――― paved road

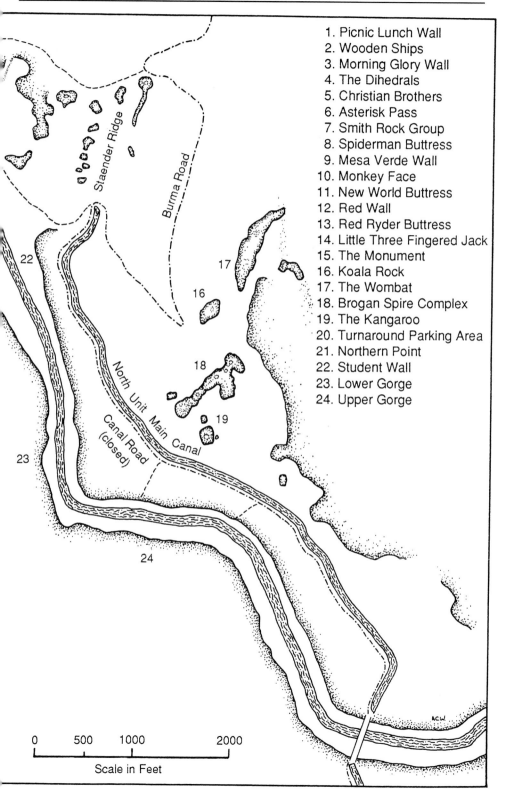

1. Picnic Lunch Wall
2. Wooden Ships
3. Morning Glory Wall
4. The Dihedrals
5. Christian Brothers
6. Asterisk Pass
7. Smith Rock Group
8. Spiderman Buttress
9. Mesa Verde Wall
10. Monkey Face
11. New World Buttress
12. Red Wall
13. Red Ryder Buttress
14. Little Three Fingered Jack
15. The Monument
16. Koala Rock
17. The Wombat
18. Brogan Spire Complex
19. The Kangaroo
20. Turnaround Parking Area
21. Northern Point
22. Student Wall
23. Lower Gorge
24. Upper Gorge

Photo: Bruce Adams

An unknown climber on Up For Grabs (5.11d).

A climber tackles Take A Powder (5.12a) in The Dihedrals.

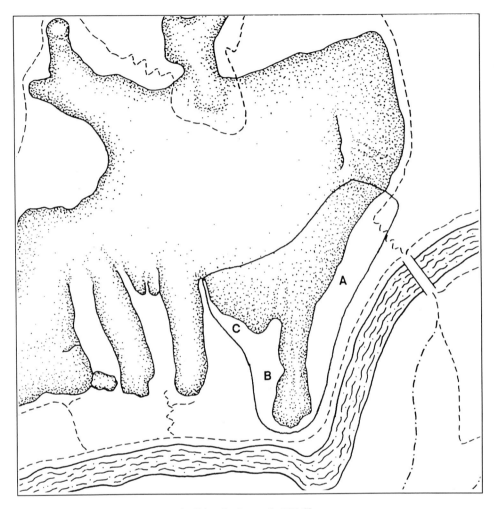

A. Picnic Lunch Wall
B. Shiprock
C. Table Scraps Wall

PICNIC LUNCH WALL AREA

N O C L I F F D O M I N A T E S the view from the Smith parking area more than Picnic Lunch Wall. Soaring nearly 700 feet above the bridge, this intimidating monolith hosts a diverse collection of routes. The multi-colored face captures the imagination of non-climbers more than any other rock at Smith. As you walk down to the bridge on a busy weekend, don't be surprised if a tourist stops you, pointing warily to the cliff, and asking, "Yuh gonna climb dat mountain?" To the climber, Picnic Lunch Wall isn't nearly as enthralling. Tons of loose rock cling precariously to its sides, turning several lines into nightmares. The crumbly rock might preclude any classics, but a pleasing variety of base routes, as well as afternoon shade, makes the wall popular on warm evenings. If you've made Picnic Lunch Wall your first stop, and the friable rock is getting you down, don't despair – most of the climbing at Smith is on far better stone.

For the big wall climber, some of Smith's few remaining aid climbs ascend the imposing arches on the left half of the cliff. Several long free lines scale the crag's less impressive right half, but these climbs usually are loose and run-out. Luckily, a throng of modern sport routes grace the base of the wall, enhancing the cliff's appeal. Nearby, the crumbling tower of Shiprock and the appropriately named Table Scraps Wall are forever ignored by sensible folk.

PICNIC LUNCH WALL

The painless approach ascends the carefully-constructed staircase rising directly above the bridge. To hike off from the top of the cliff, walk up and right to the Misery Ridge descent trail. This switchbacked, well-constructed path ultimately leads back to the base. If you ever feel the need to take out a rope, you're descending the wrong way and should keep searching for the proper trail.

A deep, black-streaked gully marks the right boundary of Picnic Lunch Wall, separating the cliff from Red Wall to the north. The first several routes start behind a couple boulders, about 50 feet left of the base of this gully.

1. SCORPIO 5.8 X Gear to 3 inches
   The scene of several epics and accidents over the years, **Scorpio** should be ignored, despite the moderate grade. The rock and protection are bad, and the climbing unaesthetic. Start below the right of two short, parallel cracks above a boulder.
   1. 5.8 Ascend a tricky, poorly protected thin crack to a belay ledge.
   2. 5.7 A short face leads into a flaring crack system. You can either climb directly, or follow easier holds to the right. Either way, the horrible protection makes the consequence of a broken hold devastating.
   3. 5.8 Face climb with no protection up a crumbly wall until reaching a dirty corner. Ascend the ugly dihedral to the top.

1a. I LOST MY LUNCH 5.9 X Gear to 3 inches
   Established by climbers unfortunate enough to get off route, this line ranks among the worst, and most dangerous, at Smith. The 180 foot lead steps right from the second pitch of the regular route and finishes in an obvious dihedral – after a nasty encounter with loose flakes. Stay away, or you might lose more than your lunch.

2. FOOL'S OVERTURE 5.9 R ★ Gear to 2.5 inches
   Identified by parallel inside corners far off the ground, this adventurous route isn't all that bad, despite some questionable rock. Start below the left of two short corners.

Picnic Lunch Wall

1. SCORPIO 5.8
1a. I LOST MY LUNCH 5.9
2. FOOL'S OVERTURE 5.9 ★★
3. HIGHWAY 97 5.12c ★★★
6. APPIAN WAY 5.12a ★★
7. NO PICNIC 5.10c ★
7a. FARMERS VAR. 5.10a
9. FREE LUNCH 5.10a ★
10. UNFINISHED
    SYMPHONY 5.12b ★★★
11. COLESLAW AND
    CHEMICALS 5.12d ★★
16. MIDNIGHT SNACK
    5.12b/c ★★
18. SOFT SHOE BALLET
    5.10a A4 ★
20. PICNIC LUNCH WALL
    5.9 A3+ ★
21. BUBBA'S IN BONDAGE
    5.7 A3 ★
22. SUICIDAL TENDENCIES
    5.11d ★
24. JOURNEY TO IXTLAN
    5.10b A5
25. EAST CHIMNEY 5.7

Photo: Bruce Adams

1. 5.8   Stem a corner past a fixed pin, then traverse up and left past an anchor. An easy, unprotected slab leads to belay bolts atop a ramp.

2. 5.9   Confront a crumbly seam to a ledge, then step across to the rightmost of two prominent dihedrals. Belay at a sloping ledge.

3. 5.8   Traverse on face holds into the left dihedral, and finish in a rotten gully.

3. HIGHWAY 97   5.12c ★★★   Bolts
Easily the finest route to the top of Picnic Lunch Wall, **Highway 97** cruises three stimulating pitches. The attractive flatiron of the final pitch is the most memorable feature, but most climbers lower after the start.

1. 5.11b   Motor up the bolted face, using pockets and tiny knobs, to a ledge.

2. 5.11d   Intense, technical moves on thin edges lead to a hand traverse right to an anchor.

3. 5.12c   Unrelenting edges with a crux of one-finger pockets snaps the concentration of most climbers.

4. LA SIESTA   5.11d ★★★   Bolts
Another bolted line rises a few feet left of the pocketed first pitch of **Highway 97.** After digesting a strenuous crank on a shallow two-finger pocket, finish with easier knobs.

5. SPARTACUS   5.12a ★★   Bolts
Despite only average quality, the short approach makes this strenuous wall popular. After a crux sequence past a small roof, the difficulty eases only slightly. Most of the loose rock plaguing early ascents pulled off long ago.

6. APPIAN WAY   5.12a ★★   Bolts
Anyone looking for a cheap 5.12 will appreciate this bolted line. Most climbers stick-clip the first bolt, and toprope through the crux. Easier knobs and pockets finish to the anchor.

7. NO PICNIC   5.10c R ★   Gear to 3 inches
This multi-pitch route is the best moderate line to the top of Picnic Lunch Wall. Unfortunately, this shouldn't be taken as a ringing endorsement, as you'll confront plenty of bad rock. Most climbers sampling this feast rap off at the first set of anchors. Start at a short, clean alcove just left of **Appian Way.**

1. 5.10c   An awkward move on great rock (crux) enters a flaring slot. Undercling left and climb a shallow dihedral, then edge on dicey knobs to an anchor.

2. 5.9   Ascend a crumbly crack to a small roof, then escape garbage by traversing right onto solid orange rock. Face climb past two bolts, then traverse left to the base of a foreboding chimney.

3. 5.8   Race up the surprisingly solid chimney, stepping right onto a ledge to avoid bad rock. Walk right, then climb a short face to a larger ledge.

4. 5.7   Hike right along the ledge and wander up moderate rock to the top.

7a. FARMERS VARIATION   5.10a X   Gear to 3 inches
On an early ascent of **No Picnic,** the leader mistakenly stumbled upon this wretched variation. If you care to relive his misfortune, don't step right out of the chimney on the third pitch. Instead plow through miserable rock to the large ledge just below the top.

8. TEDDY BEAR'S PICNIC   5.10b ★★   Bolts
This spooky face grows better with each ascent as knobs snap off on unsuspecting climbers. The friable nubbins on the first pitch are especially unnerving, but the better upper section offers some airy moves on good rock.

1. 5.10a   Romp up some large potholes and terrifying knobs to the anchors atop the first pitch of **No Picnic.**

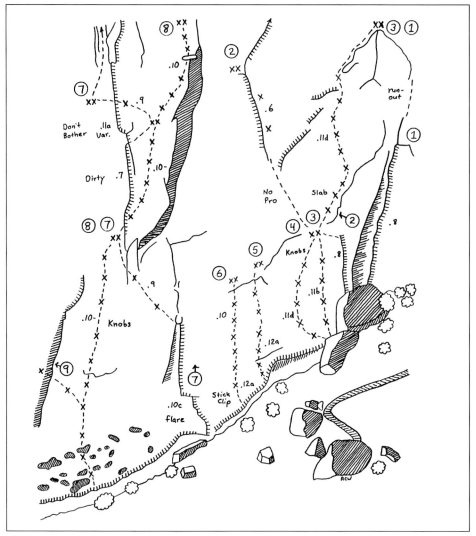

1. SCORPIO 5.8
2. FOOL'S OVERTURE 5.9 ★
3. HIGHWAY 97 5.12c ★★★
4. LA SIESTA 5.11d ★★★

5. SPARTACUS 5.12a ★★
6. APPIAN WAY 5.12a ★★
7. NO PICNIC 5.10c ★
8. TEDDY BEAR'S PICNIC 5.10b ★★

2. 5.10b Step right and jet up good rock past optional belay bolts to the highest anchor. Unfortunately, a massive loose block guards the final moves, so mantel lightly. Descend using two ropes.

9. FREE LUNCH 5.10a R ★ Gear to 3.5 inches
    As the most popular free route to the top of Picnic Lunch Wall, this meandering line pleases anyone not offended by loose rock. The climbing isn't always enjoyable, but the spacious ledges and excellent position make for some fun. A captivating fourth pitch highlights the outing. Start at the base of the same huge potholes as **Teddy Bear's Picnic**.

1. 5.10a Step gingerly past several bolts to a small, right-facing open book. Traverse left on knobs (crux) to a shallow corner leading to a belay ledge.
2. 5.9 Climb up and over a pinnacle, then step down and left to a comfortable ledge.
3. 5.9 Jam the obvious rotten crack, stemming out of an overhanging alcove to a fist crack and a small ledge.
4. 5.8 Scamper up the long crack on surprisingly solid rock to a large shelf.
5. 5.9 Grunt up an awkward wide crack and flared chimney to a two-bolt anchor at the top.

Unfinished at the time of this writing, a multi-pitch project sports dozens of bolts beginning just left of **Free Lunch**. The entire route (**Five Easy Pieces**) will offer five pitches in a direct line to the top. To date, only the first two pitchees (5.12a and 5.12c/d) go free.

10. UNFINISHED SYMPHONY 5.12b ★★ (upper pitch A3) Gear to 1 inch (#1 Friend, R.P.s, small Rocks)

The upper pitches of **Free Lunch** were originally part of an aid climb. The first pitch received a free ascent in 1982, and for two weeks held the title of Smith's hardest route. Most everyone stops at the first anchors, as the second pitch nails an ugly corner.
1. 5.12b Lieback, jam and stem the overhanging crack to an anchor. Lower off or . . .
2. A3 Aid past several bolts and fixed pins to a belay ledge.
3, 4, 5 Finish via the **Free Lunch** crack system to the top.

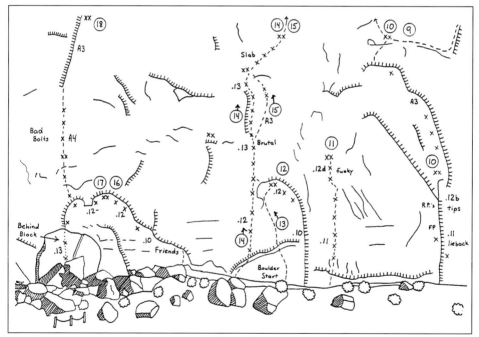

Picnic Lunch Wall – Center Base

9. FREE LUNCH 5.10a ★
10. UNFINISHED SYMPHONY 5.12b ★★
11. COLESLAW AND CHEMICALS 5.12d ★★
12. PUBIC LUAU 5.11d/12a ★★
13. PUBIC LUAU DIRECT 5.12b ★★
14. PROJECT 5.14a ?
15. ZORTEX THRUX A4
16. MIDNIGHT SNACK 5.12b/c ★★
17. SNACK CRACK 5.13b ★★
18. SOFT SHOE BALLET 5.10a A4 ★

11. COLESLAW AND CHEMICALS 5.12d ★★ Bolts
     This demanding wall left of **Unfinished Symphony** comes packed with intriguing moves held
     together with epoxy. The bizarre crux comes when you're pumped just below the anchors.

12. PUBIC LUAU 5.11d/12a ★★ Gear to 2 inches
     The name of this prominent arch refers to the style of picnic lunch preferred by the first
     ascentionist. Unfortunately, the crux sequence of underclings comes right at the slings. Most
     people just grab the webbing, but the first ascent included move, plus the strenuous anchor clip.
     The higher grade pleases the purists, while the lower grade is for everyone else.

13. PUBIC LUAU DIRECT 5.12b ★★ TR
     A comical finish caps this ignored toprope problem. Start with a tricky boulder move ten feet left
     of **Pubic Luau,** then pull tenderly on some loose face holds to a rest. The crux lunges wildly for
     the slings at the top.

14. PROJECT 5.14a ?
     When completed, this imposing free route will rate among the most difficult lines at Smith. The
     intense climbing contains everything from overhanging power moves to a technical arête section.
     The crux comes right at the top, with a wickedly hard face move pulling onto the final slab. The
     rock isn't any better than the average Picnic Lunch Wall route, but epoxy holds everything
     together.

15. ZORTEX THRUX A4 Aid rack
     Originally, **Pubic Luau** was the start of an aid route that was never completed. **Zortex Thrux** aids
     the arch, then nails an invisible seam to an anchor. A long section of aid on a slab stops one pitch
     below the top. Here, the first ascent team climbed no further, deciding retreat was a gentler fate
     than having to do some free moves. Potentially, the whole route could go free to the top
     someday.

16. MIDNIGHT SNACK 5.12b/c ★★ Gear to 3.5 inches (#1.5 to #3.5 Friends)
     This strenuous arch was the hardest route at Smith for nine months. Despite its convenient
     location, **Midnight Snack** receives few ascents; a permanent streak of bird guano, along with
     awkward moves and gear placements, turn everyone off. Bolts protect the stimulating crux
     underclings near the top.

17. SNACK CRACK 5.13b ★★ Bolts
     Smith's most technical thin crack is found behind a gigantic leaning slab. Despite the top billing,
     it receives very little attention. Originally protected by R.P.s, the start resisted all attempts until
     the addition of three bolts made it safer and less physical. Clip the first bolt with a stick, or do a
     full body stem between the wall and the leaning slab. Once you master the pin scars low, a
     strenuous undercling finishes this tasty morsel.

18. SOFT SHOE BALLET 5.10a A4 X ★ Aid rack to 2 inches
     Among Smith's most difficult aid climbs, **Soft Shoe Ballet** remains a horror show for the few who
     care to attempt it. The first pitch is very dangerous, with smashing into the slab a real possibility.
     1. A4 Aid **Snack Crack** using nuts, then exit the arch on poor pins. Nail past a few bad bolts to
     a sling belay.
     2. A4 Hard nailing up a shallow, right-leaning corner ends at an idyllic belay ledge.
     3. 5.10a A2 Mixed free and aid moves past a few bolts leads to the top.

19. PROJECT 5.15 ?
     A futuristic wall rises about thirty feet left of **Snack Crack**. It has few features other than an offset
     at one-third height. Attempted briefly in 1989, this potential free route might well be 5.15 (if
     unaltered). The climb is harder than it looks, and it looks impossible.

20. PICNIC LUNCH WALL 5.9 A3+ R ★ Aid rack to 3 inches
First done in 1969, this was the most difficult aid climb in Oregon for nearly a decade. Many additional bolts have appeared over the years, making it easier today than on the first ascent. Repeated nailings continue to turn the climb into something of an eyesore; what were once knifeblade placements now require 2.5-inch angles. Perhaps the entire route would go free, if someone didn't mind atrocious rock. Start in a pegged-out crack at the left end of a prominent, low-level roof.
1. A3+ Climb huge pin scars past a few bolts to a hanging belay.
2. 5.7 A1 Nail to the huge roof, then face traverse right to bolts leading over the ceiling to an anchor.
3. A3+ More pin pounding and bolts in a dihedral ends at another hanging belay below a small roof.
4. 5.9 A2 Keep hammering, throwing in an occasional free move, until reaching an anchor below a bolt line.
5. A1 Shaky bolts escape right to a ledge. Scramble to the top.

21. BUBBA'S IN BONDAGE 5.7 A3 ★ Aid rack to 1 inch
An aid enthusiast might enjoy this rarely-climbed direct start to **Picnic Lunch Wall**. The entire first pitch would go free if heavily cleaned. Begin 60 feet right of the regular start on a pile of boulders.
1. A3 Nail past a few bolts, then ascend a clean open book to a hanging belay.
2. 5.7 A3 Many bolts and a few pins lead past a big overhang, joining the second pitch of **Picnic Lunch Wall** just below the anchors.
3, 4, & 5 Finish **Picnic Lunch Wall** to the top.

22. SUICIDAL TENDENCIES 5.11d ★ Bolts
This crumbly face route rises just right of a right-leaning flake. Established from the ground up, the climb never received the cleaning it so desperately needed. Many holds used on the first ascent now litter the base.

23. TOUCH 5.11c ★★ Bolts
A better climb than its neighbor to the right, most of the loose rock pulled off on early ascents, leaving a fairly clean line. Start just left of the prominent, right-leaning flake, and make some tricky moves to a thin crux past the third bolt. The difficulties ease the higher you go.

24. JOURNEY TO IXTLAN 5.10b A5 X Aid rack
As the worst aid route at Smith, this overhanging wall of rubble has absolutely no redeeming qualities. Nauseated by horrible rock, the first-ascent team backed off after the first several pitches. Later, the leader returned, rapped from the top to his high point and finished the final two pitches. The entire route might never see a one-push ascent.

SHIPROCK

This landmark tower rises to the left of Picnic Lunch Wall. A dramatically different rock type than the tuff, Shiprock's rhyolite is extremely hard, but heavily fractured. If all of Smith Rock consisted of this junk, then nobody would ever climb here, as sharp chunks unexpectedly pull off in your hands. The two routes ascend opposite sides of the same chimney system, then follow a single line to the top. Don't let the grades fool you. These routes are not for beginners! Only blockheads with enough experience to know better should try.

25. EAST CHIMNEY 5.7 X Gear to 4 inches
This terrible route inexplicably attracts inexperienced climbers laden with huge racks of hexs and triple-length slings. Start at the base of the obvious chimney system separating Shiprock from Picnic Lunch Wall, then squirm up the ugly slot in two pitches. Either continue to the top via the **West Chimney,** or descend the backside by rappeling off a pile of loose boulders.

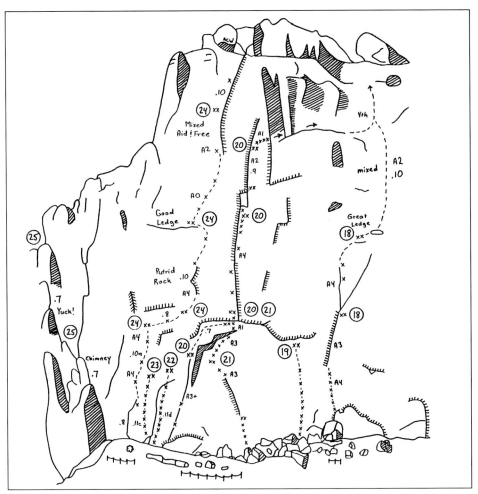

Picnic Lunch Wall – Left Side

18. SOFT SHOE BALLET 5.10a A4 ★
19. PROJECT 5.15 ?
20. PICNIC LUNCH WALL 5.9 A3+ ★
21. BUBBA'S IN BONDAGE 5.7 A3 ★

22. SUICIDAL TENDENCIES 5.11d ★
23. TOUCH 5.11c ★★
24. JOURNEY TO IXTLAN 5.10b A5
25. EAST CHIMNEY 5.7

26. WEST CHIMNEY 5.7 X Gear to 3 inches
    The **West Chimney** was the line of Shiprock's first ascent. Hike up scree along the western base of
the formation to a short chimney, then climb the fractured trough to a belay at the notch. Move
lightly up the right side of the arête on appalling rock with lousy protection to the highest of the
summit spires.

TABLE SCRAPS WALL
A small cliff called Table Scraps Wall rests atop of the gully left of Shiprock. Fortunately, the long uphill approach stops most climbers from sampling these unpalatable scraps.

27. CITY DUMP   5.7 R   Gear to 2.5 inches
    A wretched junk pile. Begin behind a flake at the base of a filthy, indistinct left-facing corner.
    1. 5.7   Climb the corn-flake crack to a belay ledge.
    2. 5.7   Clamber up a short, flaring crack to a low angle slab. Race the unprotected slab to a single bolt anchor below a right-facing corner.
    3. 5.7   Jam to the top.

28. VANISHING UNCERTAINTY   5.9 R ★   Gear to 2 inches
    Although easily the best route on Table Scraps Wall, **Vanishing Uncertainty** isn't worth the walk. Start left of the obvious face crack in the center of the wall, then traverse right on an unprotected slab past a bolt. Jam the steep flaring crack (crux), then wander up junky chimneys to the top.

29. WASTE LAND   5.8 R   Gear to 5 inches
    Rotten rock and off-width climbing plague this repulsive route. Start at the base of a large open book, and writhe to the top in one nauseating pitch.

Photo: Bruce Adams

Shiprock and Table Scraps Wall

26. WEST CHIMNEY 5.7	28. VANISHING UNCERTAINTY 5.9 ★
27. CITY DUMP 5.7	29. WASTE LAND 5.8

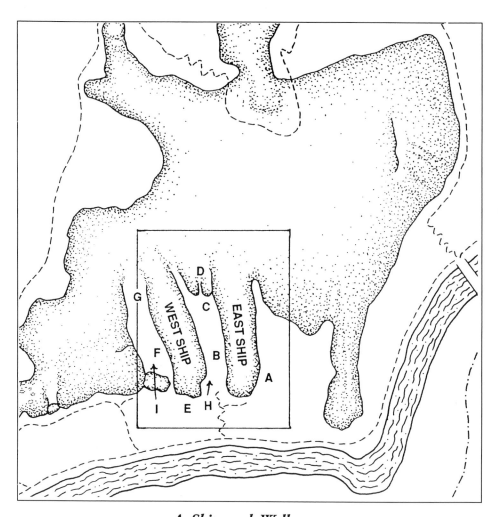

A. Shipwreck Wall
B. Aggro Wall
C. Plastic Area
D. Honeycomb Wall
E. West Ship, River Face
F. Cocaine Wall
G. Tuff Nuggets Wall
H. Aggro Gully
I. Cocaine Gully

THE WOODEN SHIPS/THE GULLIES

EXTENDING FAR DOWN the hillside left of Shiprock are two massive ribs known as the Wooden Ships. These highly-developed crags contain some of the most severe climbing at Smith, ranging from knobby faces to overhanging endurance problems. The Wooden Ships are a mecca for the sport climber, as you'll need nothing but quickdraws for 90% of the routes. These crags hold little interest for the beginner, as even the easiest bolted lines are 5.10, but they've tantalized countless climbers looking to crank the desperates.

The East Ship sits to the right and the West Ship to the left, but this area is better recognized by the three gullies cutting narrow channels through the cliff line. The right side of the East Ship borders Shiprock Gully, and contains a series of bulgy, bolted routes. Between the two crags rests the renowned Aggro Gully, with its overhanging routes on either side. Bordering the left face of the West Ship is Cocaine Gully, best known for a popular collection of vertical faces. The layout of these corridors makes the Wooden Ships a good choice year round. You usually can find sun in the winter, and avoid it during the summer by merely stepping across to the other side of the gully.

The Wooden Ships are unlike any of Smith's other top crags. While most of the routes on tuff require some cleaning, the cliffs here – especially in the Aggro Gully – are essentially walls of solidified mud. Oddly, these crumbly faces contain some of the most popular and satisfying extreme routes at Smith. On typical first ascents, climbers scoured the rock relentlessly with a brush, pulling off dozens of loose flakes to uncover a climbable line. Using epoxy, they reinforced any critical holds to ensure they won't pull off. Even with such fanatical cleaning, early ascents rain a stream of rock scraps, as climbers brush against the flaky rock between the scrubbed holds. Yet over time, the rock quality steadily improves, as solid stone lies beneath the mud on the surface. Routes like **Aggro Monkey** were originally miserable junk piles, but now are surprisingly solid.

Not all rock on the Wooden Ships requires such involved preparation. The West Ship's river face, for instance, has some excellent rock, as does the Cocaine Wall. Yet it was the collection of routes in Aggro Gully that had the biggest impact on Smith free climbing. These routes had a significance far beyond their big numbers. More than any other lines, they opened the eyes of climbers who felt that only the best rock at Smith could yield good routes. Overnight, the amount of climbable rock on the tuff increased ten-fold.

Although you'll find a variety of climbs here, the most unusual are the strongly overhanging routes of the Aggro Gully. While most of Smith's hardest lines require more technique than muscle, these climbs require plenty of pure brawn. Even if you use all the technique in the world, you'll fall flat if you can't make the lock-offs. Understandably, these climbs make an excellent training ground if you'd like to build a physique beyond the bulging forearms that other Smith desperates give you.

The new route possibilities along the walls of the Wooden Ships are many, as several sections remain almost completely untouched. Most of these routes will be 5.12 or harder, but there are moderate lines as well. A slew of 5.10 and 5.11 routes recently expanded the appeal of the area and other lines surely will follow. There are few natural gems here, but climbers willing to bring out their scrub brush won't run out of options for years to come.

EAST SHIP

The East Ship rises around the corner from Shiprock. A prominent crack system splits the entire river face of the formation. Shiprock Gully, capped by the uninspiring Table Scraps Wall, looms to the right. To the left looms the narrow Aggro Gully, with its ominous walls overhanging strongly on either side.

Shipwreck Wall

A homely wall with a collection of bolted face climbs lurks across from Shiprock. Although mediocre when first climbed, these routes quickly improved and now are justifiably popular. The following routes start far uphill, and descend in order to the foot of the East Ship:

1. PROJECT 5.13 ?
   Farthest uphill, an abandoned bolt line ascends part way up an overhang. When completed, it'll be the hardest on the Shipwreck Wall.

2. MOTHER'S MILK 5.12d ★★ Bolts
   A wild dynamic at the final bulge highlights this gymnastic route. The line attacks the left portion of the obvious overhang stretching along the upper part of the wall.

3. WALKING WHILE INTOXICATED 5.10b ★★ Bolts
   This moderate face is a good choice for climbers breaking into 5.10s. A well-protected, balancey crux on perfect rock unfortunately deteriorates into some easy junk finishing to the anchor. Start just left of a lichen-covered ramp.

4. FLIGHT OF THE PATRIOT SCUD BLASTER 5.11b ★★ Bolts
   This extremely short route, with a mouthful of a name, rises just downhill from **Walking While Intoxicated**. The only hard move cranks around an intimidating overhang past the second bolt.

5. PURPLE ACES 5.11b/c ★★ Bolts
   Continuously difficult, this series of pockets and edges keeps you thinking until the very end. The hardest moves pull around a bulge at the start.

6. MORE SANDY THAN KEVIN 5.10d/11a ★★ Bolts
   Although loose on the first ascent, the quality of this steep route improved as thin flakes snapped off. Today, it's fun, with some thin face moves following a strenuous pull around a steep section.

7. LIQUID JADE 5.12a/b ★★★ Bolts
   The best route on the Shipwreck Wall climbs an attractive line on flawless rock. After an intellectual bouldering sequence above the first bolt, the moves ease briefly before the crux cranks past a bulge on thin edges.

8. BLUE LIGHT SPECIAL 5.11a ★★★ Bolts
   This must-do route is the lowest of the bolted lines. After launching into a strenuous undercling at the start, the difficulty eases, but the moves are fun and solid to the anchor.

East Ship – River Face

Obviously lacking in potential, the river face of the East Ship features a rubble-strewn crack system and the following sport climb:

9. TIME TO POWER 5.12c ★★★ Bolts
   A pumping series of energetic moves power up this overhanging face. Unfortunately, you have to plow through an ugly approach pitch to get to the real climbing.

Photo: Bruce Adams

Shipwreck Wall

2. MOTHER'S MILK 5.12d ★★
3. WALKING WHILE
   INTOXICATED 5.10b ★★
8. BLUE LIGHT SPECIAL 5.11a
   ★★★

East Ship – River Face

9. TIME TO POWER 5.12c ★★★
10. SHIPWRECK 5.9

Aggro Gully

28. THE BURL MASTER 5.13 ?
29. MONKEY BOY 5.12c ★★
30. UP FOR GRABS 5.11d ★★★
32. TOXIC 5.11b ★★★★

West Ship – River Face

36. SOLAR 5.9 ★★
38. TIME'S UP 5.13a/b ★★★

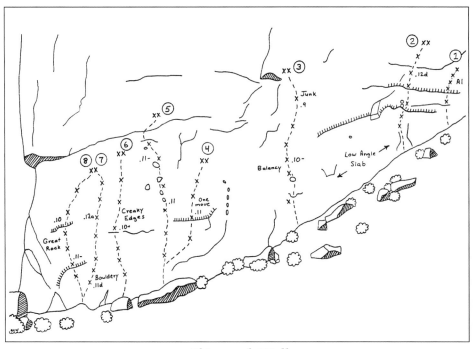

Shipwreck Wall

1. PROJECT 5.13 ?
2. MOTHER'S MILK 5.12d ★★
3. WALKING WHILE INTOXICATED
   5.10b ★★
4. FLIGHT OF THE PATRIOT SCUD
   BLASTER 5.11b ★★

5. PURPLE ACES 5.11b/c ★★
6. MORE SANDY THAN KEVIN
   5.10d/11a ★★
7. LIQUID JADE 5.12a/b ★★★
8. BLUE LIGHT SPECIAL 5.11a ★★★

10. SHIPWRECK 5.9 R Gear to 3 inches
    This junky crack splits the river face of the East Ship. The few climbers that try back off at the
    first set of anchors as the rock quickly deteriorates above. Begin below a right-leaning flake crack.
    1. 5.9 Jam and lieback a short section of brilliant rock to an arching, friable flake ending at
    anchor bolts.
    2. 5.8 Climb another few feet, then traverse sharply down and left to a rotten crack. Grovel to
    Avalanche Ledge.
    3. 5.8 Grunt up the rotten, flaring crack while showering your helpless belayer with rubble.
    4. 4th Scramble along the crest of the ridge to the top.

Aggro Gully
The steep-sided Aggro Gully separates the two Wooden Ships. The right wall gets morning and late
day shade, while the left wall sees only morning sun.

Right Side – Aggro Wall
An impressive collection of hard routes ascend the Aggro Wall. You'll find the first two lines on an
ugly face at the entrance to the gully: the remaining routes are described in order moving uphill.

11.　GHOST RIDER　5.12b ★　Bolts
　　Originally a crumbly nightmare, this bouldery route becomes more solid with every ascent. A
　　tricky start leads to an awkward crux that moves past a rock jutting out of the wall.

12.　HIGHWAY TO HELL　5.12a ★★　Bolts
　　This bulgy line rises a few feet left of **Ghost Rider.** A difficult-to-clip fourth bolt drives some
　　away, although the crux moves protect well. The rock isn't perfect, but many climbers take a
　　spin.

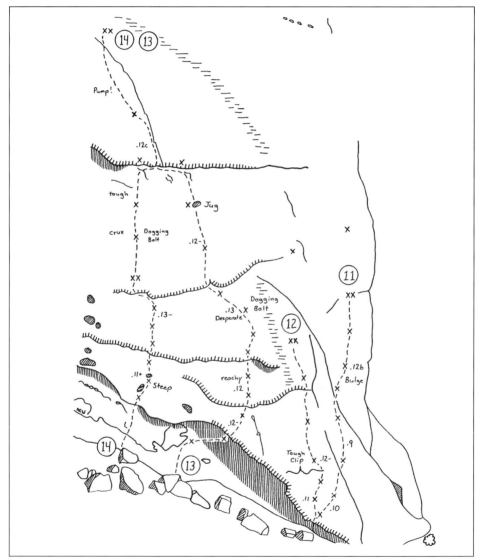

Aggro Wall - Lower Portion

11.　GHOST RIDER　5.12b ★　　　　13.　VILLAIN　5.13d ★★★
12.　HIGHWAY TO HELL　5.12a ★★　　14.　WHITE WEDDING　5.13d/14a ★★★

13. VILLAIN 5.13d ★★★ Bolts

The crux sequence of this left-leaning line ranks among the most difficult at Smith. A single crank off a sloping, two finger pocket stops most climbers cold. Although pumping, the rest of the moves aren't especially hard for such a high-grade route. If the crux comes easily, then **Villain** could be a quick tick. If not, you'll find the road to success long and frustrating, as you drop off the same move day after day.

14. WHITE WEDDING 5.13d/14a ★★★ Bolts

One of Smith's hardest routes powers up the savagely steep wall left of **Villain**. A tricky 5.13 section low saps just enough energy to make the technical crux, above the double bolts, too powerful for almost everyone. The climbing above eases, but most climbers fall off at least once past the hardest move. The eighth bolt allows you to work out the crux without taking repeated whippers. On redpoint, everyone ignores it.

15. BADMAN 5.13d/14a ★★★ Bolts

The most exciting route on the Aggro Wall climbs the pocketed face left of **White Wedding**. A powerful sequence low and a unique series of underclings and all-out dynamics highlight the crux sequences. As with every line on the wall, the rock isn't flawless, but it grows cleaner with each attempt.

16. PROJECT 5.13+ ?

This future route rises a few feet left of **Badman**. A few bolts are in place on the upper section, but a huge amount of cleaning remains.

17. AGGRO MONKEY 5.13b ★★★ Bolts

This pumping line opened the gully to climbers who previously walked by in search of better rock. Today, it's the most climbed route on the wall. After a thuggish pull over the roof, a strenuous series of cranks from jug to jug bring you to the anchors.

18. SCENE OF THE CRIME 5.13b/c ★★★ Bolts

Intriguing moves on surprisingly solid stone highlight this popular test piece. A tough boulder problem right off the ground, and a one-finger crank at mid-height, are the hardest moves, but the overall crux lies past the last bolt, where you must throw a dynamic. Tall climbers have a decided advantage here, as the final move ranges from easy to desperate, depending on whether you can make the reach.

19. CRIME WAVE 5.13c ★★★ Bolts

This direct start to **Scene of the Crime** makes an already difficult route even more demanding. If you don't possess the wingspan to make the long stretches between good holds, you might as well cross it off your list.

20. THE QUICKENING 5.12d ★★ Bolts

An invigorating sequence over a roof highlights this endurance problem. The crux itself comes higher, with a lock-off on the upper headwall. Some slick epoxy detracts from the quality of the route, but it's still worth doing.

21. PROJECT 5.13c ?

This is a much more difficult finish that shares the same start as **The Quickening,** but ends with an offset to the left. The crux will come high on the route with a big dynamic.

22. SPEWING 5.12d ★★ Bolts

This short, tricky route looms near the top of the Aggro Wall. A single, desperate move interrupts a mostly moderate sequence of good holds.

23. PROJECT 5.12 ?

The upper end of the Aggro Wall merges into an inside corner that leads into a deep chimney. A double-edged column scattered with a few bolts rises just left of this chimney, and might someday yield two routes.

24. CAUSTIC 5.12b/c ★ Bolts
This intimidating line attacks the right side of a wave of bulges downhill from the Plastic Area. Apparently it wasn't well-cleaned on the first ascent, so watch for loose holds.

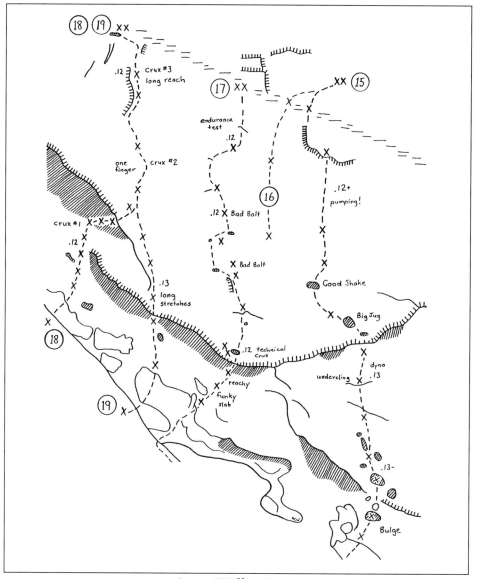

Aggro Wall – Center

15. BADMAN 5.13d/14a ★★★
16. PROJECT 5.13+ ?
17. AGGRO MONKEY 5.13b ★★★

18. SCENE OF THE CRIME 5.13b/c ★★★
19. CRIME WAVE 5.13c ★★★

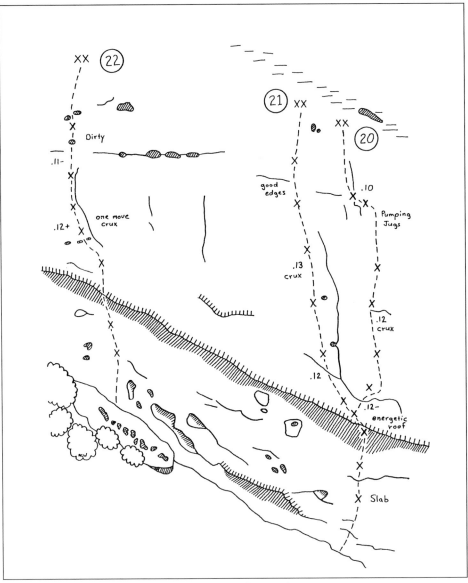

Aggro Wall – Left

20. THE QUICKENING 5.12d ★★   22. SPEWING 5.12d ★★
21. PROJECT 5.13c ?

Plastic Area

A gigantic roof of extremely dirty, flaky rock catches the eye near the top of the right side of Aggro Gully. In 1989, this roof was the scene of the most controversial routes ever established at Smith. Intent on designing a training ground for the overhanging routes of Europe, several climbers painstakingly created four routes using bolt-on, plastic holds. If you can ignore the ethical considerations, the routes are fun because they're like nothing else at Smith. Anyone searching for an upper body workout will love these thuggish jug ladders.

Obviously, it's difficult to ignore the ethical issues, as many climbers express opinions ranging from mild disgust to total outrage. Allowing this practice to spread beyond this isolated area could ruin Smith Rock. Nobody wants to see plastic holds in the Dihedrals, for instance.

Fortunately, these routes aren't overly blatant. Since they're far off the beaten path, they aren't visible from any of the trails. Most Smith Rock locals feel that in this one area, the holds should remain, but any additional plastic routes at Smith must be eliminated, if they're ever created. The thought of plastic routes throughout Smith Rock is offensive to 99% of the people who climb here. A proliferation of these artificial lines could close the park to climbing faster than anything else.

The grades of the plastic routes are always subject to change, as the holds can be rotated and changed by anyone. This makes any effort at setting a permanent grade futile. Still, at the time of this writing, the grades left to right are 5.10d, 5.13c, 5.11d, and 5.12d. Of course, when you go up to try them, the grades might be totally different, or the holds completely gone.

Honeycomb Wall

This dinky wall sits high atop the right side of the Aggro Gully. These unique climbs make an good warm-up for the more demanding climbs in the gully; they're laughably short, but a lot of fun. To approach the wall, scramble up the center of three narrow corridors, and step right to a sloping ledge system.

25. SEASONAL EFFECTIVENESS DISORDER   5.10a ★★★   Bolts
    The energetic rightmost route shouldn't be missed. A few technical moves low lead to some thrilling jugs around the crux bulge.

26. SKINNY SWEATY MAN   5.11a ★★   Bolts
    The center route contains a desperate move right off the deck and finishes with a brief flurry of jugs.

27. CRANKENSTEIN   5.11a ★★   Bolts
    A strenuous sequence of lock-offs highlights the upper of the three routes on the Honeycomb Wall. A boulder problem at the start contains the hardest move, although many ignore the original sequence by using holds to the left. Most climbers stick-clip the first bolt.

WEST SHIP

The West Ship lies on the opposite side of the Aggro Gully from the East Ship. Similar in appearance to its neighbor to the east, this formation offers many easier routes on higher-quality rock.

Aggro Gully – Left Side

A series of lines lie across the gully from the more famous routes of the Aggro Wall. An impressive bulge guards the uphill section.

28. THE BURL MASTER   5.13 ?   Project
    This route climbs a steep wall undercut by a large cave. It rises directly across the gully from the Plastic Area. The only thing lacking on this strenuous route is a start.

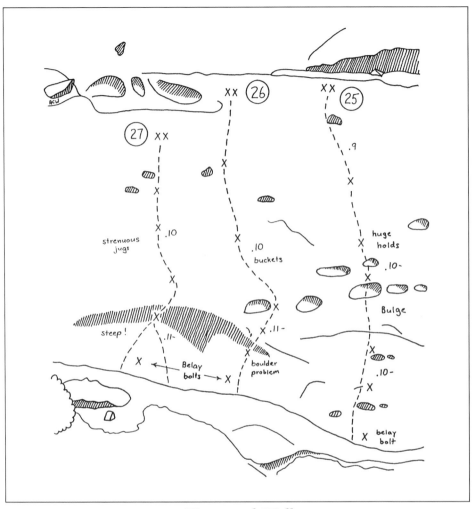

Honeycomb Wall

25. SEASONAL EFFECTIVENESS   26. SKINNY SWEATY MAN 5.11a ★★
    DISORDER 5.10a ★★★   27. CRANKENSTEIN 5.11a ★★

29. MONKEY BOY 5.12c ★★ Bolts
    This short, overhanging route rises midway up the left side of the Aggro Gully. Scramble atop the
    highest ledge system, then power up the massive bulge. The crux pulls around the lip and past the
    final bolt, although some feel the clip is more difficult than the ensuing moves.

30. UP FOR GRABS 5.11d ★★★ Bolts
    A huge dynamic caps this high-quality route, though you can avoid the lunge using holds to the
    left if you don't like flying. The technical crux comes when you must finesse a tricky bulge a few
    feet lower.

31. NO NUKES 5.10b ★   Gear to 2.5 inches

   If not for some loose flakes at the start, this crack might be worth doing. Despite appearances, the flakes don't detract much from the climbing, and the crux jams a short inch-and-a-quarter crack into a slot.

32. TOXIC 5.11b ★★★★   Bolts

   The scene of countless pumped forearms, this classic line of jugs is immensely popular. The excellent rock and athletic moves captivate everyone. The crux at the second bolt succumbs to either a wild lunge or a clever static move, although many climbers fail on good holds just below the anchor.

33. TOXIC TOPROPE 5.12a/b ★★   TR

   It's possible to toprope a powerful series of holds a few feet to the right using the **Toxic** anchors. An awkward reach-through at the crux denies most short people any chance of success.

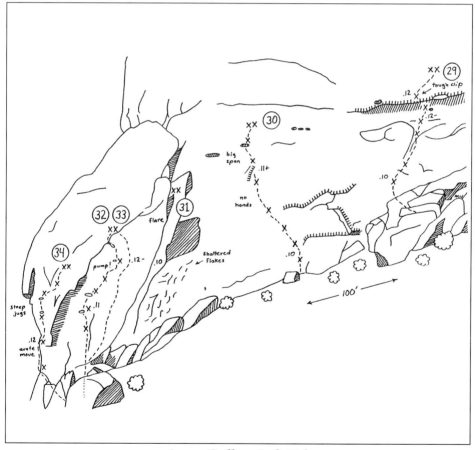

Aggro Gully – Left Side

29. MONKEY BOY 5.12c ★★
30. UP FOR GRABS 5.11d ★★★
31. NO NUKES 5.10b ★

32. TOXIC 5.11b ★★★★
33. TOXIC TOPROPE 5.12a/b ★★
34. FEET OF CLAY 5.12b ★★★

Photo: Bruce Adams

Aggro Wall – Right Side

11. GHOST RIDER 5.12b ★
14. WHITE WEDDING
        5.13d/14a ★★★
18. SCENE OF THE CRIME
        5.13b/c ★★★

West Ship – River Face

35. POWER 5.13b ★★★
37. NO DOZ 5.9 A4
38. TIME'S UP 5.13a/b ★★★

Cocaine Gully

41. SKELETON SURFER
        5.11b ★★

Cocaine Wall

45. VOMIT LAUNCH 5.11b
        ★★★

West Ship – River Face

The impressive river face of the West Ship contains the best rock on the Wooden Ships. The following routes are difficult, overhanging and excellent:

34. FEET OF CLAY 5.12b ★★★ Bolts

This short, steep wall deserves more attention than it receives. A technical crux on the starting arête leads to an exposed sequence on jugs.

35. POWER 5.13b ★★★ Bolts

This striking overhang is the most impressive section of rock on the West Ship's river face. The technical crux, a powerful two-finger pocket followed by a tough clip, comes low on the route. The holds above are good, but most find their power drained by the crux and plummet on the dash to the anchor. The original start ascended a bolted 5.9 flake from the ground, but the **Feet of Clay** approach makes more sense.

36. SOLAR 5.9 ★★ Gear to 3 inches

Spectacular but seldom climbed, **Solar** deserves more traffic. The intimidating second pitch is easier than it looks.

1. 5.8 Hand traverse to the anchor below **Power,** then climb a broken crack to a small belay ledge.

2. 5.9 Follow the obvious left-leaning corner to a belay at the crest of the ridge.

3. 4th Scramble along the ridge to the top.

37. NO DOZ 5.9 A4 X Aid rack

This forgotten aid line ascends the entire river face of the West Ship, joining **Solar** at the base of the final corner. An early attempt put a climber in the hospital with a broken leg. Since history tends to repeat itself, most climbers shy away.

38. TIME'S UP 5.13a/b ★★★ Bolts

Highly technical and surprisingly pumping, this striking wall attracts many attempts. To get to the headwall, you'll have to crank a tricky start off the ground, but a sit-down rest provides a complete recovery. Climb efficiently on the small edges low, or you'll find that your time's up when you can't hang on to good holds near the top.

39. SLIT YOUR WRIST 5.13b ★★★ Bolts

The clean, overhanging arête left of **Time's Up** yields to an intense sequence of slaps. The line shares the same start as its neighbor, but launches left at the fourth bolt into the crux section. At the sixth bolt, the difficulties ease, but the final edge of **The Blade** can foil your redpoint burn.

40. PROJECT 5.13d ?

The warm-up for this route will include the entire crux section of **Slit Your Wrist.** The main business comes higher, on the gently overhanging face above.

Cocaine Gully

The gulch between the West Ship and Morning Glory Wall offers several routes, mostly on the Cocaine Wall. A boulder the size of a large house blocks the entrance. The usual approach is a scramble up a dirty, 4th-class chimney system on the right side of the block.

41. SKELETON SURFER 5.11b ★★ Bolts

This intimidating route rises from the shadows as you enter the chimney system to the Cocaine Gully. Unusually strenuous for the grade, the **Surfer** follows a jungle gym of jugs past five bolts to a mantel over the lip. A bouldering start getting both feet off the ground is easily the hardest move, but most people pile rocks high enough to cheat past.

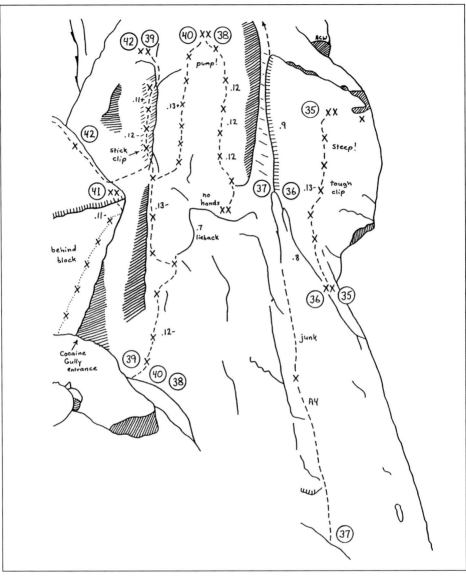

West Ship – River Face

35. POWER 5.13b ★★★	39. SLIT YOUR WRIST 5.13b ★★★
36. SOLAR 5.9 ★★	40. PROJECT 5.13d ?
37. NO DOZ 5.9 A4	41. SKELETON SURFER 5.11b ★★
38. TIME'S UP 5.13a/b ★★★	42. THE BLADE 5.12a ★★★

42. THE BLADE   5.12a ★★★   Bolts
    Extremely technical for the grade, this attractive arête baffles many attempting climbers. The crux comes right at the start, but the remaining moves will keep you perplexed. To approach, step down to a belay bolt from the top of the gigantic boulder, and stick-clip the first bolt.

Cocaine Wall

This classic, vertical face on the right side of the Cocaine Gully holds many popular routes. Morning shade makes it a good early destination on a hot day.

43. CHICKEN McNUGGETS 5.10b ★★★ Bolts

A delightful series of knobs peppers the face just right of **Cocaine Crack.** Most of the suspect nubbins blew off on early ascents, leaving behind a savory route.

44. COCAINE CRACK 5.11b ★★ Gear

For many years, this strenuous crack system was the only route on the wall. Those unfortunate enough to make the epic early ascents unwittingly pulled away all the loose boulders and flakes, leaving a clean but seldom-climbed route.

45. VOMIT LAUNCH 5.11b ★★★★ Bolts

Marred only by a tasteless name, Vomit Launch is the finest route on the Cocaine Wall. No individual move will throw you much, but the pump might make you sick. Fortunately, good holds always appear when you need them most.

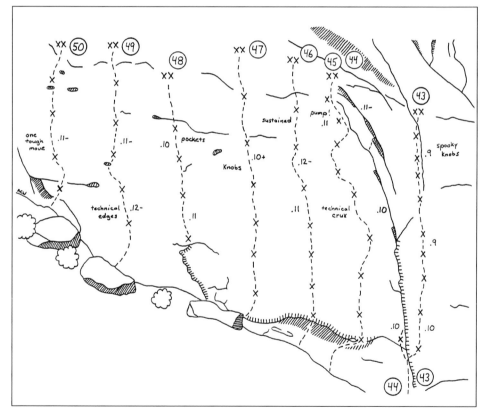

Cocaine Wall

43. CHICKEN McNUGGETS 5.10b ★★★
44. COCAINE CRACK 5.11b ★★
45. VOMIT LAUNCH 5.11b ★★★★
46. FREEBASE 5.12a ★★★★
47. POWDER UP THE NOSE 5.10d ★★★
48. SHAKE 'N FLAKE 5.11b ★★
49. RABID 5.12b ★★
50. BOUND IN BOGOTA 5.11a ★★

46. FREEBASE 5.12a ★★★★ Bolts
Another superb route ascends the attractive face a few feet left of **Vomit Launch.** The sustained difficulties peak near the top with a series of lock-offs on positive holds.

47. POWDER UP THE NOSE 5.10d ★★★ Bolts
As long as a knob doesn't blow, you'll likely enjoy this delicate face. Unfortunately, the route ascends a water streak, which makes the nubbins more friable than most.

48. SHAKE 'N FLAKE 5.11b ★★ Bolts
Popular more because of its convenient location than the quality of the moves, this unremarkable face ascends a loose flake at the start to a single hard move.

49. RABID 5.12b ★★ Bolts
A desperate, bouldery start highlights this short, thin-edged route. If you can get to the second bolt, you'll have this one in the bag.

50. BOUND IN BOGOTA 5.11a ★★ Bolts
The leftmost route on the Cocaine Wall has a tough crux above the second bolt. The climb ends shortly after it begins, after a finishing series of jugs.

Tuff Nuggets Wall

Far uphill on the right side of the Cocaine Gully are three mediocre routes. Unfortunately, this dreary face doesn't come close to matching the quality of the Cocaine Wall. But, if you're tired of waiting in line, and don't have high expectations, you might enjoy strolling uphill to sample these morsels.

51. PITCH IT HERE 5.10d ★ Bolts
Likely the best route on the wall, this face of pockets and knobs improves with every ascent as the loose holds snap off. Start downhill from the other two routes with a short offset.

52. DOUBLE EDGED SWORD 5.10c ★ Bolts
Another uninspriring bolted face rises uphill from **Pitch It Here.** After a tricky move on small edges, finish with easier knobs.

53. DESMOND'S TUTU 5.10b ★ R Bolts
The upper route on the Tuff Nuggets Wall ascends an especially ugly face just right of a chimney. The rock isn't good, and a runout on shaky knobs detracts even further from an already bad experience.

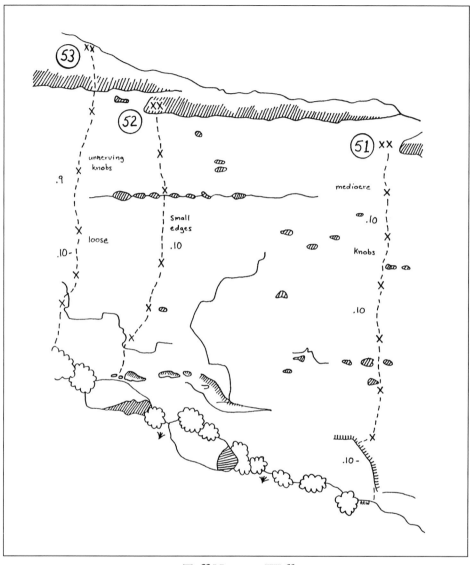

Tuff Nuggets Wall

51. PITCH IT HERE 5.10d ★   53. DESMOND'S TUTU 5.10b ★
52. DOUBLE EDGED SWORD 5.10c ★

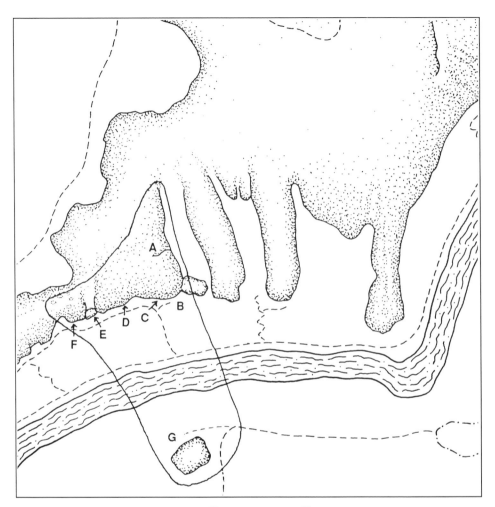

A. Rolling Stone Wall
B. Churning Buttress
C. Overboard Area
D. Zebra Area
E. The Peanut
F. Fourth Horseman
G. Rope De Dope Block

MORNING GLORY WALL AREA

MORNING GLORY WALL OFFERS a renowned selection of high quality lines. Towering 350 feet, it holds some of the most popular and developed sections of stone in the entire park. A large variety of routes, ranging from easy to extreme, attract both the beginner and the well-seasoned sport climber. The excellent rock and quick approach puts Morning Glory Wall at the forefront of Smith climbing.

Most of the hardest routes ascend a relatively small section of cliff along the right base of the wall. Known as the Churning Buttress, this area includes a remarkable collection of bolted desperates. The impressive mid-section of the crag contains several multi-pitch lines, while the moderate base routes to the left are extremely popular with intermediate climbers. A low-level traverse adds to the traffic, making this a good warm-up area and the most stylish hang in the park. If you come to Smith seeking solitude, avoid the base of Morning Glory Wall – especially in the late afternoon – as climbers pack the place.

Since the entire cliff gets sun most of the day, Morning Glory Wall is both a wonderful place to climb in the winter and an oven in the summer. Nonetheless, the routes are popular year-round. On hot days, climbers wait patiently for the evening shade, while in the dead of winter, locals bask in the sun's warmth. Even with below-freezing temperatures, it's short-sleeve weather here as long as the sun shines. Or so the legend goes . . .

Also included in this chapter are several peripheral crags. The massive boulder known as The Peanut sits left of the main wall and contains a collection of moderate, bolted routes. To the left, the river face of the Fourth Horseman offers some traditional crack climbs. Across the river from these crags sits Rope De Dope Block, a squat blob with throngs of fun routes.

MORNING GLORY WALL

This beautiful wall commands your attention as you turn the corner around Shiprock. A sign marks the exit from the main river trail, and a carefully-constructed path leads to the base.

Cocaine Gully – Left Side

The first several routes ascend steep rock on the left side of the Cocaine Gully opposite the Wooden Ships' Cocaine Wall. To approach, climb a third-class chimney on the right side of a massive boulder plugging the base of the gully. A lousy trail leads far uphill to an overhanging wall undercut with a cave. The routes are described from the top of the gully in order downhill.

1. STAND AND DELIVER 5.12c ★★ Bolts
   This odd route rises near the top of the left side of the Cocaine Gully. Clip the first bolt with a very long stick, then launch into the mindless thuggery of the crux – feet flailing through the air.

2. BEND OVER AND RECEIVE 5.13a ★★ Bolts
   The steep wall left of **Stand and Deliver** contains a mixture of artificial holds and natural rock to create a "legitimate" route. Done at the same time as the plastic routes in the Aggro Gully, this climb fortunately sits far off the beaten path. A purist's nightmare, it combines drilled pockets and modular holds at the start to get to the real rock.

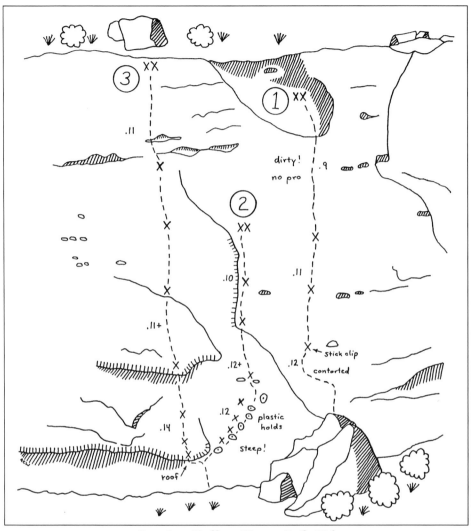

Cocaine Gully – Upper Left Side

1. STAND AND DELIVER   5.12c ★★   3. PROJECT   5.14 ?
2. BEND OVER AND RECEIVE   5.13a ★★

3. PROJECT   5.14 ?
   Destined to be another 5.14, this absurdly steep wall of pockets and edges will be among Smith's most powerful routes when completed.

4. PROJECT   5.13 ?
   After the gully trail cuts left from the Cocaine Face, it meets the left wall of the corridor below an ominous, black-streaked wall. The right of three lines follows natural holds up the right side of the streak.

5. BONGO FURY 5.13a ★★★ Bolts
    This drilled-out pegboard rises a few feet right of an ugly seam. An energetic series of pull-ups crank past the steepest section; the crux comes higher, with a nasty move on the finishing slab.

6. QUEST TO FIRE 5.12a R ★★★ Bolts
    This worthwhile climb rises 15 feet left of **Bongo Fury**. The moves are fun, but the crux sequence above the starting slab desperately needs another bolt – you might get hurt if you fall.

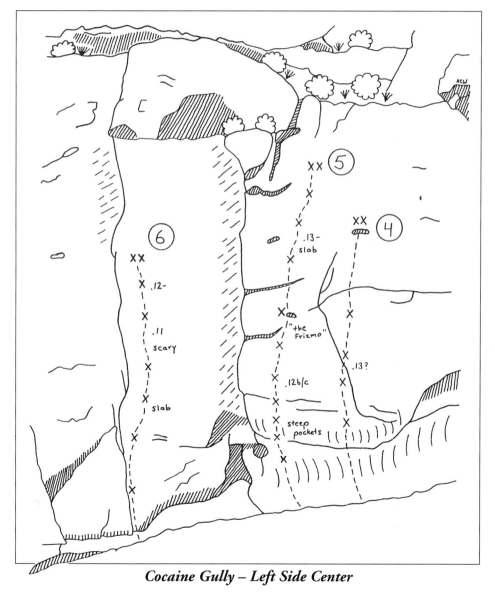

Cocaine Gully – Left Side Center

4. PROJECT 5.13 ?   6. QUEST TO FIRE 5.12a R ★★★
5. BONGO FURY 5.13a ★★★

7. HIPPO'S ON ICE   5.10a ★   Bolts
   This mediocre route lurks downhill from a break in the cliff line. The rock isn't especially solid, and lichen grows thickly, but it'll improve with time.

8. PROJECT   5.12– ?
   A vertical face capped by a five-foot bulge rises 30 feet downhill from **Hippo's on Ice**. If bolted, it might be worthwhile, with an exciting crux pulling the roof.

Rolling Stones Wall

This attractive slab rises high above the ground on the far right side of Morning Glory Wall. To reach the routes, hike up the Cocaine Gully, then make an easy boulder move onto a sloping shelf to the left. At the far left end are the following two routes:

9. GIMME SHELTER   5.11d R ★★   Bolts
   A difficult-to-clip second bolt mars this otherwise enjoyable arête. Since many feel the clip is harder than the rest of the route, **Gimme Shelter** rarely gets done.

10. EXILE ON MAIN STREET   5.11a ★★★   Bolts
    Artsy moves on good holds and an exposed position make this steep face a winner, though few climbers bother.

Churning Buttress

This celebrated section of stone at the right base of Morning Glory Wall contains a remarkable concentration of extreme routes.

11. OXYGEN   5.13a/b ★★★   Bolts
    A huge boulder leans against the main cliff on the far right side of the buttress. **Oxygen** ascends the steep face just right of this block via an offset seam. Start by stepping off the boulder, then follow a technical series of liebacks and edges to an anchor. Originally crumbly, the rock becomes better with each ascent.

12. JAM MASTER J   5.13d ★★★   Bolts
    This severe boulder problem adds a direct start onto **Oxygen**. Instead of scrambling up the giant boulder, start from the ground below an overhanging bulge. A desperately hard sequence of moves joins **Oxygen** at the second bolt. With your power drained from the start, the finish gives your stamina a real test.

13. DA KINE CORNER   5.12b/c ★★★★   Bolts
    This brilliant arête is the only "moderate" route on the entire Churning Buttress. Clip the first bolt with a long stick, unless you feel confident soloing at the crux. The moves are athletic and enjoyable, and the rock flawless.

14. WHITE HEAT   5.13c/d ★★★★   Bolts
    Most climbers find the crux of this seam too hot to handle. Start off the huge boulder, and make some awkward moves to a bouldery sequence above the fourth bolt. A small pocket crumbled slightly after the first ascent, leaving the already-intense crux even more potent. Despite the high quality of the climbing, **White Heat** sees few attempts.

15. KINGS OF RAP   5.12d ★★★★   Bolts
    This Smith classic deserves all the traffic it receives. The technical crux comes below the roof on some strenuous pocket pulls. The holds improve above, though many climbers fail near the anchors – more from the pump than the difficulty of the moves. Several bolts on the lower wall are difficult to clip, and usually sport long, fixed slings.

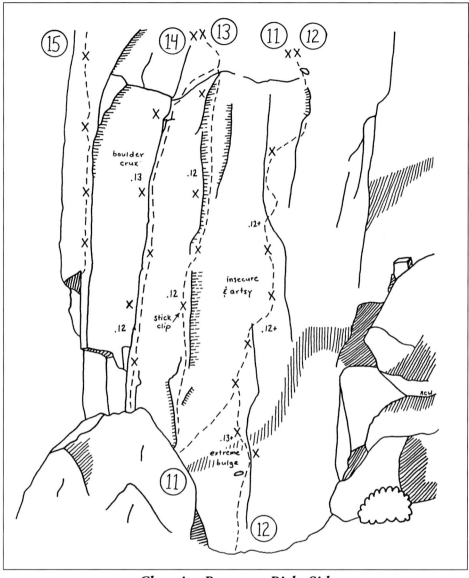

Churning Buttress – Right Side

11. OXYGEN 5.13a/b ★★★
12. JAM MASTER J 5.13d ★★★
13. DA KINE CORNER 5.12b/c ★★★★

14. WHITE HEAT 5.13c/d ★★★★
15. KINGS OF RAP 5.12d ★★★★

16. WASTE CASE 5.13b ★★★★ Bolts

Among the best routes of the grade at Smith, **Waste Case** shares climbing with both **Kings of Rap** and **Vicious Fish**. After cranking a tough boulder problem off the ground, join **Kings of Rap**, eventually stepping left around a powerful roof. If you're totally wasted, the upper arête will inevitably spit you off before you clip the anchors.

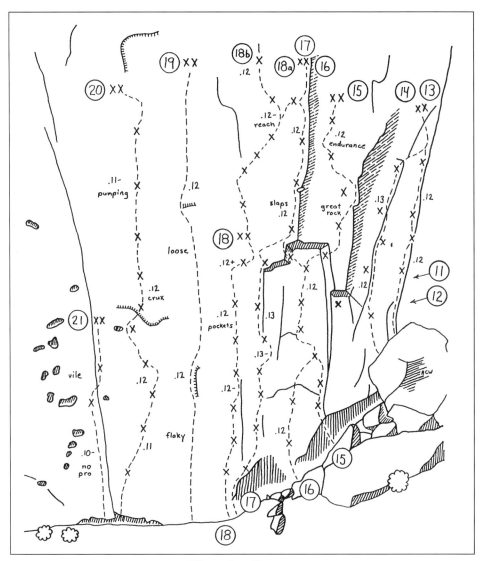

Churning Buttress

11. OXYGEN 5.13a/b ★★★
12. JAM MASTER J 5.13d ★★★
13. DA KINE CORNER 5.12b/c ★★★★
14. WHITE HEAT 5.13c/d ★★★★
15. KINGS OF RAP 5.12d ★★★★
16. WASTE CASE 5.13b ★★★★
17. VICIOUS FISH 5.13c/d ★★★★
18. CHURNING IN THE WAKE 5.13a
　　★★★★

18a. CHURNING SKY 5.13a ★★★★
18b. CHURNING IN THE OZONE 5.13b
　　★★★★
19. SIGN OF THE TIMES 5.12d ★
20. TACO CHIPS 5.12d ★★★
21. SLUM TIME 5.10a

17. VICIOUS FISH   5.13c/d ★★★★   Bolts
This fierce line sees few redpoints, despite its high quality. Pumping moves and an intense series of slaps up the steep arête lead to the jugs atop **Churning in the Wake**. Step right, then race the still-difficult arête to an anchor.

18. CHURNING IN THE WAKE   5.13a ★★★★   Bolts
Extremely popular, it's no exaggeration to say that this pocketed wall gets more traffic than the other Smith 5.13s combined. **Churning** is the entrance exam to the harder routes at Smith, and over the years, hundreds of climbers have passed the test. For those who aspire to bigger things, the line makes an excellent training route. Finishing off a day with laps on **Churning** is a ritual for many a hardman.

18a. CHURNING SKY   5.13a ★★★★   Bolts
This misdirected finish to **Churning** cuts across the upper headwall to the **Vicious Fish** arête. Because of an excellent rest, it adds little to the difficulty of the original route.

18b. CHURNING IN THE OZONE   5.13b ★★★★   Bolts
The most logical finish avoids the **Vicious Fish** arête, adding a pumping 5.12b section onto **Churning Sky**. Few climbers bother with this stretch, despite the high-quality moves. If you're looking for even more of a workout, consider approaching **Ozone** via **Waste Case**.

19. SIGN OF THE TIMES   5.12d ★   Bolts ?
Known locally as the Mud Wall, this infamous route was somehow dug out of a crumbly face. The bolts were stolen in 1989, and are still missing at the time of this writing. Hopefully, the line will get rebolted – despite all the criticism, it's not as bad as it looks.

20. TACO CHIPS   5.12d ★★★   Bolts
Horribly loose on the first ascent, many attempts at repeating this test piece fell victim to snapping holds. With dozens of ascents providing the cleaning, **Taco Chips** today comes highly recommended. A new bolt tames the previously scary crux.

21. SLUM TIME   5.10a Bolts ?
Fortunately, this wretched route never got completed to the top. There's an anchor about 45 feet up, but most of the bolts are missing hangers.

Overboard Area

The Overboard Area sits immediately left of the Churning Buttress. All the routes end after a full rope length of climbing, although none of the finishes receive much attention. The first ascents of several of these lines stirred the Smith scene, when a visiting climber placed cheap screw eyes to avoid the cost of real bolts and hangers. Designed to hang plants rather than stop falls, these "bolts" barely held body weight. After a severe reprimand from area locals, the climber decided spending the money on real bolts would be less painful than enduring continued verbal abuse; he eventually replaced the plant hangers with good bolts.

22. PROJECT   5.12 ?
A difficult, although somewhat ugly variation ascends just right of Overboard. If bolted and well-cleaned, this seam might be worth doing.

23. OVERBOARD   5.11c (5.11a/b lower part) ★★★   Bolts
This wall of jugs is the most popular climb of its grade at Smith. As a warm-up for harder lines, or an introduction for aspiring 5.11 climbers, the route sees almost non-stop traffic. The barn-door lieback at the lower crux grew more difficult when a key knob snapped off. Almost everyone lowers at the first anchors, as the rock of the more-difficult finish deteriorates rapidly.

24. MAGIC LIGHT   5.12b (5.11a lower part) ★★   Bolts
The 5.11a start to **Magic Light** sees almost as many ascents as its neighbor to the right. Most climbers stop at the mid-way anchors, ignoring the real difficulties. Although seldom attempted,

the entire route makes a worthwhile endeavor, despite imperfect rock. Many fail at a thin face move just below the anchors, with almost the whole route below them.

25. ENERGY CRISIS   5.12b ★★★   Bolts
Another popular route with a tweaky start rises a few feet left of **Overboard.** Once billed as a B2 boulder problem, the grade fell quickly after repeat ascents. After clipping the second bolt, the climbing eases to 5.11, ending at the first set of anchors.

26. SKETCH PAD   5.12d ★★★   Bolts
A worthwhile finish to **Energy Crisis** attacks a rounded lieback leading to a steep face. The attempted first ascent involved some ingenuity when the climber couldn't link the final wall before leaving Smith. Before leaving, he lowered the anchors to his high point and claimed success. He fooled no one, and someone else nabbed the route after replacing the bolts.

27. MANE LINE   5.13a ★★   Bolts
Although rarely done, this varied route offers some choice climbing. An unusually technical sequence up a low-angled slab gives most climbers fits. Begin with **Energy Crisis,** but cut left past an eye bolt to some huge potholes. Above the crux slab, a pumping crack leads to the brilliant finishing headwall.

28. LION'S CHAIR   5.11a R ★★★   Gear to 3.5 inches (two sets of R.P.s, Rocks)
This stunning line was one of Smith's first 5.11s. The start of the initial pitch makes a popular 5.10c stemming jaunt. Above the first anchors, the run-out crux delicately liebacks a rounded crack. Despite a mediocre second pitch, the entire line makes a fine diversion from the gymnasium below.
   1. 5.11a   Stem the corner 90 feet to a hanging belay.
   2. 5.10c   A crumbly dihedral leads to a move right around the roof and easy face climbing.
   3. 5.7   Solo up a low-angled face to a hanging belay beneath the final overhanging crack.
   4. 5.9   Savor the breathtaking flake crack to a good ledge and scramble to the top.
   5. 5.6   Descend Cocaine Gully to the right.

Zebra Area

The Zebra Area consists of the impressive section of rock left of **Lion's Chair.** The base routes see almost non-stop traffic, and the popular warm-up traverse cutting along the base only adds to the congestion.

29. PROJECT   5.13+ ?
Someday, this blank face left of **Lion's Chair** will fall. Most moves go free, but a few sections are depressingly thin.

30. DANDY LINE   5.12d ★★   Bolts
This eye-catching seam splits the smooth wall immediately left of **Lion's Chair.** A desperate series of moves eases quickly above the third bolt, though a loose finish tarnishes the overall quality.

31. ZEBRA SEAM   5.11d ★★★   Gear to 2.5 inches (TCUs, Friends)
Formerly a nightmarish lead, this technical seam saw very few ascents until a brush with a retro-bolter opened it to the masses.

32. ZEBRA DIRECT   5.11a ★★★   Bolts
When first climbed, this puzzling face was among Smith's most challenging lines. The popular series of rounded scoops and small edges was originally only 5.10d, but the grade rose a notch after some key holds tore off.

33. GUMBY   5.10b ★★★   Bolts
This short, pleasant face sits ten feet left of **Zebra Direct.** A deceptively tricky crux past the first bolt surprises those expecting a hike.

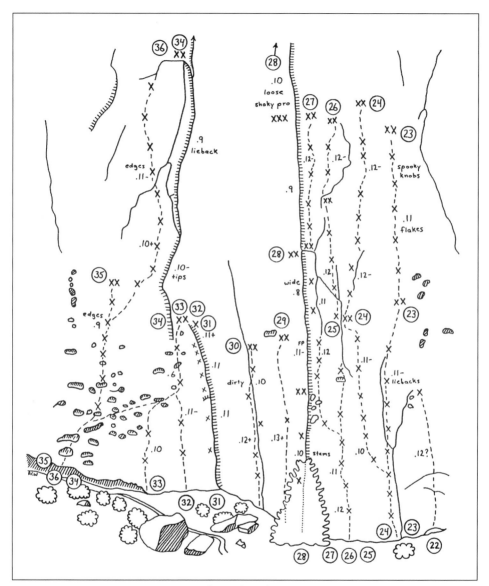

Overboard/Zebra Area

22. PROJECT 5.12 ?
23. OVERBOARD 5.11c ★★★
24. MAGIC LIGHT 5.12b ★★
25. ENERGY CRISIS 5.12b ★★★
26. SKETCH PAD 5.12d ★★★
27. MANE LINE 5.13a ★★
28. LION'S CHAIR 5.11a R ★★★
29. PROJECT 5.13+ ?

30. DANDY LINE 5.12d ★★
31. ZEBRA SEAM 5.11d R ★★★
32. ZEBRA DIRECT 5.11a ★★★
33. GUMBY 5.10b ★★★
34. ZEBRA 5.10a ★★★
35. LIGHT ON THE PATH 5.9 ★★★
36. CAT SCAN 5.11a ★

Photo: Bruce Adams

Morning Glory Wall

5. BONGO FURY   5.13a ★★★

10. EXILE ON MAIN STREET   5.11a ★★★

15. KINGS OF RAP   5.12d ★★★★

18b. CHURNING IN THE OZONE   5.13b
     ★★★★

20. TACO CHIPS   5.12d ★★★

23. OVERBOARD   5.11c ★★★

28. LION'S CHAIR   5.11a R ★★★

32. ZEBRA DIRECT   5.11a ★★★

34a. ZION   5.9 ★★★

40. LION'S JAW   5.8 ★★★

41. TAMMY BAKKER'S FACE   5.10c ★★

43. POP GOES THE NUBBIN   5.10a ★★

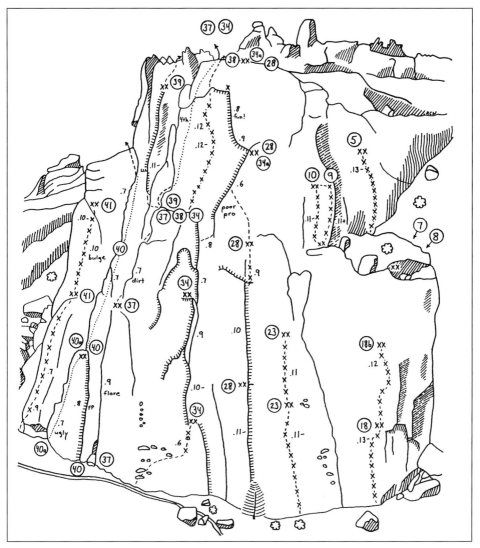

Morning Glory Wall

5. BONGO FURY 5.13a ★★★
7. HIPPO'S ON ICE 5.10a ★
8. PROJECT 5.12-?
9. GIMME SHELTER 5.11d R ★★
10. EXILE ON MAIN STREET 5.11a ★★★
18. CHURNING IN THE WAKE 5.13a
    ★★★★
18b. CHURNING IN THE OZONE 5.13b
    ★★★★
23. OVERBOARD 5.11c ★★★

28. LION'S CHAIR 5.11a R ★★★
34. ZEBRA 5.10a ★★★
34a. ZION 5.9 ★★★
37. IN HINDS WAY 5.9
38. CHOSS IN AMERICA 5.12c ★★★
39. ONE TIME TRICK 5.11a ★
40. LION'S JAW 5.8 ★★★
40a. LION'S JAW CHIMNEY 5.7
41. TAMMY BAKKER'S FACE 5.10c ★★

34. ZEBRA 5.10a ★★★ Gear to 3 inches
This striking, multi-pitch venture is a delightful diversion from the nearby desperates. To start, follow easy but run-out potholes, or take your pick of either the **Zebra Seam** (the original start), **Zebra Direct** or **Gumby**. Most climbers cap the route with the **Zion** finish.
   1. 5.6 Traverse through the huge potholes to a hanging belay.
   2. 5.10a A short crux on perfect rock leads to an impressive open book. Lieback and jam the awesome corner to a belay ledge with two bolts.
   3. 5.8 Ascend the flaring crack/chimney above to a huge ledge (or see **Zion**).
   4. 4th Step left, and hike an ugly gully to the top.

34a. ZION 5.9 ★★★ Gear to 3 inches
This spectacular line connects **Zebra** with the final pitches of **Lion's Chair**. Begin by climbing the first two pitches of **Zebra**, then traverse right on knobs midway up the third pitch. An unprotected scramble up an easy slab leads to an anchor below an intimidating crack. Hand traverse left, then lieback the exhilarating flake to a ledge, and scramble to the top.

35. LIGHT ON THE PATH 5.9 ★★★ Bolts
This moderate wall of pockets and edges grows more popular each year. A few loose holds still lurk high on the route, although most of the garbage plaguing early ascents pulled off long ago.

36. CAT SCAN 5.11a ★ Bolts
A continuation of **Light on the Path** climbs the steep face above the anchors. The line improves with each ascent as loose rock crumbles away, but it still isn't very good. You can avoid some bad rock and cut down on rope drag by starting up **Zebra Direct** and stepping left to the bolts.

37. IN HINDS WAY 5.9 Gear to 4 inches
This repulsive route sloths up a flaring, crumbly wide crack. It never gets done for obvious reasons.
   1. 5.9 Grovel up the crack to a bolt belay.
   2. 5.7 Easy climbing on rotten rock leads to the large ledge on **Zebra**. Scramble up the gully to finish.

The next two routes start far off the ground, above the big ledge atop **Zebra**. To approach, climb **Zebra**, **CAT Scan**, or **In Hind's Way** – or hike to the top and scramble down the upper chimney.

38. CHOSS IN AMERICA 5.12c ★★★ Bolts
Despite the derogatory name, **Choss in America** comes highly recommended. With the excellent position, well-protected moves and solid rock, the climb should see many more attempts. The crux comes near the top, as the rock steepens just as your forearms start to tire.

39. ONE TIME TRICK 5.11a ★ Gear to #4 Friend
This spectacular, yet forgotten hand/fist crack splits an exposed bulge. Step left from the **Zebra** ledge and jam the overhanging wide crack to a two bolt belay. Scramble along the ridge to the top.

40. LION'S JAW 5.8 ★★★ Gear to 1.5 inches
The first-pitch dihedral of **Lion's Jaw** is excellent and demanding for the grade. The rest of the route follows a repugnant, unprotected chimney that should be avoided at all costs.
   1. 5.8 Stem and jam the corner, then pull a small roof to a good ledge. Rappel off, or . . .
   2. 5.7 Battle the miserable chimney above, fighting off pigeons and stemming off crumbly walls slickened with bird guano.
   3. 5.7 Fight your way up another tight chimney, tearing up your Lycra as you go. To descend, walk left to the **Cinnamon Slab** anchor.

40a. LION'S JAW CHIMNEY 5.7 Gear to 4 inches
If you desire, it's possible to avoid the only good pitch on **Lion's Jaw** by ascending a wretched chimney just around the corner. Understandably, few people make this choice.

41. TAMMY BAKKER'S FACE 5.10c ★★ Bolts
This popular, steep buttress rises at the far left side of Morning Glory Wall. Hundreds of ascents dislodged most of the rubble plaguing early ascents, and today it isn't bad. Bring two ropes if you want to get down.
1. 5.9 Climb a short crack and step right onto a low-angled face with many bolts.
2. 5.10c An inside corner leads to a pull over a bulge on shaky holds. A deceptively tricky finish ends at an anchor.

THE PEANUT

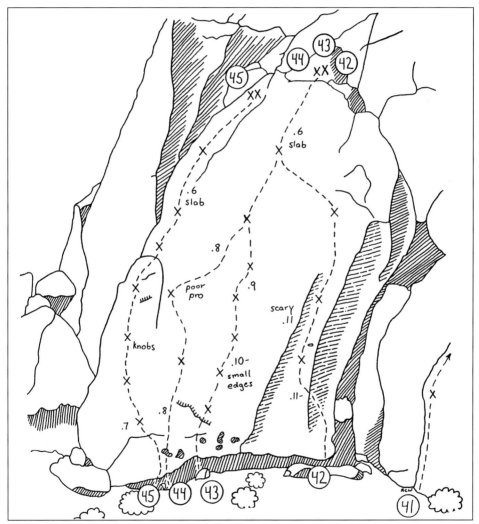

The Peanut

41. TAMMY BAKKER'S FACE 5.10c ★★   44. PEANUT BRITTLE 5.8 R ★★
42. POPISM 5.11b R ★★   45. HOP ON POP 5.8 ★★★
43. POP GOES THE NUBBIN 5.10a ★★

A gully plugged by a 65-foot boulder marks the left boundary of Morning Glory Wall. The Peanut offers several enjoyable face routes.

42. POPISM   5.11b R ★★   Bolts
This strenuous arête provides some brief entertainment. Until someone moves the poorly-located bolts, it'll never be popular.

43. POP GOES THE NUBBIN   5.10a ★★   Bolts
This thin face became popular with the addition of several bolts. Once just 5.9, enough nubbins popped off over the years to bump the grade up a notch.

44. PEANUT BRITTLE   5.8 R ★★   Bolts
The original route on The Peanut followed this knobby face. Despite some dangerous runouts, **Peanut Brittle** sees a surprising number of ascents.

45. HOP ON POP   5.8 ★★★   Bolts
If you're looking for a safe entrance into the world of 5.8, try this pleasant route. **Hop on Pop** protects with closely-spaced bolts, with the only hard move coming not far off the ground.

THE FOUR HORSEMEN

These four squat pillars sit atop the ridge left of Morning Glory Wall. Easily the most impressive spire is the Fourth Horseman, with its striking river face split by several high-quality cracks. Curiously, these routes aren't nearly as popular as they once were, since they protect naturally. Except for **Equus**, none of the river face routes top out on the actual summit. To descend, walk left to the **Cinnamon Slab** rappel anchors.

46. FRIDAY'S JINX   5.7 R ★★   Gear to 2 inches
This sinister route put a half dozen people in the hospital during the 80s. Oddly, the rock is solid and the protection reasonable, but for unknown reasons gear-ripping falls are a common occurrence on the first pitch. Start just right of a large boulder sitting below the wall.
   1.   5.7   Traverse right, and pull over a steep bulge. Climb the corner above and belay atop a large block that somehow stays attached to the wall.
   2.   5.7   Race up the quality inside corner to the top.

46a. SUNDAY'S JINX   5.7   Gear to 3 inches
If you're foolish, you may wish to swap the excellent second pitch of **Friday's Jinx** for this junk pile. The line traverses right from the first pitch anchor, then climbs a crumbly ramp.

47. CRACK OF INFINITY   5.10b ★★★   Gear to 3 inches
This varied route deserves more ascents than it receives. The first-pitch crux makes a challenging stint in its own right. You can reach the second-pitch hand crack via **Friday's Jinx**, making an exciting 5.8 route. Start below a dihedral, capped by diverging cracks.
   1.   5.10b   Climb the short dihedral and attack the right crack around a bulge. Traverse right to the belay on **Friday's Jinx.**
   2.   5.8   Start up the inside corner, then step left to a striking face crack. Jam and lieback to a nut anchor below an overhanging crack.
   3.   5.9   Lieback and jam the ominous crack to a ledge, then escape by traversing right.

47a. INFINITY VARIATION   5.10a ★★   Gear to 2 inches
An easier and far less intimidating start ascends a diagonal finger crack just right of the first pitch overhang.

48. CALAMITY JAM   5.10c ★★★   Gear to 2 inches
The finest crack pitch on the Fourth Horseman ascends a challenging arch entering a fun dihedral. If not for a mediocre finish on loose rock, it would be a four-star classic.

FOURTH HORSEMAN

FIRST HORSEMAN

SECOND HORSEMAN

THIRD HORSEMAN

51

48

46

50   49a

THE DIHEDRALS

45

THE PEANUT

41

Photo: Bruce Adams

The Fourth Horseman Area

41. TAMMY BAKKER'S FACE 5.10c ★★
45. HOP ON POP 5.8 ★★★
46. FRIDAY'S JINX 5.7 R ★★
48. CALAMITY JAM 5.10c ★★★

49a. PACK ANIMAL DIRECT 5.10b ★★★★
50. HEADLESS HORSEMAN 5.10d ★★★
51. EQUUS 5.11b ★★

48a. CATASTROPHIC CRACK 5.12a R ★★ Gear to 2 inches (Double sets of #3 through #5 R.P.s, Rocks)
This direct start to **Calamity Jam** is a serious proposition. The R.P. slots are good, but it's tough hanging out long enough to place them.

48b. SANDBAG 5.10c R ★ Gear to 2 inches
An indistinct, right-leaning slash lies left of **Catastrophic Crack.** A bolt safely protects the crux, but a freaky traverse across to **Calamity Jam** is unnerving.

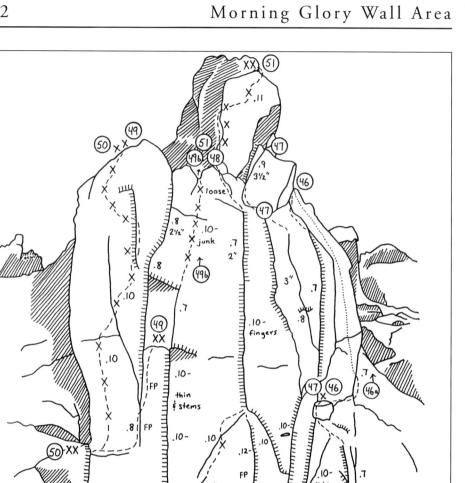

The Fourth Horseman

46. FRIDAY'S JINX 5.7 R ★★
46a. SUNDAY'S JINX 5.7
47. CRACK OF INFINITY 5.10b ★★★
48. CALAMITY JAM 5.10c ★★★
48a. CATASTROPHIC CRACK 5.12a R ★★
48b. SANDBAG 5.10c R ★

49. PACK ANIMAL 5.8 R ★★★
49a. PACK ANIMAL DIRECT 5.10b ★★★★
49b. SUNDANCER 5.10a ★
50. HEADLESS HORSEMAN 5.10d ★★★
51. EQUUS 5.11b ★★

49. PACK ANIMAL   5.8 R ★★★   Gear to 2.5 inches
Inadequate fixed pins mar the start of this otherwise entertaining route. Hopefully, they'll be replaced by bolts, as too many people depend on a single, ancient peg to keep them off the deck. The enjoyable second-pitch dihedral protects easily.
1. 5.8 Face climb past fixed pins to an anchor.
2. 5.8 Jam and stem the prominent right-facing dihedral to the top.

49a. PACK ANIMAL DIRECT   5.10b ★★★★   Gear to 1 inch
This attractive corner sits right of the regular start of **Pack Animal**. A delightful series of stems and thin jams protect scantily at the start, but give way to good slots above. For the grade, there's no better inside corner on Smith tuff.

49b. SUNDANCER   5.10a ★   Gear to .75 inch
If you prefer crumbly faces to solid cracks, you might want to try this second-pitch alternative to **Pack Animal**. Either bring a few nuts for the start, or face a long runout to the first bolt.

50. HEADLESS HORSEMAN   5.10d ★★★   Bolts
The only decent sport route on the Fourth Horseman climbs the steep buttress left of **Pack Animal**. Enjoyable moves, good rock and plenty of bolts make this route the most popular on the entire formation.

51. EQUUS   5.11b ★★   Bolts
This striking face distinguishes the summit block of the Fourth Horseman. Regrettably, the quality of the climbing doesn't do justice to the exhilarating position, as much of the route trots awkwardly up the left arête.

52. FOURTH HORSEMAN   5.7 R ★   Gear to 2.5 inches
If you'd like to stand atop this spire, you can squirm up an unremarkable chimney on the north side. Rappel down the south face from anchors just below the summit.

53. THIRD HORSEMAN   5.10b R ★   No Gear
This squat tower stands behind the Fourth Horseman. The summit comes quickly after cranking an unprotected boulder move on the north side. Don't climb up unless you can climb down, as there's no rappel anchor on top.

54. SECOND HORSEMAN   5.6 R ★   No Gear
Split by a wide chimney, this unimpressive tower yields easily after a moderate scramble. Unfortunately, you'll find no anchor on top, so you'll have to downclimb.

55. FIRST HORSEMAN   5.7 R ★   Gear to 2 inches
To reach the summit of the southernmost spire, jam a miniature dihedral and scramble up an unprotected face. Once again, there's no anchor on top.

56. RIDERLESS HORSE   5.7 X   No Gear
An insane spike that looks like it will come tumbling down when the wind blows teeters just north of the Second Horseman. I foolishly scaled this 20-foot pillar a few years back, figuring that when it fell over I'd jump clear of the rubble. Fortunately, the Horse didn't topple, but it will someday.

ROPE DE DOPE BLOCK

A squarish blob with a prominent crack splitting the river face sits across the river from the Fourth Horseman. Long popular with classes and neophytes, but ignored by everyone else, Rope De Dope today contains an excellent collection of lines. Generally solid rock, a quick approach and easily-arranged topropes make the block a natural choice.

To approach Rope De Dope Block, follow the regular trail into the canyon, but don't cross the river. Instead, hike five minutes downstream. If you're staying in the camping area, a well-maintained trail leads directly across the hillside to the back of the rock. The quickest route to the top is a tricky boulder problem on the uphill side, but if you can't climb 5.10, you'll need to lead a north-side slab route.

57. NORTH SLAB CRACK   5.3 X ★★   Gear to 2.5 inches
     A flaring crack on the low angle, north side of the block provides an easy but poorly protected route to the top.

58. HOW LOW CAN YOU GO?   5.6 ★★★   Bolts
     This simple slab makes a great first lead. After bouldering to the first bolt the climbing turns simple in a hurry.

59. SHAMU   5.8 ★★★   Bolts
     Some deceptively strenuous pulls on good holds highlight this romp up the right side of the north slab.

60. LOW BLOW   5.10b ★   TR
     The left side of the main wall offers a mediocre top rope problem. A dirty sequence on shaky holds ends with a groveling finish onto a holdless slab.

61. FLOAT LIKE A BUTTERFLY   5.10b ★★★★   TR
     This winner follows a series of side pulls and jugs up the bulging main face. Good rock, and exhilarating moves make it the best climb on the block.

62. ROPE-DE-DOPE CRACK   5.8 ★★   Gear to 3 inches
     Usually toproped, this unmistakable hand crack jams past a strenuous bulge. If you want to tie into the sharp end of the rope, you'll find good protection.

63. STING LIKE A BEE   5.10b/c ★★★   TR
     The right wall of Rope-De-Dope Crack makes a popular toprope problem. The difficulty varies depending on where you climb.

Rope De Dope Block

57. NORTH SLAB CRACK   5.3 X ★★
58. HOW LOW CAN YOU GO?   5.6 ★★★
59. SHAMU   5.9 ★★★
60. LOW BLOW   5.10b ★

61. FLOAT LIKE A BUTTERFLY   5.10b
    ★★★★
62. ROPE-DE-DOPE CRACK   5.8 ★★
63. STING LIKE A BEE   5.10b/c ★★★

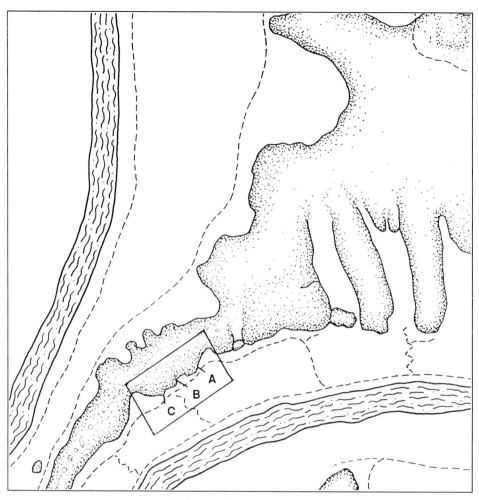

A. Latest Rage
B. Sunshine Dihedral
C. Chain Reaction

THE DIHEDRALS

A REMARKABLE COLLECTION OF STEEP FACES and sharp arêtes makes the Dihedrals the most celebrated section of stone at Smith. Serving as center stage to Smith climbing, it offers great rock and breathtaking natural lines. The relentless faces, stunning edges and classic open books appeal to everyone, regardless of ability. Excellent sport climbs from 5.5 to 5.14 tantalize both the beginner and world class climber, packing the place on busy weekends.

The Dihedrals are best known for the crucial role the area played in the history of U.S. climbing. The newer routes laid the foundations of sport climbing not just for Smith, but the entire country. Before the development of the Dihedrals, Smith climbing focused on the limited number of cracks and easier faces scattered throughout the park. Although it's hard to imagine today, it never occurred to anyone that the Dihedrals held much potential for free climbing. Without chalk marking the holds, the routes seemed impossible. Rappelling to check out the lines for unseen holds seemed like a waste of a good climbing day. Not until 1983 did it finally became clear that the true future of Smith Rock didn't lie in finishing all the cracks, but in tapping the huge volume of untouched faces and arêtes. Rappel inspections began, spurred more by desperation to find something new, than a belief that many routes would be possible. Miraculously, usable holds studded every face, and the race was on. Still, many remained skeptical. I'll never forget Alan Lester admonishing me as I bolted **Watts Tots**, saying, "You're wasting your time – you'll never be able to climb that thing!"

In 1983, the first of the classic faces began to fall. **Watts Tots** (5.12b) ushered in the sport climbing era at Smith, and two weeks later, the ridiculous arête of **Chain Reaction** (5.12c) opened the floodgates of new routes. If something as absurd as this overhanging knife edge could be climbed, it seemed anything was possible. Over the next two years, I managed more than a dozen new routes. My partner Chris Grover and I came to work every day at "The Office," the flat area at the base of **Moonshine Dihedral**. When the first hoards of visitors arrived at Smith, most of the classics stood ready and waiting. Many of these original routes combined a mixture of bolts and natural protection to avoid the time-consuming placement of hand-drilled bolts. The few naturally protected routes that remain are rarely done today, as the art of gear placement died long ago at Smith.

On an optimistic day in 1984, I turned my attention to the improbable blank face left of **Sunshine Dihedral**. After days of cleaning and intensive work, I figured out a series of relentless moves, but any attempt at linkage slapped me in the face. Just two years later, to the surprise of everyone, French climber Jean Baptiste Tribout spent a month at Smith, and left with the first free ascent of this remarkable wall. As the first 5.14 in America, **To Bolt or Not to Be** drew the attention of climbers everywhere to this small section of cliff.

By the late 80s, with the ascents of the final blank sections of stone, the development in the Dihedrals slowed. There's room for only a handful of new lines now, and climbers likely will polish these off quickly. Today, the Dihedrals serve as a monument to the '80s at Smith. In years to come, activity will be centered elsewhere, but the Dihedrals will be famous forever for bringing the world to Smith Rock.

The Dihedrals are a surprisingly small section of Smith Rock, stretching only 300 feet from end to end. Yet, because of the accordion layout of the cliff, there are more than 50 routes. The wall extends from the Fourth Horseman gully on the right to the left boundary just beyond **Vision**. However, the name often gets used as a generic reference point for all the climbing from Morning Glory Wall to Asterisk Pass. To descend from the top of the cliff, you can either make two single-rope rappels from an anchor atop Cinnamon Slab, or scramble down a moderate (5.2)slab/chimney further to the right.

1. LICHEN IT   5.7 ★★★   Bolts
   This high-quality climb is a good choice for beginners moving into lead climbing. Most rappel after the first pitch, although it's possible to finish to the top.

2. RIGHT SLAB CRACK   5.5 ★★   Gear to 2 inches
   A decent beginner's route, this line starts with a tough sequence up a vertical corner and ends with easy scrambling.
   1. 5.6 Stem and jam the crack to the same belay station as **Lichen It**. Rappel, or . . .
   2. 5.2 Continue up easy rock to the top.

3. EASY READER   5.6 ★★★   Bolts
   This low-angled face is among Smith's best beginning sport routes. With good rock and closely-spaced bolts, **Easy Reader** is a safe introduction to lead climbing. Most climbers rappel at eye bolts atop the first pitch, but you can top out after a 5.2 finish (bring gear).

4. LEFT SLAB CRACK   5.4 ★★   Gear to 2.5 inches
   Another easy climb, this vegetated crack left of **Easy Reader** doesn't match the quality of the nearby routes.

5. GINGER SNAP   5.8 ★★★   Bolts
   This enjoyable knob face provides a first-pitch alternative to **Cinnamon Slab**. Bring some gear if you don't like soloing the easy scrambling to the first bolt. Purists climb directly up the starting wall, while everyone else stems to either side (5.7).

6. CINNAMON SLAB   5.6 ★★★   Gear to 3.5 inches
   Still among the most popular easy routes at Smith, **Cinnamon Slab** introduced thousands of climbers to the sport. With the arrival of bolted faces, the popularity dwindles each year.
   1. 5.6 Jam and face climb the easily-protected **Cinnamon Slab** to a good belay ledge.
   2. 5.5 An awkward start leads to a moderate dihedral and the top.

7. CINNAMON TOAST   5.7 R ★   Gear to 3 inches
   You can step left and ascend knobs past a few bolts about 15 feet up the second pitch of **Cinnamon Slab**. This variation might be popular if not for some loose flakes near the top.

8. KARATE CRACK   5.10a ★★★   Gear to 3 inches
   This striking hand crack is a test piece for the grade. Repetitive, moderate moves build a pump that floors many climbers at the hand traverse. Be sure to protect inside the cave to make the final moves less frightening for the second.

9. PEAPOD CAVE   5.10a ★★   Gear to 4 inches
   While no classic, this solid chimney, which is capped by a committing arch, deserves more ascents than it receives. To start, either climb **Karate Crack** as a first pitch, or step left into the cave part-way up **Cinnamon Slab.**

The following four routes branch off from **Karate Crack**, ascending the steep face to the top. An anchor on top allows easy toproping with double ropes.

10. SLOW BURN   5.11d R ★★★   Gear (#3.5 and #4 Friend)
    This imposing face was the first line to the top of the Karate Wall. Although cleaned on rappel, **Slow Burn** was bolted on lead – drilling from hooks. The intent was to get a taste for the more traditional ethics of the time. The likelihood of long flyers scares everyone away, but **Slow Burn** offers excitement for bold climbers.

11. CROSSFIRE   5.12a/b R ★★★★   Gear (#3.5 Friend)
    Originally climbed almost totally with natural gear, I retro-bolted this runout nightmare in 1988, opening the line to the masses. Likely the best of the routes above **Karate Crack, Crossfire** still offers enough sporting runouts to keep your attention. Finish by stepping left to the final moves of **Power Dive.**

Photo: Bruce Adams

The Dihedrals - Right Side (Northeast) View

3. EASY READER 5.6 ★★★
6. CINNAMON SLAB 5.6 ★★★
18. WATTS TOTS 5.12b ★★★★
27. POWDER IN THE EYES 5.12c ★★★
29. SUNSHINE DIHEDRAL 5.11d ★★★★

33. MOONDANCE 5.11c ★★★
36. MOONSHINE DIHEDRAL 5.9 ★★★★
38. DARKNESS AT NOON 5.13a ★★★★
44. BUNNY FACE 5.7 ★★★

12. POWER DIVE 5.12a R ★★★★ Gear (#1.5 to #4 Friend)
    Since the moves on this top-notch line are reasonable for its entire distance, the crux comes from linking everything together. A runout section low frightens many climbers away, but bolts safely protect the upper crux.

13. KAROT TOTS 5.11b ★★★★ Gear (#4 RP, and selection of Rocks)
    As one of the first routes to venture onto the vertical faces of the Dihedrals, **Karot Tots** (the name rhymes when said correctly) hinted to the possibilities of the future. Featuring superb rock and enjoyable moves, it comes highly recommended.
    1. 5.11b Climb **Karate Crack** to within ten feet of the hand traverse and step left past a bolt, following a thin crack around a corner to a belay.
    2. 5.6 Race up easy knobs past three bolts.

Photo: Bruce Adams

The Dihedrals – Southeast Side

1. LICHEN IT   5.7 ★★★
3. EASY READER   5.6 ★★★
18. WATTS TOTS   5.12b ★★★★
20. TATOR TOTS 5.10a R ★★
21. LATIN LOVER   5.12a ★★★
26. TAKE A POWDER   5.12a ★★★
33. MOONDANCE   5.11c ★★★

39. CHAIN REACTION   5.12c ★★★★
41. RATTLESNAKE CHIMNEY   5.6 ★
43. BOOKWORM   5.7 ★★★
44. BUNNY FACE   5.7 ★★★
48. HELIUM WOMAN   5.9 ★★
50. DETERIORATA   5.8 ★
51. GO DOG GO   5.12c ★★★

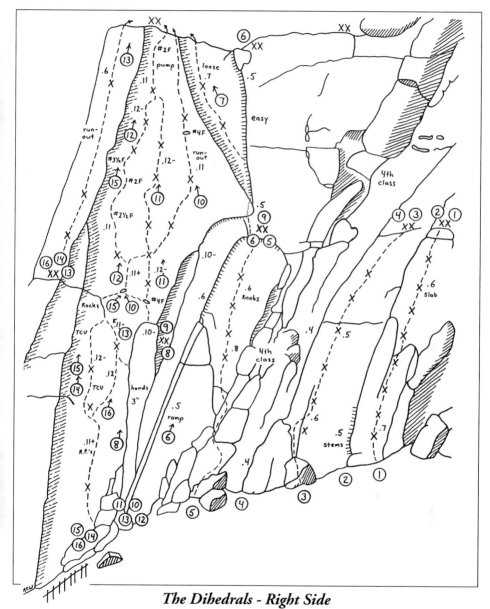

The Dihedrals - Right Side

1. LICHEN IT 5.7 ★★★
2. RIGHT SLAB CRACK 5.5 ★★
3. EASY READER 5.6 ★★★
4. LEFT SLAB CRACK 5.4 ★★
5. GINGER SNAP 5.8 ★★★
6. CINNAMON SLAB 5.6 ★★★
7. CINNAMON TOAST 5.7 R ★
8. KARATE CRACK 5.10a ★★★
9. PEAPOD CAVE 5.10a ★★
10. SLOW BURN 5.11d R ★★★
11. CROSSFIRE 5.12a/b R ★★★★
12. POWER DIVE 5.12a R ★★★★
13. KAROT TOTS 5.11b ★★★★
14. FIRING LINE 5.12b ★★★
15. KARATE WALL 5.12b ★★★★
16. LOW PROFILE 5.12b/c R ★★★★

14. FIRING LINE   5.12b ★★★   Gear (#3 & 4 RPs, TCUs, Rocks)
This thin face receives few ascents since most sport climbers shy away from placing gear. The crux involves a reach off some small clings with a protection bolt at your face. Finish by joining the Karot Tots thin crack.

15. KARATE WALL (a.k.a. POWERLINE)   5.12b ★★★★   Gear (see selection for **Firing Line** and **Power Dive**)
This stamina-exam stacks **Power Dive** onto **Firing Line**, connected by a short traverse. The entire line ranks among Smith's most captivating one pitch climbs. Unfortunately, the huge rack of gear needed takes a lot of the fun away.

16. LOW PROFILE   5.12b/c R ★★★★   Gear (#3, 4, 5 RPs, #2 Friend, Rocks)
Although totally ignored, this incipient seam was among the better ascents of the mid-80s. After stepping right from the second bolt on **Firing Line**, face climb without protection to the first bolt on **Karot Tots**. Bitterly runout at the crux, it remains unrepeated at the time of this writing.

17. LATEST RAGE   5.12b ★★★★   Bolts
An all-time classic, this attractive arête is perhaps the most popular climb of the grade at Smith. The original start (up the arête directly from the ground) and finish (to the **Karot Tots** belay) rarely get done. On early ascents, the crux came above the last bolt, climbing the left side of the arête. Today, almost everyone deviates, using better holds on the right wall.

18. WATTS TOTS   5.12b ★★★★   Bolts
As the first of the classic Dihedrals faces, this attractive wall was highly influential when first climbed. The short crux finesses a boulder sequence above the fifth bolt. The original finish went left past the final bolt, moved around the corner and joined **Tator Tots**. The newer, more intelligent ending goes right, merging with **Latest Rage** at the first set of anchors.

18a. MEGA WATTS   5.13b ★★★   TR
This series of holds is crammed too tightly between **Latest Rage** and **Watts Tots** to make a legitimate route. Still, as a toprope problem, the moves are demanding, with a blank crux coming right off the deck.

18b. KILO WATTS   5.12b ★★★   TR
This quality face suffers from the same fate as **Mega Watts**. With **Watts Tots** so close to the right, the excellent moves are almost never sampled.

19. TRIVIAL PURSUIT   5.10d R ★★   Bolts
Lost amid the better routes is this puny, undistinguished arête. Start by traversing along the same ledge as Watts Tots, then tackle a short-lived crux, leading to easy but runout knobs.

20. TATOR TOTS   5.10a R ★★   Bolts
Long before ascents of the Dihedrals' more famous face climbs, this route stepped boldly up an obvious buttress. Protected by widely-spaced bolts, **Tator Tots** deserves more respect than the average 5.10. The crux at the second bolt protects well, but the rest of the moves are dangerously runout.

21. LATIN LOVER   5.12a ★★★   Bolts
This technical wall of knobs and edges requires more finesse than power. Today, most people bypass the original crux by clipping a bolt on **Peepshow**, then traversing back right. Because of this, it feels easy for the grade. If you want to experience the original line, step out of the crack at the fifth bolt and face climb directly to the sixth.

22. PEEPSHOW   5.12a/b ★★   Bolts
If you can't get enough of **Latin Lover,** then look into this continuation, which stretches as far as a rope will reach. Extremely sustained, but never really all that hard, the route is one of Smith's ultimate tests of tedium. Be sure to use a 165-foot rope.

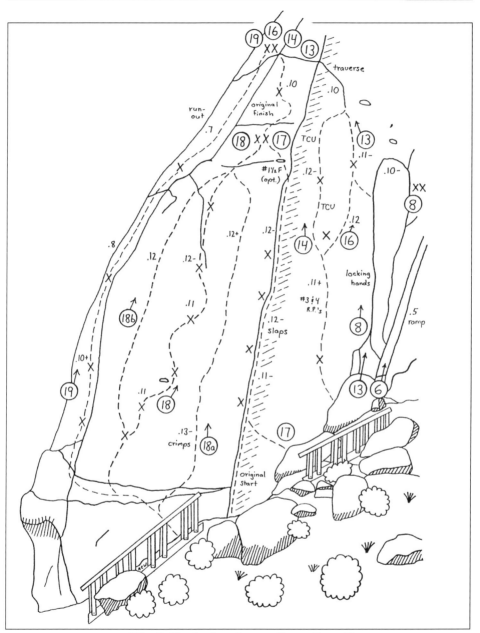

The Dihedrals – Latest Rage Detail

6.   CINNAMON SLAB 5.6 ★★★
8.   KARATE CRACK 5.10a ★★★
13. KAROT TOTS 5.11b ★★★★
14. FIRING LINE 5.12b ★★★
16. LOW PROFILE 5.12b/c R ★★★★
17. LATEST RAGE 5.12b ★★★★

18. WATTS TOTS 5.12b ★★★★
18a. MEGA WATTS 5.13b ★★★
18b. KILO WATTS 5.12b ★★★
19. TRIVIAL PURSUIT 5.10d R ★★

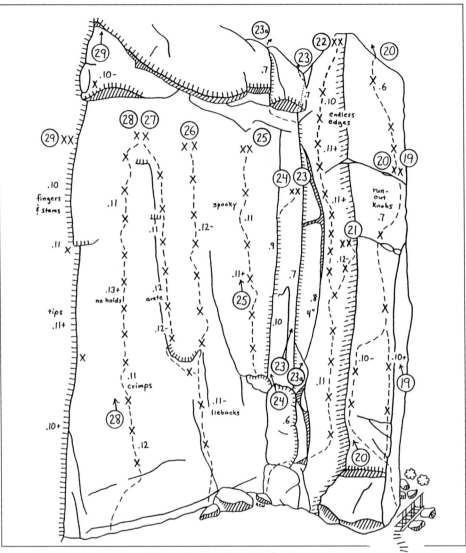

The Dihedrals – Right Center

19. TRIVIAL PURSUIT 5.10d R ★★
20. TATOR TOTS 5.10a R ★★
21. LATIN LOVER 5.12a ★★★
22. PEEPSHOW 5.12a/b ★★
23. UPPER CEILING 5.7 R ★
23a. SISTINE VARIATION 5.8 ★

24. LESTER TOTS 5.10b R ★
25. ALMOST NOTHING 5.11d R ★★
26. TAKE A POWDER 5.12a ★★★
27. POWDER IN THE EYES 5.12c ★★★
28. PROJECT 5.13d
29. SUNSHINE DIHEDRAL 5.11d ★★★★

23. UPPER CEILING   5.7 R ★   Gear to 3 inches
This unpleasant chimney system is a natural chute for the scree slope above the Dihedrals, so it collects large amounts of rubble. One look discourages most climbers, but surprising numbers go ahead and tempt fate.
1.   5.7   Jam and chimney to a belay anchor.
2.   5.7   Climb to the roof, then somehow squeeze through, trying desperately to avoid getting stuck.

23a. SISTINE VARIATION   5.8 ★   Gear to 4 inches
This two-pitch line makes a better route than its parent, but no one ever bothers. The hardest moves jam a clean fist crack on the first pitch.
1.   5.8   Start up **Upper Ceiling,** switching to a crack on the right wall. Jam and traverse left to the anchor.
2.   5.7   Scramble to the large roof, avoiding the squeeze chimney by stepping left, then jam a dirty crack to the top.

24. LESTER TOTS   5.10b R ★   Gear to 1.5 inches
Almost never climbed, this forgettable route earns the title of the most obscure line on Smith's most-travelled cliff. The climbing isn't all that bad, but some shaky protection keeps everyone away. Start with **Upper Ceiling,** then traipse up a shallow inside corner, stepping right to anchors.

25. ALMOST NOTHING   5.11d R ★★   Bolts
Once quite serious, **Almost Nothing** became much safer after someone kindly relocated the third and fourth bolts. Still, it remains a perilous undertaking, with the bolts spaced far enough apart to make whippers a distinct possibility.

26. TAKE A POWDER   5.12a ★★★   Bolts
Featuring technical moves on good rock, this steep line sees many ascents. Many avoid the thin crux past the seventh bolt by stepping right a few feet to an offset.

27. POWDER IN THE EYES   5.12c ★★★   Bolts
A baffling series of moves highlight this demanding arête/face. Start with **Take A Powder,** but step left at the roof and ascend an intricate arête on good rock.

28. PROJECT   5.13d
This desperately hard series of thin face moves is crammed tightly between **Powder in the Eyes** and **Sunshine Dihedral.** Still awaiting a redpoint lead, it will be Smith's most demanding technical exercise.

29. SUNSHINE DIHEDRAL   5.11d ★★★★   Gear (Triple set #3 to #5 RPs, Rocks, small TCUs)
This prominent dihedral is the most obvious line in the Dihedrals. Considered a top prize in the early 80s, the first free ascent gave Smith its first 5.12. Sticky rubber lowered the grade a notch, but didn't diminish the quality of the climbing. The protection to the first bolt isn't perfect, but the rest of the route protects beautifully.
1.   5.11d   Stem and jam to a three-bolt anchor. Rappel or . . .
2.   5.10a   Face climb past a bolt at the roof and follow an easy crack to the top.

30. FRENCH CONNECTION   5.13b ★★★★   Bolts (gear for **Sunshine Dihedral**)
Likely the best vertical face of the grade at Smith, this route plays second-fiddle to its more famous complete version. The extreme crux past the first bolt stops many, but the real difficulties come in trying to link the unrelenting climbing above. Oddly, many climbers are reluctant to try because they have to place gear on the approach section of **Sunshine.**

31. TO BOLT OR NOT TO BE   5.14a ★★★★   Bolts
Among the most famous free climbs in the world, **To Bolt** shook U.S. climbing in 1986. At the time, it was America's first 5.14, and it still ranks among the hardest. Originally billed as

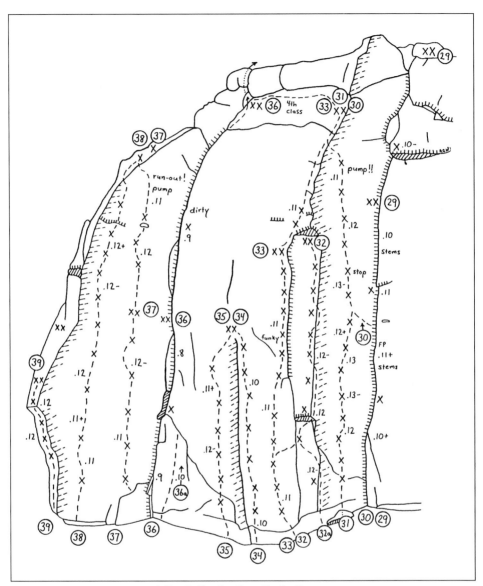

The Dihedrals – Left Center

29. SUNSHINE DIHEDRAL 5.11d ★★★★
30. FRENCH CONNECTION 5.13b ★★★★
31. TO BOLT OR NOT TO BE 5.14a
    ★★★★
32. LAST WALTZ 5.12c ★★★★
32a. LAST WALTZ DIRECT 5.12c X ★★★
33. MOONDANCE 5.11c ★★★

34. WEDDING DAY 5.10b ★★★
35. THE FLAT EARTH 5.12a/b ★
36. MOONSHINE DIHEDRAL 5.9 ★★★★
36a. MOONSHINE VARIATION 5.10b ★★★
37. HEINOUS CLING 5.12c ★★★★
38. DARKNESS AT NOON 5.13a ★★★★
39. CHAIN REACTION 5.12c ★★★★

containing the crux moves of every other route in the Dihedrals in one pitch, **To Bolt** doesn't allow a moment's rest until a shake at the tenth bolt. By then, you're tired enough that the 5.12d finish becomes a major problem in its own right.

32. LAST WALTZ 5.12c ★★★★ Bolts
Attempted with E.B.s several times, this challenging arête didn't go free until sticky rubber came around. The hardest move pulls around the roof, but many find the crux higher up, as the pump slowly builds.

32a. LAST WALTZ DIRECT 5.12c X ★★★ Bolts
Few choose to tango with this dangerously runout direct start to **Last Waltz**; a fall near the second bolt would put you on the ground. Clipping the first bolt without breaking your ankle offers a challenge in itself.

33. MOONDANCE 5.11c ★★★ Bolts
Spurned for many years due to a runout dihedral, this varied route instantly became popular when retro-bolted in 1990. The technical crux comes at the first bolt, but the climbing remains tricky the entire way. The strenuous, rarely-done upper pitch attacks an obvious triangular roof.
1. 5.11b Continuous face climbing, followed by stemming in a corner, leads to a belay.
2. 5.11c Pull over the bulge past two bolts, and solo to the top.

34. WEDDING DAY 5.10b ★★★ Bolts
Pioneered years ago with machine bolts, this arête initially received an unusually distasteful name that won't be mentioned here. These dangerous bolts got yanked to keep someone from getting hurt, and the route sat forgotten for several years. It regained popularity after it was rebolted and renamed in 1989.

35. THE FLAT EARTH 5.12a/b ★ Bolts
This strenuous line lurks just left of the **Wedding Day** arête. Unfortunately, you can cheat to the right edge in a couple places, bypassing the hardest moves. Since the rock isn't as good as a typical Dihedrals route, the crux pockets slowly crumble away.

36. MOONSHINE DIHEDRAL 5.9 ★★★★ Gear to 2 inches
This stunning dihedral shouldn't be missed. Both the rock and protection on the first pitch are perfect, with the crux coming right off the ground. Almost everyone avoids the rotten second pitch.
1. 5.9 Glide up the elegant dihedral to a hanging belay. Rappel, or . . .
2. 5.9 Move cautiously on bad rock to anchor bolts. Squeeze left through a hole, and scramble to the top.

36a. MOONSHINE VARIATION 5.10b X ★★★ Gear to 2 inches
An enjoyable but unprotected line of face holds right of the regular start makes a worthwhile diversion. (F.A. unknown)

37. HEINOUS CLING 5.12c ★★★★ Bolts
A gorgeous wall with parallel bolt lines rises just left of **Moonshine Dihedral. Heinous Cling** follows a sparsely-bolted line up the center of the face. Established on lead after cleaning, this route marked the end of a brief period of lead bolting at Smith. The lower part of the **Cling** (5.12a) sees many ascents, especially since the addition of several bolts. Originally climbed with only three bolts and natural protection, the entire route fell victim to the retro-bolting craze, erasing a part of Smith history. Still, the entire pitch is no pushover, since you'll go 40 feet if you plummet near the top.

38. DARKNESS AT NOON 5.13a ★★★★ Bolts
Smith's original 5.13 face soars just left of **Heinous Cling.** First climbed in two sections, the route later was linked in a single pitch. The demanding 5.12c start makes a good excursion in its

own right, ending with a traverse right. A no-hands rest on the left arête slashes the difficulty, but since most climbers avoid it, I've used the original grade.

39. CHAIN REACTION   5.12c ★★★★   Bolts
Easily the most photographed route at Smith, this classic knife-edge ranks among the most recognizable climbs in the world. More than any other route, **Chain Reaction** sparked the fire of Smith sport climbing. The technical crux comes at the second bolt, although almost everyone fails at least once on the powerful lunge at the roof.

40. PROJECT   5.13 ?
This unfinished line sits a few feet left of **Chain Reaction.** Although the position pales in comparison to its neighbor, the moves are even more thrilling.

41. RATTLESNAKE CHIMNEY   5.6 ★   Gear to 4 inches
For good reason, no one ever climbs this wide chimney left of **Chain Reaction.**
1.   5.6   Grovel up the dirty chimney to a scree-covered belay slot.
2.   5.4   Exit the slot, then scramble to the top.

42. ANCYLOSTOMA   5.9 ★★   Bolts
Whether you climb only on the face, or use the crack to the left (5.8), this pleasant route deserves your attention. You have the option of lowering off, or finishing via **Bookworm's** second pitch.

43. BOOKWORM   5.7 ★★★   Gear to 3.5 inches
After retro-bolting, the previously runout second pitch of this fine route became popular. The best finish follows a direct line to the top, merging with the final pitch of **Bunny Face.**
1.   5.7   After a tricky start, thrutch up a wide crack to a small ledge.
2.   5.7   Waltz up solid, well-protected knobs, finishing with either the crack or face.

43a. VARIATION   5.7 ★★   Gear to 3 inches
The original line stepped left about 30 feet up the second pitch, finishing with a solid, right-facing corner.

44. BUNNY FACE   5.7 ★★★   Bolts
The first pitch of **Bunny Face** recently dethroned **Cinnamon Slab** as the most popular beginning route at Smith. The closely-spaced bolts make this knobby slab a fine introduction to leading.
1.   5.7   Hop up big knobs to a ledge.
2.   5.6   Step right and hike the low-angled face to anchors just below the top.

45. METHUSELAH'S COLUMN   5.10a R ★   Bolts
Plagued by bad rock and poorly-spaced bolts, this unlikely line was the first bolted face in the Dihedrals. Avoid **Methuselah's** if you want to live to a ripe old age. Approach via either **Bunny Face, Rabbit Stew** or **Lycopodophyta.**

46. RABBIT STEW   5.7 ★★   Gear to 2 inches
This rarely-climbed thin crack borders the left edge of the **Bunny Face** column. If cracks suit your palate, you'll enjoy the flurry of jams.

47. LYCOPODOPHYTA   5.7 ★★   Gear to 3 inches
This unpronounceable route splits the cliff left of **Bunny Face.** The solid first pitch makes a good beginners lead. Most climbers wisely avoid the unpleasant flaring chimney of the final pitch. The odd name comes from a species of moss apparently growing on the second pitch.
1.   5.7   Scamper up the well-protected crack, stepping right past a bolt to a belay ledge.
2.   5.8   Traverse back to the crack, and grovel up the overhanging chimney to the top.

48. HELIUM WOMAN   5.9 ★★   Bolts
This unattractive buttress with parallel lines of closely-spaced bolts looms left of **Lycopodophyta.** The crux of the rightmost route comes just off the deck. It grows better with every ascent as corrupt nubbins pop off.

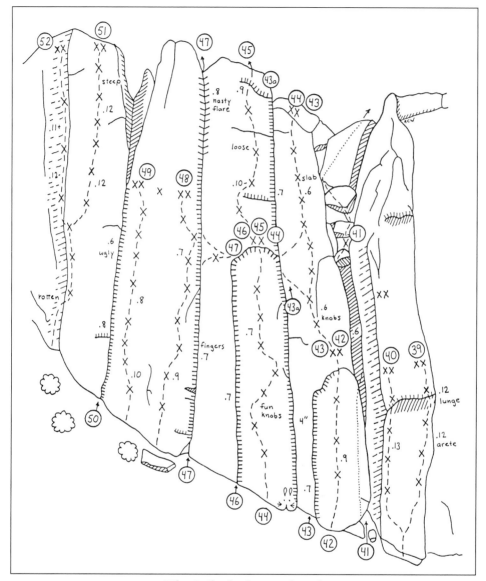

The Dihedrals – Left Side

39. CHAIN REACTION 5.12c ★★★★
40. PROJECT 5.13 ?
41. RATTLESNAKE CHIMNEY 5.6 ★
42. ANCYLOSTOMA 5.9 ★★
43. BOOKWORM 5.7 ★★★
43a. VARIATION 5.7 ★★
44. BUNNY FACE 5.7 ★★★
45. METHUSELAH'S COLUMN 5.10a R ★

46. RABBIT STEW 5.7 ★★
47. LYCOPODOPHYTA 5.7 ★★
48. HELIUM WOMAN 5.9 ★★
49. CAPTAIN XENOLITH 5.10a ★★
50. DETERIORATA 5.8 ★
51. GO DOG GO 5.12c ★★★
52. VISION 5.12b ★★

49. CAPTAIN XENOLITH   5.10a ★★   Bolts
     This knobby face sits just left of **Helium Woman.** After edging up non-existent nubbins, the climbing eases quickly above the second bolt.

50. DETERIORATA   5.8 ★   Gear to 2.5 inches
     Take a hint from the name, and avoid this junky dihedral. The moves past the crux roof are good, but the rock deteriorates rapidly near the top.

51. GO DOG GO   5.12c ★★★   Bolts
     Spectacular and popular, **Go Dog Go** combines thin edges with thuggish, overhanging jugs. The technical crux comes low on the route, although many fail on the pumpy finish.

52. VISION   5.12b ★★   Bolts
     An intimidating arête rises just left of **Go Dog Go.** The crux finesses past the fifth bolt, but the climbing remains pumping to the anchor. With its memorable position, **Vision** warrants more attention than it receives.

Scott Franklin on the first ascent of Scarface (5.14a).

Photo: Cathy Beloeil

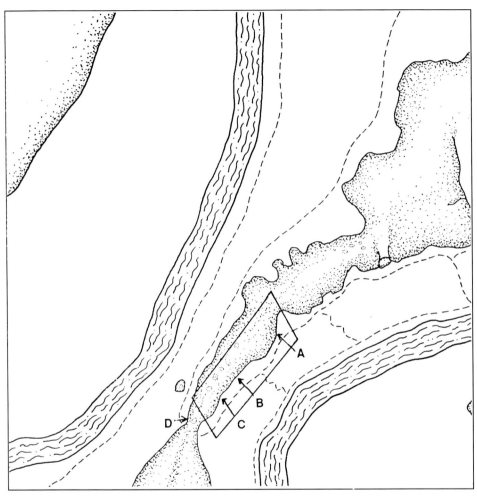

A. *Prophet Wall*
B. *Testament Slab*
C. *Combination Blocks*
D. *Asterisk Pass*

CHRISTIAN BROTHERS

EAST WALL

THE CHRISTIAN BROTHERS is a large expanse of rock immediately left of the Dihedrals. A remarkable collection of routes ascends the impressive east wall of this monolith. Capping the cliff are the five spires of the Christian Brothers themselves. From north to south are the bulbous Abbot, the Friar, the Pope, the twin spikes of the Monk, and the Priest. The summits are rarely climbed, as few lines to the top are worth doing, but the base routes are extremely popular. The variety of climbs on the east wall satisfies everyone from the beginner to the standard-setting climber. For the hardman, the best part of the cliff is the Prophet Wall. Here, an astounding series of routes line up one after another, each more impressive than the last. Further left are a throng of mostly moderate faces and cracks, which swarm with climbers of all levels.

This massive section of cliff played a crucial role in the development of Smith climbing. In the mid-sixties, the Christian Brothers inspired a generation of peak baggers, as one by one the virgin summits fell. The first exploration of the east wall came when Bob Bauman and Ken Jern climbed the dirty chimney of Gothic Cathedral in the mid-sixties. A variety of aid and easy free routes fell over the next several years, but things didn't heat up until 1972, when a new breed of free climbers arrived. First ,Tom Rogers and Clay Cox climbed the awesome crack of **Last Gasp** (5.9), then Dean Fry pushed the level higher with his ascent of **New Testament** (5.10a) in 1973. Four years later, Jeff Thomas pioneered **Shoes of the Fisherman** (5.11b), and added **Wartley's Reveng**e (5.11b) to his tick list the next year. For several years, these parallel cracks were Smith's showpieces.

Bolted face climbing came to the Christian Brothers early, when Tim Carpenter pioneered **Dancer** (5.7) and **Revelations** (5.9) in 1975. Nearly a decade passed though, before climbers realized the full potential of the area. The beautiful Prophet Wall attracted my attention in 1984; **Boy Prophet** (5.12b) was the result. The free ascent of **Double Stain,** the first 5.13 in the area, came two months later. For the first time, Smith Rock flirted with free climbing standards in the U.S. The next year, I worked out a direct start to **Boy Prophet,** but my luck ended as finger injuries kept me from nabbing the first redpoint of **Rude Boys** (5.13c). In 1986, Jean Baptiste Tribout quickly polished off the route as a warm-up for **To Bolt or Not to Be.**

In early 1988, Scott Franklin arrived on the scene, and began talking big numbers. He spied a seemingly impossible line left of **Rude Boys,** and after several weeks of effort came away with his prize – Scarface (5.14a). Again, the standards found on the East Wall of the Christian Brothers matched the top level of the day. In the last few years, this rapid development continued unabated. Routes like **Choke on This** (5.13a), **Bum Rush the Show** (5.13b), **Smooth Boy** (5.13b), and **Rude Femmes** (5.13c/d) consolidated the level here. Along with these desperate lines, an assortment of bolted faces from 5.8 to 5.12 attracted many more climbers to the area. Today, people wait in line on busy weekends for the most popular routes.

Unlike the nearby Dihedrals, the Christian Brothers still offer good new route potential. Certain areas, like the Prophet Wall and Testament Slab, will see little additional development, but other sections of stone await activity. Some year in the future, the climbs of the Christian Brothers might again stand at the top of the list. The sweeping overhang left of **Scarface** will undoubtedly catch the eye of some 5.15 climber of a future generation.

THE MONK

THE FRIAR

THE PRIEST

THE ABBOT

27

27a

25

42a

26a

42

40   31   28   21   19   13   5   2   9

COMBINATION   TESTAMENT   THE BEARD   PROPHET WALL
BLOCKS   SLAB

Photo: Bruce Adams

Christian Brothers – Northeast Side

1. DEEP SPLASH 5.11d ★★
2. RAWHIDE 5.11d ★★★
5. DREAMIN' 5.12a R ★★★★
9. SCARFACE 5.14a ★★★★
13. WARTLEY'S REVENGE 5.11b ★★★★
19. BARBECUE THE POPE 5.10b ★★★
21. REVELATIONS 5.9 ★★★
25. HEATHEN'S HIGHWAY 5.10a ★★
26a. ISLAND IN THE SKY 5.8 X

27. LAST GASP 5.9 X
27a. SAFETY VALVE 5.7 R
28. PROJECT 5.13 ?
31. OVERNIGHT SENSATION 5.11a ★★★
40. RING OF FIRE 5.11d ★★★
42. DANCER 5.7 ★★★
42a. DANCER CONTINUATION 5.8 ★

THE PRIEST

THE MONK

THE FRIAR

THE POPE

THE ABBOT

42a

25

35

42

31

38

28

COMBINATION BLOCKS

TESTAMENT SLAB

26

21

18

9

10

13

Photo: Bruce Adams

Christian Brothers – Southeast Side

9. SCARFACE 5.14a ★★★★
10. AIR TO SPARE 5.9 A4+ X ★
13. WARTLEY'S REVENGE 5.11b ★★★★
18. GOLGOTHA 5.11b R ★★★
21. REVELATIONS 5.9 ★★★
25. HEATHEN'S HIGHWAY 5.10a ★★
26. GOTHIC CATHEDRAL 5.8 R

28. PROJECT 5.13 ?
30. CHARLIE'S CHIMNEY 5.6 X ★★★
31. OVERNIGHT SENSATION 5.11a ★★★
35. DOUBLE STAIN 5.13a/b ★★★
38. HESITATION BLUES 5.10b ★★★
42. DANCER 5.7 ★★★
42a. DANCER CONTINUATION 5.8 ★

THE PROPHET WALL

This stunning face, with its assortment of difficult routes on perfect rock, looms on the right side of the Christian Brother's East Wall. The climbs are described starting far uphill and moving down and left along the base of the crag.

1. DEEP SPLASH 5.11d ★★ Bolts
   This bolted route sits above the highest point of the hillside, on the right side of the Christian Brothers. After some tweaky cranks past the second bolt, the climbing eases, but remains strenuous to the anchor. Unfortunately, the rock quality never matches the caliber of the moves.

2. RAWHIDE 5.11d ★★★ Bolts
   This strenuous traverse comes highly recommended. A snapped hold made the third bolt difficult to clip, until a Good Samaritan relocated it.

3. SMOOTH BOY 5.13b ★★★ Bolts
   A prominent, diagonal roof traverses the upper section of the Prophet Wall. Funky and technical the entire way, the crux of this unique route pulls powerfully over the lower right side of this roof.

4. CHOKE ON THIS 5.12d ★★★ Bolts
   This perplexing test piece rises a few feet downhill from **Smooth Boy.** After an ungainly crux sequence, the climbing eases above the fifth bolt, but many have choked on the finishing slab.

5. DREAMIN' 5.12a R ★★★★ Bolts
   The hardest moves of this Smith classic are in the first 30 feet, although many climbers find a blind reach around the final roof especially bewildering. The bolts are far enough apart to keep you from daydreamin' as you saunter up the 5.11 slab. Clipping into the bolt at the upper roof with a long sling avoids annoying rope drag on the final moves.

6. BOY PROPHET 5.12b R ★★★★ Bolts (TCU above final bolt)
   With flawless rock and intricate moves, this route opened the Prophet Wall in 1984. You've done the hardest moves once you clip the second bolt, but the runout 5.11 slab keeps things interesting.

7. RUDE BOYS 5.13c ★★★★ Bolts (TCU above final bolt)
   This famous test piece tempts climbers from around the world. The technical crux comes at the start, although everyone falls higher at a powerful sequence past the third bolt. A taxing finish up **Boy Prophet** caps this prestigious route. Curiously, on early repeats, many climbers with pumped forearms started calling it good at the fifth bolt, ignoring the slab that was part of the first ascent. The grade I've given reflects a complete ascent.

8. RUDE FEMMES 5.13c/d ★★★★ Bolts
   If the final slab on **Rude Boys** seems too easy, move up and left after the fourth bolt and finish on an endless 5.12 slab. Not surprisingly, few tangle with this one. Guard against rope drag by clipping the third bolt with a long sling.

9. SCARFACE 5.14a ★★★★ Bolts
   An amazing series of powerful lock-offs on overhanging pockets makes Scarface one of the most difficult free climbs in the country. The memorable first ascent marked the first time an American climber established 5.14. Although the starting wall requires the most power, the climb turns into an endurance problem above. Many feel the actual crux comes at a sick move pulling onto the final slab.

10. AIR TO SPARE 5.9 A4+ X ★ Aid rack to .75 inch
    This absurd aid route nails invisible seams on the overhanging wall left of **Scarface.** The strong possibility of a ground fall, coupled with the demise of Smith aid climbing, could mean **Air to Spare** may never see another ascent.

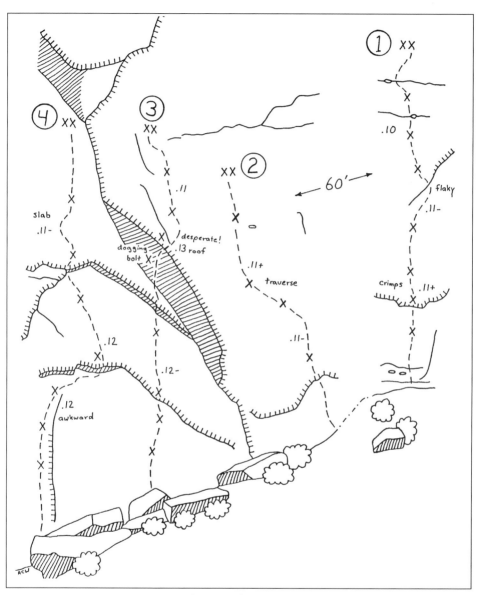

Prophet Wall – Right Side

1. DEEP SPLASH 5.11d ★★
2. RAWHIDE 5.11d ★★★
3. SMOOTH BOY 5.13b ★★★
4. CHOKE ON THIS 5.12d ★★★

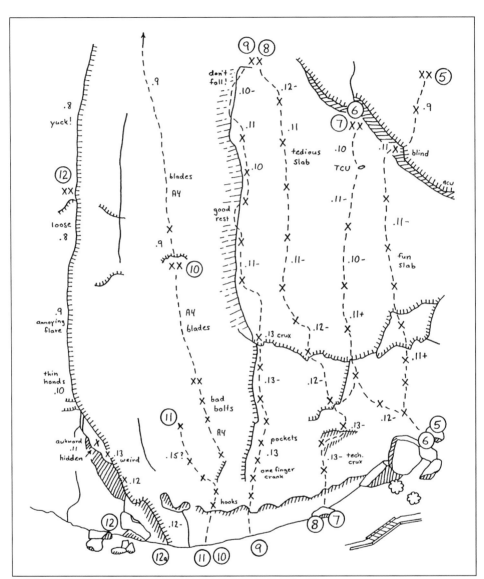

Prophet Wall – Left Side

5. DREAMIN' 5.12a R ★★★★
6. BOY PROPHET 5.12b R ★★★★
7. RUDE BOYS 5.13c ★★★★
8. RUDE FEMMES 5.13c/d ★★★★
9. SCARFACE 5.14a ★★★★

10. AIR TO SPARE 5.9 A4+ X ★
11. PROJECT 5.15?
12. SHOES OF THE FISHERMAN 5.11b
    ★★
12a. TOES OF THE FISHERMAN 5.13b

1. A4+   Nail incipient seams past bolts, rivets and dowels to an anchor below the slab.
2. 5.9 A4   Tough aid on knifeblades gives way to progressively easier free climbing. At a dirty ledge walk left into the Hobbit Hole between the Abbot and Friar.

11. PROJECT 5.15?
A few bolts on a seemingly blank wall rise just left of **Air to Spare**. Apparently a few holds exist, but a free ascent seems at least a decade away.

12. SHOES OF THE FISHERMAN 5.11b ★★   Gear to 3 inches (Doubles #1.5 through #3 Friend)
When first freed in 1977, **Shoes** earned the title of Smith's hardest route. Over the years, this awkwardly leaning crack witnessed many desperate struggles. As aspiring hardmen sought repeats, **Shoes** enjoyed a flourish of popularity in the early 80s. Today, it sees few ascents as more enjoyable 5.11s are everywhere.
1. 5.11b Jam the overhanging crack to an anchor. Rappel with two ropes, or . . .
2. 5.9 Pull over a bulge, then scramble up mud to the **Hobbit Hole**. Descend by scrambling to the **Cinnamon Slab** rappel.

12a. TOES OF THE FISHERMAN 5.13b Project
This demented variation to **Shoes** was never completed. Done with a hang in the mid-80s, the contorted finger jams discouraged anyone from maintaining interest long enough to succeed. The climbing isn't unreasonably difficult, but the moves just aren't any fun.

13. WARTLEY'S REVENGE 5.11b ★★★★   Gear to 2.5 inches
In the early 80s, no route at Smith got more attention than **Wartley's Revenge**; every aspiring 5.11 climber threw themselves at it. Although not as popular today, it's the best crack route of the grade at Smith. Except for a tricky stemming start, the holds are nothing but jugs, but the steepness causes many power failures at the final move. The upper pitches rarely get climbed, but they'd be good if they got more traffic.
1. 5.11b A technical start leads to jug hauling and a strenuous finish. Rappel, or . . .
2. 5.10a Climb a moderate crack past some loose holds to a sling belay.
3. 5.8 Jam and lieback the prominent flake, taking care not to dislodge a huge, loose block at mid-height. Step right to an anchor and scramble into the **Hobbit Hole**, descending via **Cinnamon Slab**.

THE BEARD

The Beard is an unimpressive block pasted onto the base of the wall left of **Wartley's Revenge**. Two easy routes ascend cracks up either side to a rappel anchor.

14. THE RIGHT SIDE OF THE BEARD 5.7 ★★★   Gear to 2 inches
This short, thin crack provides an excellent beginners lead or toprope problem. The tricky crux jams over a bulge at mid-height.

15. RISK SHY 5.12a X ★★★   No gear
The right arête of the Beard offers a challenging problem. Although free soloed on the first ascent, a toprope makes more sense, since a fall at the crux will leave you hurting.

16. THE LEFT SIDE OF THE BEARD 5.6 ★★★   Gear to 2.5 inches
If you've never tried to lead a route placing gear, this short, hand/finger crack provides a good introduction. The crux comes right off the ground.

17. THE CLAM 5.11b ★   Bolts
The Clam ascends the steep face directly above the Beard. The first few feet are the most difficult; while the mediocre upper wall eases considerably. Short climbers find the first move off the Beard very frustrating, as they balance on tip-toe stretching for the starting holds.

THE TESTAMENT SLAB

An appealing buttress, split by a prominent crack, rises just left of the Beard. You'd better arrive early if you plan on getting on any of these enjoyable routes on a busy weekend.

18.   GOLGOTHA   5.11b R ★★★   Gear to 1 inch (Double RPs, Rocks)

This prominent, left-leaning seam marks the right border of the Testament Slab. A bewildering crux above the final bolt gives most climbers fits. The easier lower crack protects adequately with small nuts, but more than one person has hit the ground after a gear-ripping fall.

18a.   TEMPTATION   5.10a ★★   Gear to 1.5 inches

The original line started up **Golgotha,** then traversed left across the face to join **New Testament** below the flare. For good reason, no one bothers with this exercise in rope-drag management.

19.   BARBECUE THE POPE   5.10b ★★★   Bolts

Extremely popular, this line of edges and knobs sees almost non-stop traffic during peak season. Since the original line of ascent went left of the current route, the second bolt seems annoyingly far left. Take care getting to the first clip.

20.   NEW TESTAMENT   5.10a ★★★   Gear to 3 inches

This obvious crack splits the face of the Testament Slab. When first freed, it was the most difficult route on the Christian Brothers. Climbers routinely fly off the deceptively tricky final moves, so protect well before launching into the groove.

21.   REVELATIONS   5.9 ★★★   Bolts

This rounded arête was Smith's first fully-bolted sport route. Bolted on rappel long before the practice gained acceptance, **Revelations** instantly became popular. The original intent was to face climb directly past the bolts, but almost everyone uses the arête now. Bring some small Rocks if you don't like the length of the runout to the first bolt. One rope reaches the ground if you stay left when rapping off.

22.   IRREVERENCE   5.10a ★★★   Bolts

This bolted line up the center of the wall rises a few feet left of Revelations. A ticklish series of knobs and pockets gives many climbers the jitters.

23.   NIGHTINGALE'S ON VACATION   5.10b ★★   Bolts

A deceptively tricky crux highlights this trip up the left arête of the Testament Slab. After a moderate start, a short sequence above a ledge leads to easy climbing. Hopefully, the closely-spaced bolts will keep you off the ledge if you plummet.

24.   OLD TESTAMENT   5.7 ★★   Gear to 3 inches

The easiest and worst of the routes on the Testament Slab follows a hand crack in a tight, left-facing corner. After crawling right along a ledge, romp up easy knobs or continue in the crack to the anchors.

25.   HEATHEN'S HIGHWAY   5.10a ★★   Gear to 3 inches

This long, varied route ascends to the top of the Friar. Most climbers bypass the upper two pitches, as only the second pitch stands out. Still, the entire line makes a pleasant diversion from the bustle below, and deserves more attention than it receives.

1.   Climb any of the Testament Slab routes to the anchor atop **Revelations.**
2.   5.10a   A crazy line of bolts zigzag on jugs to a hanging belay.
3.   5.9   Face traverse right to a crack and climb to the gap between the Friar and the Pope.
4.   5.6   Grotesque climbing protected by ancient bolts leads to the summit of the Friar. To descend, rappel north into the **Hobbit Hole** and make a complicated scramble to the **Cinnamon Slab** rappel.

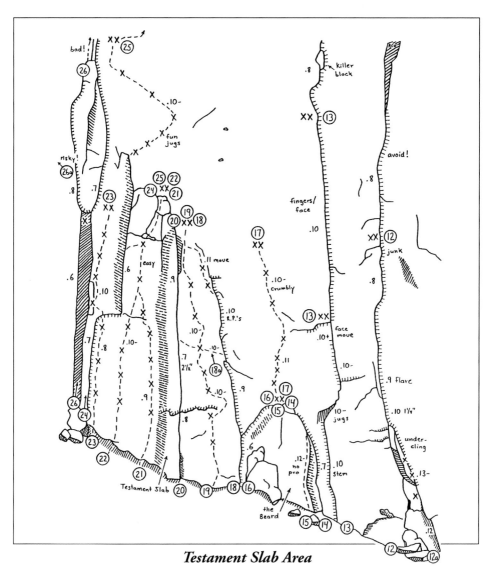

Testament Slab Area

12. SHOES OF THE FISHERMAN 5.11b ★★

12a. TOES OF THE FISHERMAN 5.13b

13. WARTLEY'S REVENGE 5.11b ★★★★

14. THE RIGHT SIDE OF THE BEARD 5.7 ★★★

15. RISK SHY 5.12a X ★★★

16. THE LEFT SIDE OF THE BEARD 5.6 ★★★

17. THE CLAM 5.11b ★

18. GOLGOTHA 5.11b R ★★★

18a. TEMPTATION 5.10a ★★

19. BARBECUE THE POPE 5.10b ★★★

20. NEW TESTAMENT 5.10a ★★★

21. REVELATIONS 5.9 ★★★

22. IRREVERENCE 5.10a ★★★

23. NIGHTINGALE'S ON VACATION 5.10b ★★

24. OLD TESTAMENT 5.7 ★★

25. HEATHEN'S HIGHWAY 5.10a ★★

26. GOTHIC CATHEDRAL 5.8 R

26a. ISLAND IN THE SKY 5.8 X

26. GOTHIC CATHEDRAL 5.8 R   Gear to 4 inches
This horrendous rubble-gully splits the entire east face of the Christian Brothers. Atrocious rock, inadequate protection and awkward climbing make any ascent a foolish mistake.
1. 5.7 Stem the chimney past a roof to an anchor.
2. 5.8 Grovel up the righthand crack to the slot between the Pope and the Friar. Either do the **Christian Brothers Traverse**, or rappel the route using two ropes.

26a. ISLAND IN THE SKY 5.8 X   Gear to 2.5 inches (Friends)
Plagued by bad rock and even worse protection, the airy traverse to the **Island in the Sky** ledge rarely sees traffic. Start up the first pitch of **Gothic Cathedral**, stepping left to the dangerous face traverse. Rappel with two ropes.

27. LAST GASP 5.9 X   Gear to 6 inches
Perhaps the most striking feature of the East Wall of the Christian Brothers is an impressive wide crack splitting the Priest. Nicknamed **Crack of Doom**, this awe-inspiring pitch involves enough unprotected climbing on horrible rock to scare away generations of climbers.
1. 5.7 Climb the first pitch of **Gothic Cathedral.**
2. 5.6 Traverse left to a belay below the wide crack.
3. 5.9 Stem between the crack and right wall, then commit into the off-width. Unprotected thrashing leads into the **Crack of Dawn**. An ugly exit and a quick face move ends on the summit. Rappel off the west side of the Priest using two ropes.

27a. SAFETY VALVE 5.7 R   Gear to 3 inches
If you're trying **Last Gasp** and realize part way up you've made a poor choice, **Safety Valve** provides a painless escape. Rather than committing to the **Crack of Dawn**, continue up a corner to the notch between the Priest and Friar.

28. PROJECT 5.13 ?
The impressive wall left of the Testament Slab eventually will contain several high-quality routes. Most of the moves already go on the first of these lines.

COMBINATION BLOCKS AREA
Two massive blocks, stacked one atop the other, lean against the base of the Christian Brothers. Several high-quality routes ascend every possible side of this unique formation.

29. PRIVATE TRUST 5.11c R ★★★   Bolts
This fine route would be popular if the first bolt wasn't so far off the ground. The crux finesses a complicated bouldering sequence below the first clip, so with any mistake, you hit the dirt.

30. CHARLIE'S CHIMNEY 5.6 X ★★★   Gear to 3.5 inches
The right edge of Combination Blocks forms a distinctive, knife-edge flake. After liebacking boldly up this flake, squeeze through a tight hole to the top. The 30-foot runout off the ground keeps most people away from this otherwise enjoyable route.

31. OVERNIGHT SENSATION 5.11a ★★★   Bolts
A technical finish highlights this romp up the high-quality main face of Combination Blocks. A few bolts are tough to clip, but this doesn't diminish the route's popularity.

32. TINKER TOY 5.9 X ★★★   Gear to 3 inches
The striking left arête of Combination Blocks can be climbed on either the right or left side. **Tinker Toy** follows a high-quality, but very poorly-protected, line up the right side of the edge.

33. DOUBLE TROUBLE 5.10b ★★   Bolts
Ascending the left side of the arête makes a much safer endeavor than **Tinker Toy**. Facing right, lieback an intimidating sequence past many bolts to the anchor.

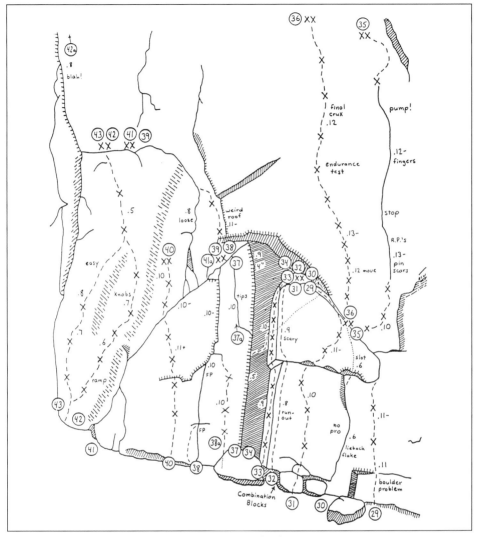

Combination Blocks Area

29. PRIVATE TRUST 5.11c R ★★★
30. CHARLIE'S CHIMNEY 5.6 X ★★★
31. OVERNIGHT SENSATION 5.11a ★★★
32. TINKER TOY 5.9 X ★★★
33. DOUBLE TROUBLE 5.10b ★★
34. BOWLING ALLEY 5.5 ★★
35. DOUBLE STAIN 5.13a/b ★★★
36. BUM RUSH THE SHOW 5.13b ★★★
37. TOYS IN THE ATTIC 5.9 ★★

37a. CHILD'S PLAY 5.10c ★★
38. HESITATION BLUES 5.10b ★★★
38a. BLUE BALLS 5.10b X ★★
39. ATTIC ANTICS 5.11b ★★
40. RING OF FIRE 5.11d ★★★
41. TOY BLOCKS 5.10a ★★
42. DANCER 5.7 ★★★
42a. DANCER CONTINUATION 5.8 ★
43. JETE 5.8 ★★★

34. BOWLING ALLEY 5.5 ★★ Gear to 3.5 inches
The easiest line to the top of Combination Blocks thrashes up a squeeze chimney on the formation's left side. Start up the obvious corridor via either crack, then fling your body into a slot behind the upper block.

The following two routes start from the top of Combination Blocks and tackle the streaked overhanging wall above. Approach these lines by climbing any of the routes to the top of the block.

35. DOUBLE STAIN 5.13a/b ★★★ Gear to 1 inch (Double set of RPs, Rocks)
When first freed, this pin-scarred tips crack was Smith's first 5.13. Today, few climbers risk fumbling with the gear and stay away. The split-grade indicates the difference between a true redpoint lead and an ascent with pre-placed gear. The first ascent involved an unusually powerful nut placement, followed by a difficult down climb. Understandably, no one bothers with this insane exercise in gear-placement skills.

36. BUM RUSH THE SHOW 5.13b ★★★ Bolts
The impressive, overhanging wall left of **Double Stain** contains this extreme route. After a technical crux low, the climbing remains strenuous enough to keep the outcome in doubt until the final moves.

37. TOYS IN THE ATTIC 5.9 ★★ Gear to 4 inches
The wide alley on the left side of Combination Blocks culminates in a massive roof. After jamming the steepening crack, hand traverse down and left to an anchor. You'll be chastised by your second if you fail to protect the traverse, as the climb is scarier to follow than lead.

37a. CHILD'S PLAY 5.10c ★★ Gear to 2.5 inches
Hidden from view, this entertaining thin crack ascends the left wall of **Toys in the Attic.** Start up **Toys,** but step left after 30 feet, jamming the diagonal crack to the anchor.

38. HESITATION BLUES 5.10b ★★★ Gear to 2 inches
A pleasant crack splits the wall left of Combination Blocks. Justifiably popular, this strenuous line frustrates those who hesitate. The fixed pins should be replaced with bolts before they pull out on someone.

38a. BLUE BALLS 5.10b ★★ Gear to 2 inches
This short seam lurks a few feet right of the start of **Hesitation Blues.** Originally a bold undertaking, recent bolts eliminate any danger.

39. ATTIC ANTICS 5.11b ★★ Gear to 2.5 inches
This neglected pitch cranks over the intimidating roof above the **Hesitation Blues** anchors. After pulling awkwardly over the lip, a quick stemming sequence ends with a traverse left to anchors.

40. RING OF FIRE 5.11d ★★★ Bolts
The most popular route of its grade at Smith, this steep face sees almost non-stop activity on a busy day. The popularity comes more from the closely-spaced bolts and unassuming look than the brilliance of the climbing.

41. TOY BLOCKS 5.10a ★★ Gear to 2.5 inches
An obvious hand traverse slashes across **Ring of Fire.** Once plagued by a teetering block (now long gone), the route ascends in relative safety up smaller loose flakes to the anchor atop **Dancer.**

41a. SELF PRESERVATION VARIATION 5.10a ★★★ Gear to 2.5 inches
If you're wise, you'll avoid the shaky flakes on **Toy Blocks** by continuing the hand traverse right to the **Hesitation Blues** anchor. Although rarely done, the rock and climbing are excellent.

42. DANCER   5.7 ★★★ Bolts

This knobby slab makes an excellent choice for aspiring sport climbers. A steep bulge past the third bolt makes you think for a moment, but the finish comes easy.

42a. DANCER CONTINUATION   5.8 ★   Gear to 3 inches

For good reason, this mediocre second-pitch finish to **Dancer** never gets done. Nonetheless, if summits are important to you, ascend the left of two crumbly cracks to the south shoulder of the Priest. Either rappel down the west side, or take the **Christian Brothers Traverse.**

43. JETE   5.8 ★★★ Bolts

A few bolts protecting a pleasant, knobby face are just a jump left of **Dancer.** After a crux above the third bolt, **Jeté** joins its partner to the right.

Jason Karn on Rude Boys (5.13c).   Photo: Cathy Beloeil

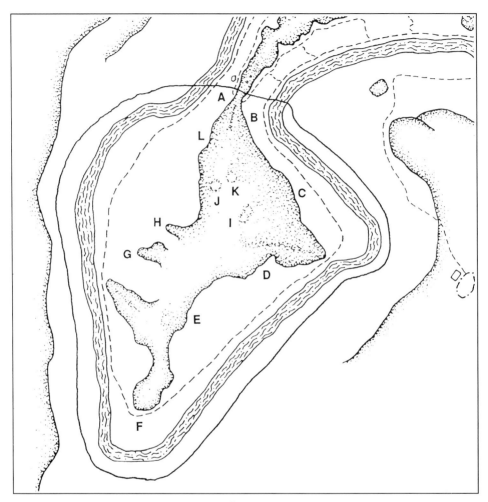

A. *Asterisk Pass*
B. *Northeast Face*
C. *Phoenix Buttress*
D. *Vulture Ridge*
E. *Grover Wall*
F. *Southern Tip*
G. *Cod Rock*
H. *Flounder Block*
I. *Smith Summit*
J. *Arrowpoint*
K. *The Platform*
L. *Northwest Face*

SMITH ROCK GROUP

THE SMITH ROCK GROUP encompasses the massive complex of multi-colored spires and cliffs south of Asterisk Pass. The area contains huge expanses of rock that, unfortunately, are far more interesting to bird watchers than climbers. With a few notable exceptions, the rock doesn't match the quality found elsewhere at Smith. Still, the sheer volume of stone suggests that isolated pockets of great climbing might be found here. During the 90s the area surely will see development as the choices dwindle elsewhere.

Especially stunning when viewed from the Dihedrals, the ominous northeast wall rises far above the river. The castellated spikes of Vulture Ridge connect with the double spires of Smith Summit, while the Platform and Arrowpoint tower to the right. Despite the grandeur of this face, the few routes to the top plow through garbage. The most notable exceptions are the multi-pitch crack lines nearest Asterisk Pass and the outstanding rock of the Phoenix Buttress. Following the river downstream, the stone deteriorates into a mixture of low-grade tuff and shattered rhyolite. While these colorful walls are strikingly beautiful, they're generally far too junky to climb. Fortunately, some exceptions exist here as well, as the southern end of the peninsula contains a few snazzy lines. Around the bend, the cliffs on the west side aren't nearly as spectacular, with only a few isolated crags worth visiting. Moving back toward Asterisk Pass, the cliff line again captures the eye. Here, several steep but forgotten cracks soar far above the ground.

Several routes in the area, especially those near **Sky Ridge,** are off-limits in the spring and early summer as birds of prey make their nests nearby. The park service posts signs at the base of these closed sections of cliff. Please check with the ranger before attempting nearby routes, as they might be in the restricted zones.

To descend from the routes topping out near **Sky Ridge,** scramble up a third-class gully and continue south around the base of the Platform and Arrowpoint. Eventually, a scree chute cuts down the west side to a trail leading back to Asterisk Pass. Be sure you can see all the way to the bottom of the gully you start down, as several end in steep cliffs. If you can't stand walking in your rock shoes, a fixed rappel station just over the top of **Sky Ridge** allows two double-rope rappels down the west side.

ASTERISK PASS
Separating the Christian Brothers from the Smith Rock Group is Asterisk Pass, with its precariously balanced bulb. An easy but exposed fourth-class scramble leads to the west side routes.

1. THE ASTERISK   5.7 X ★   No Gear
    Among Smith's most recognizable features, this bulbous rock somehow sits atop Asterisk Pass without toppling over. Foolhardy climbers occasionally make a few exposed moves up the back of the head. No anchors are in place, so make sure you can climb down.

EAST SIDE ROUTES
By far the most popular routes in the Smith Rock Group are on the east side. The following climbs start at Asterisk Pass and continue a half mile downstream to the Southern Tip:

2. SKY RIDGE   5.8 R ★★   Gear to 2 inches
    Two decades before anyone heard of sport climbing, this striking arête sported Smith's first rappel-placed bolts. Despite the breathtaking position, it sees few ascents. A runout on easy, rotten rock at the start makes the climb more serious than the typical 5.8, but the remaining moves protect well. To start, scramble up the ridge to a belay niche.

1. 5.8 Climb delicately up the arête until bolts lead to better rock on the right wall. After rejoining the edge, finish to a belay on the crest of the ridge.

2. 5.7 Amble up an easy crack on the left to an exposed traverse below the final summit block. Hand traverse if you're wise, or foot shuffle if you're foolish, thirty feet to the left.

2a. SKY RIDGE VARIATION 5.8 R ★ Gear to 3 inches
You can avoid the best climbing on the first pitch by stepping right to a forgettable crack leading to the belay anchor.

2b. SKY DIVE 5.10c ★★★ Bolts
The original finish to **Sky Ridge** aided a bolt line on the overhanging summit block. **Sky Dive** frees this bulge with a short sequence of exposed, bouldery moves.

Northeast Face

The next several climbs ascend the prominent northeast face of the Smith Rock Group. With only a few exceptions, most of the multi-pitch routes are serious ventures on bad rock.

3. SKY WAYS 5.10a R Gear to 6 inches
One look at this ominous crack discourages sensible climbers from sampling **Sky Ways**. Several loose boulders await those who try. Begin by moving left from the belay niche below **Sky Ridge**.

4. BY WAYS 5.8 R Gear to 4 inches
Despite some atrocious rock, someone climbed this unaesthetic traverse a few years back. If you avoid it, you'll have a much better day of climbing.
1. 5.8 From the belay below **Sky Ridge**, traverse far left along a dirty crack to **Sky Chimney**.
2. 5.7 Finish up the second pitch of **Sky Chimney**.

5. SKY CHIMNEY 5.7 ★★ Gear to 3 inches
This prominent crack system makes a fine multi-pitch choice. The upper two pitches are solid, well-protected and enjoyable. Take care not to dump rock on your belayer when emerging onto the scree slope above the final pitch. To approach, cut left across the hillside below Asterisk Pass to a distinctive block sticking out from the base of the wall.
1. 5.6 Grunt up an unpleasant chimney system to a massive ledge.
2. 5.7 Lieback a solid right-facing corner and disappear into a tight belay hole.
3. 5.7 Fly up the dihedral above to a gravel-covered belay ledge just below the top.

5a. SKY CHIMNEY VARIATION 5.7 R Gear to 6 inches
You can avoid the unpleasant first pitch of **Sky Chimney** by climbing a much worse corner to the right.

6. WHITE SATIN 5.9 ★★★ Gear to 2.5 inches
The brilliant upper pitch of **White Satin** more than makes up for the mediocre approach. The excellent rock and fine position make a memorable route.
1. 5.6 Climb the unpleasant chimney to a huge ledge.
2. 5.7 Ascend a shallow inside corner, then make an exciting hand traverse around a large flake. Belay a few feet higher in an uncomfortable slot.
3. 5.9 Glide up the overhanging corner. At the final bulge, either step right or attack it directly.

7. GRETTIR'S SAGA 5.10a X Gear to 2.5 inches
With bad rock, monster runouts and intolerable rope drag, this obscure route is a serious proposition. Start downhill 20 feet from the detached pillar below **Sky Chimney**, at a short, left-facing dihedral.

8. BLACK VELCRO 5.9 R ★ Gear to 2.5 inches
Likely unrepeated, **Black Velcro** ascends a devious crack system far left of **White Satin**. The route isn't all bad, as the lower dihedral contains some good rock, but it makes a poor choice for the budding 5.9 climber.

SMITH SUMMIT

VULTURE RIDGE

THE PLATFORM

ARROWPOINT

THE ASTERISK

PHOENIX BUTTRESS

Photo: Bruce Adams

Smith Rock Group – Northeast Face

2. SKY RIDGE 5.8 R ★★
6. WHITE SATIN 5.9 ★★★
8. BLACK VELCRO 5.9 R ★
9. SNIBBLE TOWER 5.9 A1 ★
10. CONDOR 5.10c ★★

12. 100% BEEF 5.13 ?
13. SMITH SUMMIT – EAST WALL 5.8 X
14. CARABID 5.6 R ★★
16. PHOENIX 5.10a ★★★★

  1. 5.5 Climb the first pitch of **Sky Chimney.**
  2. 4th Traverse far left along a scary ledge system to a belay beneath a curving corner.
  3. 5.8 Ascend a right-facing dihedral to a bolt belay.
  4. 5.9 Continue up the dihedral, then face climb right over a bulge. Step lightly up a rotten corner to an anchor.
  5. 5.7 A short face leads to the top.

9. SNIBBLE TOWER 5.9 A1 R (fifth pitch ★★★★; other pitches, no stars) Gear to 2.5 inches
If the fifth pitch of this route were right off the ground, it would rank among the best climbs at Smith. Unfortunately, it sits atop four pitches of junk. The entire climb goes free by avoiding the third-pitch bolt line, pushing directly up a rotten corridor to the left. It makes more sense to avoid this tasteless stretch by following the regular route. Start below an ominous chimney system left of the only pine tree at the base of the wall.
  1. 5.6 Scramble left up a ramp 30 feet to belay bolts.

2. 5.7 Traverse right to a disgusting chimney, then sloth up a flare, escaping right to a belay.
3. A1 5.6 Shaky aid bolts rejoin the crack system.
4. 5.7 Climb the solid ramp and step around a few bulges to a belay beneath the classic open book.

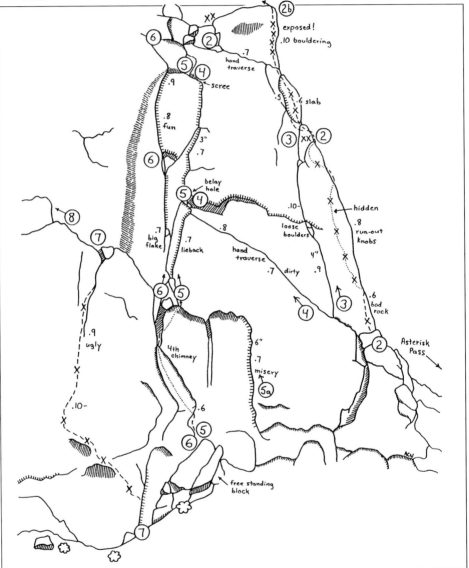

Smith Rock Group – Northeast Face Detail

2. SKY RIDGE 5.8 R ★★
2b. SKY DIVE 5.10c ★★★
3. SKY WAYS 5.10a R
4. BY WAYS 5.8 R
5. SKY CHIMNEY 5.7 ★★

5a. SKY CHIMNEY VARIATION 5.7 R
6. WHITE SATIN 5.9 ★★★
7. GRETTIR'S SAGA 5.10a X
8. BLACK VELCRO 5.9 R ★

5. 5.9   Soar up incredibly good rock to a ledge.
6. 4th   Traverse down and left, then hike up a boulder-filled gully. Walk off to the west.

10. CONDOR   5.10c ★★   Gear to 3 inches
A huge gully splits the wall between the Platform and Smith Summit. **Condor** ascends a crack system about 100 feet left of the steep wall at the base of this gully. Start beneath the right of two parallel cracks and jam solid rock, finishing up the left side of a huge tooth.

11. LIVIN' LARGE   5.13 ?   Project
An impressive overhang, capped by a roof rises around the corner left of **Condor.** This appealing line ascends great rock up the center of this face.

12. 100% BEEF   5.13 ?   Project
Destined to be a popular test piece, this rounded arête entails powerful slaps up the left side of the clean, overhanging wall.

13. SMITH SUMMIT – EAST WALL   5.8 X   Gear to 2.5 inches
Among the worst routes at Smith, this wall has nothing to offer but a life-threatening experience. Repugnant rock and poor protection earn the East Wall its reputation as an Oregon death tour. Start just left of the bolted sport routes, below a colorful lichen-covered corner.
1. 5.8   Climb the corner, then make a tricky face traverse right to the base of an imposing hand crack.
2. 5.8   Jam the strenuous crack on okay rock to an anchor.
3. 5.6   Romp up a loose ramp 160 feet to a ledge.
4. 5.8   Step right and climb a filthy crack leading to dangerous face moves and a belay.
5. 5.6   Scramble up a steep wall of scree to the top of the east tower of Smith Summit. Descend by rappeling south into a huge gully. Either hike out, or scramble down to a short, roped pitch below a single bolt.

Phoenix Buttress

Amid some of the worst stone at Smith rises this small section of incredibly solid, reddish/purple rock. The excellent collection of routes see almost non-stop traffic. Midday shade makes the Phoenix Buttress a fine destination in the hot summer.

14. CARABID   5.6 R ★★   Gear to 2.5 inches
If not for some runout stretches, this enjoyable face would be a fine beginner's lead. Start by scrambling into the gully right of the Phoenix Buttress, then ascend a discontinuous crack system on good rock to an anchor. Rappel using two ropes.

15. DRILL 'EM AND FILL 'EM   5.10a ★★   Bolts
An enjoyable series of edges rises above a large, detached flake on the right side of the buttress. Most climbers bypass the original crux by stepping left at the second bolt. Bring a #3 Friend if you don't like soloing to the first clip.

16. PHOENIX   5.10a ★★★★   Bolts (optional #3 Friend)
Excellent rock and intriguing moves make this steep face a must. For the grade, there's no better route at Smith. The level recently rose a notch when a flake pulled off past the third bolt. Most climbers wisely lower off at the first set of anchors, but you can cheapen the experience by continuing up mediocre cracks to the **Carabid** belay (bring gear).

17. LICENSE TO BOLT   5.11b ★★★   Bolts
This challenging line of pockets and edges rises left of **Phoenix.** The technical crux comes right at the start with a long lockoff, but the moves stay tricky the whole way.

18. FRED ON AIR   5.10d ★★★   Bolts
     Crammed tightly a few feet left of **License to Bolt**, this pocketed face is a worthwhile jaunt. The
     hardest moves finesse past a bulge at the start, but it's easy to cheat left.

19. FLAKE CHIMNEY   5.6 R   Gear to 4 inches
     A massive flake leans against the wall 100 feet left of the Phoenix Area. For reasons unknown,

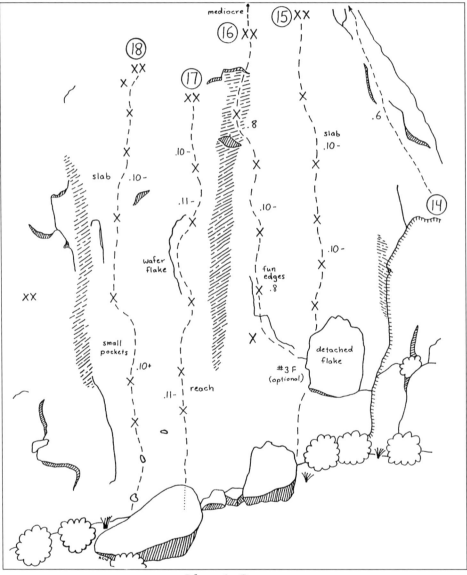

Phoenix Buttress

14. CARABID   5.6 R ★★   17. LICENSE TO BOLT   5.11b ★★★
15. DRILL 'EM AND FILL 'EM   5.10a ★★   18. FRED ON AIR   5.10d ★★★
16. PHOENIX   5.10a ★★★★

someone once climbed a miserable corridor up the right side of this flake, rappeling from a sling wrapped around the top.

20. VULTURE RIDGE   5.6 X   Gear to 3.5 inches
    This offbeat route treads lightly along the crest of the spiked ridge extending east from Smith Summit. Uncommonly dangerous, the arête features terrible rock, bad protection and inadequate belay anchors. Move gingerly up the huge crux flake, or the whole thing might peel away. To get to the base, hike around the corner a quarter of a mile beyond the Phoenix Buttress and scramble up the first gully on the right.

The Grover Wall

South of the Phoenix Buttress, the cliff line degenerates into impressive walls of mud. No route ascends a quarter mile section of cliff here. However, in 1990, Chris Grover slogged up the scree, exploring a steep white face rising above a slab. No routes other than his original bolt line ascend this wall, but the potential exists for several extreme climbs.

SOUTHERN TIP

At the southern end of the Smith Rock Group, the Crooked River turns 180 degrees, heading back along the west side of the formation. The Southern Tip contains a surprisingly solid section of stone. The route selection isn't all that great, but you'll find the area peacefully isolated.

21. YODERIFIC   5.11d ★★   Bolts
    An impressive open book dominates the Southern Tip. A tolerable series of holds leads past several bolts on the right wall of the dihedral. The few climbers that bother encounter a holdless crux getting past the third bolt.

22. KUNZA KORNER   5.10c ★★★★   Gear to 2 inches
    This brilliant dihedral stands in sharp contrast to the rubble found for hundreds of yards to either side. For the grade, it's the best stemming pitch on Smith tuff. The first syllable of Kunza rhymes with June.

23. WAVE OF BLISS   5.11d X ★★★   Gear (#1 through #2.5 Friend, two #3 Friends, #2 to #5 RPs)
    The stunning left arête of **Kunza Korner** would be popular if not for some shaky protection. Far too few bolts, interspersed with laughable natural gear, protect a fine series of moves to the top of the cliff. The climb will likely fall victim to the retro-bolting craze someday, but until then – don't take it lightly.

24. YODER EATERS   5.10d   Bolts
    This bulgy bolt line lurks about 40 feet left of the obvious corner. Since you won't find a single solid hold on the entire route, you'll wonder why anyone bothered with this stinker.

25. PROJECT 5.12 ?

Three bolts litter the crumbly wall left of **Yoder Eaters.** On the aborted preparation, climbers drilled holds into blank stone, then lost interest, leaving a mess behind. All in all, it's among the worst displays of out-of-control ethics at Smith.

26. CRUMBLE PIE 5.9 R ★ Bolts

This uninspiring face looms just around the corner to the left of the preceding routes. A few delicate moves on a low-angled slab lead to anchor bolts.

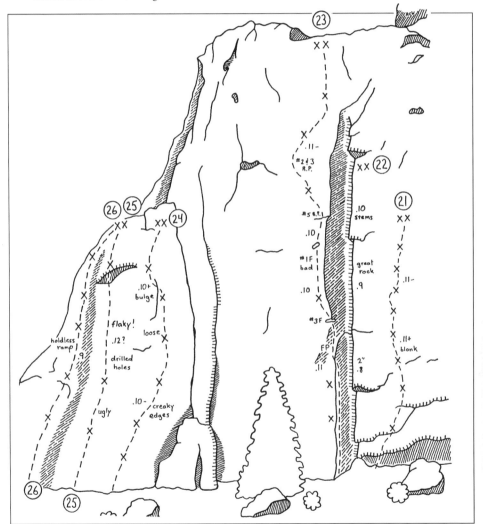

The Southern Tip

21. YODERIFIC 5.11d ★★
22. KUNZA KORNER 5.10c ★★★★
23. WAVE OF BLISS 5.11d X ★★★
24. YODER EATERS 5.10d
25. PROJECT 5.12 ?
26. CRUMBLE PIE 5.9 R ★

WEST SIDE ROUTES

The west side of the Smith Rock Group pales in comparison to the massive walls on the east side. Still, you'll find some worthwhile routes here, and won't need to wait in line for anything. To approach all the west side routes, scramble over Asterisk Pass and follow a trail south along the base of the cliff.

Northwest Wall

Scattered along the northwest face are the test pieces of the Smith Rock Group's west side. Most of the rock is junk, but a few impressive cracks split the upper faces. In the early 80s, as climbers polished off

Photo: Bruce Adams

Smith Rock Group – Northwest Face

2. SKY RIDGE 5.8 R ★★	31. NO BRAIN, NO PAIN 5.10d R ★★
27. SKYLIGHT 5.10c ★★	32. NO PAIN, NO GAIN 5.11c ★★
28. BITS AND PIECES 5.7 X ★	33. ZIGZAG 5.8 ★
28a. BITS OF FECES 5.8 R	34. CULL'S IN SPACE 5.10c ★★★
29. STAGEFRIGHT 5.12a ★★	
30. TEARS OF RAGE 5.12b ★★	

Smith's more accessible cracks, they turned in desperation to the northwest wall. These memorable pitches, reached only after miserable approaches, never caught on and today sit completely forgotten.

27. SKYLIGHT 5.10c ★★ Gear to 2.5 inches
     Hindered only by its remote location, the exposed final pitch of **Skylight** comes highly recommended. Unfortunately, mediocre approach pitches guard the route, keeping everyone away. Start right of parallel, right-leaning cracks behind a juniper tree.
     1. 5.6 Scamper up a lichen-covered face, then step left to a belay spot.
     2. 5.7 Continue up a steepening crack, circling right to a belay atop a huge, detached block.
     3. 5.10c Move down and left to the obvious overhanging corner. Locking hand jams lead to an awkward crux exiting right.

28. BITS AND PIECES 5.7 X ★ Gear to 2.5 inches
     The enjoyable start to this lackluster route would make a fine beginning lead if it weren't so sparsely bolted. The meandering upper pitch protects poorly. Begin below a distinctive, water-stained groove.
     1. 5.5 Romp up some easy knobs past a couple of bolts to a slot. Exit right, and face climb to an anchor.
     2. 5.7 Step right, jamming a dirty crack, then wander left (with no protection) to the finishing crack.

28a. BITS OF FECES 5.8 R Gear to 2.5 inches
     This short stretch adds an unappealing third pitch to **Bits and Pieces**. Step right high on the second pitch to a belay at the base of an obscure slab crack. Ascend poor rock to the top in one bowel-tightening pitch.

29. STAGEFRIGHT 5.12a ★★ Gear to 1 inch
     If the rock were better, this wildly overhanging thin crack would be a Smith classic. Even so, the outstanding position makes it a memorable experience. The crux comes on the final moves with a lunge past a bolt. The quickest approach ascends **Bits and Pieces**, stepping left just below the top to a belay on a massive block. Perhaps the best access climbs **Sky Ridge**, **Sky Chimney** or **White Satin**, then steps down easy rock on the west side.

30. TEARS OF RAGE 5.12b ★★ Gear (Bring four #1s, two #1.5s, and a #2 Friend)
     This impressive, arching line is one of Smith's better finger cracks. The crux battles a series of locking jams on an overhanging wall, but the disgusting approach keeps everyone away. Only a few thin-crack connoisseurs have weathered the start to sample the charms of the third pitch.
     1. 5.6 Climb the first pitch of **Bits and Pieces**.
     2. 5.7 Start up the second pitch of **Bits and Pieces**, but step right after 60 feet. Keep traversing around a corner to an anchor beneath the arching crack.
     3. 5.12b Race up the crack, trying desperately to exit left before pumping out. Delicate 5.10 knobs lead past two bolts to an anchor.
     4. 5.7 Climb the unprotected slab to a bolt, then pull over a steep bulge to the top.
     5. 4th Walk right around an exposed gendarme to easy ground.

31. NO BRAIN, NO PAIN 5.10d R ★★ Gear to 3 inches
     As the first of the west-side cracks to be developed, this striking line enjoyed a brief flurry of popularity before it drifted into obscurity. If you don't mind a nasty approach, the overhanging hand crack above is spectacular. If you have a brain, you'll tape for this skin-shredder. Start on the right side of a huge boulder at the base of the wall.
     1. 5.4 Scramble right up an easy ramp to a ledge.
     2. 5.7 A devious, poorly-protected traverse on bad rock leads left to the base of the hand crack.
     3. 5.10d Jam the crack in one strenuous pitch to a bolt belay. Either rappel using two ropes, or continue to the top via **No Pain, No Gain.**

32. NO PAIN, NO GAIN 5.11c ★★ Gear to 2.5 inches
   Strenuous, painful and radically overhanging, this thin crack might be popular if it weren't such a
   chore to get here. The best access climbs **No Brain, No Pain**, but it's quicker to follow the first
   two pitches of **Tears of Rage**.
   1, 2 & 3. Climb **No Brain, No Pain** to a large ledge below the overhanging wall.
   4. 5.11c Jam the steep hand/finger crack past three bolts to an anchor on a low-angled slab.
   5 & 6 5.7 Finish with the final two pitches of **Tears of Rage**.

33. ZIGZAG 5.8 ★ Gear to 3.5 inches
   As you hike south from Asterisk Pass, the cliff line recedes just beyond a section of appealing
   rock. As you start uphill, a crack system splits the wall above a cluster of juniper trees. This
   abandoned route climbs to a belay horn, then backs off. The zigzagging crack above awaits a first
   ascent, but loose flakes guard the upper stretches.

Several small crags clutter the hillside beyond the northwest wall. The following left-leaning crack
comes into view far uphill just as the main cliff recedes:

34. CULL'S IN SPACE 5.10c ★★★ Gear to 2.5 inches
   Once popular, this traversing crack sits neglected today. The gymnastic moves are fun, and the
   climb deserves more attention than it receives.

Flounder Block

Leaving the northwest wall behind, the trail passes below this diminutive crag, with its obvious corner.

35. FLOUNDER CORNER 5.2 ★ Gear to 2.5 inches
   This simple scramble up a forgettable inside corner isn't worth the walk. To descend, hike uphill.

36. HOOK, LINE AND SINKER 5.7 ★ Gear to 2 inches
   A crack splits the left wall of **Flounder Corner**. A quick flurry of contrived jams ends on top.

Cod Rock

After passing beneath Flounder Block, a bigger crag comes into view to the south. Two routes – one
junk pile and one classic – adorn the river face of this crag.

37. SUNSET BOULEVARD 5.8 ★ Gear to 2.5 inches
   This prominent crack splits the center of Cod Rock. The bad rock and unaesthetic climbing
   keeps everyone away.

38. SUNSET SLAB 5.9 ★★★★ Bolts
   A thoroughly-scrubbed, bolted face rises on the right side of Cod Rock. Well-worth the hike, this
   charming line makes a fine way to escape the crowds.

SMITH ROCK GROUP SUMMIT PINNACLES

Capping the northern end of the Smith Rock Group are the twin spires of Smith Summit, the
Arrowpoint and the Platform. When viewed from the east, these summits are spectacular spires, but
from the west they appear little more than insignificant hummocks. Still, you might enjoy hiking here
on a crowded day to sample the alpine setting. The approach hikes over Asterisk Pass and heads south
along a rough trail leading up the hillside between Flounder Block and Cod Rock. At the plateau atop
the hill, you'll see Smith Summit straight ahead. The Arrowpoint sits to the left, hiding the Platform
from view.

39. SMITH SUMMIT – WEST

The twin towers of Smith Summit continue to elude climbers hoping to stand on the highest point of the Smith Rock Group. The only line to the top of the east summit follows the deadly east wall, and no real route exists to the top of the west tower. The humorous first ascent of the west spire involved little climbing skill. Using a bow and arrow, a determined group of climbers shot a thin wire over the top, and managed to pull over a rope. They tied off one end, and captured their prize by prussiking up the other. A reasonable free line exists on the west face, but some atrocious rock discourages anyone from trying.

Arrowpoint & The Platform

From the east, this small spire hides behind the Platform, but viewed from the west, it dominates the skyline. Of the three summits, the Arrowpoint holds the greatest interest to the climber, since the rock is solid. To approach, hike north along a narrow ridge of rock from the Smith Rock Group summit plateau.

40. NORTHWEST CORNER   5.2 ★★   Gear to 3 inches

The easiest line to the top romps up a solid crack system on the northwest side. You'll find two rusted bolts on top, but most climbers scramble down the way they came, rather than trusting this ancient anchor.

41. SHAFT   5.10b ★★   Gear to 1.5 inches

You'll feel shafted if you hike all the way up here just to do this route, but it makes a pleasant detour after topping out on nearby climbs. Start below the north face and jam an extremely short, high-quality finger crack.

42. SOUTH FACE   5.0 A1 ★★   Gear to 1 inch

Rising above a slab, this left-leaning seam splits the puny south side of Arrowpoint. The climb would easily go free, and might be fairly good.

43. THE PLATFORM   5.1 R ★   Gear to 2.5 inches

Viewed from the Dihedrals, the Platform towers impressively above the cliff line. The disappointing backside offers a simple, unexposed scramble up blocky rock. To approach the route, hike around the northwest side of the Arrowpoint, and drop down to the base of the Platform's southwest face.

Alan Watts on the first ascent of Split Image (5.12c/d).

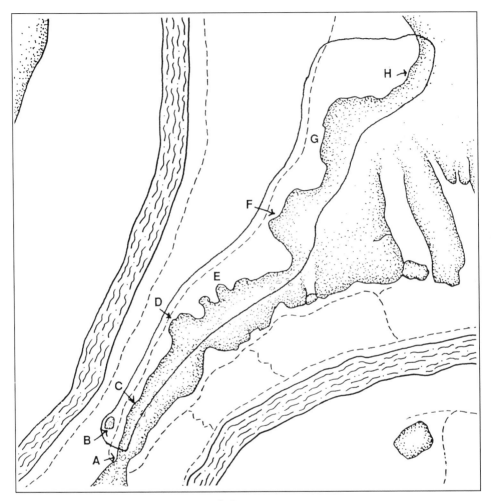

A. Asterisk Pass
B. The Awl
C. Christian Brothers – West Side
D. Snake Rock
E. Fallen Angel Buttress
F. Spiderman Buttress
G. Mesa Verde Wall
H. Pleasure Palace

WEST SIDE CRAGS

SMITH ROCK'S WEST SIDE CRAGS offer an unsung collection of mostly moderate routes. Stepping over Asterisk Pass to the west side is like moving back ten years in Smith history. Since a longer approach guards these cliffs, they haven't seen near the growth of the more accessible areas. Only a few walls contain bolted lines, and large expanses of stone are almost completely untouched. Yet the seclusion isn't the only reason why the development lags behind here. With a few notable exceptions, these crags lack the stunning lines found on the east side. Most of the options are lichen-covered slabs or vertical faces, with few overhanging walls. Still, despite the lack of eye-catching routes, the potential for new lines is almost limitless. During the nineties, climbers will inevitably brave the extra few minutes of walking, and expand the appeal of these varied cliffs.

The West Side Crags contain many different rocks spread over a half-mile distance. Just over Asterisk Pass rises the leaning spike of the Awl, with the west side of the Christian Brothers towering above. Further north along the trail sits the high-quality Snake Rock, the Angel Flight Crags and the first-rate routes of the Spiderman Buttress. After the dominating, 350-foot Mesa Verde Wall, the cliff line eventually recedes into the short climbs of the Pleasure Palace. Just to the north rises the amazing spire of Monkey Face, detailed in the next chapter.

Although the west side surely will grow more popular, much of the appeal lies in its remoteness. When weekend climbers pack the Dihedrals, most west-side routes are vacant. The entire area also is an excellent morning destination during warm spells. Most climbs stay in the shade past noon, and even on 100-degree days, you'll find early temperatures agreeable. By the same token, the routes freeze in winter's chilling breezes, as they get only late-day sun.

THE AWL
This leaning spike, with its obvious short dihedral, rises just beyond Asterisk Pass.

1. INSIDE CORNER   5.10c ★★   Gear to .75 inch
   Even today, most climbers find the moves up the starting corner desperate. Above a belay ledge, easy but unprotected face moves lead to the captivating summit. Descend by rappeling off the overhanging uphill side.

2. PROJECT   5.13 ?
   Several bolts litter the steep, uphill face of the Awl. Years ago, someone aided the left side of this face (called **Merkin's Jerkin**), using a few pins at the start and many quarter-inch bolts. This line and others will likely go free someday. The best route will power up horrible pockets on the obvious rounded arête.

THE MONK
THE FRIAR
THE PRIEST

5
3
19
1
11
8
12
10 9 7 6
13
18 17
SNAKE ROCK
CHRISTIAN BROTHERS
WEST SIDE
THE AW

Photo: Bruce Adams

Christian Brothers – West Side and Snake Rock

1. INSIDE CORNER 5.10c ★★
3. CHRISTIAN BROTHERS TRAVERSE
   5.7 X ★
5. ROOTS OF MADNESS 5.11a R ★
6. HOT MONKEY LOVE 5.11a ★★
7. FALLEN ANGEL 5.10c R ★★
8. MODERN ZOMBIE 5.10d ★★★
9. MIDRIFF BULGE 5.10a ★★

10. MANIC NIRVANA 5.10c ★
11. MONK CHIMNEY 5.7
12. THE SNAKE 5.9 R ★★
13. THE GOLDEN ROAD 5.11b ★★
17. A DESPERATE MAN 5.9 ★★
18. HEMP LIBERATION 5.10d ★★
19. LORDS OF KARMA 5.12c ★★★

CHRISTIAN BROTHERS - WEST SIDE

The mediocre rock and lichen-grown walls of the Christian Brothers west face stand in sharp contrast to the striking lines of the opposite side. The only worthwhile routes ascend short crags scattered along the base of the wall. The far right side of the cliff provides a starting point for the following multi-pitch odyssey:

3. CHRISTIAN BROTHERS TRAVERSE   5.7 X ★   Gear to 3 inches
If you're looking for a day of adventure far above the crowds, consider this extravaganza. A peak-baggers dream, the traverse crosses the summits of all five Christian Brothers: the Priest, the Monk, the Pope, the Friar and the Abbot. The rock and protection are horrible in places, forcing sensible beginners to cross this venture off their list. Still, fine position and unique character make the Christian Brothers Traverse worth doing once in every Smith climber's lifetime. Start by scrambling to the highest ledge directly above the Awl.
1.   5.5   Easy rock leads to diverging cracks. It's best to ascend the wide crack on the left, though some climbers grovel up bad rock (5.6) on the right instead. Belay at bolts on the Priest's south buttress.
2.   5.4   Romp up simple potholes, then leap across a frightening gap to a low-angled slab. Climb big holds to a belay on the crest of the ridge.
3.   5.7   After traversing left, a miserably rotten crack regains the ridge. A face move protected by a bolt ends on the summit of the Priest. Rappel north into a notch.
4.   5.6   A scary traverse right leads to a squeeze chimney between the Monk's twin summits. Writhe up the slot to top, and rappel into another low notch to the north. If you'd like to bypass the top of the Monk, you can continue the scary traverse to the Monk/Pope notch.
5.   5.4   Chimney, then climb dirty rock to the top of the Pope. Rappel into the slot at the base of the Friar. The original route bypassed the summit of the Pope via an unprotected face traverse left.
6.   5.6   Stroll up rotten rock past several ancient bolts to the top of the Friar. Abseil north into the Hobbit Hole – a large amphitheater between the Friar and Abbot. Boulder out of the gully to a sloping ledge below the east face of the Abbot.
7.   5.6 A2   Follow a ridiculous line of shaky bolts (several are missing) over a bulge to the teetering summit of the Abbot. Most bypass this spire and make a fourth-class scramble north to the **Cinnamon Slab** rappel.
No one has managed (or perhaps even tried) to reverse the Christian Brothers Traverse (going north to south). Getting to the summit of the Priest would be the only major resistance. The following two routes will get you started by climbing the eastern face of the Friar. Approach from the top of **Cinnamon Slab** via a fourth-class scramble.

4. ABBOT GULLY   5.5 A2 X   Gear to 2 inches
    The first ascent of the Friar followed this harrowing line up the east wall. Hike to the Hobbit
    Hole between the Abbot and Friar, then climb a crack to the notch separating the two pinnacles.
    Traverse far left on easy ledges to a belay in a shallow hole. A short line of terrifying bolts over a
    bulge leads to easy face climbing and the top.

4a. NORTHEAST ARETE   5.6 X   Gear to 2 inches
    A free alternative ascends directly up the grotesque northeast ridge. Start by climbing to the notch
    between the Friar and Abbot, then continue, with very poor protection, to the top.

The following routes ascend directly above the trail skirting the west face of the Christian Brothers:

5. ROOTS OF MADNESS   5.11a R ★   Gear to 2.5 inches
    An accident just waiting to happen, this ignored line involves poorly-protected moves on flaky
    rock, ending at a woefully inadequate anchor. On the second ascent, after narrowly averting a
    ground fall at the crux, the anchor pins pulled out in the hands of the horrified climber. Start by
    scrambling up blocks above the Awl to the base of a distinctive, right-arching crack system.

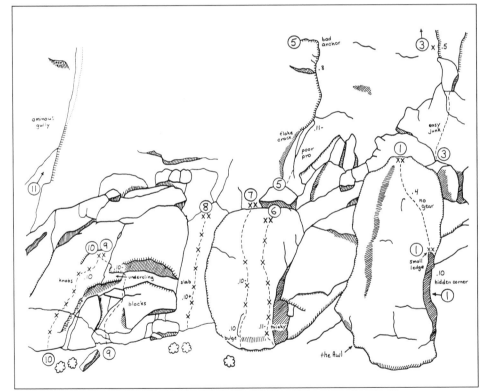

Christian Brothers – West Side Base Routes

1. INSIDE CORNER   5.10c ★★
3. CHRISTIAN BROTHERS TRAVERSE
    5.7 X ★
5. ROOTS OF MADNESS   5.11a R ★
6. HOT MONKEY LOVE   5.11a ★★

7. FALLEN ANGEL   5.10c R ★★
8. MODERN ZOMBIE   5.10d ★★★
9. MIDRIFF BULGE   5.10a ★★
10. MANIC NIRVANA   5.10c ★
11. MONK CHIMNEY   5.7

6. HOT MONKEY LOVE 5.11a ★★ Bolts
Just beyond the Awl sits the appealing Fallen Angel Buttress. After a deceptively tricky crux at the start, the right arête succombs to a series of well-protected knobs.

7. FALLEN ANGEL 5.10c R ★★ Bolts
Rising above a distinctive starting bulge, this sparsely-bolted face sees few ascents. An energetic crux getting to the first clip stops many climbers in their tracks.

8. MODERN ZOMBIE 5.10d ★★★ Bolts
A swath of well-scrubbed holds leads up a narrow, low-angled face just beyond the Fallen Angel Buttress. A pleasant series of miniature knobs finesse past many bolts to an anchor.

9. MIDRIFF BULGE 5.10a ★★ Gear to 1.5 inches
An unmistakable roof system, split by a crack, rises above the trail. Some taxing underclings lead to an awkward sequence around the lip.

10. MANIC NIRVANA 5.10c ★ Bolts
This odd route traverses above the lip of the **Midriff Bulge** roof. Although protected by closely-spaced bolts, the moves are unnerving because the roof drops away below your feet.

11. MONK CHIMNEY 5.7 Gear to 4 inches
This ugly corridor splits the entire northwest face of the Christian Brothers. Start at the high point of the hillside and follow double cracks, confronting rotten rock, to the notch between the Monk and Friar.

SNAKE ROCK

Beyond the Christian Brothers, a large buttress split by an obvious crack comes into view. The cliff's name comes from a snake-head boulder guarding the base of the wall. Snake Rock contains a small yet appealing selection of modern sport routes, and will likely see further development in the future. A fixed rappel station atop the north side offers a quick descent.

12. THE SNAKE 5.9 R ★★ Gear to 5 inches
This varied route climbs the prominent crack system splitting the south side of the buttress. A short dihedral at the start of the second pitch contains the hardest moves, but a runout lieback below scares most people away.
1. 5.7 An easy crack leads to a strenuous lieback ending at an anchor.
2. 5.9 Stem the steep dihedral, then slither up a dirty, flaring chimney to the top.

12a. VENOM 5.10b ★★ Gear to 2.5 inches
Parallel steep cracks rise several feet right of the regular start. A series of thin hand jams gives way to a moderate flake system.

12b. REPTILE 5.8 R ★ Gear to 2 inches
A crack in a shallow dihedral rises just around the corner left of **The Snake**. After jamming the mediocre corner, climb unprotected knobs to the first-pitch anchor.

13. THE GOLDEN ROAD 5.11b ★★ Bolts
This attractive, golden face grew more difficult each year after the first ascent as small edges crumbled. Today, the few remaining holds are solid.

14. SPLIT IMAGE 5.12c/d ★★★★ Bolts
Easily one of Smith's most classic arêtes, this stunning line once was the hardest route in the park. Originally climbed largely on the right side of the edge, repeat ascents discovered better holds on the left wall. Everyone uses this new sequence now, but it makes clipping the second bolt desperate. The baffling crux now comes at the first bolt, because a gouged pocket has decreased the potency of the final moves.

15. MADE IN THE SHADE 5.12c ★★★ Bolts
This tip-splitting face ascends the left wall of **Split Image.** First, crank a tweaky boulder problem off the ground; the holds become huge above the first bolt.

16. CLING ON 5.9 ★★★ Gear to 4 inches
An impressive dihedral capped by a huge roof dominates the center of Snake Rock. The

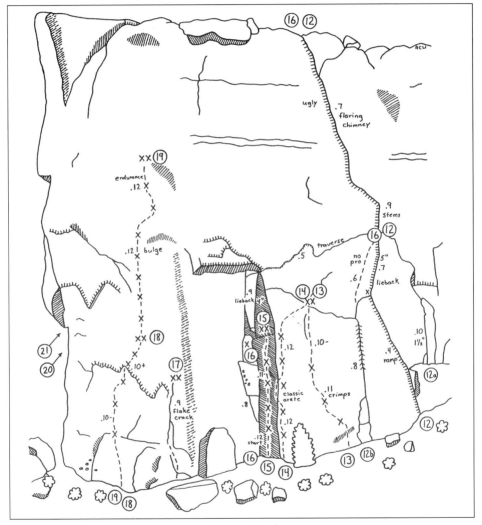

Snake Rock

12. THE SNAKE 5.9 R ★★
12a. VENOM 5.10b ★★
12b. REPTILE 5.8 R ★
13. THE GOLDEN ROAD 5.11b ★★
14. SPLIT IMAGE 5.12c/d ★★★★
15. MADE IN THE SHADE 5.12c ★★★

16. CLING ON 5.9 ★★★
17. A DESPERATE MAN 5.9 ★★
18. HEMP LIBERATION 5.10d ★★
19. LORDS OF KARMA 5.12c ★★★
20. STRUNG OUT 5.9 ★
21. STRUCK OUT 5.6 X

strenuous lieback off the deck is a popular jaunt on perfect rock, but almost no one tangles with the wide crack of the second pitch.

1.   5.8   Jam, stem, and lieback the flake crack to a ledge.

2.   5.9   Either jam the overhanging crack above, or execute a committing lieback to a ledge. Traverse right to the first belay on **The Snake.** Rappel, or . . .

3.   5.9   Follow the upper pitch of **The Snake** to the top.

17.   A DESPERATE MAN   5.9 ★★   Gear to 1 inch
A large boulder leans against the clean left wall of the Cling On dihedral. Just left of this block looms a series of discontinuous cracks. A brief flurry of liebacks and jams on solid rock ends at an anchor, not far off the ground.

18.   HEMP LIBERATION   5.10d ★★   Bolts
This well-protected line pulls over the roof system on the left portion of Snake Rock. Although intimidating in places, you'll always find good holds where you need them most.

19.   LORDS OF KARMA   5.12c ★★★   Bolts
A challenging finish to **Hemp Liberation** attacks the sweeping wall above the anchor. You can climb the entire route in one pitch by using a long sling on the bolt under the lower roof, and unclipping the first bolt past the lip.

20.   STRUNG OUT   5.9 ★   Gear to 4 inches
The quality of Snake Rock deteriorates quickly as you walk uphill along the base of the bulging north face. The only route of any consequence ascends an ominous flare splitting the wall. Among the most physical climbs of the grade at Smith, this wildly-overhanging bombay chimney asks more of you than the typical 5.9.

21.   STRUCK OUT   5.6 X   Gear to 2.5 inches
A low-angled, flaring crack without a start rises uphill from **Strung Out.** Begin uphill on lichen-covered face holds, then grovel up the dirty crack to an anchor. You'd be better off if you never even came to bat for this one.

ANGEL FLIGHT CRAGS

North of Snake Rock, the cliff line gives way to several small, gully-split crags. There aren't many routes here, since lichen grows thick on any face that doesn't overhang. Still, with wire brush in hand, you might uncover some good routes.

22.   PROJECT   5.13 ?
Leaving Snake Rock, you'll first come to a large pillar with a steep river face. A stunning arête on the downhill side of the block sports a few bolts and awaits a free ascent.

23.   HEAVEN CAN WAIT   5.7 R ★   Gear to 1.5 inches
Most climbers wisely ignore this lackluster route. Hidden from view until you're standing at the base, the climb starts atop the second gully left of Snake Rock.

1.   5.7   Traverse left along a ledge, then jam an inside corner.

2.   5.7   Move left 20 feet on unprotected face holds, then climb past a bolt to the top.

24.   ANGEL FLIGHT BUTTRESS   5.8 R ★★   Gear to 1 inch
The second crag beyond Snake Rock is this low-angled, lichen-covered slab. An enjoyable, though rarely climbed line moves directly up the face past a few widely-spaced bolts. Start uphill and left of the lowest point on the buttress.

1.   5.8   A tricky start leads to easier knobs and a simple crack. Continue up the slab to a bolt belay.

2.   5.7   A crumbly face move past a single bolt ends on top.

25. FOLLIES OF YOUTH (a.k.a. HIGH SAGE) 5.9 R ★ Gear to 3 inches
    A squarish, lichen-plastered block with a single route up the center rises a few feet left of **Angel Flight Buttress.** A bolt protects the crux, but the runout finish discourages most attempts. Descend by scrambling left.

Spiderman Buttress and Angel Flight Cracks

22. PROJECT 5.13 ?
23. HEAVEN CAN WAIT 5.7 R ★
24. ANGEL FLIGHT BUTTRESS 5.8 R ★★
25. FOLLIES OF YOUTH (a.k.a. HIGH SAGE) 5.9 R ★

28. TARANTULA 5.11d ★
29. SPIDERMAN 5.7 ★★★★
34. IN HARM'S WAY 5.7 ★★★
36. CORNERSTONE 5.11d ★★

SPIDERMAN BUTTRESS

After skirting the base of Snake Rock, the trail heads uphill past Angel Flight Crags to the rotund Spiderman Buttress. Several moderate routes adorn this solid face, making it the most popular west-side destination. To descend, drop into a gully on the right to a short 4th class scramble.

26. COMMON HOUSEHOLD FLY 5.5 ★ Gear to 3 inches
Parallel, low-angled junk cracks are at the far right side of the Spiderman Buttress. The boring right line falls after a short stint of jams.

A triangular roof rises above a massive, square block pasted against the base of the right side of the buttress. The following two routes undercling around opposite sides of this roof:

27. ARACHNID BOOGIE 5.9 ★ Gear to 3 inches
Cutting right around the big roof provides a few entertaining moments, but the finish deteriorates into a battle with bad rock and rope drag.
1. 5.6 Climb the clean chimney up the right side of the square block to a large ledge.
2. 5.9 Jam a short crack to the base of the roof, then undercling right around a corner. Follow a rotten crack right 40 feet to the top.

28. TARANTULA 5.11d ★ Gear to 2.5 inches
Perhaps Smith's most awkward route, this intimidating crack was once among the hardest climbs in the park. Despite good rock and an exhilarating finish, the contorted crux at the lip stays in your mind long after the good memories fade.
1. 5.7 Squirm up the chimney to a ledge.
2. 5.11d Stem to the roof, then undercling left to a bolt. Thrash into a slot, then lieback past another bolt to the top.

29. SPIDERMAN 5.7 ★★★★ Gear to 3 inches
An attractive, low-angled buttress split by cracks on either side leans against the lowest part of the cliff. Spiderman jams the right side of the buttress and the stunning crack above in two fun-filled pitches. This Smith classic blends great rock, intimidating moves and good protection into a breathtaking line.
1. 5.7 Cruise a low-angled hand crack, then follow the dogleg crack above past a strenuous bulge to belay bolts on a slab.
2. 5.7 Step slightly right and climb the exposed crack to a roof. Execute a wild lieback and scramble up loose rock to the top.

29a. SQUASHED SPIDER 5.7 X ★★ Gear to 3 inches
As a variant to the regular start, you can climb unprotected knobs directly up the face of the lower buttress.

29b. SPIDERMAN VARIATION 5.7 ★★★ Gear to 3 inches
An easier, but less-exciting version of **Spiderman** escapes the second-pitch roof via a moderate crack system to the left. Since the moves aren't nearly as intimidating as the regular route, many unnerved climbers take this option.
1. 5.7 Hike up the left side of the low-angled buttress, and join the regular route to the anchor.
2. 5.6 Ascend the ramp around a corner to the left, then frolic up the crack system to anchor bolts on top.

30. WIDOW MAKER 5.9 R ★★★ Gear to 2 inches
This invigorating lieback flake is exciting and strenuous for the grade. It protects reasonably well, though you might have trouble hanging out long enough to place satisfying gear.
1. 5.9 Begin up the lefthand start to **Spiderman**, then step left into the crack. Jam and lieback past two small roofs to a ledge.
2. 5.5 Waltz up easy cracks to the top.

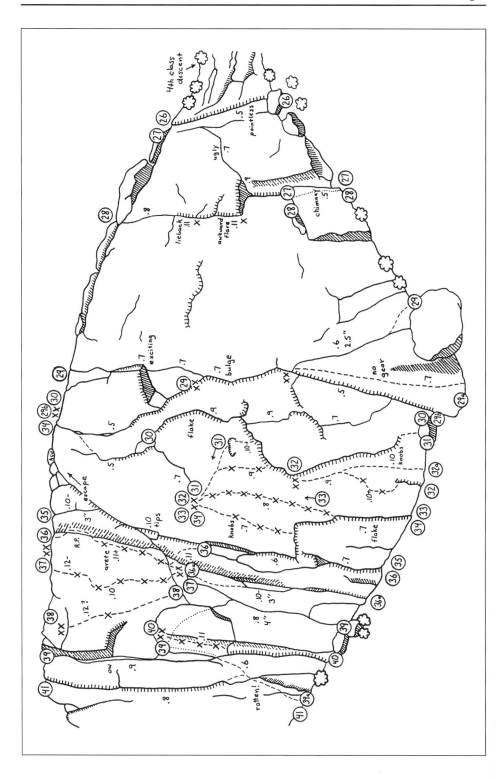

Spiderman Buttress

26. COMMON HOUSEHOLD FLY 5.5 ★
27. ARACHNID BOOGIE 5.9 ★
28. TARANTULA 5.11d ★
29. SPIDERMAN 5.7 ★★★★
29a. SQUASHED SPIDER 5.7 X ★★
29b. SPIDERMAN VARIATION 5.7 ★★★
30. WIDOW MAKER 5.9 R ★★★
31. BEST LEFT TO OBSCURITY 5.10a R
32. EXPLOSIVE ENERGY CHILD 5.10d R ★★★
32a. MORE OR LESTER 5.10c ★★ TR
33. OUT OF HARM'S WAY 5.8 ★★★

34. IN HARM'S WAY 5.7 ★★★
35. LITTLE FEAT 5.10b ★★
36. CORNERSTONE 5.11d ★★
36a. CORNERSTONE VARIATION 5.10a ★★
37. DEATH TAKES A HOLIDAY 5.12a ★★★
38. PROJECT 5.11/12 ?
39. DOCTOR DOOM 5.9 R ★★
39a. DOCTOR DOOM VARIATION 5.6
40. WHAT'S UP DOC? 5.11 ? ★★
41. NECROMANCER 5.8 ★

31. BEST LEFT TO OBSCURITY 5.10a R Gear to 1.5 inches
If you decide to try this route, you've made a poor choice. Start with a tricky move above a small pillar, then follow an arching flake crack past an anchor to a dangerous exit on teetering blocks. Fight rope drag on the long traverse left to rappel bolts.

32. EXPLOSIVE ENERGY CHILD 5.10d R ★★★ Gear to 1 inches
This technical thin face thrills those who love Smith nubbins, and torments those who don't. Bolts protect the crux moves, but a runout finish on easier knobs might wrinkle your brow. Most climbers ignore the second pitch.
1. 5.10d Delicate face climbing past two bolts leads to a thin crack and a hanging belay.
2. 5.9 Move up an arching crack, then make a tricky move to a bolt. After another bolt, traverse left to an anchor. Rappel.

32a. MORE OR LESTER 5.10c ★★ TR
From the anchors atop the first pitch of **Explosive Energy Child,** you can toprope a series of knobs just right of the regular line.

33. OUT OF HARM'S WAY 5.8 ★★★ Gear to 1.5 inches
Hopefully, the closely-spaced bolts on this enjoyable knobby face will keep you free from harm. Start in a shallow, right-facing dihedral just left of **Explosive Energy Child,** then step right onto the face. Stroll up knobs, and traverse left to an anchor.

34. IN HARM'S WAY 5.7 ★★★ Gear to 2 inches
The first pitch of this admirable route is highly-recommended. Wisely, most rappel off at the first anchors instead of finishing the lackluster upper pitch. Start at the same right-facing corner as **Out of Harm's Way.**
1. 5.7 Jam the miniature dihedral to a large ledge, then wander on big knobs past three bolts to an anchor. Rappel or . . .
2. 5.7 Move right and make one awkward move to easy cracks.

35. LITTLE FEAT 5.10b ★★ Gear to 2.5 inches
An obvious, right-facing corner splits the left side of the **Spiderman Buttress.** The neglected crux tackles a stimulating series of finger jams past a solid bulge. Unfortunately, some mediocre rock lower down detracts from the experience. To finish, step left and jam an exciting hand crack, or weasel off to the right.

36. CORNERSTONE 5.11d ★★ Gear to 1.5 inches
A finishing sequence up a tricky, bolted arête highlights this ignored route. Some climbers split the upper pitch in two with a belay at a set of chains.
1. 5.7 Climb the **Little Feat** dihedral to a belay atop a pedestal.
2. 5.11d Make a few hard moves (5.11c) protected by wires to a large ledge. Rest, then finesse past four bolts on the crux arête, protecting the final moves with RPs.

36a. CORNERSTONE VARIATION 5.10a ★★ Gear to 3 inches
The original line bypassed the hard moves off the pedestal by climbing a sweeping hand crack to the left.

37. DEATH TAKES A HOLIDAY 5.12a ★★★ Bolts
This enjoyable route rises just left of the final section of Cornerstone. Moderate, well-protected moves lead to a strenuous crux just below the top. The best approach rappels from above, although it's possible to use the **Cornerstone Variation.**

38. PROJECT 5.11/12 ?
The wall left of **Death Takes a Holiday** will soon yield another steep route.

39. DOCTOR DOOM   5.9 R ★★   Gear to 6 inches
This unmistakable wide crack splits the far left side of the Spiderman Buttress. The upper pitch might be Smith's finest off-width, though that's not saying much. Start on the right side of a large pillar.
1. 5.8   Climb a short, solid fist crack leading into a chimney.
2. 5.9   Step left and thrash up the off-width on high-quality rock.

39a. DOCTOR DOOM VARIATION   5.6   Gear to 3 inches
An alternate start scrambles up easy trash on the left side of the block.

40. WHAT'S UP DOC?   5.11 ? ★★   Gear to 3 inches
An sharp arête rises just below the ominous off-width of **Dr. Doom**. A fine series of bolt-protected moves ends at an anchor atop a flat pillar. The start ascends an uninspiring crack to the left, though someone will surely add a direct line.

41. NECROMANCER   5.8 ★   Gear to 3 inches
Despite a clean finish, this corner left of **Dr. Doom** isn't likely to raise the spirits of anyone, as the opening sequence plows through garbage.

MESA VERDE WALL
Easily the most impressive of the West Side Crags is the majestic Mesa Verde Wall. With its collection of modern and traditional lines, this monolith makes a good choice on a summer morning, as many routes stay shaded well past noon. Inexplicably, this cliff was the scene of the worst accidents in Smith history. In 1987, three climbers died in two tragic accidents just weeks apart. The reactionary editor of a Bend newspaper called for a ban on Smith climbing, and reporters dubbed Mesa Verde Wall "death hill." Fortunately, the furor died down since climbers didn't continue to fall to their deaths with the regularity that the editor of *The Bulletin* predicted. Apart from **Western Chimney** and **Palo Verde** none of the routes ascend to the top of the wall. All climbs on the northwest side end at a massive ledge system stretching across the upper portion of the face. To descend from these routes, scramble left around a corner across a low-angled slab to a single bolt (exposed third class). Downclimb the fifth-class chimney below, and hike down easy ledges.

42. CAPTAIN FINGERS   5.10a R ★   Gear to 2 inches
A small wall rises above the high point of the hillside midway between Mesa Verde Wall and Spiderman Buttress. **Captain Fingers** jams an obscure thin crack splitting this face. An ugly finish on creaky face holds detracts from an otherwise worthwhile route.
1. 5.5   Scramble up a left-facing corner to a ledge.
2. 5.10a   Glide up the painful thin crack to the top of a small pillar and make a dangerous face move to top.

43. WESTERN CHIMNEY   5.5 R ★★★   Gear to 3 inches
A gigantic flake system leans against the right side of Mesa Verde Wall. Two clean, runout pitches chimney behind the left side of this flake. Good rock and enjoyable climbing make it unlike the typical Smith rubble-chimney.

44. CHUCK'S SMELLY CRACK   5.10b R ★   Gear to 1.5 inches
A small, left-facing corner that disappears after 50 feet rises immediately left of the **Western Chimney**. After a tricky start with freaky protection, jam to an anchor.

45. PALO VERDE   5.6 A3 ★★   Aid rack to 1.5 inches
If you want to climb the impressive main face of Mesa Verde Wall, this nail-up is your only option. Except for the final section, the climb features better-than-average rock for a Smith aid route. Someone added several bolts and a hanging belay midway up the third pitch, eliminating the original A4 crux.

1. 4th   Scramble to the base of the crack in the center of the wall.
2. 5.6 A3   After a few free moves, resort to aid in a shallow dihedral. Nail over a roof to a hanging belay.
3. A2   Keep on nailing past some crumbly rock to the top.

46.   PETROGLYPH CRACK   5.7 ★   Gear to 3 inches
      Two flake systems leading to a long ledge are below the largest portion of Mesa Verde Wall. The right route climbs short triple cracks past some loose blocks. There really aren't any petroglyphs here, so don't bother looking.

47.   COWS IN AGONY   5.11a/b ★★   Bolts
      Although somewhat contrived, this route offers some enjoyable moves on good rock. The difficulty varies depending on how close you stay to **Cliff Dwelling Crack** on the left; the further right, the harder the route.

Photo: Bruce Adams

Mesa Verde Wall and The Pleasure Palace

42.   CAPTAIN FINGERS   5.10a R ★
43.   WESTERN CHIMNEY   5.5 R ★★★
44.   CHUCK'S SMELLY CRACK   5.10b R ★
45.   PALO VERDE   5.6 A3 ★★
47.   COWS IN AGONY   5.11a/b ★★
51.   DESOLATION ROW   5.11a ★★
57.   MINAS MORGUL   5.11d ★★

60.   SCREAMING YELLOW ZONKERS
      5.10b ★★★★
62.   TREZLAR   5.10a ★★★★
65.   RED SCARE   5.10b ★★
68.   BOP TILL YOU DROP   5.11a ★★★
70.   AGGRO BUMBLY   5.10d ★★★

48. CLIFF DWELLING CRACK 5.8 ★★ R Gear to 4 inches
An obvious flake crack rises just left of **Cows in Agony**. Difficult protection detracts from an otherwise fine series of lieback moves up this wide crack.

49. JUNIPER FACE 5.11d ★★ Bolts
Hidden from view by a juniper tree, this tricky line climbs a series of pockets on a smooth face just right of a large, inside corner.

50. CHIMNEY DE CHELLY 5.10a R ★★ Gear to 2.5 inches
This multi-pitch route ascends the unmistakable dihedral system bordering the left side of the main face. Unfortunately, a lousy second pitch takes away from an otherwise good climb. The first two pitches are runout enough to get you into trouble, but the crux moves protect well.
1. 5.10a A tough, thin section past a bolt leads to easier but runout climbing through potholes. Make a hard face move right to an anchor.
2. 5.9 Clip a bolt, then make unprotected face moves up and left to a belay below a large dihedral.
3. 5.8 Stem the corner and solid chimney above to a huge ledge. Descend the north side ledges.

51. DESOLATION ROW 5.11a ★★ Gear to 2 inches
This direct line avoids the poorly-protected climbing on **Chimney De Chelly**. The bolted crux tackles a wild lieback up a steep pinch-edge.
1. 5.11a Start with **Chimney De Chelly**, but continue straight up an awkward flare to a triangular roof. Clip a bolt, and race to a belay ledge.
2. 5.8 Follow the excellent third-pitch corner of **Chimney De Chelly** to the top.

52. SHADOW OF DOUBT 5.12a ★★★ Bolts
The most difficult free line on the entire cliff ascends great rock on the left wall of **Chimney De Chelly**. A continuous section of delicate moves leads to a weasel traverse left to anchor bolts. Hopefully, someone eventually will continue further up the face to a more logical stopping point.

53. REASON TO BE 5.10d ★★★ Bolts
The appealing left arête of the **Chimney De Chelly** corner makes a fine one-pitch jaunt. It's possible to start directly up the edge, but everyone traverses in from the right instead.

54. TALE OF TWO SHITTIES 5.10a ★★★ Gear to 2.5 inches
Highlighted by an excellent inside corner, this enjoyable line offers three varied pitches. The second pitch contains the hardest moves, but a devious finish on face holds is more intimidating. Start uphill from the lowest part of the wall atop a block below a small, left-facing corner.
1. 5.7 Jam a discontinuous series of cracks to a belay spot below the attractive dihedral.
2. 5.10a Strenuous jams on great rock end at a small ledge.
3. 5.9 A balancey series of moves past three bolts leads to a knobby finish. Descend the north side ledges.

55. SUNDOWN 5.9 ★★★ Gear to 2 inches
This clean, shallow dihedral is highly recommended. Start right of a massive block on either a difficult direct line or easier face holds to the left. Once in the corner, locking jams on good rock end with a hand traverse left to an anchor.

56. DOWN'S SYNDROME 5.10a R ★★ Gear to 2 inches
Rather than escaping left at the top of the **Sundown** dihedral, attack the knobby face above in one pitch from the ground. The bolts are far enough apart to raise your pulse as you edge up the nubbins. Step left past the last bolt to a hanging belay atop the crux pitch of **Minas Morgul**.

57. MINAS MORGUL 5.11d ★★ Gear to 2.5 inches
For several years, this line was a sought-after test piece, but it drifted into obscurity as climbers turned to bolted routes. The crux pitch tackles a strenuous series of thin jams capped by a roof.

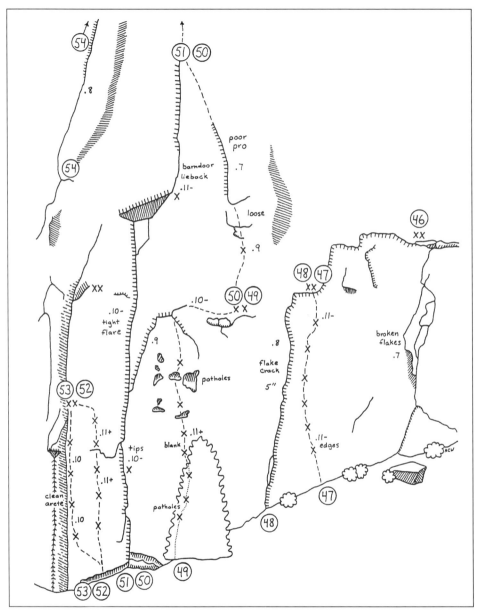

Mesa Verde Wall – Base Detail

46. PETROGLYPH CRACK   5.7 ★
47. COWS IN AGONY   5.11a/b ★★
48. CLIFF DWELLING CRACK   5.8 R ★★
49. JUNIPER FACE   5.11d ★★
50. CHIMNEY DE CHELLY   5.10a R ★★

51. DESOLATION ROW   5.11a ★★
52. SHADOW OF DOUBT   5.12a ★★★
53. REASON TO BE   5.10d ★★★
54. TALE OF TWO SHITTIES   5.10a ★★★

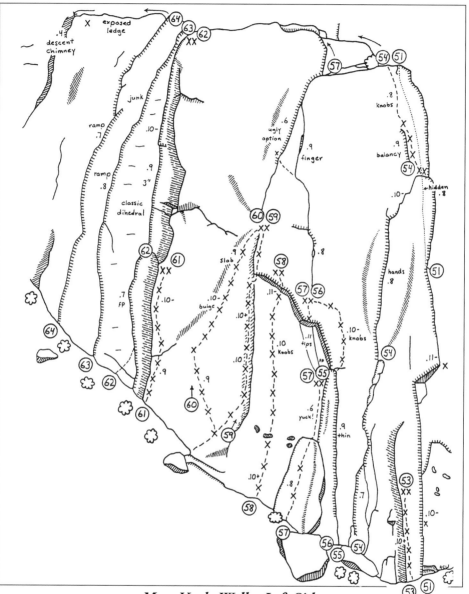

Mesa Verde Wall – Left Side

51. DESOLATION ROW 5.11a ★★
53. REASON TO BE 5.10d ★★★
54. TALE OF TWO SHITTIES 5.10a ★★★
55. SUNDOWN 5.9 ★★★
56. DOWN'S SYNDROME 5.10a R ★★
57. MINAS MORGUL 5.11d ★★
58. BAD MOON RISING 5.11a ★★★

59. MOONS OF PLUTO 5.10d ★★★★
60. SCREAMING YELLOW ZONKERS
    5.10b ★★★★
61. COSMOS 5.10a ★★★
62. TREZLAR 5.10a ★★★★
63. FOUR Fs 5.8
64. LICHEN PERSUASION 5.7

You'll find good protection if you can hang out long enough to place it. Start at the base of a large block leaning against the wall.

1. 5.8 Face climb directly up the block past two bolts, then continue on bad rock to an anchor. The first ascent followed the flaring chimney behind the block, although no one goes this way anymore. Another option ascends **Sundown** to the same anchors.

2. 5.11c Climb the finger crack splitting the overhanging wall to a hanging belay.

3. 5.9 Stroll up a low-angled crack on good rock past a small roof, then jam a steep finger crack. The original finish avoided the final crack by climbing a slovenly corner (5.6) to the left. Don't make the same mistake.

58. BAD MOON RISING 5.11a ★★★ Bolts
Just left of a massive boulder rises this engaging face climb. The perplexing start frustrates anyone who can't reach the holds, but the crux pulls around a small roof higher up.

59. MOONS OF PLUTO 5.10d ★★★★ Bolts
For years, people either loved or hated this attractive arête, depending on whether they blew a knob. Today, with the bad nubbins gone, you can't help but like **Moons of Pluto**. The insecure crux hits near the top of the arête, as positive holds grow scarce. Rappel from two bolts using double ropes.

60. SCREAMING YELLOW ZONKERS 5.10b ★★★★ Bolts
This stunning face ranks among the best 5.10 routes at Smith. If you enjoy knobs, you won't want to miss the well-protected moves, but you might have to wait in line. Bring two ropes to get down.

61. COSMOS 5.10a ★★★ Bolts
Another fun route, **Cosmos** ascends a popular series of knobs right of an arête. The crux comes just below the anchors at a bulge.

62. TREZLAR 5.10a ★★★★ Gear to 2.5 inches
This unmistakable dihedral lies on the shaded north side of Mesa Verde Wall. You'll have to wade through an unpleasant approach to get to the real climbing, but don't let this stop you. The grade of the upper pitch comes more from the continuity than the difficulty of the individual moves. Start slightly uphill from the base of the corner.

1. 5.7 Traverse right across the slab to a dirty crack and stem the poorly-protected corner to a ledge.

2. 5.10a Stem and jam the impressive corner to a bolt belay. Descend the north-side ledges.

63. FOUR Fs 5.8 Gear to 2 inches
Two shallow dihedrals are immediately left of **Trezlar**. **Four Fs** follows the right corner to the top in one dirty pitch that totally lacks any redeeming qualities.

64. LICHEN PERSUASION 5.7 Gear to 2 inches
This unappealing line ascends the left of the two corners uphill from **Trezlar**. The large amounts of lichen and dirt will likely persuade you to leave it alone.

THE PLEASURE PALACE

The north face of Mesa Verde Wall quickly peters out the farther you walk uphill. Beyond lies a section of uninspiring, reddish-purple rock called the Pleasure Palace. A small collection of bolted face climbs grace the cliff line. The quickest approach from the parking lot hikes up and over Cocaine Gully.

65. RED SCARE 5.10b ★★ Bolts
When hiking uphill from **Trezlar**, you'll come first to the largest of the Pleasure Palace walls. The longer of two bolted lines provides some good entertainment as it pulls around a few steep bulges.

66. WE BE TOYS 5.10a ★ Bolts
A few feet left of Red Scare rises this unremarkable, low-angle face. Some forgettable moves up a seam end abruptly at anchor bolts.

67. LITTLE WICKED THING 5.10a ★ Bolts
Further uphill, the Pleasure Palace deteriorates, until you come to a line of routes rising above the highest point of the hillside. **Little Wicked Thing** follows a junky face right of a steep arête.

68. BOP TILL YOU DROP 5.11a ★★★ Bolts
The best route on the crag follows an appealing, overhanging edge. It easily justifies the long uphill slog to the Pleasure Palace, as the moves are delightful and the rock solid.

69. MATTHEW 7:24 5.10b ★★ Bolts
This comically short route rises immediately left of **Bop Till You Drop**. A few exceedingly well-protected jugs lead to a pull over the crux bulge. Many climbers will feel silly roping up for this boulder problem.

70. AGGRO BUMBLY 5.10d ★★★ Bolts
With good rock and strenuous moves, this face pleases almost everyone. A few unwise climbers risk a bad fall by stepping right; it's much better to attack the crux head on.

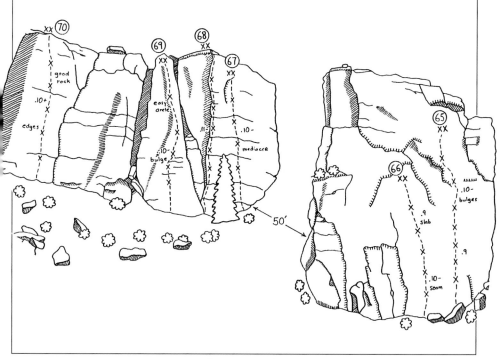

Pleasure Palace

65. RED SCARE 5.10b ★★
66. WE BE TOYS 5.10a ★
67. LITTLE WICKED THING 5.10a ★

68. BOP TILL YOU DROP 5.11a ★★★
69. MATTHEW 7:24 5.10b ★★
70. AGGRO BUMBLY 5.10d ★★★

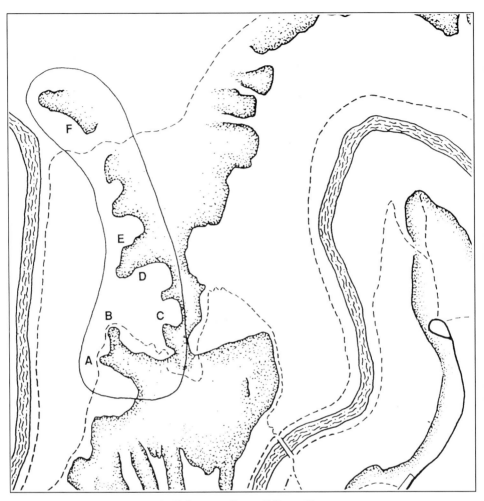

A. *Diamonds and Rust Buttress*
B. *Monkey Face*
C. *Fairy Tale Tower*
D. *Great Expectations*
E. *Kiss of the Lepers Area*
F. *New World Buttress*

MONKEY FACE AREA

THE MOST REMARKABLE CHUNK of stone at Smith is the 350-foot spire of Monkey Face. Visitors send thousands of postcards each year bearing the likeness of this natural wonder. Viewed from the south, the four-sided pinnacle bears a striking resemblance to a grinning monkey, complete with mouth, nose and eyes. For the climber, Monkey Face holds some brilliant routes with solid rock and unmatched positions. The overhanging arêtes, sweeping faces and stunning thin cracks offer something for everyone.

The rock itself is unlike anything else at Smith. The lower portion consists of an extremely solid, light-colored stone with sharp-cut edges and few pockets. Higher, it changes into a heavily-featured, reddish-purple rock bulging dramatically on all sides. The combination makes every route to the top highly diverse, as small-edged vertical faces give way to overhanging thuggery. Unlike Smith's typically mediocre multi-pitch lines, the longer routes here usually are good from bottom to top. Yet despite the rave reviews, Monkey Face receives far less traffic than the Dihedrals or Morning Glory Wall. A long hike discourages many from climbing here, so you'll likely have Monkey Face all to yourself. The exposed spire receives even less attention during the winter, as the howling west wind makes climbing impossible. Yet during warmer months, there's no finer place to climb at Smith, as you'll usually find it breezy and cool.

The easiest line to the summit follows the amazing bolt ladder of the **Pioneer Route**. Despite appearances, even climbers with little aid experience find Monkey Face a great place to learn. Massive five-eighths inch bolts with oversized hangers help pacify fears about the frightfully exposed position. Some take the route lightly – a nine-minute solo blitz, and at least one nude ascent were two of the better stunts. Still, the length and exposure of Monkey Face gets beginners into trouble. After all, an ascent of **Bunny Face** does little to prepare you for mind-numbing exposure of **Panic Point**. Perhaps the most unusual feat performed here involved no actual climbing. In 1987, Adam Grosowsky strung a tight-wire between the overlook to the south – the Springboard – and the Monkey's mouth. After several rehearsals, he walked without a belay across the nauseating exposure of the gap, as a sweaty-palmed friend watched nervously.

Over the last three decades, Monkey Face played a leading role in Smith climbing. No other crag matched the steady stream of influential, standard-setting routes pioneered here. It all began in January 1960, when Dave Bohn, Jim Fraser and Vivian Staender first reached the summit. Spread over seven days, and capped with an icy bivouac in the mouth cave, their ascent was a much larger undertaking than anything previously attempted at Smith. They battled sub-freezing temperatures, rigged a comical series of belay lines from the parent cliff and pioneered the use of etriers in Smith aid climbing. Their ascent wasn't any breakthrough in standards though, as they drilled bolt ladders on easy 5th class rock. Some argue that other climbers of the era could have succeeded with far fewer bolts, but the team deserves credit for their ingenuity and perseverance.

Within a decade of the first ascent, the main faces succumbed to hammer-swinging, Yosemite-inspired hardmen. Dean Caldwell, Byron Babcock and Bill Lentsch climbed the **West Face** in 1962, a route remarkable only because they drilled nearly 100 holes on a 350-foot face. A few shaky, original bolts remain in use today, though shortly after the first ascent Lentsch wrote, "These (bolts) were treated roughly and cannot be counted upon to support a climber. It is strongly urged other climbers not attempt to use them."

The next year, Dave Jensen and Bob Martin voiced their response to the Monkey Face bolt lines with an inspired ascent of **Bohn Street/West Face Cave**. Obviously trying to avoid drilling, they nailed an incipient seam left of the Pioneer Route almost entirely on poor pins. Their ascent sent the message that it was possible to climb Monkey Face using boldness and skill rather than relying on the drill.

Later ascents of the **East Face, North Face** and **Southwest Corner** (now called **Astro Monkey**) followed suit, crowning the aid-climbing era on Monkey Face.

During the seventies, free ascents of the original aid lines became Smith's greatest prizes. Jeff Thomas opened the door in 1977 when he freed the awesome third-pitch dihedral of the **Southwest Corner** (5.11a). But the most obvious goal wasn't a free ascent of any particular aid pitch, but instead Monkey Face itself. In early 1979, Chris Jones led an exposed pitch into the **West Face Cave**, and discovered an overhanging line of holds to the top. A few weeks later he returned and, along with Bill Ramsey, created **Monkey Space** (5.11b). This thrilling route was easily Smith's hardest face climb, with two 5.11 pitches. Primed from his breakthrough ascent, Jones next turned to a thin crack on the east side of the spire. After three days, he boosted the standards of Smith by two full letter grades with **Rising Expectations** (5.11d).

After following Chris on **Rising Expectations** as a 19-year-old wannabe, I set my sights on Monkey Face. In 1980, two weeks after quitting college, I freed the technical start of the **Southwest Corner** (5.11d), and the next year led the **West Face's** first pitch (5.12a). But it wasn't until an optimistic day in 1982, when I rappelled every side of Monkey Face, that I saw the amazing potential. I immediately began work on the **East Face**, an impossible-looking seam opened by two decades of nailings. The first pitch (5.12c) went in 1983, but the rest of the route seemed unreasonably hard, so I looked elsewhere. Along with Chris Grover, I managed a free ascent of **Astro Monkey**, Smith's hardest long free route at the time, with four pitches of 5.11. That same year, Alan Lester grabbed a piece of the Monkey Face pie with his free ascent of the impressive second pitch of the **North Face** (5.11d). Exposed and tricky to protect, this was the pillar's most serious venture.

The next year, after jumaring to the first-pitch anchors countless times, I finally freed the second pitch of the **East Face**. This strenuous crack far exceeded the difficulty of any other Smith route, and served as a tune-up for the events of the coming year. In August 1985, I returned to the spire, nabbing **Close Shave** (5.12c), and **Young Pioneers** (5.12d). A few weeks later, with my calves bulging from so many hikes over Misery Ridge, I realized my dream of freeing the entire **East Face** (5.13c/d), linking the first and second pitches into a single lead. With this ascent, Smith Rock stood atop U.S. free climbing. That same year, Hidetaka Suzuki boosted the level of Smith's longer routes, linking all four pitches of the **Northwest Passage** (5.12a, 5.11c, 5.11d, 5.11b).

Since 1985, the new route activity on Monkey Face dwindled, more from a lack of convenience than a shortage of lines. In 1989, Ron Kauk freed **The Backbone** for NBC's "SportsWorld." With a pitch of 5.13, and three of 5.12, this will be Smith's most difficult long free route for years to come. Finally, in 1992, Jean-Baptiste Tribout again brought Monkey Face international acclaim. His free ascent of Just Do It (5.14c) on the bulging east wall ranks among the hardest free climbs in the world.

In the future, Monkey Face should see other significant new routes, though they may be slow in coming. If the spire were nearer the parking lot, it would contain many more lines, almost all at the higher end of the spectrum. But the long hike discourages the typically lazy climber from launching into a new project here. These brilliant new routes await a generation unafraid of a long walk. Several one-pitch base routes stretch across the lower west face, making fine warm-ups for the harder lines. Unfortunately, these climbs often lack the flawless stone found above, as the edges are notoriously friable. I've also included several crags that lie nearby in this chapter. These include the Diamonds and Rust Buttress, the anemic Fairy Tale Tower, the putrid Kiss of the Lepers Area and the New World Buttress.

The most common approach to Monkey Face heads over Asterisk Pass (fourth-class) and follows a trail along the base of the West Side Crags. A shorter, but far more arduous approach storms directly over the switchbacked path of the Misery Ridge trail, then back down the west side. Either alternative takes from 25 to 30 minutes from the parking lot.

Every route to the summit shares the same descent. From the top, make a short rappel south over the massive nose boulder to an anchor. Next comes the 140-foot free rappel that many consider the highlight of the entire climb. Finally, from a ramp below the east wall, either scramble down a short 4th class section, or make another rappel to easy ledges.

DIAMONDS AND RUST BUTTRESS

This prominent, multi-spiked rib lurks across the hillside north of Mesa Verde Wall and just south of Monkey Face. Only two grisly routes blemish this unappealing crag.

1. SLOW TRAIN 5.7 ★ Bolts
    Starting at the foot of the buttress, make a deceptively tricky high step onto an easy face. Perhaps, if someone replaced the stolen hangers, the climb might be worth doing, but then again, probably not.

2. DIAMONDS AND RUST 5.8 R Gear to 2.5 inches
    The only route to the top of the buttress is no gem. Lousy rock and runout climbing plagues every pitch of this garbage dump. The line starts below the obvious roof at the base of the buttress and underclings right to an easy face. After a belay, grovel up three more pitches to the top.

MONKEY FACE

The impressive Monkey Face complex rises left of the Diamonds and Rust Buttress. The first several routes are 100 feet right of the main spire.

3. PERPETUAL MOTION 5.9 ★ Gear to 2.5 inches
    An impressive, white-streaked arch system dominates the southern portion of the Monkey Face complex. **Perpetual Motion** jams part way up this solid crack to an anchor. Unfortunately, the route starts with a horrible traverse from the right.

4. DOLF'S DIHEDRAL 5.8 ★★ Gear to 2.5 inches
    A brilliant crack in a corner rises a few feet left of **Perpetual Motion.** The route might be popular, but an unpleasant traverse guards the dihedral and the locking jams end shortly after they begin.

5. POTENTIAL ENERGY 5.10b R ★★ Gear to 3.5 inches
    This obscure line deserves more attention. Despite some runout moves on the second pitch, you'll have a bolt at your face on the crux. The original start aided a direct line up a thin seam. Today, most of this pitch goes free via **Flex Your Head,** and the remainder would succumb easily.
    1. 5.10a Lieback a left-leaning flake, then join **Dolf's Dihedral** for 15 glorious feet. Make a tricky mantle left onto a large ledge, and belay at two bolts.
    2. 5.10b Scamper up second-rate rock past several bolts to a hard move on solid stone. Easy but unprotected face climbing ends at belay bolts.
    3. 5.9 Ramble up and right on low-angled ramps, then pull over a couple of small roofs to the top.

6. FLEX YOUR HEAD 5.11c ★★ Bolts
    This free version of the original start to **Potential Energy** rises above a juniper tree. The delicate, sustained moves really aren't that enjoyable, but they're well-protected. A #5 RP provides optional protection between the third and fourth bolts.

7. PROJECT 5.12 ?
    A couple of bolts pepper the blank wall immediately left of **Flex Your Head.** Eventually, a worthwhile route might grace this thin face, but for now it sits abandoned.

Several westside routes end in a low notch separating Monkey Face from its parent cliff. From here, either continue to summit, or escape off the backside. To descend, rappel or downclimb (5.4) to a slanting ramp running along the east wall. Scramble down ledges (4th class), or make a short rappel from anchor bolts.

8. KING KONG 5.9 R ★★ Gear to 6 inches
    Although rarely done, **King Kong** offers several memorable sections. A monstrous off-width on

Photo: Bruce Adams

Monkey Face – West Side

5. POTENTIAL ENERGY   5.10b R ★★
6. FLEX YOUR HEAD   5.11c ★★
8. KING KONG   5.9 R ★★
11. BLOW COCOA   5.11c ★
13. WEST FACE VARIATION   5.8 ★★★
15. MOVING IN STEREO   5.11d ★★★

16. ASTRO MONKEY   5.11d ★★★
17. POSE DOWN   5.12c ★★★
18. WEST FACE   5.12a A1 ★★★★
29. PIONEER ROUTE   5.7 A1 ★★★★
32. MONKEY SPACE   5.11b ★★★★

the third pitch keeps many away, though it's easy to bypass this section. The actual crux traverses tiny knobs on the second pitch. Start below vegetated, double cracks.

1. 5.8 Scamper up easy cracks past a bulge to belay bolts.

2. 5.9 Step right on face nubbins and sidestep past three bolts to an anchor.

3. 5.8 Chimney, then off-width a sinister crack and traverse 45 feet left to a belay on a good ledge. As an alternative, step left below the off-width and climb a flake.

4. 5.8 The first ascent team followed a 5.6-crack system to the top of the parent cliff. Today, most climbers finish to the notch via an exposed traverse.

5. Continue to the summit or descend the east side.

8a. KING KONG DIRECT 5.10a R ★ Gear to 2.5 inches
Bushes choke this once-desirable start to **King Kong**. A formerly delightful sequence edged past a bolt to a widening jam crack. Unfortunately, it would take a major archaeological dig to uncover this artifact of Smith climbing.

9. GODZILLA 5.8 ★ Gear to 3 inches
If you enjoy squirming up dirty, flaring chimneys, this might be the route for you. An exhilarating undercling exits the second-pitch chimney, but the approach stinks.

1. 5.8 Ascend the first pitch of **King Kong**.

2. 5.8 Flail up the chimney, fighting testy pigeons. Undercling around a large block and scramble to a belay platform.

3. 5.8 Traverse left to the notch or continue up the crack system (5.6) to the top of the cliff.

10. SMAUG 5.10b ★ R Gear to 1.5 inches
A few dangerously loose blocks detract from this otherwise passable route. The crux finesses a technical sequence in a shallow corner, followed by a runout section on jugs. Start just left of **Godzilla** below a right-facing, block-plugged corner.

1. 5.10b Climb the crack, moving cautiously around some shaky flakes, and cut left to a belay.

2. 5.7 Move back right and climb a runout shallow corner to a roof. Skirt to the right, then step back left to a belay ledge.

3. 5.8 Traverse left to the notch, or follow cracks (5.6) to the top of the cliff.

11. BLOW COCOA 5.11c ★ Bolts
The first attempts to repeat this friable wall ended in failure, as holds broke with every go. As the crumbly edges snap off, the climb grows better and more difficult each year.

12. MONKEY FARCE 5.10b R ★★ Gear to 1.5 inches
This ridiculous line traverses the west face of Monkey Face to a tiny ledge, then raps off. The first-pitch finger crack gets done occasionally, but almost no one tangles with the poorly-protected finish. Start below a diagonal crack just left of the **Blow Cocoa** bolt line.

1. 5.10b Make a tricky face move past a comical fixed pin, then jam the strenuous crack. When possible, move left onto a lichen-covered ramp, and step delicately to an anchor.

2. 5.9 Face traverse left on low-angled knobs past an anchor. Some frightening moves lead to the belay atop the first pitch of the **West Face**. Rappel using two ropes.

13. WEST FACE VARIATION 5.8 ★★★ Gear to 2.5 inches
The most popular of the moderate routes on the west side of Monkey Face makes a fine choice for intermediate climbers. The rock and protection are good, and the moves charming. Finishing to the summit via the **Pioneer Route** makes one of the most enjoyable long routes at Smith.

1. 5.7 Start on the left side of some neatly-stacked blocks and swing right to easy cracks and a ledge. After a clean corner, pull past two bulges to a bolt belay. A slightly more difficult variant (5.8) ascends the right side of the starting block.

2. 5.5 Step left then hike an easy slab until forced to circle right below a roof. Cut back left to a belay, fighting horrendous rope drag.

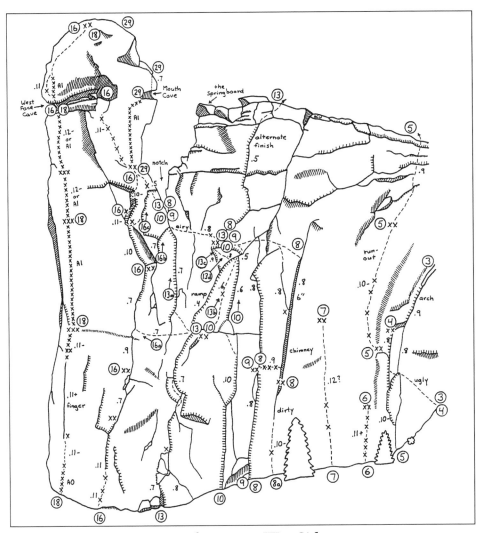

Monkey Face – West Side

3. PERPETUAL MOTION 5.9 ★
4. DOLF'S DIHEDRAL 5.8 ★★
5. POTENTIAL ENERGY 5.10b R ★★
6. FLEX YOUR HEAD 5.11c ★★ Bolts
7. PROJECT 5.12 ?
8. KING KONG 5.9 R ★★
8a. KING KONG DIRECT 5.10a R ★
9. GODZILLA 5.8 ★
10. SMAUG 5.10b ★ R
13. WEST FACE VARIATION 5.8 ★★★

13a. VARIATION 5.8 ★★★
13b. VARIATION 5.7 X ★★
13c. VARIATION 5.9 R ★★
13d. VARIATION 5.8 X ★
16. ASTRO MONKEY 5.11d ★★★
16a. VARIATION 5.7 X ★
16b. VARIATION 5.7 ★★
16c. VARIATION 5.11a ★★★
18. WEST FACE 5.12a A1 ★★★★
29. PIONEER ROUTE 5.7 A1 ★★★★

3. 5.8 Either climb a moderate crack system to the top of the cliff (5.6), or make a tricky face move past a bolt and continue traversing left to the notch. Follow the **Pioneer Route,** or descend the east side.

13a. VARIATION 5.8 ★★★ Gear to 2 inches
You can ignore pitches two and three on the regular route, and step left, jamming an excellent crack leading directly to the notch. Many prefer this direct line, as it avoids the rope drag of the second pitch.

13b. VARIATION 5.7 X ★★ Gear to 2 inches
This second-pitch variant swaps rope drag for poor protection by climbing a low-angled slab to the right. The rock is solid, but the single bolt sticks halfway out.

13c. VARIATION 5.9 R ★★ Gear to 1 inch
You can climb directly over the second pitch roof by attacking a short, overhanging thin crack in a corner and manteling onto the belay ledge.

13d. VARIATION 5.8 X ★ Gear to 3 inches
A foolhardy way to pull the second-pitch roof crawls right to left along a huge, detached flake to the finishing mantel.

14. DRUG NASTY (a.k.a. DEAN'S DREAM) 5.11c ★ Bolts
A mediocre, bolted face route rises just left of the **West Face Variation.** Easily the greatest challenge here lies in climbing the wall without snapping off a hold. As with most knobby faces, **Drug Nasty** will improve with time, but it'll never be a classic. Stick-clip the first bolt or risk a broken ankle on the starting block.

15. MOVING IN STEREO 5.11d ★★★ Bolts
Far better than its neighbor to the right, this left-leaning offset comes highly recommended. A moderate series of holds on good rock leads to a perplexing crux above the final bolt.

16. ASTRO MONKEY (a.k.a. SOUTHWEST CORNER) 5.11d ★★★ Gear to 2 inches
This challenging climb combines the original **Southwest Corner** with **Monkey Space** in six high-quality pitches. The start makes a decent base route, and most climbers rappel from the first anchors without venturing higher. The wildly exposed third pitch is the most exciting on the route, but every section has its charms.
1. 5.11d Edge past three bolts on small holds, then jam pin scars in a shallow corner moving around a roof to an anchor. Lower off, or continue on a runout slab to a higher set of bolts.
2. 5.9 Jam a brilliant finger crack, then climb easier rock to a belay beneath an overhanging dihedral.
3. 5.11a Attack the corner on locking finger jams, then make some wild moves left around a roof.
4. 5.10a Stem a short dihedral and swing right around a roof, mindful of a rope-eating slot. Belay on **Bohn Street.**
5. 5.11a Follow **Monkey Space** into the **West Face Cave.**
6. 5.11b Continue up **Monkey Space** to the top.

16a. VARIATION 5.7 ★ X Gear to 2 inches
You can reach the top of the first pitch by making a long traverse down and left from the first belay on the **West Face Variation.** By traversing a little higher, you'll join the second pitch of **Astro Monkey** just above the steep thin crack.

16b. VARIATION 5.7 ★★ Gear to 2 inches
If the third pitch proves too intimidating, escape right up short, parallel cracks. Follow a low-angled ramp to the notch and an easy descent.

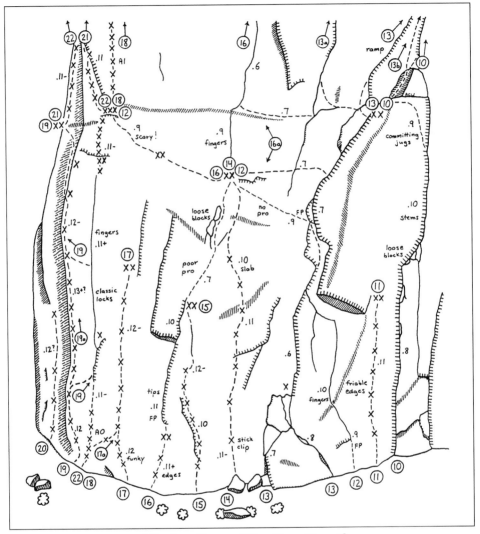

Monkey Face – West Face Detail

10. SMAUG 5.10b R ★
11. BLOW COCOA 5.11c ★
12. MONKEY FARCE 5.10b R ★★
13. WEST FACE VARIATION 5.8 ★★★
13a. VARIATION 5.8 ★★★
13b. VARIATION 5.7 X ★★
14. DRUG NASTY 5.11c ★
15. MOVING IN STEREO 5.11d ★★★
16. ASTRO MONKEY 5.11d ★★★
16a. VARIATION 5.7 X ★

17. POSE DOWN 5.12c ★★★
17a. VARIATION 5.12a/b A0 ★★★
18. WEST FACE 5.12a A1 ★★★★
19. SHEER TRICKERY 5.12b ★★★
19a. PROJECT 5.13+ ?
20. PROJECT 5.12 ?
21. THE BACKBONE 5.13a ★★★★
22. NORTHWEST PASSAGE 5.12a A0 (or 5.12b) ★★★★

16c. VARIATION 5.11a ★★★ Gear to 2 inches
Many ascents of the **Southwest Corner** cut right, not left, at the third pitch roof. After a hand traverse on pin scars, belay immediately or face intolerable rope drag on the easy scramble to **Bohn Street.**

17. POSE DOWN 5.12c ★★★ Bolts
This studly face is excellent, with an intellectual crux getting to the second bolt. The climbing above is less cerebral, but stays tricky to the finish.

17a. VARIATION 5.12a/b A0 ★★★ Bolts
Many climbers ignore the free start by aiding the first few moves of the **West Face** and cutting right past a bolt, joining the regular route.

18. WEST FACE 5.12a A1 ★★★★ Gear to 2 inches
Smith's most awe-inspiring bolt line ascends four pitches of perfect rock up the blank west wall of Monkey Face. Although somewhat of an eyesore, the bolt ladders on the upper pitches provide exhilarating climbing whether done aid or free. You'll have to aid the second-pitch bolt ladder unless you can climb 5.17, but the rest of the route goes free. The first-pitch finger crack makes a fine climb in its own right. Curiously, the original bolt line at the start still hasn't gone free; everyone begins by aiding a short bolt line to the first pin scars. If you dislike aid starts to free climbs, begin with the first few moves of **Sheer Trickery.**
1. 5.12a A0 Aid the first five bolts to a thin crack. Free the classic finger crack to a bolted finish on face holds.
2. A1 Clip a line of ratty bolts on a featureless wall to a ledge.
3. 5.12a An airy free pitch on great rock leads past a ledge to an energetic finish into the **West Face Cave.**
4. 5.11b Power out of the cave on overhanging pockets, clipping two bolts. The original line aids a bolt ladder a few feet right, providing an easy out if you can't crank another free move. Easy scrambling ends at bolts just below the summit.

19. SHEER TRICKERY 5.12b ★★★ Gear to 1.5 inches
A prominent, bolted arête that shares the same first moves as the **West Face** rises immediately left of the start of the **West Face. Sheer Trickery** fools you by not climbing the edge in its entirety, but the line of least resistance. An extreme section low leads to a traverse right into the West Face crack. After 30 feet of jamming, step back left and finish the arête to an anchor. To descend, rappel with two ropes.

19a. PROJECT 5.13+ ?
The entire edge of **Sheer Trickery** remains undone. A bleak sequence on perfect rock between the third and sixth bolts foils all attempts.

20. PROJECT 5.12 ?
A few bolts litter the face around the corner left of the **Sheer Trickery** arête. After someone scrubs lichen from the finishing dihedral, it should fall at a reasonable grade.

21. THE BACKBONE 5.13a ★★★★ Bolts
This remarkable arête surely must rank among the world's most stunning free climbs. Separating the west and north faces of Monkey Face, this razor-edge combines a fearfully-exposed position with extreme climbing. While the second pitch stands out as the real gem, the entire route is the most difficult multi-pitch venture at Smith. On early attempts, climbers ignored ledges on either side of the arête, trying to slap wildly up both edges (5.13c) without pulling around to rest. Unfortunately, there are several places where you can step around the corner, slashing the grade considerably. Still, you can't avoid the crux – a desperate series of slaps up the right arête.

1.   5.12b   Climb **Sheer Trickery** to belay bolts, or hike in from the northeast corner of the spire (5.6).
2.   5.13a   Soar up the breathtaking arête past many bolts to an anchor at a small ledge.
3.   5.12a   Step right, joining the **West Face** bolt line, and attack the fearfully-exposed wall into the **West Face Cave.**
4.   5.12a   Several bolts dot a strongly overhanging wall 20 feet right of the normal exit. A lunge off the deck yields to jug hauling and the top.

22.   NORTHWEST PASSAGE   5.12a A0 (or 5.12b)   ★★★★   Gear (Friends to #2.5, Rocks, triple RPs)
Without rival, the **Northwest Passage** is Smith's finest long crack climb. Varied moves, perfect rock and an exposed position make this the best free route to the summit. The line links the first pitch of the **West Face,** with the **North Face** via a memorable connection pitch. The exposed position makes for some chilly climbing on a cold day, so leave this well-shaded route for warmer times. Even in midsummer, it remains cool and breezy, as long as you do the first pitch early.
1.   5.12a A0 (or 5.12b)   Climb the first pitch of the **West Face,** or use the **Sheer Trickery** free start.
2.   5.11c   An exciting, barn-door lieback up the razor-edged arête leads left around the corner to the **North Face** crack. Strenuous jams end at a hanging belay.
3.   5.11d   Jam the intense upper section of the **North Face** to the **West Face Cave.**
4.   5.11b   Pure thuggery up the standard exit ends on top.

23.   NORTH FACE   5.12a   ★★★★   Gear (Friends to 2.5 inches, Rocks, triple RPs #3 through #5)
This flake crack splits Monkey Face's north wall. Originally done in two pitches to the cave, the best version bypasses the hanging belay, preferably with a 55-meter rope. On the first ascent, a pointless bolt line gained the crack by arching across the lower face. Today, everyone begins by traversing to an anchor on the northwest corner. The first 20 feet above the mid-pitch anchors protect stubbornly, but the upper part eats small wires.
1.   5.6   Start below the northeast corner and traverse right on bad rock to an anchor.
2.   5.12a   Step right and climb the arête past a few bolts into the flake crack. Never-ending jams and liebacks lead to a crux move below the cave. Cut right and belay in the **West Face Cave.**
3.   5.11b   Gorilla up a short, overhanging wall to easy climbing.

23a. ORIGINAL START   A1
For reasons unknown, the first-ascent team avoided the natural line with a line of prehistoric bolts arching in from the left.

24.   SPANK THE MONKEY   5.12a R   ★★★★   Bolts
This delicate arête separates the overhanging east wall from the north face. Airy moves, well-spaced bolts and a razor-sharp edge make the route more exciting than the typical 5.12a. Some climbers put their minds at ease with double ropes. Bring a few wires if you'd like to protect the final moves to the anchor.

25.   EAST FACE   5.13c/d   ★★★★   Gear (5 #3 RPs, 8 #4 RPs, Rocks)
A breakthrough route for Smith when first freed, the **East Face** was America's hardest free climb for 14 months. Despite a superb position, the climb is rarely attempted due to the lack of bolts. A true redpoint ascent (placing all gear on lead) still hasn't gone, since everyone pre-places the nuts. The original first pitch makes a fine 5.12c, with locking jams and good protection. The upper portion begins with a desperate sequence above the anchors leading to powerful jams up the overhanging wall; the crux hits when you're totally gassed on the final traverse.
1.   5.13c/d   Jam the beautiful thin crack past a set of anchors, then power past a few bolts to the finishing arête. Rappel using two ropes, or . . .
2.   5.10b   Easy face moves past a few bolts lead to a ledge. Free a steep bolt ladder on good holds, and hike a dirty slab to the top.

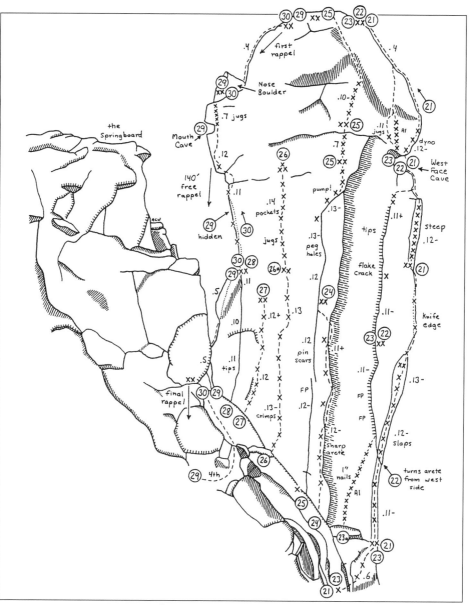

Monkey Face – North/East Faces

21. THE BACKBONE   5.13a ★★★★
22. NORTHWEST PASSAGE   5.12a A0 (or 5.12b) ★★★★
23. NORTH FACE   5.12a ★★★★
23a. ORIGINAL START   A1
24. SPANK THE MONKEY   5.12a R ★★★★
25. EAST FACE   5.13c/d ★★★★

26. JUST DO IT   5.14c ★★★★
26a. JUST DO IT   (lower part)   5.13c ★★★★
27. MEGALITHIC   5.12d ★★★★
28. RISING EXPECTATIONS   5.11d ★★★★
29. PIONEER ROUTE   5.7 A1 ★★★★
30. CLOSE SHAVE   5.12c R ★★★

26. JUST DO IT   5.14c ★★★★ Bolts
The awesome, overhanging wall left of the **East Face** contains the most difficult climbing in America. The upper section rates 5.14 in its own right, but the route goes in one pitch from the ground, using the 5.13c slab as a warm-up. The crux involves an outrageous series of lockoffs on one- and two-finger pockets.

26a. JUST DO IT (lower part) 5.13c ★★★★ Bolts
The start of **Just Do It** makes a fine route in its own right, ending at an anchor at the rock's color change. A tweaky section low leads to a good shake, with the crux coming at a tough dynamic off a small pocket.

27. MEGALITHIC   5.12d ★★★★ Bolts
A line of bolts starting with a left-facing offset rises left of **Just Do It**. A tough series of moves, broken by good shakes, ends at an anchor part-way up the lower wall. The face above appears blank, but who knows?

28. RISING EXPECTATIONS   5.11d ★★★★   Gear to 2 inches
This excellent crack was Smith's hardest route for nearly two years. Finger jams at the start fluster many climbers, but the crux comes higher, pulling around the final bulge.

29. PIONEER ROUTE   5.7 A1 ★★★★   Gear to 1.5 inches
The original route to the summit is a great way to spend a day. The outrageous exposure and uncommonly safe climbing make it extremely popular. The tempting bolt ladder attracts neophytes, but don't take the climb lightly – backing off halfway up isn't easy. **Panic Point** is the most exciting 5.7 pitch you'll ever do; timid climbers savor the nauseating exposure from the security of their aiders. Approach by hiking up scree on the backside of the spire to a large ledge.
1.   4th   Make an exposed step to easy scrambling up a slanting ramp.
2.   5.5   Climb a short corner to the notch, then face climb past a pin and bolt to a ledge called **Bohn Street**.
3.   A1   Blitz the chrome-moly bolt line to an awkward entrance into the mouth cave. All the moves go, but the pitch awaits a free ascent (5.13 ?).
4.   5.7   From the east side of the mouth, step out over the eerie void and tremble past several bolts to a ledge at the Monkey's nose.
5.   5.4   Step right around a huge boulder to a large, unexposed ledge. Easy, unprotected scrambling ends on top.

29a. YOUNG PIONEERS 5.12d ★★★ Bolts
A strenuous pitch frees into the mouth cave just right of the **Pioneer Route's** chrome-moly bolt line. The crux launches for the lip of the cave, followed by a strenuous mantel. Despite some crumbly pockets, the exhilarating position warrants far more attention.

30. CLOSE SHAVE   5.12c R ★★★ Bolts
An unmatched arête ascends the underside of the Monkey's neck and chin. **Close Shave** frightens away almost everyone, since only four bolts protect 65 feet of climbing, but you'll have a bolt at your face on the crux. The hardest moves tackle severe slaps up the arête, with nothing but air below your feet. At the mouth cave, join **Panic Point** for the final section to the rappel anchor at the nose boulder.

31. BOHN STREET–WEST FACE CAVE   5.12a R ★   Gear to 1 inch (RPs, Rocks, TCUs)
This formerly bold aid route fell victim to repeated nailings; today, it frees grotesque "angle scars." A flip of the rope will knock out most of the gear, since nothing sets properly in the flaring peg holes.
1.   5.5   Ascend to **Bohn Street**.
2.   5.12a   Step left and jam the seam past a bulge to a bolt. Traverse left to the **West Face Cave**.
3.   5.11b   Muscle up an overhanging bolt line at the back side of the cave and scramble to the top.

Photo: Bruce Adams

Monkey Face – Northeast Side

21. THE BACKBONE   5.13a ★★★★
23. NORTH FACE   5.12a ★★★★
25. EAST FACE   5.13c/d ★★★★
26. JUST DO IT   5.14c ★★★★

28. RISING EXPECTATIONS   5.11d ★★★★
29. PIONEER ROUTE   5.7 A1 ★★★★
30. CLOSE SHAVE   5.12c R ★★★

31a. ORIGINAL FINISH   A2
The original third pitch followed a line of shaky pins and bolts out the south side of the **West Face Cave.** Gravity dislodged several fixed pieces over the years, and those that remain await the next climber foolish enough to test them.

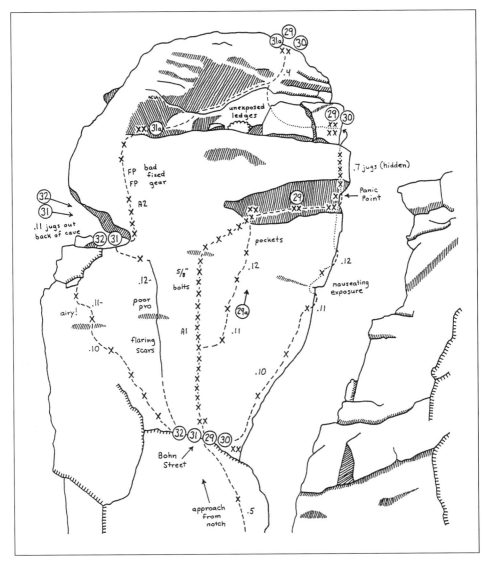

Monkey Face – South Face Detail

29. PIONEER ROUTE   5.7 A1 ★★★★
29a. YOUNG PIONEERS   5.12d ★★★
30. CLOSE SHAVE   5.12c R ★★★
31. BOHN STREET–WEST FACE CAVE
     5.12a R ★

31a. ORIGINAL FINISH   A2
32. MONKEY SPACE   5.11b ★★★★

32. MONKEY SPACE 5.11b ★★★★ Bolts (optional gear to 2 inches)
This historic route was the line of Monkey Face's first free ascent. The amazing position, good rock and exciting moves makes it an undisputed Smith classic. The memorable second pitch traverses over nothingness from **Bohn Street** and face climbs into the **West Face Cave**. The actual crux comes on a short, bouldery wall out the north side of the cave.
1. 5.5 Climb to **Bohn Street**.
2. 5.11a Step left and move past several bolts to a strenuous pull over an exposed bulge. A short flake cracks ends in the **West Face Cave**.
3. 5.11b Gorilla up a short, bolt-protected wall to the top.

FAIRY TALE TOWER

A large hunk of stone, reeking of rotten rock rests near the top of the scree slope uphill from Monkey Face. Although two routes ascend the buttress, it'll remain forgotten happily-ever-after.

33. CHICKEN LITTLE 5.6 ★ Gear to 2 inches
It's not the sky that's falling . . . only stones from above. Start up a prominent dihedral on the left side of the buttress and climb two lackluster pitches to the top.

34. MR. TOAD'S WILD RIDE 5.9 R ★ Gear to 2.5 inches
This humdrum route starts on face holds just right of the **Chicken Little** dihedral. Traverse right and scamper past a few spaced bolts to easier climbing.

KISS OF THE LEPERS AREA

To the north lies a huge amount of stone that's every bit as bad as Monkey Face is good. Understandably, almost no one ever visits. Named for head-shaped "kissing" spires, the Kiss of the Lepers Area contains a mercifully small collection of routes. A few sections of good rock exist, but they're broken with large amounts of garbage.

35. GREAT EXPECTATIONS 5.7 ★★ Gear to 2.5 inches
The upper of three staircased crags atop the ridge north of Monkey Face contains a clean, left-leaning open book with two distinct bulges.

36. FUNGUS ROOF 5.10c X Gear to 2.5 inches
As you walk along the base of the Kiss of the Lepers Area, you'll first come to a large, crack-split roof. This forgotten route face climbs past a couple bolts, then jams the dirty ceiling crack. After pulling over the lip, continue up disintegrating rock to an anchor.

37. SCABIES 5.8 X Gear to 3 inches
Avoid this diseased climb at all costs. Start about 50 feet left of the **Fungus Roof** at a short left-facing corner leading into some large potholes. Stagger up rotten, poorly-protected rock for two sickening pitches.

NEW WORLD BUTTRESS

This prominent, optimistically-named crag rises above the river far to the north of Monkey Face. Some reconnaissance trips in the late 70s caused a few idealistic climbers to proclaim this cliff the future of Smith Rock. Fortunately, they were wrong. Two routes of mixed quality ascend this hunk of stone, though absolutely no one bothers.

38. HAWKLINE MONSTER   5.10a R ★   Gear to 2.5 inches
The line on the New World Buttress follows the rightmost of two massive corners on the river face. Despite sections of good climbing, there's enough bad rock below to sour the whole experience.
1. 5.9   Follow the left-facing dihedral past a ledge to a bolt belay.
2. 5.10a   Jam a finger crack crux to a rotten ramp, and move up and left to an anchor.
3. 5.8   Face climb to the top of the buttress.

39. NEW WORLD   5.8 R ★   Gear to 2.5 inches
Despite some sections of passable climbing, this five-pitch odyssey contains far too much junk to justify the long approach hike. Start on the north side of the buttress with a short traverse right, and climb to the top via an obscure crack system. The enjoyable third pitch splits a steep slab, but it's not enough to rescue **New World** from obscurity.

Photo: Cathy Beloeil

Erik Johnson on Spank The Monkey (5.12a).

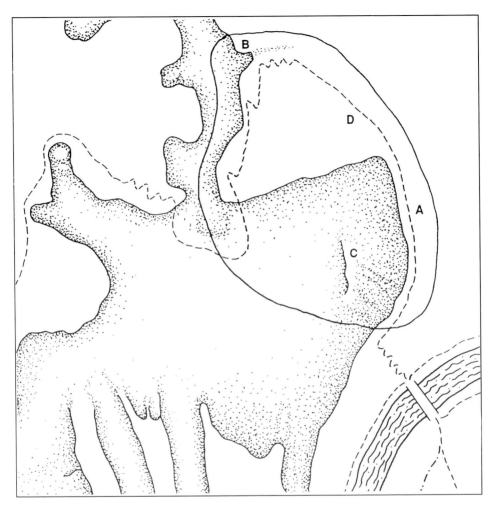

A. Red Wall
B. Red Ryder Buttress
C. Easy's Playhouse
D. Misery Ridge Trail

RED WALL AREA

THE ATTRACTIVE, REDDISH–PURPLE FACE of Red Wall towers immediately right of Picnic Lunch Wall. From the turnaround parking area, this aptly-named 300-foot cliff dominates the view. The iron-rich rock offers a different climbing experience from the normal tuff. The best portions are solid and well-featured, with excellent beginning lines and moderate bolted faces. Yet despite the great stone and quick approach, Red Wall hasn't seen the intense development of Smith's better-known crags. The steepest faces are dismally blank and since the best-looking new routes are slabs, most climbers look elsewhere for first ascents.

Between February and July, the park service protects active nesting sites by closing portions of Red Wall. The restricted climbs are on the right side of the crag, including **Moscow** and **Peking**. A sign marks the closed areas, and the ranger can provide additional information on what routes are off-limits. Please use restraint during these months and go elsewhere – the future of Smith climbing depends on it.

Many of the more popular Red Wall routes top out. A fixed anchor above Super Slab allows a quick descent with two double-rope rappels. Most climbers avoid the rappels with a trip down **Misery Ridge**. To find the descent trail, weave uphill through junipers and sagebrush bearing right, looking for the unmistakable staircase. If you're ever compelled to use a rope on the descent, you'll know you're lost and should keep searching for the proper trail.

RED WALL

1. TITANIUM JAG 5.10b ★★ Gear to 2 inches
   This arching dihedral splits the upper portion of Red Wall's left side. Despite good rock, mostly fixed protection and varied climbing, it sees few ascents. Start by scrambling to a ledge left of a large circular flake.
   1. 5.8 Climb an indistinct seam past a fixed pin to the crest of the ridge. Easy climbing leads left around the corner to a belay spot.
   2. 5.9 Scamper up an attractive ramp past a bolt to a belay beneath a roof.
   3. 5.10b Face climb left past three bolts to a crux move around the roof, and scramble to the top.

2. BILL'S FLAKE 5.10a ★★ Gear to 3 inches
   This obvious circular flake rests along the base of the left portion of the wall. The original route underclings, liebacks and jams great rock on the left side.

3. FINGER PUPPET 5.10a ★★ Bolts
   A quick series of edges leads up the face of **Bill's Flake**. After a tricky crux past the first bolt, delightful holds end at an anchor.

4. PHANTASMAGORIA 5.10b ★ Bolts
   This steep wall of friable edges rises above **Bill's Flake**. After starting up **Finger Puppet**, step right past the second bolt and follow a series of balancey, unrelenting edges to an anchor.

5. POP ART 5.10c ★ Bolts
   Parallel bolt lines on a short pillar rise just off the trail below **Bill's Flake**. The run-of-the-mill left route follows knobs past a bulge to cold-shut anchor bolts.

6. DANCES WITH CLAMS 5.10a ★★ Bolts
   The rightmost of two bolt lines climbs simple edges to an exciting finish on jugs. The moves are enjoyable as long as the holds don't pull off in your face.

Photo: Bruce Adams

Red Wall

1. TITANIUM JAG   5.10b ★★
6. DANCES WITH CLAMS   5.10a ★★
7. PAPER TIGER   5.10a ★★
8. SUPER SLAB   5.6 ★★★★
11. AMPHETAMINE GRIP   5.7 R ★★★

14. HELTER SKELTER   5.10c R ★★
15. RIDE THE LIGHTNING   5.11b ★★★
18. SOLE SURVIVOR   5.11b ★★★
21. SHANGHAI   5.10a X ★
25. MOSCOW   5.6 ★★★

7. PAPER TIGER   5.10a ★★   Gear to 2.5 inches
This varied jaunt ascends the most obvious weakness up the left section of Red Wall. The start plows through some uninspiring rock, but the upper wall is solid. You can bypass the crux first pitch by scrambling left from **Super Slab** along an obvious ledge system. The regular start begins below a short corner right of a bolted pillar.
1. 5.10a Scurry up the corner to a slot, then jam a solid crack to an alcove. Pull over the intimidating roof on creaky face holds to belay bolts.
2. 5.9 Cut left on unprotected buckets, then move right past a sagebrush. Bypass a roof on the left, and finish up the obvious crack system.

7a. KARL MARX VARIATION   5.10a R   Gear to 2.5 inches
This pointless variant avoids the simple corner at the start with run-out edges to the right. A single bolt protects the crux, before cutting back left to the security of the crack.

8. SUPER SLAB 5.6 ★★★★ Gear to 2.5 inches
Many feel this charming climb is the best route of the grade at Smith. **Super Slab** blends excellent rock, good protection and aesthetic moves into a memorable line. The first two pitches aren't special, but the elegant final slab leaves you totally satisfied. You can either rappel the route with double ropes, or scramble up a deceptively difficult (5.7), unexposed slab in the exit gully.

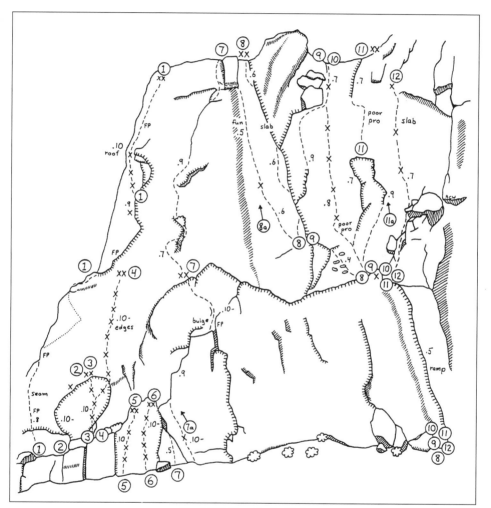

Red Wall – Left Side

1. TITANIUM JAG 5.10b ★★	8. SUPER SLAB 5.6 ★★★★
2. BILL'S FLAKE 5.10a ★★	8a. VARIATION 5.6 X ★★★★
3. FINGER PUPPET 5.10a ★★	9. PANAMA EXPRESS 5.9 ★★
4. PHANTASMAGORIA 5.10b ★	10. PANAMA RED 5.8 R ★★
5. POP ART 5.10c ★	11. AMPHETAMINE GRIP 5.7 R ★★★
6. DANCES WITH CLAMS 5.10a ★★	11a. GRIPPED 5.9 ★
7. PAPER TIGER 5.10a ★★	12. RED ROVER 5.7 R ★★
7a. KARL MARX VARIATION 5.10a R	

1. 5.6 Start below a shattered amphitheater and ascend a ramp past a bulge to a ledge.
2. 5.3 Step left around the corner to a big ledge, then climb runout potholes to a belay slot behind a block.
3. 5.6 Savor the super slab to the top.

8a. VARIATION 5.6 X ★★★★ Gear to 2.5 inches
This obscure route ascends the clean face just left of **Super Slab's** upper pitch. Unfortunately, a single bolt protects the entire lead, making it a free solo for the leader. If fully bolted, it would rank among Smith's best easy pitches.

9. PANAMA EXPRESS 5.9 ★★ Gear to 2.5 inches
If **Super Slab** seems too easy for your tastes, you can up the ante by stepping right not far up the third pitch. Scamper up a crack and ramp to a massive block, then move right and face climb to the top.

10. PANAMA RED 5.8 R ★★ Gear to 2.5 inches
This enjoyable route wanders past five bolts on the slab right of **Super Slab's** third pitch. A dangerous runout getting to the first bolt keeps all but the most stout-hearted climbers away.

11. AMPHETAMINE GRIP 5.7 R ★★★ Gear to 2 inches
Highly varied and challenging for the grade, this solid route follows a meandering crack above the first belay on **Super Slab**. The upper pitch protects poorly, but if you're solid on 5.7, you'll enjoy the pleasant climbing.
1. 5.6 Romp up the first pitch of **Super Slab.**
2. 5.7 An easy scramble leads to a left-leaning crack. Jam and lieback around a bulge to a belay ledge.
3. 5.7 Some easy moves lead to a traverse left and a tricky finish up a corner of light rock.

11a. GRIPPED 5.9 ★ Gear to 2 inches
A more-difficult, less-enjoyable second pitch pulls around an awkwardly flaring slot to the right before joining the regular line.

12. RED ROVER 5.7 R ★★ Gear to 2.5 inches
This forgotten line never caught on, despite some fun climbing. After approaching with the first pitch of **Super Slab**, scramble up huge blocks to the right and boulder to a bolted slab. Rappel from an anchor below the top

13. IRON CURTAIN 5.9 R ★★ Gear to 1.5 inches
This worthwhile route begins sixty feet downhill and to the right of **Super Slab**, below a shallow, left-facing corner. After finessing a likable crux sequence with a blend of stems and finger jams, finish on creaky flakes to a large ledge. Rappel with two ropes from anchor bolts.

14. HELTER SKELTER 5.10C R ★★ Gear to 2.5 inches
This serious, multi-pitch line attracts few ascents, though adventure-seekers might enjoy the climbing. Closely-spaced bolts protect steep edges on the crux second pitch, but the rest of the route protects poorly. The first pitch alone provides a runout, but high-quality jaunt on small holds. Start right of **Iron Curtain** below a short, curving flake.
1. 5.10a Romp past a bolt to a seam, then finesse tiny holds past a fixed pin. Force a traverse left and follow runout edges to a large ledge.
2. 5.10c Move left into a bowl and face climb past four bolts to a belay in an alcove.
3. 5.7 An unnerving runout on so-so rock leads far left to a lone bolt. Cut back right to a belay bolt on the upper slab.
4. 5.8 Scramble up the simple slab, then jam a short, left-facing corner to the top.

14a. VARIATION 5.8 Gear to 2.5 inches
If you'd like to climb the upper pitches without messing with the start, this ugly variation meets your needs. Begin far left of the regular start by scrambling into a large amphitheater, then traverse right past two bolts.

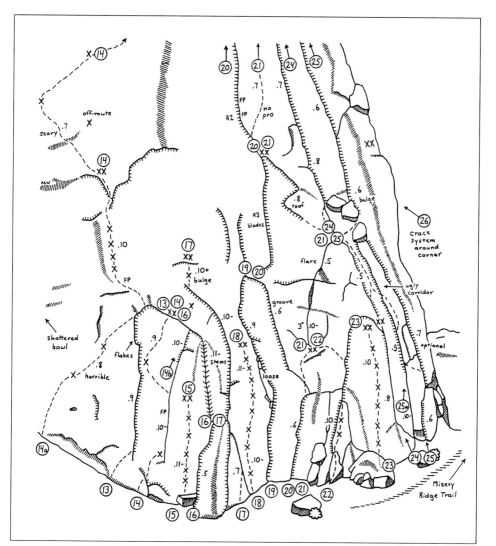

Red Wall – Right Side Base Routes

13. IRON CURTAIN 5.9 R ★★
14. HELTER SKELTER 5.10c R ★★
14a. VARIATION 5.8
14b. IF SIX WERE NINE 5.10b ★★
15. RIDE THE LIGHTNING 5.11b ★★★
16. CHAIRMAN MAO'S LITTLE RED
BOOK 5.11a ★★★
17. FINGERS OF FATE 5.10d ★★★
18. SOLE SURVIVOR 5.11b ★★★

19. GONE WITH THE FLAKE 5.9 ★
20. HO CHI MINH TRAIL 5.7 A3 R
21. SHANGHAI 5.10a X ★
22. CARTOON DEFICIENCY 5.10c ★
23. LET'S FACE IT 5.10b ★★★
24. PEKING 5.8 ★★
25. MOSCOW 5.6 ★★★
25a. MONGOLIANS 5.10b R ★★
26. HAVANA 5.6 ★

14b. IF SIX WERE NINE   5.10b ★★   Gear to 1 inch
A better-protected and more logical version of **Helter Skelter's** first pitch continues up the seam without veering left. A tricky sequence past a small roof ends at anchor bolts.

15. RIDE THE LIGHTNING   5.11b ★★★   Bolts
The original Red Wall sport climb follows a line of crimpers just left of a short inside corner. Closely-spaced bolts and good rock make this electrifying route popular.

16. CHAIRMAN MAO'S LITTLE RED BOOK   5.11a ★★★   Gear to 1 inch
For many years, this blank dihedral was the hardest route on Red Wall. Short but intense, **Mao's** ranks among Smith's best stemming sessions. The climbing favors those with well-developed calves.
1.   5.6   Stroll up a short, left-facing corner just right of **Ride the Lightning** to the base of the **Little Red Book.**
2.   5.11a   Jam and stem the polished dihedral, then traverse left to an anchor. Rappel with two ropes.

17. FINGERS OF FATE   5.10d ★★★   Gear to 2 inches
Despite an exhilarating finger crack on perfect rock, this line sees few ascents. The actual crux muscles a single, overhanging boulder move to the anchor.
1.   5.7   Start on the right side of a small buttress and climb a short, leaning crack to a ledge.
2.   5.10d   Step right, then jam the increasingly difficult, left-arching crack. Mantel to a jug and power over the bulge on creaky holds with a bolt at your chest. Rappel with two ropes.

18. SOLE SURVIVOR   5.11b ★★★   Bolts
This bolted wall makes a fine choice for face climbing connoisseurs. After a runout start, the level eases to a crux bulge just below the anchor.

19. GONE WITH THE FLAKE   5.9 ★   Gear to 4 inches
An ominous, left-leaning flake rises a few feet right of **Sole Survivor.** After an unnerving encounter with loose blocks midway up, disappear into a memorable bombay chimney crux. Rappel from a huge horn using two ropes.

20. HO CHI MINH TRAIL   5.7 A3 R   Gear to 2.5 inches
The most-neglected route on the entire wall nails an indistinct corner above **Gone with the Flake.** Perhaps someone will rescue the **Trail** from obscurity with a free ascent, but for now it sits forgotten. Starts a few feet right of **Gone with the Flake** below a short, right-leaning crack.
1.   5.6   Scramble up the easy crack, then climb a wide groove on the right side of a huge flake to an anchor.
2.   A3   Move right and nail an inside corner to a belay beneath the final slab.
3.   5.7 A2   Mixed aid and free climbing ascends the prominent right-facing dihedral. Cut right below the top to a belay spot.
4.   4th   Weave through boulders to the top.

21. SHANGHAI   5.10a X ★   Gear to 3 inches
First done by off-route climbers intent on nabbing a free ascent of **Ho Chi Minh Trail,** this lackluster route entices few attempts. A brilliant hand crack starts the second pitch, but the rest of the route is loose and runout.
1.   5.6   Start up the same crack as **Ho Chi Minh Trail,** but avoid the big flake by stepping right to an anchor on a slab.
2.   5.10a   Jam the clean, overhanging hand crack and make an awkward entrance into a slot. Scramble up a rotten corridor to a ledge.
3.   5.8   Ramble left to an undercling around an obvious roof and continue to a belay ledge.
4.   5.7   Follow the **Ho Chi Minh Trail** dihedral for a few feet, then traverse right onto an unprotected, dangerously loose death-slab. When possible, step right to a belay.

5. 4th   Easy scrambling leads to the top.

22.   CARTOON DEFICIENCY   5.10c ★   Gear to 1.5 inches
Just left of a short dihedral rises an insignificant, right-leaning corner above some broken boulders. Two inadequate quarter-inch bolts protect the crux, making the route far more serious than it need be. Above the corner, easy rock leads to a traverse left to anchor bolts.

23.   LET'S FACE IT   5.10b ★★★   Bolts
This excellent bolted wall rises left of a clean crack after the trail rounds a corner and starts uphill. A pleasant sequence of well-protected knobs and edges makes **Let's Face It** the best of its grade on Red Wall.

24.   PEKING   5.8 ★★   Gear to 2.5 inches
Perhaps this route should be modernized and renamed Beijing? The line follows the left of parallel crack systems splitting the right side of Red Wall. The start of the first pitch jams an elegant hand/finger crack to rappel anchors. The rest of the route doesn't match the quality of the opening stint, but it's worth doing.
1.   5.8   Hand traverse left to an attractive crack and jam perfect stone to an anchor. Rappel, or scramble on mediocre rock to a high ledge.
2.   5.8   A hard move over a bulge enters the prominent, left-facing dihedral. You'll need a 165-foot rope to reach the belay above the corner in one pitch.
3.   4th   Scramble to the top.

25.   MOSCOW   5.6 ★★★   Gear to 3.5 inches
The first line to the top of Red Wall followed the rightmost of the parallel crack systems. The solid rock, excellent protection and varied climbing makes a fine choice for climbers seeking a long entry-level route. Start below an obvious, blocky dihedral.
1.   5.6   Power up the steep starting corner on jugs, then either attack the clean open book above (5.7), or bypass it to the left. When possible, step left to avoid bad rock, and face climb to a ledge.
2.   5.6   Move right, then jam and stem the clean, left-facing dihedral to a belay ledge.
3.   5.6   Continue up the corner, following a low-angled wide crack to a belay above all difficulties.
4.   4th   Scramble to the top on easy rock.

25a. MONGOLIANS   5.10b R ★★   Gear to 1 inch
No one bothers with this preposterous start to **Moscow**. Begin a few feet left of the initial inside corner, and follow a surprisingly tricky seam before joining the regular line.

26.   HAVANA   5.6 ★   Gear to 2.5 inches
This rarely-climbed route wanders up an obscure crack system on the north face of Red Wall. Start uphill to the right of **Moscow** below an ugly trough and climb two pitches to the top.

Red Ryder Buttress

27. METAMORPHIC MANEUVERS 5.9 ★
28. I ALMOST DIED   5.11a ★★★
29. RED RYDER   5.8 R ★★
29a. FLEX   5.9 ★★★

30. THE YOUNG AND THE RESTLESS   5.9
     R ★
30a. THE YOUNG AND THE WORTHLESS
     5.7 X

RED RYDER BUTTRESS

A dismal buttress of reddish/purple rock rests high up the hill right of Red Wall. No route ascends the main face – with the exception of some solid stone low, the rock stinks. The high-quality base routes are worth visiting if you can tolerate the long slog up Misery Ridge. The first two routes rise above the trail as it cuts left along the base of the buttress.

27. METAMORPHIC MANEUVERS 5.9 R ★ Gear to 2 inches
When the trail first reaches the base of the main wall, you'll spot an insignificant, left-facing corner a few feet right. Start with some unprotected face moves, then climb great rock up the eight-foot corner. After a blocky exit, hike past a pin to an anchor.

28. I ALMOST DIED 5.11a ★★★ Gear to 2.5 inches
Immensely popular a few years back, few sport climbers weather the approach to this short, roof-capped corner. Despite a name suggesting otherwise, it ascends perfect rock on locking jams with great protection.

The next four routes ascend an appealing slab on the right side of the Red Ryder Buttress. Although mostly solid, these climbs are too runout for casual enjoyment. Approach the wall by stepping right off the Misery Ridge trail at the last switchback before the trail cuts left. Scramble to a ledge below the slab.

29. RED RYDER 5.8 R ★★ Gear to 1.5 inches
If you don't mind sparse protection, you'll enjoy this crafty thin face. Most climbers wisely lower from the first anchors instead of venturing onto the ugly upper pitch.
1. 5.8 Edge past two bolts on the left side of the wall to an anchor.
2. 5.7 Step left and grunge up a lousy crack to rappel anchors.

29a. FLEX 5.9 ★★★ Gear to .75 inch
An enjoyable variation jams a low-angled seam left of the regular start. A deceptively tricky sequence ends far too quickly at the first set of bolts.

30. THE YOUNG AND THE RESTLESS 5.9 R ★ Gear to 2.5 inches
If not for some loose flakes on the upper pitch, this route might be worth doing. The low-angled, runout first pitch makes a worthwhile jaunt in its own right.
1. 5.7 Start at the right side of the slab and climb lichen-covered knobs past a couple bolts to a ledge.
2. 5.9 Step left past a bolt on loose flakes and pull over two intimidating roofs. Continue traversing to the anchor atop **Red Ryder.**

30a. THE YOUNG AND THE WORTHLESS 5.7 X Gear to 3 inches
A really grotesque alternative to the upper pitch grovels directly up a crumbly crack system to the top of the cliff.

EASY'S PLAYHOUSE

A small, overhanging cliffband packed with powerful sport routes sits atop Red Wall. The athletic moves and closely-spaced bolts make the area a popular destination – despite the monster approach. East-facing and sitting high above the canyon, Easy's Playhouse makes a great summer afternoon trip. The easiest approach hikes to the top of Misery Ridge, cutting sharply left on a faint trail above the final staircase. Hike downhill, skirting a slab, until you spot the crag on your right. Since the cliff sits atop the gully separating Red Wall from Picnic Lunch Wall, any route topping-out nearby makes a painless approach if you hate walking uphill.

31. PROJECT 5.12 ?
    An unfinished route stretches between rounded holds on the right side of the crag. By the time you visit, it'll likely be a free climb.

32. BUGGING OUT 5.12d ★★★ Bolts
    The hardest line at Easy's Playhouse climbs a jungle gym of good holds right of an obvious dihedral. The crux muscles an awkward pull entering and exiting a sloping flare.

33. BOYS IN THE HOOD 5.11d ★★★★ Bolts
    This brawny line rises immediately left of a steep inside corner. A relentless series of jugs on perfect rock ends quickly at an anchor.

33a. ADAM SPLITTER 5.12c ★★ TR
    This toprope problem powers past some dirty pockets just left of **Boys in the Hood.**

34. BIG BOSS MAN 5.12a ★★★ Bolts
    Essentially a roof, this pull-up contest unfortunately lacks a start. Most climbers just hoist themselves to the initial holds, but it's possible to start legitimately with a traverse from jugs on the right.

35. STRAIGHT OUT OF MADRAS 5.12c ★★★ Bolts
    The left route cranks an athletic series of jugs, and underclings. As with **Big Boss Man**, the undercut cave lacks a decent start, although a free variant grovels in from the left.

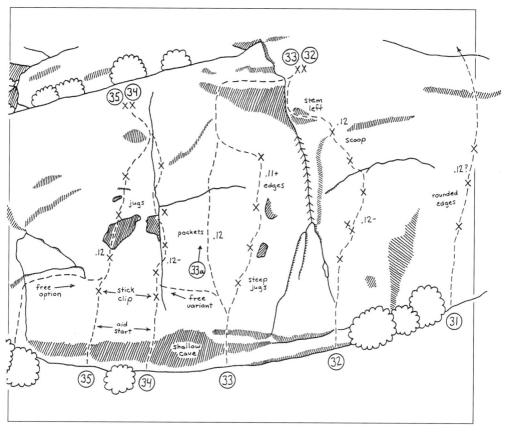

Easy's Playhouse

31. PROJECT 5.12 ?
32. BUGGING OUT 5.12d ★★★
33. BOYS IN THE HOOD 5.11d ★★★★
33a. ADAM SPLITTER 5.12c ★★

34. BIG BOSS MAN 5.12a ★★★
35. STRAIGHT OUT OF MADRAS 5.12c ★★★

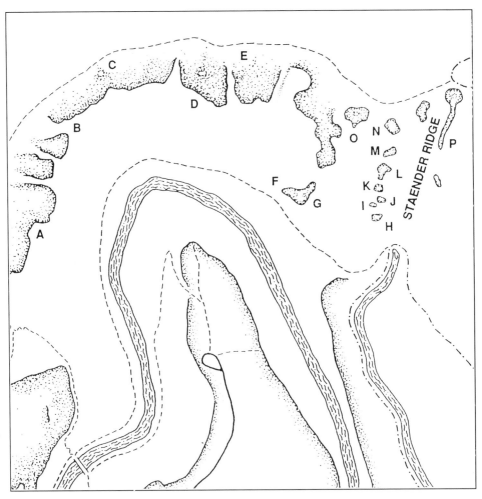

A. Cajun Cliff
B. London Tower
C. Little Three Fingered Jack
D. The Monument
E. Osa Thatcher's Needle
F. Liberty Bell
G. Juniper Spire
H. Adit Rock

I. Control Tower
J. Independence Tower
K. The Mole
L. Bette's Needles
M. Flattop
N. Staender Ridge
O. French Tent Rock
P. The Dinosaur

THE MONUMENT
AREA AND
STAENDER RIDGE

A HUGE ARRAY of impressive faces and spires, curving around a bend in the Crooked River, lies upstream right of Red Wall. Despite their rugged beauty, rotten bands split most of these walls, making them totally unsuitable for climbing. Fortunately, lurking amid the garbage are some true gems. Staender Ridge not only offers some great routes, but it sends you back in Smith history. You'll rarely see another soul, and can marvel over ancient bolts with tin-foil hangers.

The rock beyond Red Wall degenerates quickly into a series of crumbly gullies and unappetizing faces. The solid Cajun Cliff is the only worthwhile section of rock in this large expanse. Shortly before the bend in the river, the faces grow more impressive, with the striking wall of Little Three Fingered Jack and the 600-foot south face of the Monument rising above. Further upstream, the rock again worsens as the imposing faces give way to ugly gullies and shattered rhyolite plugs. Just after the river finishes its 180-degree turn, the pinnacles of Staender Ridge rise neatly one after another just left of the switchbacked Burma Road.

In the early years, this was the best place to sample Smith climbing. For decades, access to Smith Rock was via the Burma Road. Apparently, old-timers hated long approaches as much as we do today, as the spires nearest the parking lot received most of the attention. The pioneers pitched their tents at the old climbers' camp, nestled among some pines at the northern bend of the Crooked River. Eventually, locked gates blocked the Burma Road access, cutting the routes off from the masses. Today, these rarely-climbed relics of Smith's early days are almost totally ignored.

The approach hikes vary from 15 minutes for the Cajun Cliff to 40 minutes to the top of Staender Ridge. A much quicker approach during low-water conditions fords the river below the Northern Point. For this approach, drive to the turnaround parking area and walk north through the rimrock.

CAJUN CLIFF
A huge amount of non-descript, horrible rock rests to the right of Red Ryder Buttress. Surprisingly, in the middle of this squalor rises a section of clean stone called the Cajun Cliff. The following two routes are worth doing, and make a fine change of pace from the regular circuit. Approach by walking right along the river from the bridge about one-half mile to a massive pine tree. Hike a short scree slope up to the base of the light-colored crag.

1. DEFINITELY CAJUN 5.12a ★★★ Bolts
   This challenging line climbs a vertical arête on the left part of the wall. The spicy crux sequence finesses some strenuous side pulls past the second bolt, and is followed by pumping edges.

2. PLEASURE PRINCIPLE 5.10d ★★ Bolts
   A bolted thin face rises a few feet right of **Definitely Cajun**. With each ascent the rock quality improves, as friable edges continually crumble away.

The next two routes are located beyond Cajun Cliff.

3. LONDON TOWER   5.10a R   Gear to 4 inches
    Beyond the Cajun Cliff, gullies split several unappealing hunks of stone. London Tower, with its obvious crack system rises immediately right of the last gully. After two dreary pitches, the crux steps delicately up a series of edges entering the obvious flare.

4. DEAD BABY BUBBAS   5.10a ★   Gear to 2 inches
    A nameless monolith, split by ominous cracks, lurks right of London Tower. Just right of this face sits a short, south-facing thin crack that ends after 40 forgettable feet.

LITTLE THREE FINGERED JACK

The river face of Little Three Fingered Jack is the most stunning section of rock between Red Wall and the Monument. The summit spires themselves are unimpressive, but the right-leaning corner of the 350-foot main face catches the eye.

5. NORTHWEST RIDGE   3rd class ★
    The easiest route to the highest finger involves a simple scramble along the backside ridge. To approach this blob, hike up a gully left of the Monument and skirt behind the cliff line.

    CHOCKSTONE CHIMNEY   4th class ★   Gear to 3 inches
    A slightly-more difficult route drops left from the summit ridge, finishing with a short, chockstone-plugged chimney.

Photo: Bruce Adams

Cajun Cliff, London Tower and Little Three Fingered Jack

1. DEFINITELY CAJUN   5.12a ★★★
2. PLEASURE PRINCIPLE   5.10d ★★
3. LONDON TOWER   5.10a R
4. DEAD BABY BUBBAS   5.10a ★
6. HOWL   5.12a R ★★
7. VICTORY OF THE PROLETARIAN PEOPLE'S AMBITION ARETE   5.7 X
8. BRUCE'S TRAVERSE   5.7 X ★

6. HOWL   5.12a R ★★   Bolts
    This intellectual edge slaps past several bolts to an anchor. Despite stimulating climbing, no one bothers because the moves to the third bolt are dangerously runout.

7. VICTORY OF THE PROLETARIAN PEOPLE'S AMBITION ARETE   5.7 X   Gear to 2.5 inches
    This so-called "route for the common man" is anything but that. The horrible rock, poor protection and repugnant climbing will turn a pleasant day into an ordeal. Start below a ramp on the left side of Little Three Fingered Jack's main face.
    1. 5.7   Climb the ramp on dicey rock to belay bolts.
    2. 5.7   Ascend the mangy crack above, trying to avoid the inevitable stone fall.

8. BRUCE'S TRAVERSE   5.7 X ★   Gear to 2.5 inches
    At the time of the first ascent, this obscure route was Smith's longest free climb. Start by scrambling into the gully right of the main face, then climb an unprotected slab to a crack system. After a belay, the upper pitch cuts across the prominent, left-leaning slash to the base of the summit spire.

9. A LITTLE SEDUCTION   5.12a ★★★   Bolts
    Two unclimbed walls rise between Little Three Fingered Jack and The Monument. At the right end of these cliffs, just before the Monument gully, sits a detached rib of rock with an overhanging face. Highly recommended, the remarkably polished and solid stone makes the route unlike any other at Smith.

THE MONUMENT

This beautiful tower is a Smith Rock landmark. The awesome six hundred foot south face rivals Picnic Lunch Wall for the title of Smith's biggest wall. Unfortunately, bands of miserable rock cut across the face, turning every route on the main wall into an epic.

10. THE NORTH RIDGE   4th Class ★★   Gear to 3 inches
     The back side of the Monument offers a simple scramble to the summit. Walk up the 2nd-class gully to the left of the tower, then hike the north ridge, dropping right to a moderate chimney.

10a. NORTH RIDGE DIRECT   5.2 ★★★   No gear
     A better, but unprotected line to the summit heads up the crest of the north ridge to some fun moves on a solid, pocketed wall.

11. ABRAXAS   5.11a A0 R ★   Gear to 3.5 inches (double Friends, wires)
     This imposing route takes a direct line up the Monument's southwest face. Sadly, poor rock and funky protection plague several pitches, keeping everyone away. The climb nearly goes free, with only a few hangs on the crux pitch. The highlight is the Tombstone Wall. This gently overhanging hand crack jams flawless rock with a breathtaking position. Some climbers ignore the lower pitches and make two, double-rope rappels from the top to take a crack at this gorgeous pitch.

     1. 5.6   Start in huge potholes and diagonal right to an anchor.
     2. 5.10d   Step right into a chimney. Climb deplorable rock past quarter-inch bolts, then hand traverse left to an anchor. Belay here, or continue up miserable seams to a pedestal.
     3. 5.11a A0   A long pitch of mixed aid and free climbing leads up a seam past several shaky bolts to an alcove.
     4. 5.10d   Step right and jam the spectacular Tombstone Wall in one long pitch to an anchor.
     5. 5.5   An easy ramp ends on top.

THE
MONUMENT
OSA THATCHER'S
NEEDLE
LITTLE
THREE FINGERED JACK
16
17
8
9
11
12
14 13

Photo: Bruce Adams

The Monument and Osa Thatcher's Needle

8. BRUCE'S TRAVERSE 5.7 X ★
9. A LITTLE SEDUCTION 5.12a ★★★
11. ABRAXAS 5.11a A0 R ★
12. SANDS OF TIME 5.7 A4 R

13. SOUTHEAST FACE 5.7 A3 X
14. PROJECT 5.12 ?
16. BIRD DUNG CHIMNEY 5.4 X
17. DECEPTION CRACK 5.10a ★

12. SANDS OF TIME 5.7 A4 R Aid rack to 3 inches
First climbed in a multi-day solo effort, this route aids the prominent crack system right of **Abraxas**. Despite some stretches of good rock, there's enough garbage to ensure eternal obscurity.

13. SOUTHEAST FACE 5.7 A3 X Gear to 3.5 inches
Perhaps Smith's worst route, this impressive wall is best appreciated through binoculars. The climb begins in a deep chimney on the right side of the wall and wanders up several dangerous pitches to the top. The cadaverous rock, grisly protection and gruesome anchors are the stuff of nightmares. A climber died here in the early 70s, so take this warning seriously.

14. PROJECT 5.12 ?
A smooth slab rises just left of the Southeast Face's starting chimney. The route saw some toprope attempts in the late 80s, but now sits abandoned.

OSA THATCHER'S NEEDLE

A large, unnamed formation reeking of bad rock is immediately right of The Monument. The slender spire of Osa Thatcher's Needle clings precariously to the left side of the buttress.

15. OSA THATCHER'S NEEDLE 5.7 X No gear
Starting on the backside of the formation minimizes the bad rock, but it's still a harrowing experience. Hike up the easy gully right of the Monument and make a complicated 4th-class scramble to a notch. A quick stint on bad rock protected by an ancient peg ends on the anchorless summit.

16. BIRD DUNG CHIMNEY 5.4 X Gear to 4 inches
One look should you change your mind if you somehow develop an interest in this trash pile. Climb the obvious chimney joining the backside route. This is midway up the gully right of The Monument.

17. DECEPTION CRACK 5.10a ★ Gear to 3 inches
This prominent crack separates Osa Thatcher's Needle from its parent cliff. Walk up the gully east of The Monument and wade through bad rock to the base of a thin crack. Jam to a belay in a chimney, then scramble off the backside.

18. BRAIN SALAD SURGERY 5.11a ★★★ Gear to 6 inches
Several gully-split rubble cliffs are right of The Monument. Remarkably, this stunningly solid gem rises amidst some of the worst rock on Earth. The bizarre crux liebacks and underclings the leaning off-width into a flaring slot. To find it, hike up the third gully right of The Monument and look for the unmistakable wide crack on the left side of the ravine.

19. STREET WALKER 5.6 Gear to 3 inches
This sordid, left-leaning crack sits just downhill from **Brain Salad Surgery**. A cheap pitch ends atop the ridge. To get off, scramble uphill on easy rock.

LIBERTY BELL/JUNIPER SPIRE COMPLEX

The trail curves around the bend in the Crooked River past The Monument. On the right is the old climbers' camp. The spires of Liberty Bell and Juniper Spire tower just above the path on the left.

Liberty Bell

This dark, double-peaked lump sits a few feet west of the slender spike of Juniper Spire. The upper portion of Liberty Bell is solid, but bad rock guards the lower reaches.

20. JUNIPER GULLY 5.6 A1 X ★ Gear to 2.5 inches
Scramble up the scree slope above the trail to the base of the gully separating Liberty Bell from Juniper Spire. Climb so-so rock past an anchor to a notch below the summit. An ancient aid bolt leads to an unprotected arête ending on the lower summit. It would easily go free, but the bolt might not hold a fall.

21. LIBERTY BELL CHIMNEY 5.5 X ★ Gear to 2.5 inches
The original route to the highest summit of Liberty Bell stems the wide chimney on the uphill side of the crag. A crux pull over a chockstone followed by a squeeze through a hole ends on the shattered summit. There's no suitable anchor on top, so downclimb to a rappel horn.

Photo: Alan Watts

Liberty Bell and Juniper Spire

20. JUNIPER GULLY 5.6 A1 X ★
22. THE EAR 5.7 R ★
23. THE PRODUCT 5.13a ★★★★

24. PROJECT 5.13 ?
25. JAMBOREE 5.8 ★★
26. RIB TRAVERSE 5.6 X ★★★

Juniper Spire

This distinctive, willowy tower, with its gorgeous south face, rises immediately right of Liberty Bell. All routes to the top rappel with double ropes down the overhanging south wall.

22. THE EAR   5.7 R ★   Gear to 2.5 inches
    Start on the downhill side and climb the trough between Liberty Bell and Juniper Spire to a single bolt at the notch. The unnerving crux pitch climbs a delicate arête on the right, passing behind a small "ear" to a finishing crack. Simple scrambling along the summit ridge leads to the top.

22a. VARIATION   5.4   Gear to 3 inches
    If the ear pitch seems too scary, you can escape right with an easy finish up a shattered chimney.

23. THE PRODUCT   5.13a ★★★★   Bolts
    This exquisite arête on Juniper Spire's south face rises far off the beaten path. Split with good shakes, **The Product** finesses an endless series of intricate moves to a powerful finish up a diagonal crack. Despite the closely-spaced bolts, perfect rock and cerebral moves, the route sees few attempts since it sits so far from Smith's free-climbing arena.

24. PROJECT   5.13 ?
    The right arête of Juniper Spire's south face will someday yield another amazing route. Some of the moves already go free on toprope.

25. JAMBOREE   5.8 ★★   Gear to 2 inches
    A crack in a shallow corner separates the southeast side of Juniper Spire from the connecting rib to the right. A flurry of jams and stems on decent rock ends on the backside arête. Either follow the ridge to the top, or walk off.

26. RIB TRAVERSE   5.6 X ★★★   Gear to 2.5 inches
    The easiest route to the summit scrambles along a rib on the uphill side of the tower. After weaving past several gendarmes on great rock, climb to the appealing summit. Rappel off the south face using two ropes.

STAENDER RIDGE

Rising above the irrigation tunnel left of the Burma Road is a row of pinnacles known as Staender Ridge. From bottom to top, Adit Rock, Control Tower, Independence Tower, the Mole, Bette's Needles, Flattop and Staender Summit sit neatly along the crest of the ridge. Once popular, these spires receive little attention today, despite some high-quality routes. For the climber looking for easy 5th-class lines, Staender Ridge offers the best selection in the park. If you shy away from crowds, you might enjoy sampling Smith's early history in these alpine surroundings.

The main reason why Staender Ridge sees so little activity is the long, uphill slog. The hike varies from 25 to 40 minutes, depending on how far you venture up the ridge. To approach, follow the trail right from the bridge, embarking on a mile-long jaunt around the northern bend of the river. After passing below Juniper Spire, the path heads uphill to the canal tunnel at the Burma Road's first switchback. An indistinct trail cuts up the ridge, along the east side of the spires.

Adit Rock

Closest to the canal sits this blob of great rock. A chimney splits the crag into two portions – a downhill chunk containing most of the routes, and a rounded uphill piece offering limited potential. To reach the top, either stem a short chimney or scramble up the backside (both grade 3).

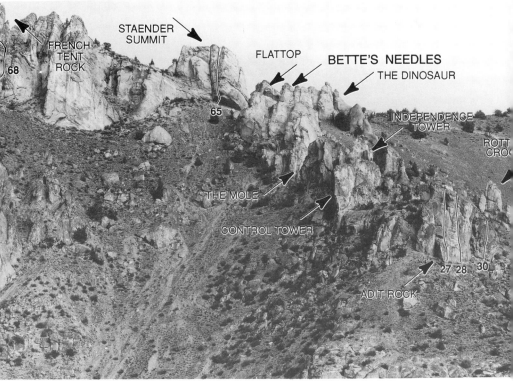

Photo: Bruce Adams

Staender Ridge

27. INSTANT REPLAY 5.6 ★★★
28. PARKING LOT CRACK 5.8 ★★
30. MUNCHKIN LAND 5.7 ★★

65. SMUT 5.12c/d ★★★
68. SOUTH BOWL 5.5 X

27. INSTANT REPLAY 5.6 ★★★   Gear to 1.5 inches
    The leftmost of the parallel cracks on the downhill face starts behind a leaning pillar. A fine
    beginner's route, **Instant Replay** jams solid rock with good protection.

28. PARKING LOT CRACK 5.8 ★★   Gear to 4 inches
    The rightmost of Adit Rock's parallel cracks was once the closest route to the old parking area. If
    you aren't up for the finishing off-width, escape right on easy face holds.

29. PROJECT 5.12 ?
    The attractive, southeast arête rises just left of a short arch. A bouldery start opens what promises
    to be a top-notch sequence on perfect rock.

30. MUNCHKIN LAND 5.7 ★★   Gear to 2 inches
    This miniature leaning corner arches across the right side of Adit Rock. Unless you're a
    munchkin, you'll need only make a couple moves to reach the anchor.

31. LOLLYPOP LEAGUE 5.5 X ★★★★   No gear
    This detached pillar balances against the right side of Adit Rock. A wonderful, but totally
    unprotected series of pockets and edges lead up the face to an anchor. If bolted, it would be a
    perfect first lead.

32. ORANGE PLANET 5.12 ? Project
    The only prospect on the bulbous uphill block of Adit Rock follows a rounded arête just right of
    a chimney. A single bolt right off the deck tempts any sport climber walking by.
Two unnamed 15-foot pillars are uphill from Adit Rock. You can reach the top of either spire with a
quick, 4th-class move. Next in line are two pinnacles, Control Tower on the left, and Independence
Tower on the right.

Control Tower

A prominent, wavy crack splits the south side of this small pinnacle. The backside offers a simple, 3rd-
class scramble, while the longer west face contains the following route:

33. OUT OF CONTROL 5.10c ★★ Gear to 2.5 inches
    This strenuous climb ascends a leaning crack above a bolt on Control Tower's bulging west side.
    The moves are deceptively taxing, as more than one leader has lost control in the pumping crack
    above the crux.

Independence Tower

This chunk, capped by a slender pillar, rises a few feet uphill from Control Tower. The most obvious
feature is a huge dihedral on the west face.

34. FREE SPIRIT 5.8 ★★ Gear to 2 inches
    This appealing line jams good rock up a thin crack on the southwest corner of the spire. To reach
    the base, scramble down a crumbly, 3rd-class gully between Independence Tower and Control
    Tower.

35. SCOOP ROUTE 5.4 X ★ Gear to 2 inches
    This is a simple route that follows the path of least resistance up the south side.

36. MIDNIGHT RIDER 5.10a R ★ Gear to 1 inch
    This mediocre climb follows a direct line up the south face of the tower. Start just left of the east
    corner, then face climb on unprotected holds to a large ledge. A tricky boulder move up a
    miserable seam pulls onto the summit.

37. NORTH SIDE 5.5 ★★★ Gear to 2 inches
    The original route to the top scrambles up solid rock on the uphill face. The hardest moves are
    right off the ground.

38. D.A.R. CRACK 5.10a ★★ Gear to 4 inches
    An attractive, right-facing dihedral splits the west side of Independence Tower. **Daughters of the
    American Revolution Crack** climbs tolerable rock up this corner, then liebacks a finishing off-
    width.

The Mole

The rounded Mole sits next in line above Independence Tower. Despite its humble stature, this block
contains several routes on great rock.

39. SUNJAMMER 5.10b ★★★ Gear to 1 inch
    Stimulating finger jams on perfect rock highlight this jaunt up an overhanging dihedral. Start at
    the notch between Independence Tower and the Mole, and step over to the base of the corner.

40. SOUTH FACE 5.6 X ★ Gear to 2.5 inches
    A simple, but run-out line starts off a boulder and climbs face holds up the southeast side of the
    block. To finish, traverse right to a short hand crack above **Chopper.**

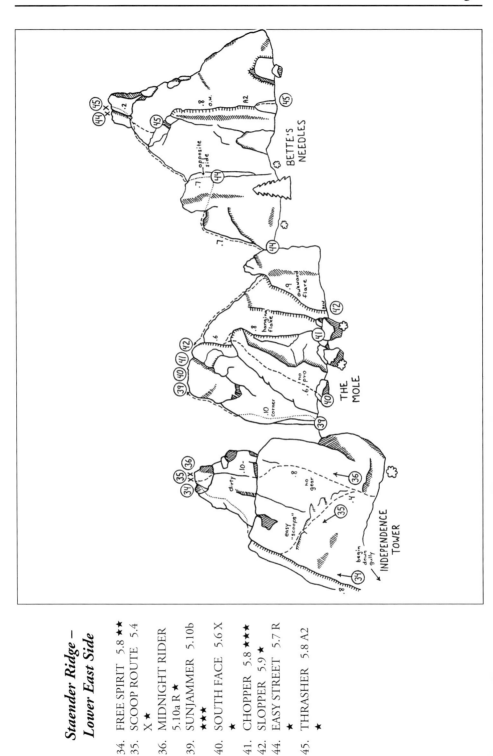

Staender Ridge –
Lower East Side

34. FREE SPIRIT 5.8 ★★
35. SCOOP ROUTE 5.4
    X ★
36. MIDNIGHT RIDER
    5.10a R ★
39. SUNJAMMER 5.10b
    ★★★
40. SOUTH FACE 5.6 X
    ★
41. CHOPPER 5.8 ★★★
42. SLOPPER 5.9 ★
44. EASY STREET 5.7 R
    ★
45. THRASHER 5.8 A2
    ★

41. CHOPPER 5.8 ★★★ Gear to 2.5 inches
A striking corner plugged with a razor-edged flake splits the east side of the Mole. Despite enjoyable moves, the detached pillar might dissuade you – you'd get the chop if it pulled off.

42. SLOPPER 5.9 ★ Gear to 1 inch
This silly, right-leaning arch is immediately right of **Chopper**. Despite some solid rock, the moves are awkward and unrewarding.

43. NORTH RAMP 4th class ★★
The easiest route to the top follows a short 4th-class ramp on the uphill side, then face climbs on low-angled holds.

43a. VARIATION 5.0 ★★ Gear to 3 inches
A simple alternative to the **North Ramp** begins a few feet left and marches up a short, flaring crack to the top.

43b. SILLY CRACK 5.8 ★★ Gear to 2.5 inches
A short crack splitting a bulge rises on the lower reaches of the Mole's north side. Some thin hand jams lead to easy scrambling.

Bette's Needles

The largest, and most spectacular of the Staender Ridge towers rises uphill from The Mole. The 150-foot south face looms impressively above the trail. The rock isn't as solid as nearby spires, but it's the best summit of them all.

44. EASY STREET 5.7 R ★ Gear to 3 inches
This circuitous route winds along the south arête of Bette's Needles. Start just left of the ridge, below double seams.
1. 5.7 Climb a short pitch up the low-angled crack, and traverse a big ledge along the west face to a chimney.
2. 5.7 A short, overhanging slot up double cracks ends on the south arête. Romp up simple rock to the top.

45. THRASHER 5.8 A2 ★ Gear to 6 inches
A prominent, right-facing open book splits the south face of Bette's Needles. The starting corner would go free, but the rock and protection are bad.
1. 5.8 A2 A short section of nailing leads into a grotesque off-width. Thrash to a good belay ledge.
2. 5.2 Scramble up the south face to the top.

46. LIMESTONE CHIMNEY 5.2 ★★ Gear to 1 inch
The easiest route to the summit follows a simple chimney system on the uphill side of the tower.

46a. VARIATION 5.6 ★ Gear to 2 inches
A more challenging variant climbs an inside corner slightly right of the regular line.

47. JUNIPER SNAG 5.6 R ★★ Gear to 2.5 inches
The best route on Bette's Needles ascends a series of corners up the west face. Start at a gnarled juniper snag halfway down the western base of the spire.
1. 5.6 A thin face move up a shallow groove gains a scree-covered ledge. Climb a tight open book to a belay spot.
2. 5.5 Jam the double cracks up a steep, flaring chimney to a ledge, then scamper to the top.

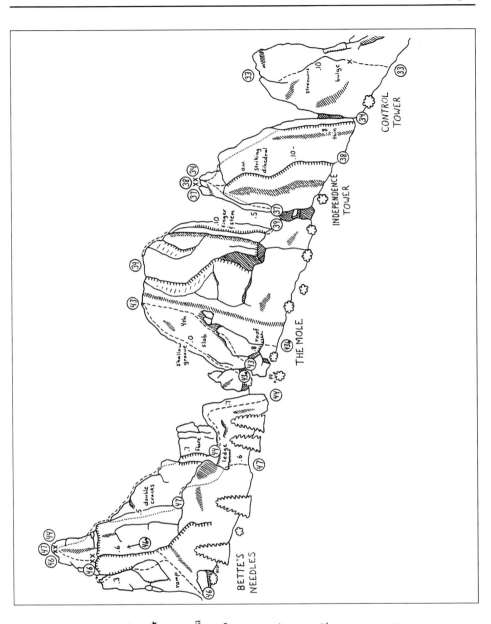

Staender Ridge –
Lower West Side

33. OUT OF CONTROL
    5.10c ★★

34. FREE SPIRIT 5.8 ★★
    ★★★

37. NORTH SIDE 5.5

38. D.A.R. CRACK 5.10a
    ★★

39. SUNJAMMER 5.10b
    ★★★

43. NORTH RAMP 4th
    class ★★

43a. VARIATION 5.0 ★★

43b. SILLY CRACK 5.8
     ★★

44. EASY STREET 5.7 R
    ★

46. LIMESTONE
    CHIMNEY 5.2 ★★

46a. VARIATION 5.6 ★

47. JUNIPER SNAG 5.6
    R ★★

Flattop

This aptly-named, square-cut block rests next in line above Bette's Needles. Adorned with ten routes, it's the most developed on Staender Ridge. The westside routes are extremely short; the east wall offers some longer climbs. The actual summit sits atop the north side of a flat plateau. Overhanging on all sides, this bulbous, ten-foot pillar can be climbed by any of three routes up the northwest, west, and southeast sides (5.5 to 5.7). Most climbers crank the boulder move once, then settle for the summit plateau on future ascents.

48. EAST CHIMNEY 5.4 X ★★★ Gear to 1 inch
    Surprisingly, this dismal-looking chimney is one of Smith's finest. Start up a zig-zag ledge below the east side and stem to the flat bench below the summit block.

49. SKID ROW 5.7 ★ Gear to 2 inches
    Worse than the average Flattop route, **Skid Row** follows a left-facing dihedral up the east side. Start atop a smooth block below a corner and climb one mediocre pitch to the top.

50. LOST FOX 5.9 ★★★ Gear to 2.5 inches
    Highly recommended, this appealing crack splits Flattop's east buttress. Start below a short left-facing corner, then jam the solid 5.8 crack. The actual crux finesses a bolted boulder move just below the summit block.

51. BUMP AND GRIND 5.9 ★★ Gear to 6 inches
    This off-width in a right-facing corner lurks on the uphill side of Flattop's east face. Lieback and stem solid rock up the 5.7 crack, then cut left to the same bouldering crux as **Lost Fox**.

52. DELIVERANCE 5.9 ★ TR
    This unlikely line up the northwest side was first toproped by someone desperate for something new. After pulling atop a starting block, make some tricky face moves on small edges to the top.

53. DIRECT NORTHWEST CRACK 5.4 ★★ Gear to 2 inches
    This comically short route climbs the left of parallel cracks on the west face. Below the summit block, cut either left or right to the top.

54. LIEBACK FLAKE 5.4 ★ Gear to 2 inches
    Neither a lieback nor a flake, this block-plugged corner splits the center of Flattop's pint-sized west face.

55. PRUNE FACE 5.7 ★★ Bolts
    This rare, bolted Staender Ridge route follows good knobs to the summit plateau.

56. LOWER WEST CHIMNEY 5.7 R ★ Gear to 3 inches
    This counterpart to the East Chimney climbs the opposite side of the same slot. An annoyingly tricky entrance gains the simple, unprotected chimney.

57. SOUTH BUTTRESS 5.3 X ★★★ Gear to 1 inch
    Essentially a free solo, this enjoyable route storms the pint-sized south buttress. A quick traverse right along a ledge leads to fun knobs and the summit shelf.

Staender Summit

This large chunk of stone, with its undercut roof along the southwest side, caps Staender Ridge. A variety of routes ascend the many cracks splitting every side of the block. There's no anchor on top, so you'll have to scramble down the simple North Chimney.

58. PEANUTS 5.8 ★★ Gear to 2.5 inches
    The left of several crack lines on Staender Summit's east side jams great rock up an opening flare. Finish with a left-facing corner.

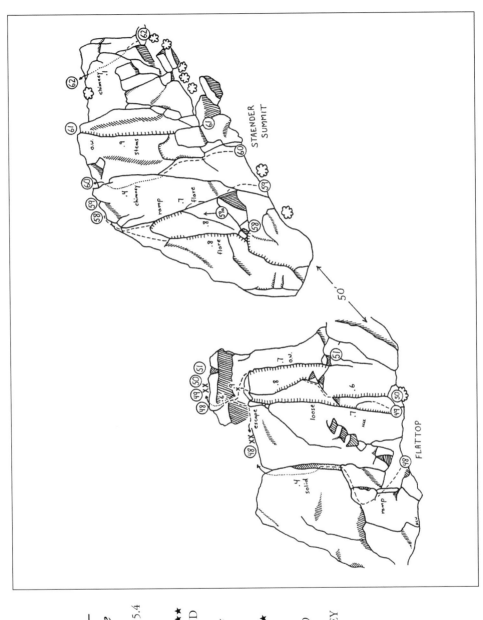

Staender Ridge –
Upper East Side

48. EAST CHIMNEY 5.4
     X ★★★
49. SKID ROW 5.7 ★
50. LOST FOX 5.9 ★★★
51. BUMP AND GRIND
     5.9 ★★
58. PEANUTS 5.8 ★★
59. DEFECATION
     CRACK 5.7 ★★
59a. NUT CASE 5.8 ★★
60. EAST SIDE
     CHIMNEY 5.4 ★
61. DESIDERATA 5.9
     ★★
62. NORTH CHIMNEY
     5.1 ★★

59. DEFECATION CRACK 5.7 ★★ Gear to 2.5 inches
Better than the name implies, **Defecation Crack** climbs a short flare to a left-leaning ramp.

59a. NUT CASE 5.8 ★★ Gear to 2.5 inches
A pleasant start to Defecation Crack jams good rock up a right-leaning crack to the finishing ramp.

60. EAST SIDE CHIMNEY 5.4 ★ Gear to 3 inches
A mediocre slot splits the upper part of Staender Summit's east wall. While no classic, at least the double cracks protect easily.

61. DESIDERATA 5.9 ★★★ Gear to 3.5 inches
This attractive dihedral dominates the east side of the crag. Don't let the awkward off-width move at the top scare you away from sampling this stemming treat.

62. NORTH CHIMNEY 5.1 ★★ Gear to 2.5 inches
The original route to the top of Staender Summit follows a short groove on the uphill side of the block.

63. NORTHWEST CORNER 5.3 ★★ Gear to 3 inches
A short hand crack on the tiny north face of Staender Summit follows the right side of a pillar.

63a. WEST LEDGES 5.1 ★ Gear to 3 inches
A simple alternative foot-shuffles right to a huge ledge system just below the summit.

64. FALLING ROCK ZONE 5.6 R Gear to 3 inches
A repugnant, flaring chimney rises a few feet left of **Smut**. If the sight of this slot doesn't scare you away, then flail up an abominable pitch to the top.

65. SMUT 5.12c/d ★★★ Gear to 1 inch (Rocks, #1 Friend)
This finger-crack roof is the best-known route on Staender Ridge. Most climbers bypass terrible jams at the crux start by piling cheater stones high enough to reach the first decent slots. A rocky landing makes a tempting solo a risky gamble. Ignore the junky, 5.6 finish by lowering off anchor bolts.

66. AFFLICTION 5.6 A4 R ★ Aid rack (bring a crash pad)
If you enjoy bashing pins risking a certain ground fall, then you'll love this ludicrous aid route. Start just right of **Smut** and nail a faint roof seam into a scoop. Easy, unprotected face climbing leads to the top.

French Tent Rock (a.k.a. No Name)

This multi-peaked spire sits across the gully to the left of Staender Summit. A short, third-class scramble polishes off the highest summit, but the slender pillar to the west offers the only real climbing.

67. NORTH LEDGE 5.6 R ★ Gear to 2 inches
The only sensible route to the top of French Tent Rock starts on the backside of the spire. After liebacking a short, left-facing corner above a ledge, follow the easy west ridge to the summit anchors.

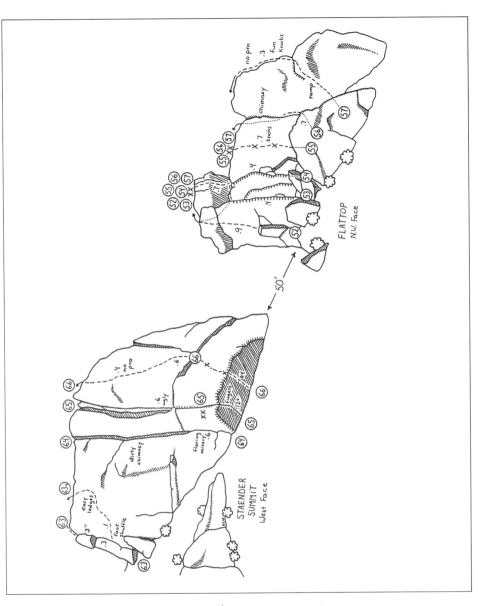

Staender Ridge – Upper West Side

52. DELIVERANCE 5.9 ★

53. DIRECT NORTHWEST CRACK 5.4 ★★

54. LIEBACK FLAKE 5.4 ★

55. PRUNE FACE 5.7 ★★

56. LOWER WEST CHIMNEY 5.7 R ★

57. SOUTH BUTTRESS 5.3 X ★★★

63. NORTHWEST CORNER 5.3 ★★

63a. WEST LEDGES 5.1 ★

64. FALLING ROCK ZONE 5.6 R

65. SMUT 5.12c/d ★★★

66. AFFLICTION 5.6 A4 R ★

68. SOUTH BOWL 5.5 X Gear to 2.5 inches
    This harrowing line has absolutely nothing going for it. You'll find the route by circling below the North Ledge to the south face. After a short scramble, climb an obvious flare on some of Smith's worst rock to an unexposed bowl. To finish, cut left to the summit ridge.

Rotten Crack
An isolated pinnacle lurks right of Staender Ridge about midway up the hillside. The following routes are certain to haunt anyone foolish enough to try.

69. ROTTEN CRACK 5.8 X Gear to 1 inch
    The original route to the summit follows a lousy seam on the west side of the tower. Either follow a direct line up a wide crack, or step in from the backside, and make some poorly-protected moves to the top.

70. FRICTION ARETE 5.4 X No gear
    This terrible route tempts fate by climbing boldly up the downhill arête. The repulsive rock makes it a serious gamble.

The Dinosaur
This unusual formation sits above Rotten Crack and just left of the crest of the Burma Road. Split into two distinct segments, the upper part is a small pinnacle, while the low-angled slab of the Dinosaur's tail extends far downhill. A 5.2 route scrambles up the backside to the highest point.

71. ORANGE PEEL 5.6 X Bolts (bring quarter-inch hangers)
    A lousy route that climbs a low-angled slab on the west side of the Dinosaur's tail. Start just uphill from the lowest of several juniper trees, and traverse right into a scoop. A few friction moves lead past hangerless bolts to an easy scramble along the top of the ridge. Ignore the upper pinnacle by hiking down a simple groove.

72. LEMON PEEL 5.8 X ★ Bolts
    This holdless slab rises about 20 feet uphill from **Orange Peel,** behind a second juniper tree. Smear past two bolts to a meandering crack leading to the crest of the ridge. Downclimb an easy groove.

73. BROWN COW 5.6 X Gear to 3 inches
    A grotesque chimney splits the south side of the Dinosaur's upper pinnacle. A harrowing pitch on bad rock ends on top.

74. COW PIE 5.6 X Gear to 1 inch
    The west face of the Dinosaur's upper segment offers a second ugly chimney to the summit. Enter the slot with a face move to the left, and wallow up a low-angled, sparsely-protected groove.

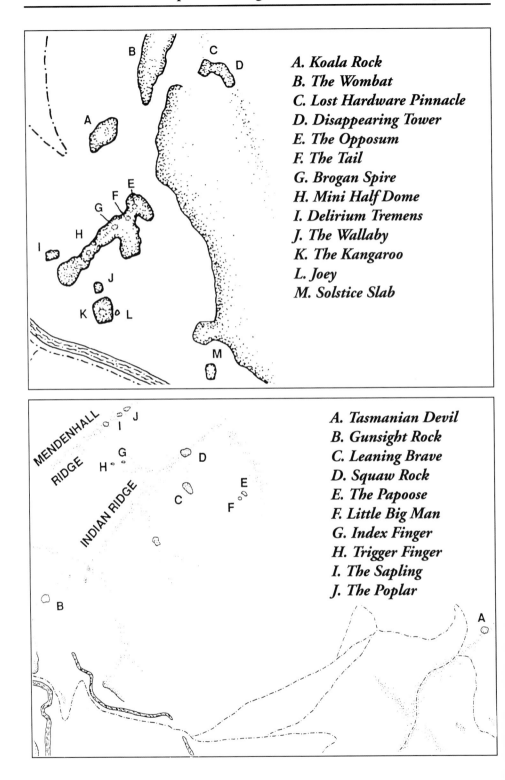

A. Koala Rock
B. The Wombat
C. Lost Hardware Pinnacle
D. Disappearing Tower
E. The Opposum
F. The Tail
G. Brogan Spire
H. Mini Half Dome
I. Delirium Tremens
J. The Wallaby
K. The Kangaroo
L. Joey
M. Solstice Slab

A. Tasmanian Devil
B. Gunsight Rock
C. Leaning Brave
D. Squaw Rock
E. The Papoose
F. Little Big Man
G. Index Finger
H. Trigger Finger
I. The Sapling
J. The Poplar

MENDENHALL RIDGE

INDIAN RIDGE

THE MARSUPIAL CRAGS & SURROUNDING AREAS

FAR FROM SMITH'S chalk-choked sport routes are walls and spires that only the most adventurous climbers visit. The Marsupial Crags are the best of these areas. Prominently displayed on the hillside east of the park, this collection of pinnacles contains many remote routes. Along with Staender Ridge, the Marsupials once offered Smith's most accessible climbing. Today, with the Burma Road blocked, anyone who hates long approaches avoids the place. This pleases the rare visitors, as the pinnacles offer fun routes without the Smith crowds. Since it sits high above the rest of the park, an added bonus are the marvelous views of the Central Oregon desert and the Cascade volcanoes.

Even more remote are the pinnacles of Indian and Mendenhall Ridges. Located far to the north of Smith Rock State Park, these high ridges contain several impressive, but rotten towers. The spires are the most visible landmarks at Smith, standing out on the horizon for 40 miles to the north and south. The rock isn't special, but you'll never find a more pristine part of Smith Rock. Anyone visiting here experiences climbing unchanged from the days of the earliest pioneers.

THE MARSUPIAL CRAGS

Strewn across the hillside east of the parking lot are the Marsupial Crags. Here, you'll find Koala Rock, the Wombat, Opossum, Wallaby and Kangaroo. The normal approach follows the trail right from the bridge below the main parking area. Walk around the northernmost bend of the Crooked River, then hike uphill to the irrigation tunnel below the Burma Road. The crags rest on the hillside to the right. Allow at least 30 minutes to Koala Rock, and 90 minutes to the remote Tasmanian Devil. An alternate approach hikes along the canal road from the south.

Koala Rock

This large hunk of stone, which offers several enjoyable routes, sits just above the most prominent switchback on the Burma Road. The easiest line to the top scrambles up 3rd-class rock on the backside.

1. HEATSTROKE 5.10b ★★ Gear to 1.5 inches
   The south face of Koala Rock contains a single route up an obvious, left-facing corner. A bolt appeared at the start after the first ascent, taming the entrance from face holds to the left. After jamming the attractive crack, cut left around a roof and finish to rappel anchors.

2. THIN AIR 5.9 ★★★ Gear to 2.5 inches
   This remote jewel easily justifies the long approach. Most climbers rappel after the first pitch, ignoring a runout finish. Start below a buttress at the lowest part of Koala Rock.
   1. 5.8 Edges and thin jams on great rock lead over a small roof. Jam the widening crack to a large ledge.
   2. 5.9 Wander past two widely-spaced bolts to an anchor.

THE WOMBAT

KOALA ROCK

BROGAN SPIRE COMPLEX

MINI-HALF DOME

KANGARO(

DELERIUM TREMENS

Photo: Bruce Adams

Marsupial Crags

3. CATTY CORNER 5.8 ★ Gear to 4 inches
   Parallel cracks in a large, left-facing dihedral rise left of the lowest buttress. The unappealing wide crack on the right jams awkwardly past some chockstones to **Thin Air's** first anchor. Either rappel or downclimb 4th-class slabs to the left.

4. CRAZIES 5.7 ★★ Gear to 3 inches
   The leftmost of parallel cracks in a corner follows a slot past a bolt to a low-angled lieback. A killer block once guarded the moves, but today its remnants litter the base.

5. DESERT SOLITAIRE 5.9 X ★ Gear to 1.5 inches
   This intimidating route follows a direct line up the center of Koala Rock. The physical second pitch protects sparsely, and scares almost everyone away. Start below a short, water-stained groove.
   1. 4th Boulder up a groove, then zig-zag up easy ramps, belaying beneath an ominous bulge.
   2. 5.9 Good holds muscle past two bolts to the base of an inside corner.
   3. 5.8 Romp up the crack to the top. Either downclimb or rappel off the backside.

Koala Rock

1. HEATSTROKE 5.10b ★★
2. THIN AIR 5.9 ★★★
3. CATTY CORNER 5.8 ★
4. CRAZIES 5.7 ★★
5. DESERT SOLITAIRE 5.9 X ★
6. ROUND RIVER 5.4 ★★★
6a. ROUND RIVER DIRECT 5.8 X

6. ROUND RIVER 5.4 ★★★ Gear to 1.5 inches
This is a delightful route that wanders up three pitches of low-angled slabs on the left side of Koala Rock. Though too runout for the first-time leader, it makes a great outing for anyone else. Start behind a small juniper tree.
1. 5.4 Face climb solid rock past three well-spaced bolts to an anchor.
2. 5.3 Move past another bolt to a fun slab with huge pockets.
3. 5.4 Wander onto the north face along a simple slab, then zigzag along steep ledges to the top. Either scramble or rappel down the backside.

6a. ROUND RIVER DIRECT 5.8 X Gear to 2 inches
You can ruin a great route by continuing directly up the northwest edge, ignoring the third-pitch slab. Poor protection and mediocre rock makes this a dangerous proposition.

The Wombat
This foreboding monolith dwarfs the other members of the Marsupial Crags. The massive northwest face ranks among Smith's most impressive walls, but, unfortunately, it mostly consists of junk. Despite a couple of enjoyable routes, most climbers appreciate the Wombat only from a distance. The easiest route to the summit follows a short, fourth-class ridge on the backside after a crux uphill slog.

7. CATFIGHT CRACKS 5.9 R Gear to 3 inches
Once an extremely bold undertaking, the second pitch of this ugly route was essentially a free solo. Friends make the line a lot less fearsome, but the climbing is just as bad as ever. Start at the lowest part of the Wombat, below a disgusting groove.
1. 5.7 Climb a dirty flare rising above a small tree to a bolt belay.
2. 5.9 Step across to the miserable right crack, and fight to a belay stance.
3. 5.8 Traverse right onto the south face of the Wombat, and climb to the notch behind an obvious, detached spire.
4. 5.7 A few face moves lead out the notch to easy scrambling and the top.

Photo: Bruce Adams

The Wombat – Northwest Face

7. CATFIGHT CRACKS 5.9 R
8. C.L. CONCERTO 5.9 A4 R
9. SANTIAM HIGHWAY LEDGES 5.10a ★

10. GREEN GULLY 5.6 ★
11. WHITECLOUD 5.7 R ★★
12. THE THUMB 5.7 ★★

8. C.L. CONCERTO 5.9 A4 R   Aid rack to 3 inches
Very rarely climbed, this aid route nails a direct line up the largest face on the Wombat. With
plenty of bad rock and offensive climbing, the **Concerto** makes a serious endeavor. Start below an
unappealing, flaring crack just left of a dark, sagebrush-covered ledge.
1. 5.9 Jam the awkward crack and scramble to a bolt on the highest ledge.
2. A3 Nail repugnant seams to bolts and a hanging belay.

3. A4   Difficult aid leads up and left to an anchor.

4. 5.6 A2   Continue aiding left, and move around a corner to easy free climbing.

9. SANTIAM HIGHWAY LEDGES   5.10a ★   Gear to 3 inches

This forgotten route cuts across the main face of the Wombat. Start uphill from **C.L. Concerto** at a large ledge system stretching across the wall.

1. 4th   Traverse right across big ledges to a belay beneath a short wall.

2. 5.8   A quick pitch ends at a higher ledge, below a bolted face.

3. 5.10a   Some face moves lead up and right past several bolts to a crack system. Jam the crack past a crux bulge and belay.

4. 5.8   Move right over a sloping bulge into a notch behind the obvious thumb.

5. 5.7   Boulder out a steep face, and scramble several hundred feet to the top.

10. GREEN GULLY   5.6 ★   Gear to 3 inches

A menacing, overgrown gully rises halfway along the base of the Wombat's west face. The short stretch of good rock on the second pitch isn't worth the ordeal required to get there.

1. 5.5   Scramble up a dirty corridor, then thrash through a groove to a belay below diverging cracks.

2. 5.6   Step left and jam a corner to the top.

11. WHITECLOUD   5.7 R ★★   Gear to 3 inches

This remote route makes a good choice for climbers who want to get away from it all. The runout start isn't special, but the crux jams solid rock. Hike to the left skyline of the west face, and cut right across a ledge to a tree.

1. 5.7   Climb a flaring crack to a bolt, then storm a corner to anchor bolts. Use a 165 foot rope.

2. 5.4   A short chimney leads to the top.

12. THE THUMB   5.7 ★★   Gear to 2 inches

Only the most obsessive peak baggers will bother with this silly spire jutting out from the southwest face. After hiking to the top of the Wombat, scamper (4th class) down the summit ridge to a steep wall above a notch. Rappel into the slot, then stroll to the top of the Thumb. The actual crux comes on the retreat, reversing the first rappel with a few free moves.

Brogan Spire Complex

The triple peaks of the Brogan Spire Complex are across the hillside to the right of Koala Rock. They are called the Opossum, the Tail, and Brogan Spire. Better than average rock makes these towers the best of the Marsupial summits. To approach the complex, hike up the Burma Road to the obvious switchback below Koala Rock, and cut across the hillside to the south.

Brogan Spire – North Face

This classic, flat-topped tower is the lowest and most appealing of the three spires. The next three routes ascend good rock on the overhanging north wall.

13. THE GREAT ROOF   5.6 A3 ★★★   Gear to 1 inch

Smith's last great crack problem still awaits a free ascent. Despite excellent quality rock, the inconvenient location deters any attempts. The entire route might go free, as the second pitch cuts around the roof rather than pulling over it. Start below the obvious seam extending down from a large roof, midway along the north wall.

1. A3   Aid a series of pin scars past several bolts into a left-facing corner. Belay beneath the big roof.

2. 5.4 A1   Traverse out the right wall on bolts and continue up easy rock to an anchor.

3. 5.4   Easy scrambling on good stone leads to the top. Descend by reversing to the anchor atop the second pitch, and rappel with two ropes.

14. PIN BENDER   5.8 A2 ★   Aid rack to 1 inch
This obscure aid seam rises 50 feet right of the Great Roof . Remarkable only because someone
bothered to climb it, **Pin Bender** sees very few ascents. Start behind a juniper, on a pocketed wall.
1.   A2   Nail a seam and a shallow right-facing corner to an anchor.
2.   5.8   Some tricky face moves past a couple of bolts give way to easier climbing and the top.
Use the Great Roof descent.

15. PROJECT   5.12 ?
This future free route sports a few bolts on the attractive face right of **Pin Bender.** The gently
overhanging wall may someday see several desperate lines.

Photo: Bruce Adams

Marsupial Crags – Northwest Side

13. THE GREAT ROOF   5.6 A3 ★★★
14. PIN BENDER   5.8 A2 ★
15. PROJECT   5.12 ?
16. WEST FACE   5.5 X ★★★

21. DOGFIGHT CRACK   5.8 R
24. EYE SORE   5.12a
25. DELIRIUM TREMENS   5.10a ★★★★

16. WEST FACE 5.5 X ★★★ Gear to 3 inches
The downhill side of Brogan Spire offers a delightful romp up mostly solid rock. Start at the Mini Half Dome notch and climb gingerly past a ratty bolt. Two hundred feet of easy scrambing ends on top.

Brogan Spire – South Face
The southern side of Brogan Spire offers some great routes, mostly in the lower grades. The distinguishing feature is a narrow, low-angled buttress extending far south from the summit horn.

17. WEST GULLY 5.10c ★★★ Gear to 1 inch
A strenuous boulder problem out of the starting cave highlights an otherwise easy route to the top of Brogan Spire. Approach by walking uphill into a huge amphitheater on the southwest side of the monolith.

Photo: Bruce Adams

Marsupial Crags – Southwest Side

16. WEST FACE 5.5 X ★★★
17. WEST GULLY 5.10c ★★★
18. SOUTH BUTTRESS 5.5 X ★★★★

19. CAVE ROUTE 5.6 X ★★★★
20. DIAGONAL CRACK 5.4 X ★
29. SOUTH FACE 5.6 X

1.　5.10c　Crank the powerful start out a steep bulge, and stroll to a unique hole. Simple (5.4) free climbing up a groove ends at anchors on the summit ridge.

2.　5.4　Wander up great rock without protection to the summit. Rappel the route.

17a. VARIATION　5.7 ★★　Gear to 3 inches

If you can't manage the bouldering start, climb a short crack to the left.

18.　SOUTH BUTTRESS　5.5 X ★★★★　Bolts

Despite non-existent protection, this is the best route of the grade at Smith Rock. With consistently solid rock and creative route finding, the **South Buttress** makes a great choice if you're comfortable soloing 5.5. Start at the far south end of the buttress at a burnt-out juniper snag.

1.　5.5　A crux move off the ground leads to an easy scramble as far as a rope will reach. If you're confused about where to go, always veer right.

2.　5.3　Pass over the top of a tunnel, and climb past a bolt to an anchor on the summit ridge.

3.　5.4　Stroll up perfect rock to the top. Rappel.

19.　CAVE ROUTE　5.6 X ★★★★　Gear to 2 inches

The sparse protection and remote location deny this wonderful route the attention it deserves. The attempted first ascent ended only a few feet from the summit, as lightning prompted a hasty retreat. Approach by skirting around the south buttress of Brogan Spire, then passing through a tunnel. Continue uphill to the base of a short, steep wall in a large amphitheater.

1.　5.6　Solo the vertical face on good holds to an anchor.

2.　5.3　Pass through a unique hole and climb an easy groove to anchor bolts on the summit ridge.

3.　5.4　Race to the top on good holds. Rappel the route.

The Opposum

The highest of the three summits on the Brogan Spire Complex features two mediocre routes starting on the uphill side. An alternate line to the top skirts from Brogan Spire around the north face of the Tail to a short face climb (5.4).

20.　DIAGONAL CRACK　5.4 X ★　Gear to 3 inches

An insignificant ramp cuts across the uphill face of the Opossum. Walk, then crawl, to an intimidating hand traverse crux. Rappel from anchor bolts.

21.　DOGFIGHT CRACK　5.8 R　Gear to 2.5 inches

Easily one of Smith's ugliest routes, this harrowing line jams bad rock to the top. Start at the northeast corner of the Opossum, right of **Diagonal Crack.**

The Tail

This unimpressive lump sits between Brogan Spire and the Opossum. To approach the following route, either climb the Opossum and rappel into a notch, or traverse along the north face from Brogan Spire.

22.　OPOSSUM NOTCH　5.0 ★　No gear (on summit pitch)

The simple face moves above the Opossum notch are insignificant compared with the involved approach. The descent either reverses to the top of the Opossum, or rappels to anchors in the Brogan Spire notch.

Mini Half Dome

A rounded block below the lowest point of the Brogan Spire Complex looks vaguely like Half Dome's southwest face.

23. MINI HALF DOME 5.8 R ★★ Bolts
     This route follows a ramp past some prehistoric bolts on the uphill side of the block.

24. EYE SORE 5.12a Bolts
     The seven artificial holds bolted onto the sweeping north face are totally out of place in these pristine surroundings. Whoever erases this piece of vandalism will earn a Smith Rock good-citizen badge.

Delirium Tremens

A massive, unnamed chunk of stone rises below Mini Half Dome. This small block, with an impressive dihedral on the west side, looms just above the canal to the left of the unnamed chunk.

25. DELIRIUM TREMENS 5.10a ★★★★ Gear to 2.5 inches
     The namesake of the block jams a gorgeous pitch up a bulging corner. The perfect rock, excellent protection and unrelenting moves make this the finest climb in the Marsupial Crags.

26. BLURRED VISION 5.12a ★★ Bolts
     The Marsupials' only sport route edges on thin holds up the right wall of **Delirium Tremens**. The first-ascent team finished directly above the final bolt, avoiding an arête just to the right. Today, almost everyone ignores this contrivance by using anything within reach.

The Wallaby, Kangaroo & Joey

These three spires rise near the canal, downhill and right of the Brogan Spire Complex. Furthest north sits the bulbous-topped Wallaby. The massive Kangaroo lies just to the right, while the insignificant gendarme of Joey is hidden from view on the Kangaroo's backside.

27. WALLABY 5.9 ★ Bolts
     The Wallaby might be the best of the three towers, but it still isn't much fun. Start on the north ridge, then face climb junky rock past inadequate bolts to a belay below the summit block. A deceptively tricky boulder move on the east side mantels onto the top.

The Kangaroo

This large tower offers nothing but two terrible routes to the summit. Hopefully, some potential free climbs up the attractive west wall will someday rescue the Kangaroo from mediocrity. Two anchors are already in place above this impressive face.

28. NORTH LEDGES TRAVERSE 5.6 X Gear to 3 inches
     This intimidating line makes a very poor choice for the beginner – or anyone else for that matter. Start with some pockets on the backside that lead into an amphitheater, and scramble to the notch between the Kangaroo and Joey. Crawl and hand traverse along a dirty, right-leaning ramp to the top, praying nothing will pull off in your hands. A few lousy bolts protect the pitch, but don't count on them to stop a fall.

29. SOUTH FACE 5.7 X Gear to 2 inches
     The other way to the summit of the Kangaroo follows a line just as miserable as the preceding route. Start below the south side and traverse left past a bolt on repugnant rock onto the low-angled south face. Follow the line of least resistance directly to the top in two pitches.

30. JOEY – SOUTHWEST SIDE 5.4 X Bolts
This small spire clings to the east side of the Kangaroo. Start by bouldering into an amphitheater on the uphill side, then climb junky flakes to a notch between the two pillars. Easy face moves on putrid rock lead past a bolt to the top. Lasso the summit horn with webbing, and rappel off.

Above and south of the Brogan Spire Complex stretches a large expanse of bad rock. Despite the huge volume of stone, no route exists here except for the following line at the south end of the cliff:

31. SOLSTICE SLAB 5.8 ★ Gear to 2 inches
An isle of decent rock in a sea of trash lurks a quarter mile south of the Kangaroo. You'll find this south-facing ramp at the entrance to the northernmost hiking gully that extends through the cliff line. A freaky face move at the start leads to good jams, which end at a rappel block.

Lost Hardware Pinnacle & Disappearing Tower

Two dinky spires joined by a connecting rib are hidden behind the Wombat, high atop the ridge to the south. Lost Hardware Pinnacle is the highest peak; Disappearing Tower sits just down the ridge. From the west, these pinnacles are impressive, but the backside view will make you wonder why you bothered hiking here. The monstrous approach takes about an hour. Walk along the entire west face of the Wombat, eventually passing through a notch to the east side. Drop downhill and veer right to the backside of the two blobs.

32. LOST HARDWARE ROUTE 5.6 R ★ Gear to 1.5 inches
Begin on the short, uphill side of the spire and foot-shuffle right along a ledge to the southwest corner. An exposed face move leads to an easy final slab.

33. OVER THE HILL 5.7 R ★★★ Gear to 2 inches
This enjoyable route climbs the obvious arête on the downhill side of Lost Hardware Pinnacle. The crux move near the top protects with a hidden bolt around the corner to the right.

34. THE FAR SIDE 5.9 R ★★ Bolts
A spooky face protected by a few widely-spaced bolts lurks a few feet right of **Over the Hill**. Move left near the top, nearing but never using the arête.

35. DISAPPEARING TOWER 5.7 X ★ Gear to 3 inches
The only route to the top of this pillar starts at the notch between the two spires. After a dangerous face move pulls into a miniature corner, a crack leads to the teetering summit. Rappel.

Tasmanian Devil

A pillar of decent rock atop a remote ridge sits nearly a mile northeast of the Wombat. Despite obvious potential, you'll only be let down if you hike here hoping for a productive day of climbing.

36. POCKET HOLD ROUTE 5.3 X ★★★ Gear to 3 inches
The only route to the top follows good holds on the east side to a finishing slot. You'll need to reverse the moves to get down, since there's no rappel anchor.

37. DEVIL IN DISGUISE A1 ★★ Gear to 1 inch
An attractive aid seam splits the north face of the Tasmanian Devil and ends at an anchor. If it wasn't such a long walk, this crack would be a high-quality free route, blending tip jams and stemming.

INDIAN & MENDENHALL RIDGES

Smith's earliest climbs took place on the isolated pinnacles of Indian and Mendenhall Ridge, far north of today's state park. The rock on these weathered spires doesn't compare with Smith's main area, but the alpine position is unmatched. The fastest approach is along the canal road from the north. To reach this road, turn east off Highway 97 on Park Lane, just north of the Crooked River Gorge. Unfortunately, locked gates now block this approach, cutting it off to the public. The only legal access today is a torturous two-hour hike through Sherwood canyon from the main Smith parking area.

Indian Ridge

Viewed from Smith's main parking area, Indian Ridge dominates the distant northern horizon. From bottom to top, the pinnacles include Gunsight Rock, Squaw Rock, Leaning Brave and the Papoose. A variety of unnamed blobs pepper the ridge, offering mediocre third- and fourth-class scrambles.

38. GUNSIGHT ROCK 5.1 ★ No gear

The first pillar of any consequence on Indian Ridge is this aptly-named tower. Zigzag up easy ledges on the north side to the notch between the two peaks, and make some face moves on good rock. To descend, reverse the route.

Photos: Bruce Adams

Indian/Mendenhall Ridge – Southwest View

Squaw Rock

Smith's most visible spire overlooks the entire Central Oregon area. The rock isn't great, but the dominating position is unsurpassed. If you like alpine scenery, you might enjoy spending a day climbing this landmark. Besides, you can't call yourself a true Smith Rock veteran until you stand atop the proud summit.

39. SPIRAL 5.1 X ★★★   Gear to 2 inches
    Although sparsely-protected, this pleasant route spirals up mostly good rock to the summit. Start just left of a juniper tree near the east corner of the pillar. A few face moves lead left, then back right to a large ledge. Follow a simple ramp around to the west face, and race up solid face holds to the top. As with most alpine climbs, there aren't any convenient belay or rappel anchors. Fools rappel from slings draped around loose boulders, but most climbers reverse the route.

39a. DIRECT VARIATION 5.5 R ★   Gear to 3 inches
    A more difficult variant follows a direct line up the east face. Begin below an ugly groove a few feet right of the regular start.

Squaw Rock – East Face

39. SPIRAL 5.1 X ★★★
39a. DIRECT VARIATION 5.5 R ★
39b. SOUTH SPIRAL 5.3 X ★

Photo: Alan Watts

1. 5.4 Climb the awkward crack to a large ledge at the Squaw's lap.

2. 5.5 Follow a mediocre crack splitting the east side directly to the summit.

39b. SOUTH SPIRAL 5.3 X ★ Gear to 2.5 inches
Similar to the original route, this series of ledges winds the opposite direction to the summit. Use the same start, but instead of cutting back right, climb a crumbly right-facing corner to a big ledge. Circle across the south side to the west face, then scramble to the top.

40. SOUTH FACE 5.3 X ★ Gear to 2.5 inches
This intimidating route-finding exercise follows easy ledges directly up the southwest face. Despite poor protection, the rock is mostly solid, and the moves enjoyable. Start at the crest of the ridge at the lowest point of the spire.

LITTLE FINGER
INDEX FINGER

Photo: Bruce Adams

Squaw Rock and Indian Ridge from the south.

Leaning Brave, Papoose & Little Big Horn

Three spires sit south of Indian Ridge near Squaw Rock. The massive Leaning Brave rises just downhill, while the twin spires of the Papoose and Little Big Horn sit further away to the southeast.

41. LEANING BRAVE 5.7 X Gear to 1.5 inches
If this tower sat atop Indian Ridge, it would dominate the skyline just as much as Squaw Rock; instead, it rises anonymously to the south. An unusually dangerous route starts by traversing from the uphill ridge to a notch below the north side. A crux traverse leads right to a large ledge cutting across the face. Easy but unprotected scrambling on trashy rock finishes to the top.

42. PAPOOSE, SOUTHEAST RIDGE 5.1 X Gear to 2 inches
Twin spires stand about a quarter mile southeast of Squaw Rock. The highest tower is the Papoose. A terrible route follows junky rock on the southeast edge. There's no suitable anchor on the shattered summit, so you'll have to downclimb.

43. LITTLE BIG HORN 5.3 X Gear to 2 inches
A smaller version of the Papoose rises a few feet downhill. The only route climbs suicidal flakes on the east side to the anchorless summit.

Indian Ridge / Mendenhall Ridge Gully

Smith's most obscure spires lurk hidden from view on the right side of the draw between Indian and Mendenhall Ridges. They aren't worth a special trip by any stretch of the imagination, but they make a fun detour on the hike to the Poplar. There are several rock blobs here – mostly second- and third-class – and the following slender spires:

44. LITTLE FINGER 5.6 X ★★★ No gear
     Hidden from view slightly downhill from a large rock mass balances this delightful needle. A great route on the south arête follows twenty feet of solid rock to the top. Descend by reversing the moves.

45. INDEX FINGER 5.4 X ★ No gear
     This slender spire capped by a small boulder sits near the bottom of the cluster. Simple, but unprotected moves scramble 30 feet up the east side to the anchorless summit.

Mendenhall Ridge

Mendenhall Ridge rises across the draw to the north of Indian Ridge. Two spires – the spike-topped Sapling and the classic Poplar – dominate the skyline. A few other rock masses (third- and fourth-class) make worthwhile scrambles if you'd like to tick the entire ridge.

The Sapling

A distinctive summit horn caps the lowest of the two adjacent spires atop Mendenhall Ridge.

46. TILTED SLAB 5.3 X No gear
     Start on the uphill side of the pinnacle and face climb unprotected junk 25 feet to the tilted slab. Circle around and scale the precarious spike from the south, then reverse to a rappel anchor on the slab.

The Poplar

Among Smith's most impressive spires, this bulbous tower balances atop Mendenhall Ridge just uphill from The Sapling. When driving along Highway 97 just south of the Crooked River Gorge, this eye-catching pinnacle stands out on the horizon.

47. SOUTH CHIMNEY 5.7 R ★ Gear to 3 inches
     A chimney splitting the south face is an easy route to the summit. The crux stems past the initial bulge on bad rock. Rappel with double ropes.

THE POPLAR

THE SAPLING

46

47

Photo: Alan Watts

Mendenhall Ridge, looking west

46. TILTED SLAB 5.3 X   47. SOUTH CHIMNEY 5.7 R ★

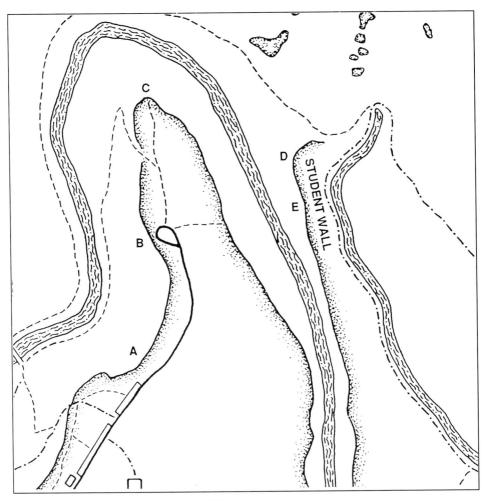

A. *Hidden Crag*
B. *Overlook Area*
C. *Northern Point*
D. *Reproductive Wall*
E. *The Textbooks*

BASALT RIMROCK

THE BASALT RIMROCK lining the Crooked River gets no respect. Overshadowed by the towering tuff and aesthetic basalt columns, these puny bands get lost in the crowd. They might receive acclaim if they didn't compete for attention with the rest of Smith; instead, they wallow in obscurity. After all, it's hard to take anything named the Student Wall or Practice Area seriously.

Of the miles of rimrock along the canyon, only two sections contain any routes. The first cliff, the Practice Area, rests along the rim just north of the turnaround parking area. A flat, 150-yard approach makes this Smith's most accessible crag. The best of the rimrock though, lies on the opposite side of the canyon slightly further upstream. Here, the Student Wall offers dozens of unheralded but enjoyable routes on great rock.

The rimrock's reputation as a novice area usually keeps more experienced climbers away. This is a shame, since the basalt makes an excellent choice for 5.9 to 5.11 climbers wanting to hone their crack skills. The recent addition of several bolted face routes might finally bring the rimrock the attention it deserves.

The Practice Area and Student Wall differ from the more attractive columns found upstream. Easily overlooked, the jumbled rimrock lacks eye-catching lines. The routes usually protect easily on lead, but almost everyone opts for a toprope. This makes the rimrock especially attractive for classes, and for anyone uncomfortable with the sharp end of the rope.

Climbers first visited the Student Wall in the 1950s. Because of its proximity to the old climbers' camp and parking lot, the crag saw heavy activity; sadly, no one kept track of first ascents. The only recorded routes during the early days were two remarkable climbs in 1971. In an effort far ahead of its time, Del Young pulled off **Theseus** (5.10c) and **Minotaur** (5.10d), tearing apart Smith's free-climbing standards. Until sticky rubber lowered the grade, **Minotaur**, a Yosemite-style tips crack, was Oregon's first 5.11. Oddly, Young's routes never received recognition in accounts of the development of Smith climbing. If they where anywhere else in the park, these climbs would be well-known, but their location on the Student Wall doomed them to obscurity.

Nothing has changed over the past two decades, as the cracks fell quietly to anonymous climbers. Chuck Buzzard chronicled a few of the routes in his guide to Smith basalt, *Basalt and Boulders,* but the crowds never came. The sport climbing era didn't arrive until 1991, when Jeff Frizzell and Chip Brejc bolted several face routes. Their lines will inevitably become popular, since they blend good rock and closely-spaced bolts with a painless approach. Oddly, a major reason the rimrock attracted so little attention was that few routes had names. Most climbers won't bother with an unidentified crack, but they'll eagerly try anything with a name and grade. I've taken the liberty of naming any unnamed lines, hoping this might help legitimize them.

With the exception of the Textbooks on the Student Wall, there aren't many anchor bolts along the rim. Fortunately, you can arrange a top rope using juniper trees as anchors. Always bring an extra rope as the trees are far back from the edge.

PRACTICE AREA

The basalt cliffs of the Practice Area are across the river from Red Wall and the Monument. A quick approach and easily-arranged topropes makes this rimrock a convenient place to sample your first basalt. If you decide to climb here, expect a barrage of preposterous questions from bewildered tourists as you pull over the top. The sometimes-sandy rock isn't as good as Smith's better basalt, but it's still plenty solid. There are three main cliffs in the Practice Area. The Hidden Wall rises slightly north of the main entrance into the canyon, while the dinky Overlook Crag drops off directly west of the turnaround. The best routes are at the Northern Point, overlooking the Monument and Staender Ridge.

Hidden Wall

This puny crag sports a single route, reached after Smith's shortest approach hike. Park in the third day-use parking lot, and cut downhill along a fence into a draw.

1. SOFT ASYLUM 5.12b ★★★ Bolts

    A desperate route follows an overhanging arête rising above a massive boulder. Some insecure stems at the start lead to a powerful crux on pockets and edges. Pumping slaps finish to an anchor.

Overlook Crag

The turnaround parking area is a popular scenic spot for anyone visiting Smith Rock, since Red Wall dominates the view to the west. Dropping off sharply below the viewpoint is the Overlook Crag, with its small collection of routes. The approach hikes south, then skirts back north along the base of the cliff.

2. FLICKER FLASH 5.10a ★ Gear to 3 inches

    Hike along the base of the broken rimrock until you arrive at an insignificant, right-leaning hand crack above a pile of boulders. Over in the blink-of-an-eye, **Flicker Flash** jams and liebacks past a few loose blocks.

3. FLASH IN THE PAN 5.11a/b ★ TR

    Parallel, right-leaning seams rise immediately left of **Flicker Flash**. The tricky right crack succumbs to a short-lived sequence of liebacks, stems and face holds.

4. LIGHTNING 5.11a ★ TR

    A short, but powerful sequence of liebacks, thin jams and high steps polishes off the leftmost of the parallel seams. Above a ledge, fight through a sagebrush to the top.

5. RAMBO ROOF 5.12b ★★★ TR

    Continue hiking north for about 100 feet along the base of the crag until you pass under a fin jutting out from the wall. Ahead, the **Rambo Roof** splits an overhang rising above a huge, pyramid block. The wimp-proof crux muscles an undercling to a horribly flaring jam and a distinctive, detached stone. If bolted, **Rambo** would be popular, but as a toprope problem few climbers bother.

6. PROJECT 5.12+ ?

    This bolted arête promises to be the best route on the Overlook Crag. It rises a few feet left of **Rambo Roof**.

The Northern Point

Many short cracks of all sizes split the rimrock of the Northern Point. The quick approach makes these routes Smith's most accessible moderate lines. Since the climbs face north, the Point makes an intelligent choice on a hot day when you're trying to escape the sun. To approach the crag from the turnaround, hike north toward the Monument along a well-worn path. Continue to the northern rim, and peer over the edge, searching for a gigantic, weathered snag leaning against the wall. Just west of this snag (left as you face the Monument) is a break in the rimrock. An easy, third-class scramble takes you down to the base of the crag. You'll find the following 17 routes in order as you leave the leaning snag behind you, and skirt downstream along the base of the rimrock:

7. GREENHOUSE 5.8 X ★ Gear to 2 inches
   Much better toproped than led, this pint-sized route starts above some blocks just right of the approach chimney. Pull past an energetic bulge on moss-covered ledges, then master a crux face move at the top.

8. JERSEY SHORE 5.7 ★★ Gear to 2.5 inches
   The first crack right of the approach chimney cuts around the left side of a small fin. After an entertaining lieback clears a bulge, a few thin jams end at a crux mantel.

8a. VARIATION 5.8 R ★ Gear to 2.5 inches
   An awkward, poorly-protected variant climbs around the right side of the fin.

9. LEAN CUISINE 5.6 ★★ Gear to 3 inches
   Next in line beyond **Jersey Shore** are short, left-leaning double cracks. Despite appearances, a charming sequence of stems and jams on good rock leads to the top.

10. LITTLE WONDER 5.10b ★★ Gear to .75 inch
    Although laughably short, this thin crack in a shallow open book is no pushover. Start atop a block just right of a broken, left-leaning crack, then jam and stem 15 desperate feet to easy climbing.

11. THUMPER 5.8 ★★ Gear to 3 inches
    An exciting sequence of liebacks mixed with hand jams tames this appealing line. Begin by stepping off a boulder across a void to a small corner, then hand traverse left to the base of a steep crack.

12. BLOCK HEAD 5.7 ★ Gear to 3 inches
    A fractured corner lurks downhill a few feet beyond **Thumper**. After cranking on wedged blocks at the start, lieback around an easier bulge to the top.

13. MEAT GRINDER 5.8 ★★ Gear to 3.5 inches
    A distinctive, arching hand traverse at the start guards this energetic route. After moving left, make an awkward exit move, then jam, stem and lieback the finishing fist crack.

14. DOUBLE TIME 5.7 ★ Gear to 2.5 inches
    An obvious weakness splits the rimrock just after a sharp arête. Start with a clean jam crack, then scramble into the slot. **Double Time** avoids the simple, chimneying finish by cutting right and stemming to a crux mantel.

15. DEVIL'S DELIGHT 5.9 R ★ Gear to 4 inches
    This overhanging, block-filled wide crack lurks around the corner right of a break in the rimrock. Start by climbing to a ledge, then crank past intimidating blocks – you'll have to pull on them.

16. SWAN SONG 5.10b ★★ Gear to 2 inches
    Flanked by wide cracks, this enjoyable line follows a short, but powerful crack splitting a steep wall. Hopefully, the detached block defending the crux will stay there as you jam on by.

Northern Point – Right Center

7. GREENHOUSE 5.8 X ★
8. JERSEY SHORE 5.7 ★★
8a. VARIATION 5.8 R ★
9. LEAN CUISINE 5.6 ★★
10. LITTLE WONDER 5.10b ★★
11. THUMPER 5.8 ★★
12. BLOCK HEAD 5.7 ★
13. MEAT GRINDER 5.8 ★★
14. DOUBLE TIME 5.7 ★

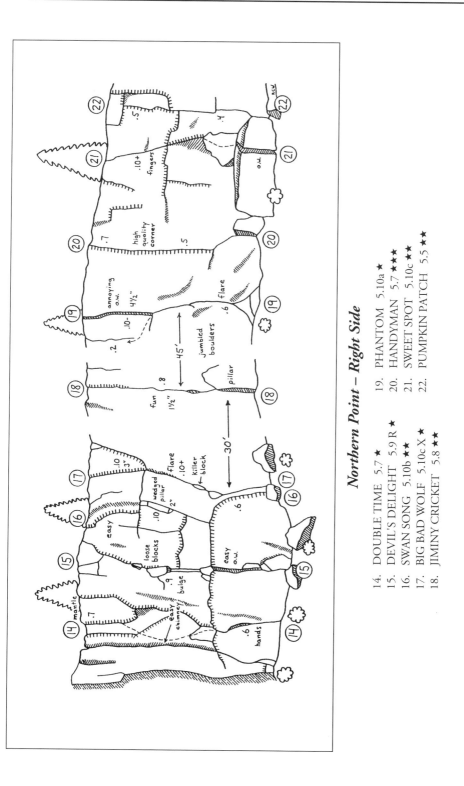

Northern Point – Right Side

14. DOUBLE TIME 5.7 ★
15. DEVIL'S DELIGHT 5.9 R ★
16. SWAN SONG 5.10b ★★
17. BIG BAD WOLF 5.10c X ★
18. JIMINY CRICKET 5.8 ★★

19. PHANTOM 5.10a ★
20. HANDYMAN 5.7 ★★★
21. SWEET SPOT 5.10c ★★
22. PUMPKIN PATCH 5.5 ★★

17. BIG BAD WOLF   5.10c X ★   TR
    You've got good reason to fear the **Big Bad Wolf**. The crux pulls a detached flake to your waist, then reaches awkwardly for face holds. Since the only gear is behind this block, you'd be a fool to go for the lead.

18. JIMINY CRICKET   5.8 ★★   Gear to 2 inches
    This highly varied crack rises just left of a large boulder about 30 feet beyond the flaring **Big Bad Wolf**. Somehow, in the course of 30 feet, it takes in finger/hand jams, face moves, stems, and liebacks.

19. PHANTOM   5.10a ★   Gear to 4 inches
    After scrambling around some huge blocks obstructing the path, you'll spot a 15-foot wide crack near the top of the cliff. **Phantom** starts up an easy flare, then launches into the intimidating off-width. If you're spooked, you can always step left to an easy escape.

20. HANDYMAN   5.7 ★★★   Gear to 2.5 inches
    This attractive crack, set in a shallow dihedral, rises around the corner to the right of **Phantom**. Big face holds slash the difficulty as you glide up delightful stems and jams to a crux finish.

21. SWEET SPOT   5.10c ★★   Gear to 1.5 inches
    This tricky problem jams a short, diagonal crack above a small roof. You'll reach the starting jams by balancing atop an obvious triangular block. The pull around the roof comes easily, but the crux hits hard on the final moves.

22. PUMPKIN PATCH   5.5 ★★   Gear to 3.5 inches
    Just before the rimrock disappears, a low-angled crack system splits a patch of orange rock a few feet right of **Sweet Spot**. An easy scramble leads to a single muscle move at the top.

After scrambling down the third-class approach chimney to the base of the Northern Point, walk toward the massive snag leaning against the rimrock. You'll find the following seventeen routes by skirting upstream along the base of the cliff:

23. WHO PUDDING   5.8 R ★★   Gear to 2.5 inches
    A few puny cracks, barely worth bothering with, are near the opposite exit of the approach chimney. The rightmost of two routes located here starts left of a hand crack below a small inside corner plugged by a miniature spike. A few jams mixed with good jugs tame the right-leaning crack.

24. WHO HASH   5.8 R ★★   Gear to 2.5 inches
    The left of two insignificant routes follows the line of least resistance just left of **Who Pudding**. After an awkward crux cranks past a seemingly detached block, cut right and finish on easier rock.

25. PLAYING WITH FIRE   5.7 ★★   Gear to 4 inches
    A series of worthwhile cracks are just past the leaning snag. The first line stems and liebacks a surprisingly easy off-width.

26. BURN BABY BURN   5.10a ★★★   Gear to 2.5 inches
    This shallow dihedral rises around the corner and left of the obvious wide crack. Start with a simple scramble to a hole, then lieback and jam the high quality crux to the top.

27. FIRESTARTER   5.10d ★★   Gear to 2 inches (wires)
    The leftmost of three parallel cracks is by far the most challenging. If you miss the critical face holds past the undercling at the crux you'll probably plummet.

28. LIFEGUARD   5.7 R ★★   Gear to 2.5 inches
    This moderate climb follows the easiest line left of several attractive cracks. Start behind a juniper tree and scramble to a deceptive crux that catches unwary climbers off guard. Keep your fingers crossed, pull softly around a massive block at the top.

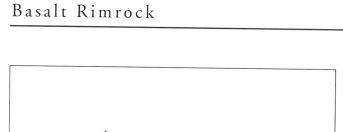

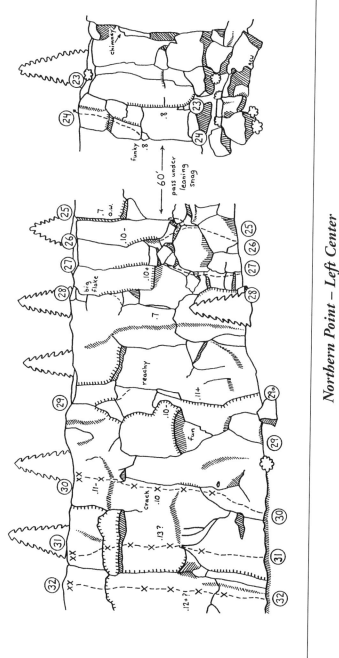

Northern Point – Left Center

23. WHO PUDDING 5.8 R ★★
24. WHO HASH 5.8 R ★★
25. PLAYING WITH FIRE 5.7 ★★
26. BURN BABY BURN 5.10a ★★★
27. FIRESTARTER 5.10d ★★
28. LIFEGUARD 5.7 R ★★

29. IF I RAN THE CIRCUS 5.10b ★★★
29a. RUNAWAY BUNNY 5.11d. ★★
30. WOMAN IN THE MEADOW
    5.11a ★★
31. THE HEATHEN 5.13 ?
32. PROJECT 5.12 ?

29. IF I RAN THE CIRCUS   5.10b ★★★   Gear to 3 inches
This undercling around a roof is among the best and most obvious lines on the Northern Point. Start with a few jams up an inverted triangular block, then launch into an energetic sequence past the roof to a liebacking crux.

29a. RUNAWAY BUNNY   5.11d ★★   TR
This contrived toprope problem in a shallow corner rises a few feet to the right. After some desperate moves on polished rock, finish with long stretches between positive holds. Purists totally ignore the hand crack only inches to the left.

Just beyond **If I Ran the Circus,** the traditional crack climbs give way to several bolted sport routes. The following lines make good choices on a summer afternoon:

30. WOMAN IN THE MEADOW   5.11a ★★   Bolts
Far better than it looks, this enjoyable line follows a gray seam splitting the face. It makes a good warm-up for the harder climbs, as big holds at the start gradually shrink to a crux move just below the anchor bolts.

31. THE HEATHEN   5.13?   Project
This attractive wall, rising above a sweeping triangle, will someday contain a desperate route. Most of the moves go free, but the linkage awaits a Herculean effort.

32. PROJECT   5.12?
This future free route, which goes up a rounded bulge, lurks five feet left of a strongly overhanging dihedral.

33. HANG IT LOOSE   5.10b R ★★   Gear to 3 inches
A flaring roof, split by a crack sits 50 feet upstream from the bolted routes. After romping up a slab-plugged corner, crank the memorable roof on great holds. Don't celebrate your success too soon, since the crux hits unexpectedly with a tricky high step well above a quarter-inch bolt.

34. JUNGLE FEVER   5.11b ★★   Bolts
This bolted seam rises about 40 feet left of **Hang It Loose.** Start up a pillar, then follow pumpy liebacks and edges to a crux reach past the final bulge. The original line cranked directly, but many climbers cut left at the top.

35. TORRID ZONE   5.12a ★★★   Bolts
You'll need more brawn than brains on the steep wall just left of **Jungle Fever.** After an easy slab start, turn on your power, reaching between big jugs – feet flailing in the air.

36. HAVANA SMACK   5.13 ?   Project
The eye-catching line left of **Torrid Zone** will eventually free increasingly difficult moves up a steep, bolted wall.

37. THE FOUR NYMPHS   5.12a/b ★★   Bolts
A demanding route rises above a few massive, flat-topped boulders about fifty feet beyond the preceding routes. Start with an arête, then battle past artsy, unrelenting moves on sloping holds.

38. SIDEWALK CAFE   5.11c ★★   Bolts
A short fingertip traverse to a rounded arête highlights the last route on the Northern Point. Start with easy, shattered jugs leading into a corner, then commit right to the crux moves.

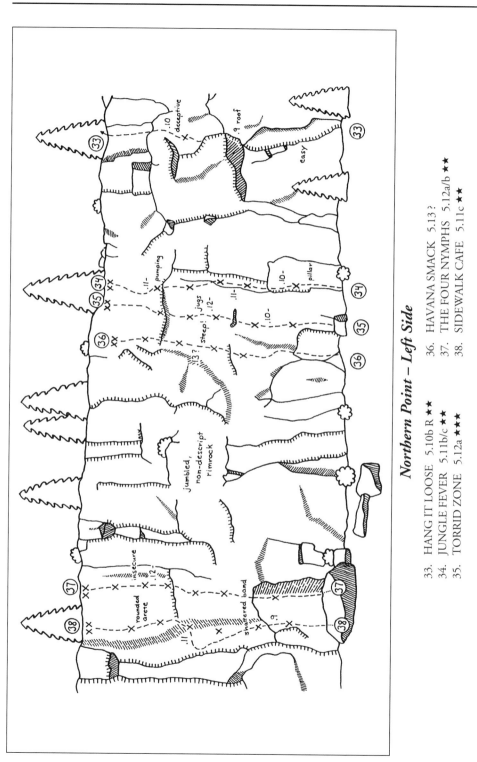

Northern Point – Left Side

33. HANG IT LOOSE 5.10b R ★★
34. JUNGLE FEVER 5.11b/c ★★
35. TORRID ZONE 5.12a ★★★

36. HAVANA SMACK 5.13?
37. THE FOUR NYMPHS 5.12a/b ★★
38. SIDEWALK CAFE 5.11c ★★

STUDENT WALL

The high-quality, weathered basalt of the Student Wall stretches across the river upstream from the Northern Point. A popular destination with classes for the past three decades, this crag offers Smith's finest rimrock climbing. The left portion, known as the Reproductive Wall, contains the longest routes and the only bolted sport climbs. The rimrock of the mid-section is only 20 feet high, but the Textbooks on the right end contain an excellent group of cracks.

Since the entire crag faces west, it makes a good morning choice in the summer and a late-day destination during the winter months. The best approach cuts across the river below the Northern Point, then hikes uphill to the base. During high-water conditions the river is impassable, forcing a longer hike from the bridge below Picnic Lunch Wall.

Reproductive Wall

A collection of cracks, along with some sport routes and bolt ladders, makes this the most varied section of the Student Wall. The climbs start on the upper left side and are listed in order moving right along the base.

39. SPRING BREAK   5.5 ★★   Gear to 3 inches
    A fine beginner route, this dinky, left-facing corner is over before you know it. Start at the far left side of the cliff and scramble up simple boulders to some fun jams and stems.

40. FLUNKED OUT   5.6 ★★   Gear to 3 inches
    This simple climb wanders up the easiest path just left of several parallel cracks. After a crux traverse cuts right from the starting corner, finish on simple rock.

41. CRAM SESSION   5.8 ★   Gear to 2.5 inches
    Several parallel jam cracks, all starting after an easy scramble, mark the left portion of the Reproductive Wall. To climb the left crack, cruise a water-worn groove, then jam around a hanging column to frothy jugs.

42. FIST FIGHT   5.8 ★★   Gear to 3 inches
    The neighbor to **Cram Session** shares the same start, but jams and liebacks a better-quality hand crack just to the right.

43. FRAT JERKS   5.8 ★★   Gear to 4 inches
    Although intimidating, this wide crack set in a right-facing corner is more of a lieback/stemming problem than an off-width. Begin with a simple trough directly below the chockstone-plugged crack.

44. BON FIRE   5.8 ★★   Gear to 3.5 inches
    This appealing line is tucked in a left-facing corner right of **Frat Jerks**. After a simple scramble, fun jams above a bolt end with a short wide section.

45. PASSING GRADE   5.9 ★★★   Gear to 3 inches
    This quality line deserves more than just a passing grade. Start at some yellow splotches of lichen and jam a short, attractive crack. Some face moves past two hangerless bolts lead to an enjoyable flurry of jams up a left-facing dihedral.

46. PUPPET MASTER   5.11a ★★★   TR
    Although rarely tried, **Puppet Master's** meandering seam makes a great toprope problem. The hardest moves come in the first 20 feet, with insecure liebacks and awkward face holds. Start downhill and around the corner right of several parallel cracks.

47. POP QUIZ   5.11c ★★   Gear to 3 inches (wires)
    This unmistakable arch is the most-imposing crack on the Reproductive Wall. Most climbers flunk out on the contorted, thin-hand jams at the start, but you'll ace the test if you can claw past.

48. FIGHT SONG 5.10a ★★★ Gear to 2.5 inches
This exceptional flake crack lurks just left of a gray, bolted wall. An awkward start up a short, right-leaning corner gives way to exciting jams and liebacks at the crux.

49. EMBRYONIC 5.11d ★★★ Bolts
The center of the Reproductive Wall offers a couple of high-quality sport climbs. The left route starts with a bolted crack, then attacks the pocketed wall, pulling over a sequential bulge near the top.

Photo: Bruce Adams

Student Wall: Reproductive Wall – Left Side

39. SPRING BREAK 5.5 ★★
40. FLUNKED OUT 5.6 ★★
41. CRAM SESSION 5.8 ★
42. FIST FIGHT 5.8 ★★
43. FRAT JERKS 5.8 ★★
44. BON FIRE 5.8 ★★
45. PASSING GRADE 5.9 ★★★
46. PUPPET MASTER 5.11a ★★★
47. POP QUIZ 5.11c ★★
48. FIGHT SONG 5.10a ★★★
49. EMBRYONIC 5.11d ★★★
50. DRILLING ZONA 5.11c ★★★★
50a. PROJECT 5.13 ?

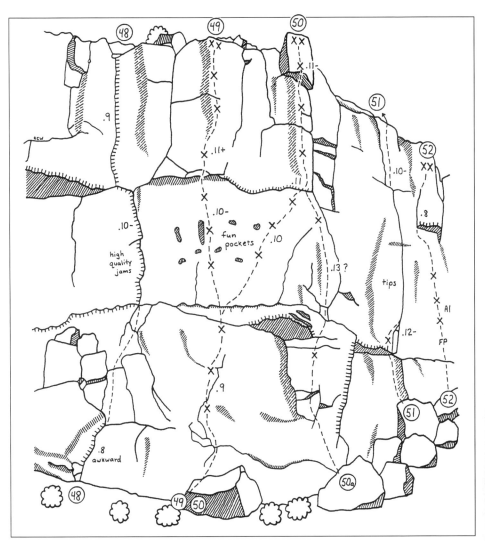

Reproductive Wall – Center

48. FIGHT SONG   5.10a ★★★   50a. PROJECT   5.13 ?
49. EMBRYONIC   5.11d ★★★   51. CLASS DISMISSED   5.12a ★★
50. DRILLING ZONA   5.11c ★★★★   52. FIRST AID   5.8 A1 ★★

50. DRILLING ZONA   5.11c ★★★★   Bolts

The best route on Smith rimrock attacks the striking buttress in the center of the wall. Start up the same crack as **Embryonic**, but veer right on fun pockets until a tricky move gains the arête. Exciting moves on big holds lead to a final crux just below the anchors.

50a. PROJECT   5.13 ?

This direct start will someday bring 5.13 to the Student Wall. Start by climbing jumbled rock to a roof, then levitate 20 feet up a blank dihedral and arête before joining the regular line.

51. CLASS DISMISSED   5.12a ★★   Gear to 1 inch (TCUs, small wires)
Despite being Smith's hardest rimrock route for a full decade, this appealing thin crack sees few attempts. The starting moves on friable jugs aren't much fun, but the puzzling, bolt-protected crux saves the day. Unless you're a thin crack expert, expect a tussle getting to a ledge just below the top.

52. FIRST AID   5.8 A1 ★★   Gear to 2.5 inches (small wires)
A line of fixed pins and bolts ending at an anchor below the rim garnishes the wall right of **Class Dismissed**. It makes a good place to sample aid climbing, but expect some strenuous free moves pulling around a roof.

53. CARDIAC FIB   5.10c ★★   Gear to 3.5 inches
Set in a corner, this overhanging crack rises just right of the **First Aid** bolt line. After jamming around a heart-stopping bulge, cruise easier rock to the top.

54. CARDIAC KID   5.8 ★★   Gear to 3 inches
This odd line starts below **Cardiac Fib**, then underclings right under a roof to an annoyingly awkward crux. Finish with simple stemming in a corner.

A flat face sporting dozens of quarter-inch studs sits on the right side of the Reproductive Wall, just right of **Cardiac Kid**. Some twisted individuals came here years ago and spent days honing their drilling skills. There are two main routes, but with the grid pattern of bolts you can aid almost anywhere – as long as you bring lots of hangers. Both lines would obviously go free (5.11/5.12), but the littering of bolts ruins their appeal.

55. THE LIVING END   5.10b ★★   Gear to 2 inches
The last climb of any consequence on the Reproductive Wall follows an attractive crack above a boulder-plugged slot. A humbling sequence of inch-and-a-quarter jams highlights the route.

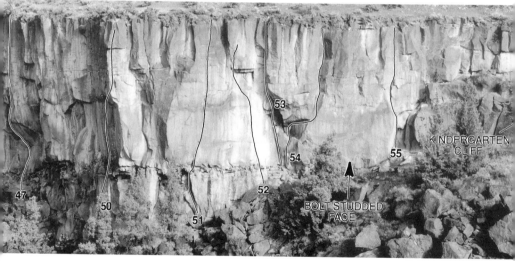

Photo: Bruce Adams

Student Wall: Reproductive Wall – Right Side

47. POP QUIZ 5.11c ★★
50. DRILLING ZONA 5.11c ★★★★
51. CLASS DISMISSED 5.12a ★★
52. FIRST AID 5.8 A1 ★★

53. CARDIAC FIB 5.10c ★★
54. CARDIAC KID 5.8 ★★
55. THE LIVING END 5.10b ★★

Kindergarten Cliff

The 200-foot mid-section of the Student Wall contains dozens of options, from tough bouldering traverses to simple scrambles. Ranging from 15 to 25 feet in height, this puny cliff makes a good place to introduce someone to climbing, even though it's a little too short for legitimate routes.

The Textbooks

The corners at the right end of the Student Wall are among Smith's best-kept secrets. Perfect basalt, varied climbing and plenty of bolt anchors make the crag a pleasant place to develop crack climbing skills. Most routes protect easily on lead, but almost everyone brings out the toprope. The Textbooks start right of a fourth-class descent chimney, just as the base trail drops downhill.

56. CHEAT SHEET   5.11a ★★ Gear to 2.5 inches
     This short thin crack sits a few feet right of a break in the rimrock. A desperate sequence of flaring jams, liebacks and edges stretches between widely-spaced slots.

57. SCHOOL'S OUT   5.7 ★★   Gear to 3 inches
     Double cracks split the first inside corner on the left side of the Textbooks. Most climbers stem across to the off-width on the right, but you can contrive matters by jamming either crack separately (5.10a left; 5.8 right).

Photo: Bruce Adams

Student Wall: The Textbooks – Left Side

56. CHEAT SHEET 5.11a ★★	62a. CHARM SCHOOL 5.7 ★★
57. SCHOOL'S OUT 5.7 ★★	63. PANIC SEIZURE 5.11b ★
58. PROM NIGHT 5.7 ★★★	64. LITTLE BLACK SAMBO 5.9 X ★★
59. DOOR KNOB PEOPLE 5.7 ★★	65. GLOBAL MOTION 5.10b ★★★
59a. SLAM DANCE 5.8 ★	66. HOMECOMING QUEEN 5.7 ★★
60. RAGE 5.7 ★★	67. SILLY BOY 5.10b ★★★
61. DUNCE CAP 5.8 R ★★	68. HEART THROB 5.7 ★★★
62. BAD MANNERS 5.7 ★★	68a. DANCING HEARTS 5.10b ★★

58. **PROM NIGHT** 5.7 ★★★ Gear to 1.5 inches
This fun route follows locking finger jams up a shallow corner, aided by huge face holds. Begin with a boulder move onto a large, square ledge.

59. **DOOR KNOB PEOPLE** 5.7 ★★ Gear to 3 inches
A few stems and jams exiting a flaring slot highlight this chimney in a deep-set corner. The route looks gross, but it's not bad.

59A. **SLAM DANCE** 5.8 ★ Gear to 3 inches
A hand traverse midway up **Door Knob People** cuts left to an annoying entrance into a clumsy slot. Don't bother.

60. **RAGE** 5.7 ★★ Gear to 1.5 inches
Two routes, sharing the same start up a very short, arching crack, are right of the **Door Knob People** chimney. The easier left crack follows face holds and jams in a shallow, right-facing corner.

61. **DUNCE CAP** 5.8 R ★★ Gear to 1 inch (small wires)
This poorly-protected seam starts up **Rage,** then jams the thin crack on the right, finishing with some scary face moves.

62. **BAD MANNERS** 5.7 ★★ Gear to 3.5 inches
An obvious chimney slices through the rimrock immediately left of a gray wall. Despite its slovenly appearance, the stems and knobs in the flaring slot aren't bad.

62a. **CHARM SCHOOL** 5.7 ★★ Gear to 3 inches
A more refined variant to **Bad Manners** swings left onto a ledge and polishes off a few thin-hand jams in a short corner.

63. **PANIC SEIZURE** 5.11b ★ Gear to 3.5 inches (small wires)
The Textbooks are exceptionally solid, except for this dirty section of gray rock. **Panic Seizure** plows around a bulging sand dune on hand jams to a solid finish. The confusing crux comes near the top, with a desperate sequence of edges and side pulls above a crucial one finger pocket.

64. **LITTLE BLACK SAMBO** 5.9 X ★★ Gear to 1 inch (small wires)
Distinguished by an oblong hole a few feet off the ground, this sparsely-protected route follows a leaning crack above a bouldering start.

65. **GLOBAL MOTION** 5.10b ★★★ Gear to 3 inches
A right-leaning crack splits the rimrock just before a large boulder blocks the approach path. The high-quality crux reaches between good slots in the starting corner.

66. **HOMECOMING QUEEN** 5.7 ★★ Gear to 2 inches
After walking around a massive boulder at the base of the cliff, you'll spot this unsightly, block-plugged crack. After a short lieback enters a slot, step past the loose flake to a crux finish up either of two cracks.

67. **SILLY BOY** 5.10b ★★★ Gear to 2.5 inches
An attractive crack rises just left of an unmistakable inside corner. After a desperate undercling at the start, lieback and jam good rock to a ledge. Choose between an easy finish to the left or a tougher direct line.

68. **HEART THROB** 5.7 ★★★ Gear to 3 inches
This short dihedral capped by a roof is the most conspicuous route on the Textbooks. An elegant hand crack ends far too quickly at an anchor 30 feet off the ground. Many climbers lower off here, but the finish cuts left around an intimidating roof on jugs.

68a. DANCING HEARTS   5.10b ★★   Gear to 2 inches
An alternate ending to **Heart Throb** underclings a short, but desperate sequence around the right side of the roof.

69.   DEAD WEEK   5.8 ★★   Gear to 3 inches
This right-facing corner lurks 10 feet right of **Heart Throb**. Begin atop a small block and make a few liebacks to easier climbing.

70.   THESEUS   5.10c ★★★   Gear to 2 inches
This demanding line helped boost standards over two decades ago. Along with nearby **Minotaur**, it stood atop Smith free climbing for several years. After storming the crux finger crack, finish by cutting right past a fixed pin.

71.   LITTLE BO PEEP   5.10c ★★★   Gear to 2.5 inches
Some tough moves up a prominent, right-leaning corner highlight this enjoyable crack. Cut right near the top when the holds disappear.

72.   DEEP SLEEP   5.8 ★★★   Gear to 3 inches
A fun route jams a locking hand crack in a shallow corner, just right of **Little Bo Peep's** leaning start. Above the start, finesse a few face moves to the top.

73.   THE VIRGIN SLAYER   5.9 ★★★   Gear to 3.5 inches
The most impressive feature on the right side of the Textbooks is an imposing roof capping a short, right-facing corner. The easiest route weasels awkwardly left, then jams an exquisite hand/finger crack.

74.   LABYRINTH   5.10b ★★★   Gear to 3 inches
A burly undercling cuts right around an intimidating roof to a strenuous exit. Finish with easier double cracks in a corner.

75.   MINOTAUR   5.10d ★★   Gear to 2 inches (TCUs, wires)
Once a standard-smashing route, this tame-looking thin crack was Smith's first 5.11. Sticky rubber dropped the grade a notch, but the desperate tip jams humble climbers even today.

76.   BIG MAN ON CAMPUS   5.9 ★★★   Gear to 1 inch (small wires)
This high-quality line sits behind a leaning, free-standing pillar. Start by chimneying a unique slot, then make a few tricky face moves to the top.

77.   ASTRO BUNNY   5.10b/c ★★   TR
A leaning, inside corner rises right of a free-standing pillar. After a crux of side pulls, thin jams and stems, some perplexing face moves finish to the rim.

78.   BLOCK PARTY   5.10b ★★   TR
This toprope problem climbs a shallow groove past a detached block. Don't pull on the flake, since it's smarter to risk a fall skirting left than gamble with death. Once safely past this obstacle, wonderful jugs finish to the rim.

79.   SPLASH   5.10c ★★   Gear to 2 inches (wires)
A tough series of thin-hand jams up a left-facing corner highlights this attractive route. Move cautiously past some loose blocks after the crux and finish on moderate edges.

80.   AVANT GARDE   5.11a ★★   Gear to 2 inches (wires)
The last route on the right side of the Textbooks jams a parallel-sided crack right off the deck. Thin-crack masters hike the crux, but everyone else struggles.

Photo: Bruce Adams

Student Wall: The Textbooks – Right Side

68. HEART THROB 5.7 ★★★
69. DEAD WEEK 5.8 ★★
70. THESEUS 5.10c ★★★
71. LITTLE BO PEEP 5.10c ★★★
72. DEEP SLEEP 5.8 ★★★
73. THE VIRGIN SLAYER 5.9 ★★★
74. LABYRINTH 5.10b ★★★

75. MINOTAUR 5.10d ★★
76. BIG MAN ON CAMPUS 5.9 ★★★
77. ASTRO BUNNY 5.10b/c ★★
78. BLOCK PARTY 5.10b ★★
79. SPLASH 5.10c ★★
80. AVANT GARDE 5.11a ★★

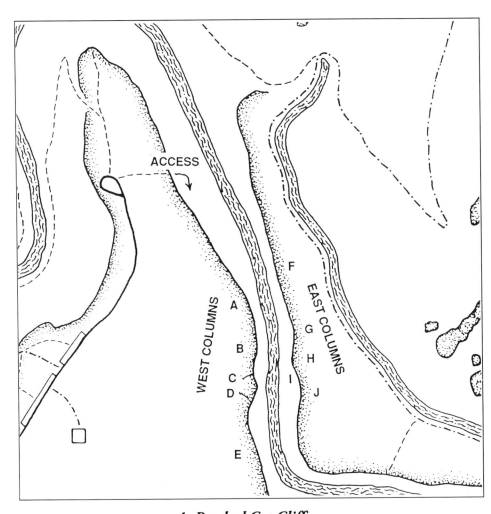

A. *Parched Cat Cliff*
B. *Wildfire Wall*
C. *Catwalk Cliff*
D. *Star Wall*
E. *Jungleland*
F. *Solo Wall*
G. *Windfall Wall*
H. *Hand Job Wall*
I. *Arrington Columns*
J. *Shakespeare Cliff*

THE LOWER GORGE

T H E   B A S A L T   C O L U M N S of the Gorge are hidden in the canyon up the Crooked River. This area adds tremendously to the appeal of Smith Rock, since the climbing bears little resemblance to the more famous tuff routes. Excellent vertical cracks, calf-burning stemming corners, technical faces, and outrageous arêtes tantalize everyone who visits. Square-cut edges and wavy, textured ripples make even the blankest looking routes possible. While some feel that columnar basalt gets repetitive after awhile – since one corner or crack resembles another – others get so hooked they rarely venture elsewhere. For everyone, the Gorge provides a fine diversion from tendon-tweaking pockets. When you drop into the narrow canyon, you'll feel you've left Smith Rock and traveled to a completely different area.

Since the routes are rarely overhanging, the Gorge taxes your creativity more than your upper body. The hardest lines involve a little of everything, favoring a well-rounded, thoughtful approach over brute strength. The consistent steepness and isolation of the columns makes the Gorge a poor choice for the beginner, as the better climbs start at 5.10a and almost nothing exists below 5.8. The rimrock of the Practice Area and the Student Wall (see Chapter 12) provide a better introduction for the novice.

Most Gorge climbs protect naturally. Since only the newest lines sport totally fixed gear, you'll need more than a handful of quickdraws when climbing here. A rack of Friends, TCUs, R.P.s (#2 through #5) and Rocks are essential for many routes. Most of the climbs protect easily, but some are both technically demanding and tricky to protect. Sometimes you'll have to stop in the middle of a desperate sequence to fiddle with a small R.P. placement. You can almost always spot these nightmares by the fact that they don't have a hint of chalk on them.

The earliest climbing on Smith basalt occurred on the Student Wall during the 60s. It wasn't until 1973 that anyone decided to hike upstream to check out the larger cliffs. Wayne Arrington was the first to come under the spell of the Gorge, and he pioneered 30 routes over three years. His climbs ranked among the boldest and most difficult at Smith. Exactly what Arrington climbed remains a mystery, since he rarely documented his climbs. Along with many other 5.9s, his leads of **Taxdor** and **Titus** were tremendous feats for the time. Without the benefit of today's wide crack protection, these off-widths were free solos. At the time, 5.9 wasn't far below Smith's highest standard.

Soon, the word spread about the outstanding climbing in the Gorge and others began exploration. Rained out on a trip to Yosemite, Paul Landrum and Ken Currens settled for Smith instead; within a week they forever changed Gorge climbing. When the dust settled, their best ascents, including **Wildfire** (5.10b), **Prometheus** (5.10b) and **Morning Star** (5.10c), became instant test pieces. The Gorge now contained the greatest concentration of hard routes at Smith.

By the end of 1981, after ascents of **Dark Star** (5.11d/12a), and **Neutron Star** (5.12a), the Gorge stood atop Smith free climbing. Still, most climbers viewed the Gorge as more of a diversion from the park than a place to center their efforts. What the Gorge really needed was someone to dedicate themselves to the basalt, instead of merely visiting now and then. Enter Chuck Buzzard. Possessed with a passion for the basalt, Buzzard devoted three years to developing the Gorge, pioneering more than 60 routes in the process. He didn't come away with the hardest routes of the time, but he first recognized the basalt's true potential. Rarely venturing elsewhere, Buzzard painstakingly cleaned overgrown walls, hacked trails through the brush, and published *Basalt and Boulders,* his cryptic guide to Central Oregon basalt.

By the mid-eighties, Gorge climbing began dying out. I ticked **Masquerade** and **Jonny and the Melonheads** (both 5.12b) in 1984, then didn't return for several years. After climbing **Zealot** (5.12a), even Chuck Buzzard moved on, leaving the Gorge without any driving forces. If not for the efforts of John Rich, new route activity would have completely ceased. A math teacher with legendary stemming ability, Rich became Mr. Gorge in 1986, with his ascent of **Cry of the Gerbil** (5.12b). During the next few years, he pioneered several hard routes, and instantly changed Gorge climbing the day he brought a power drill into the canyon.

Despite the temptations of the power drill, the prevailing attitude is to leave the older routes as they are, instead of retro-bolting the entire Gorge. The rusted pins that protect many cruxes on the older routes are methodically getting replaced with bolts. As the freezing and thawing of the Gorge's columnar joints inevitably loosens any fixed pin, this re-bolting makes good sense. Still, once climbers replace the suspect pins, the traditional lines – no matter how runout – should be left as they are. Ideally, both types of routes will peacefully co-exist in the future and new generations of Gorge climbers won't turn the bolder routes of yesterday into today's bolted warm-up.

Despite the undeniable charm of the Gorge, several problems detract from the experience. The most troublesome issue involves the ownership. The West Columns are privately owned by those living above the rimrock. Fortunately, access exists through the state park, so you'll never need to hike through back yards to get here. If climbers continue to respect the rights of the landowners by entering the Gorge only from the designated areas and never topping out on any west-side routes, there might be no confrontation. If you ignore the rights of the owners and start traipsing through their yards and belaying off their back porches, climbing in the Gorge will cease. If you're ever confronted by a landowner, please be polite and respect their wishes. The future of climbing in the Gorge may well depend on your behavior. On a positive note, the park service recently purchased the entire east side of the Lower Gorge, including it within the boundaries of Smith Rock State Park.

A more repugnant annoyance also afflicts the Lower Gorge. Some people living above the west side rim occasionally use the area as a garbage dump. They've turned portions of this once-pristine place into a smelly, rubbish pile. Unfortunately, since we're trespassing on their land, there's nothing we can do. The plummeting debris poses a risk to climbers below, so take cover if the garbage starts to fall.

The Gorge consists of two main sections, located upstream and downstream from a 90 degree bend in the Crooked River. This chapter covers the traditional columns on both sides of the river in the Lower Gorge. Chapter 14 details the new, bolted routes upstream from the bend in the Upper Gorge.

WEST COLUMNS

An amazing concentration of high-quality routes (every six feet for nearly 300 yards!), greet anyone visiting the West Columns. Since the entire area gets afternoon shade, it's a good destination on a warm day.

To approach the West Columns, drive past the main parking area to the turnaround parking lot. Follow a trail 50 yards east to the rim, and search for a fourth-class descent slot sporting three steel rungs glued into the rock. Below the rim, follow an indistinct trail and hop boulders 200 yards upstream to the first wall.

Parched Cat Cliff (a.k.a. Cox Rocks)

As you're strolling across the boulder field, you'll see the Parched Cat Cliff ahead. Named in memory of a slowly-decomposing cat at the base, this small crag contains a modest collection of neglected routes.

1. LITTLE ORPHAN JAMMIES 5.10d ★★ Gear to 2.5 inches
   This forgettable line features a short crux of stems and painful jams. Start with a thin crack to a ledge, then move right into the crack-split corner. Finish with a traverse left to an anchor.

2. SQUEAL AND PEAL 5.11c ★★ Gear to 2 inches (small wires)
   Insecure stems usually thwarts the few climbers trying this desperate line. After jamming dirty, converging cracks to a ledge, storm the blank corner above to anchor chains.

3. CRETIN'S RETREAT (a.k.a. CRETIN'S REVENGE) 5.10c ★★ Gear to 2.5 inches
   Some painfully sharp jams master a prominent corner in the center of the crag. The first ascent team retreated at a bolt below the current anchors, naming the route after their abortive effort.

4. ORIFACE 5.10b ★★★ Gear to 2.5 inches
   As the only route topping out on the West Columns, this steep face above **Cretin's Retreat** desperately needs anchor bolts below the rim. Whether you do the route in one pitch or two, the exposure makes the bolted wall a unique Gorge experience.

5. THE FERRET'S DEAD 5.9 ★★ Gear to 2.5 inches
   Clumsy moves lead to a ledge; once past these, romp up an appealing crack splitting a slab left of **Cretin's Retreat.**

6. COX ROCKS 5.8 ★ Gear to 4 inches
   The original climb on the cliff follows an ignored off-width, rising above a jumbled ledge at mid-height.

7. THREE FINGERED HACK 5.10c ★★ Gear to 3 inches (wires & TCUs)
   This attractive finger crack splits the face of the column left of Cox Rocks. Jam a starting hand crack, then move left under a block and savor the lichen-covered corner to an anchor.

8. HACK ATTACK 5.12b ? Project
   A desperately blank corner rises directly below the upper crack of **Three Fingered Hack.** Attempted only on toprope, the climb hasn't seen a continuous ascent. Despite dirty rock, someone will surely lead the seam someday – if only because it's hard.

9. VULTURE CREST 5.9 ★ Gear to 3.5 inches
   Two unappealing flake cracks starting off a small, rectangular column are on the left side of the Parched Cat Cliff. The first line jams a crack just right of some razor-edged flakes to a pedestal. Finish with simple jams to an anchor.

10. TERROR BONNE 5.10a R ★ Gear to 3.5 inches
    Some intimidating flakes, splitting a flat face are immediately left of **Vulture Crest.** After shaking through the crux, climb an easy crack to a rappel anchor.

11. PHYSICAL ABUSE 5.10a ★★ Gear to 2.5 inches
    As the Parched Cat Cliff recedes, you'll spot an appealing crack dividing two detached columns. The climbing would be pumping, but the abuse ends abruptly after only 25 glorious feet.

Photo: Bruce Adams

Parched Cat Cliff

1. LITTLE ORPHAN JAMMIES   5.10d ★★
2. SQUEAL AND PEAL   5.11c ★★
3. CRETIN'S RETREAT   5.10c ★★
4. ORIFACE   5.10b ★★★
5. THE FERRET'S DEAD   5.9 ★★

6. COX ROCKS   5.8 ★
7. THREE FINGERED HACK   5.10c ★★
8. HACK ATTACK   5.12b ?
9. VULTURE CREST   5.9 ★
10. TERROR BONNE   5.10a R ★

Wildfire Wall

Leaving the Parched Cat Cliff behind, you'll arrive at the start of the real climbing – the Wildfire Wall. The full length, parallel cracks are among the best in the Gorge. The right section contains some great crack climbs, while the mid-portion offers difficult stemming corners, and bolted sport routes. Far to the left, the wall fizzles out at a narrow passage called the Catwalk.

12. BYRNE'S REVENGE   5.11b R ★★   Gear to 1 inch (small wires, TCUs)
Some short, crackless corners mark the right side of the **Wildfire Wall.** The only route here starts left of a detached pillar and finesses past a bolt-protected crux. The runout finish discourages anyone from repeating this scary line.

13. MAD MAN   5.8 ★   Gear to 6 inches
When first done, this obvious wide crack/squeeze chimney up the right side of a column was totally unprotected. With today's offwidth technology it's much safer, but no one ever tries.

14. WILDFIRE   5.10b ★★★★   Gear to 2.5 inches
This early Gorge classic comes highly recommended. The crux stems and jams up the tight, starting dihedral. After a final finger crack, move right around a blind corner to an anchor.

15. LA VIE DANSANE   5.11d R ★★   Gear to 2 inches (small wires)
Crammed tightly left of **Wildfire,** this poorly-protected seam stays separate the entire way. To finish, either cut right or move up and left to a higher set of slings.

16. CRIME WAVE   5.11b ★★★   Gear to 1.5 inches (wires & TCUs)
A delightful, pin-protected crux of tip jams and edges end this fun route. Start below a missing chunk of column and pull around a small roof at the base. The first ascent skipped out on the final corner by traversing left to **Gruff;** a new anchor allows a more aesthetic direct finish.

17. GRUFF   5.10a ★★★   Gear to 3 inches
This enjoyable, easily protected crack contains the most locking jams you'll ever experience. Either start directly with a few finger slots, or hand traverse in from the left.

18. RIM JOB   5.10b ★★★   Gear to 3 inches (wires)
Another appealing corner with a technical crux near the start rises just left of **Gruff.** The upper section looks tough from below, but hidden ledges slash the grade.

19. IRON CROSS   5.11b ★★   Gear to 3 inches (small wires)
Named for the extreme palming at the crux, **Iron Cross** contains one desperate move. Hopefully, someone will yank a critical knifeblade, and drill a good bolt.

20. NEUTRAL ZONE   5.11a ★★   Gear to 3 inches (TCUs)
Left of Iron Cross are converging cracks forming a wide slot between two columns. After stemming the chimney, master painful finger jams up the finishing dihedral, and step left to an anchor.

21. BADFINGER   5.10b ★★★★   Gear to 2.5 inches
A long-time Gorge classic, this attractive face crack features excellent rock, bomber protection, and three intriguing crux bulges. Start just left of an obvious wide slot.

22. SOFT TOUCH   5.10d ★   Gear to 3 inches (wires)
A dangerously loose block once guarded the corner immediately left of **Badfinger.** The crux originally involved delicate, life-threatening stemming around the flake. Although safer today, it still isn't very good.

23. ORGAN GRINDER   5.10a ★   Gear to 3 inches
This meandering lesson in rope drag management misses the best parts of three separate routes. Start up the converging cracks of **Neutral Zone,** then cut left past **Badfinger** and finish **Soft Touch's** upper corner.

24. ON THE ROAD 5.11a ★★★★ Gear to 2.5 inches (small TCUs)
Among the Gorge's best lines, this attractive crack splits a steep buttress. As the first 5.11 in the area, **On the Road** enjoyed a flurry of activity during the 80s. The technical crux exits a flare at the start, but a finger crack at three-quarters height consistently mows down unfit climbers.

25. EDGE OF THE ROAD 5.12c ★★★ TR
For several years, this toprope column was the hardest exercise on Smith basalt. Start atop a precariously balanced pillar left of **On the Road**, and tackle a desperate move on the razor-edged arête. The difficulties ease only slightly before you are slapped with a holdless crux near the top.

Photo: Bruce Adams

Wildfire Wall – Right Side

12. BYRNE'S REVENGE 5.11b R ★★	19. IRON CROSS 5.11b ★★
13. MAD MAN 5.8 ★	20. NEUTRAL ZONE 5.11a ★★
14. WILDFIRE 5.10b ★★★★	21. BADFINGER 5.10b ★★★★
15. LA VIE DANSANE 5.11d R ★★	22. SOFT TOUCH 5.10d ★
16. CRIME WAVE 5.11b ★★★	23. ORGAN GRINDER 5.10a ★
17. GRUFF 5.10a ★★★	24. ON THE ROAD 5.11a ★★★★
18. RIM JOB 5.10b ★★★	25. EDGE OF THE ROAD 5.12c ★★★

Photo: Bruce Adams

Wildfire Wall – Center

21. BADFINGER 5.10b ★★★★
24. ON THE ROAD   5.11a ★★★★
25. EDGE OF THE ROAD   5.12c ★★★
26. TITUS 5.9 ★
27. SPLIT DECISION   5.12a ★★★
28. PURE PALM   5.11a ★★★★

29. CORNERCOPIA   5.10b ★★★
30. TEACHERS IN SPACE   5.11d ★★
31. BOLD LINE   5.10c ★★
31a. PASS OVER   5.10c ★★
32. RESUSCITATION   5.12b/c ★★★

26. TITUS 5.9 ★ Gear to 6 inches
This obvious wide crack protected scantily when first climbed nearly two decades ago. Modern technology safely protects the off-width, but the moves are just as awkward as ever.

27. SPLIT DECISION 5.12a ★★★ Gear to 1 inch (TCUs)
The baffling corner left of **Titus** wins most decisions when climbers go to battle. Begin atop a detached pillar, then step across to a thin crack. The crux involves some bizarre, insecure stemming protected by four fixed pegs.

28. PURE PALM 5.11a ★★★★ Bolts
Easily among the Gorge's most classic lines, you shouldn't ignore this unique corner. Originally protected entirely with fixed pins, the climb was mercifully bolted, making it much less nerve-wracking. The crux, like every other move, is a palming problem.

29. CORNERCOPIA 5.10b ★★★ Gear to 1.5 inches
A similar, but much easier stemming box rises left of **Pure Palm**. A bouldering crux at the start leads to easier, well-protected jams and stems.

30. TEACHERS IN SPACE 5.11d ★★ Gear (TCUs, Rocks)
The teacher who did the first ascent of this challenging line spent plenty of time flying through space before succeeding. After some painfully wide stems at the start, the crux cranks good edges past some fixed pins. Unfortunately, bat excrement slickens the walls, spoiling a decent route.

31. BOLD LINE 5.10c ★★ Gear to 2.5 inches
An intimidating crack system leading to a small roof rises about 15 feet left of **Teachers in Space**. After a few thin jams, **Bold Line** cuts right at the roof and stems a corner to anchors. The moves are easier than they look from the ground, and not in the least bit bold.

31a. PASS OVER 5.10c ★★ Gear to 2.5 inches
An alternate finish to **Bold Line** cuts left around the roof to a couple bolts. The original line stopped here, but a new ending pulls around another roof to a higher anchor.

32. RESUSCITATION 5.12b/c ★★★ Bolts
As the hardest route in the Lower Gorge, this test piece leaves most climbers breathless. Start atop a pile of rubble just left of **Bold Line**. Sustained, technical moves up the clean face lead to a trick move getting past the fourth bolt.

33. PROJECT 5.12 ?
Left of **Resuscitation** sits an anchor atop an abandoned corner. After an aid ascent, a potential sport route never panned out, but this shallow dihedral would go free if heavily cleaned.

34. WHITE TRASH 5.12a ★★★★ Bolts (with a fixed peg)
Technical and highly varied, this well-protected line deserves its reputation as a Gorge classic. After starting atop a small block leaning against the wall, sustained moves lead to a crux sequence getting past a fixed pin.

35. LION OF JUDAH 5.11d ★★★ Bolts
This open book rises above an obvious roof at the base of the cliff. After stick clipping the bolt at the lip, the crux pulls around the left side of the roof, leading to an unrelenting stemming finish.

35a. JUDAH DIRECT 5.12a ★★ TR
A more difficult variation pulls directly over the roof from an inside corner on the right. Until someone places a separate protection bolt, no one will lead this start.

36. CRY OF THE POOR 5.11a ★★★★ Gear to 2 inches (small wires)
This exquisite seam, with its thin-edged crux at mid-height soars just left of Lion of Judah. Oddly, despite the quality of the moves and protection, the climb sees few ascents.

37. JUST SAY YES 5.12a ★★★ Bolts
This bolted line attacks a flat face left of the **Lion of Judah** roof. After starting below a corner on the left, cut right past a bolt to good edges, then give in to a delicate crux near the top. Initially a toprope problem, the 5.12b original line included a desperate direct start.

38. OUT OF DARKNESS 5.11a ★★★ Gear to 2 inches (small wires)
A fine stemming corner rises between two bolt lines. After a fun dihedral, the first crux hits just below a traverse under a roof. An insecure palming move in the corner to the right finishes to the anchor.

Photo: Bruce Adams

Wildfire Wall – Left Side

32. RESUSCITATION 5.12b/c ★★★	39. TRY TO BE HIP 5.12a ★★★★
33. PROJECT 5.12 ?	40. JESSIE'S LINE 5.11b/c R ★★
34. WHITE TRASH 5.12a ★★★★	41. COME TO THE QUIET 5.10d ★★
35. LION OF JUDAH 5.11d ★★★	42. ON EAGLES WINGS 5.11c X ★
35a. JUDAH DIRECT 5.12a ★★	43. SEAM OF DREAMS 5.11b ★★
36. CRY OF THE POOR 5.11a ★★★★	44. FLUTTER BY 5.11b ★
37. JUST SAY YES 5.12a ★★★	45. SEND YOUR CLONE 5.10c R ★
38. OUT OF DARKNESS 5.11a ★★★	

39. TRY TO BE HIP 5.12a ★★★★ Bolts
    Everyone raves over this excellent, bolt-protected column. Start with Out of Darkness, then step left onto the face after thirty feet. Split by good rests, the enchanting series of intellectual cruxes never let up until you clip the anchors.

40. JESSIE'S LINE 5.11b/c R ★★ Gear (#4 Friend, wires)
    A frightening start, protected by a lousy Friend, blemishes this otherwise enjoyable inside corner. You have the option of either attacking thin jams at the crux directly (5.11c), or weaseling around to the right.

41. COME TO THE QUIET 5.10d ★★ Gear to 1.5 inches
    Beyond Jessie's Line, the unbroken, full-length corners give way to a row of shorter columns. The first of these condensed routes jams a thin crack to an awkward, committing crux pulling around a bulge.

42. ON EAGLES WINGS 5.11c X ★★ Gear to 1 inch (double R.P.s)
    This nightmarish corner lurks above the Come to the Quiet anchor. Horrible R.P.s protect insecure stems above a nasty, ankle-snapping flake. If you still want to try despite my warning, climb in one pitch from the ground.

43. SEAM OF DREAMS 5.11b ★★ Gear to 1 inch (small wires)
    This obscure seam splits the face just left of Come to the Quiet. Start up frothy, ugly jugs, then face climb a low-angled, incipient crack. The crux moves are fun, but they're nothing to dream about.

44. FLUTTER BY 5.11b ★ Gear to 1 inch (small wires)
    Protected by a bolt, this puny, chalkless face doesn't turn many heads. The moves past the bolt aren't bad, but the crux comes higher, above a critical #3 R.P. placement.

45. SEND YOUR CLONE 5.10c R ★ Gear to 1.5 inches
    Grown over and disgusting looking, this dirty, right-leaning thin crack has nothing going for it. A rusty fixed pin protects the crux sequence.

46. BOLDERDASH 5.10a ★ Gear to 1.5 inches
    This stunted line ascends the last crack before the Catwalk. The brief flurry of jams won't leave much of an impression on you.

Catwalk Cliff

Beyond the Wildfire Wall, the trail narrows to a small ledge skirting precariously above the water. Known as the Cat Walk, this tight passage leads to the brilliant lines beyond. Be sure and check your shoelaces, or you might accidently tumble into the drink.

47. PROMETHEUS 5.10c ★★★ Gear to 2.5 inches
    The first route beyond the Cat Walk follows an obvious hand crack leading to a stemming box. The crux surprises you near the top, just when you think the hardest moves are below.

48. NORTHERN LIGHTS 5.11d ★★★ Bolts
    This attractive, bolted seam splits the prominent column left of Prometheus. An entertaining series of crack and face moves lead to a bizarre crux pulling around a bulge.

49. LAST CHANCE 5.10c ★★★★ Gear to 2 inches
    This brilliant open book shouldn't be missed. Perfect rock, bomber protection, and locking jams make Last Chance a Gorge classic. The moves aren't difficult, but the continuity leaves pumped forearms in its wake.

50. STRIKE FORCE 5.12a R ★★ Gear to 1.5 inches (wires)
    Another corner guarded by a roof rises left of Last Chance. The climb begins with a vengeance, assaulting a flaring lieback to a depressingly blank face move. Only a rusty peg keeps you off the

deck, so use caution until someone adds a badly-needed bolt. The upper corner eases quickly, and ends with a traverse right to the **Last Chance** anchors.

51. SILENT HOLOCAUST   5.11c ★★   Gear to 1.5 inches (small wires)
Much like its neighbor to the right, the crux here cranks around an awkward roof near the ground. Again, the moves protect with inadequate pins about ready to fall out. Above the roof, some moderate climbing leads right to **Strike Force.**

Photo: Bruce Adams

Catwalk Cliff – Right Side

47. PROMETHEUS   5.10c ★★★
48. NORTHERN LIGHTS   5.11d ★★★
49. LAST CHANCE   5.10c ★★★★
50. STRIKE FORCE   5.12a R ★★
51. SILENT HOLOCAUST   5.11c ★★
52. DIMINISHING RETURNS   5.10c ★★
53. SPIRITUAL WARFARE   5.11a ★★★
54. THE PEARL   5.11b ★★★★
55. NUCLEAR   5.11d ★★★

56. FULL COURT PRESS   5.12a ★★★
57. BABY FIT   5.11c ★★
58. BAT FLAKE   5.10a ★
59. SATAN'S AWAITING   5.11a ★★
60. RISING STAR   5.10b ★★
61. WHITE DWARF   5.11b/c R ★★
62. NIGHT SHIFT   5.11b ★★★
63. GROUND ZERO   5.10d ★★★

52. DIMINISHING RETURNS 5.10c ★★ Gear to 4 inches
This meandering route takes in part of **Silent Holocaust,** and finishes with **Strike Force** after traversing right from double wide cracks in a corner.

53. SPIRITUAL WARFARE 5.11a ★★★ Gear to 3 inches
The crux of this deceptively strenuous route battles over an intimidating bulge on finger jams. Start up the same wide crack as **Diminishing Returns,** but instead of stepping right, power directly to an anchor.

54. THE PEARL 5.11b ★★★★ Gear to 2.5 inches (wires)
This quality seam left of converging wide cracks contains three distinct crux sections. An insecure lieback near the top isn't much harder than the moves below, but it consistently stops attempting climbers.

55. NUCLEAR 5.11d ★★★ Gear to 2 inches (wires)
The blank corners left of **The Pearl** feature several difficult lines. The right route finesses past bolts, pegs and a few nuts to a reachy crux stretching past a holdless section of rough rock. Finish by cutting left around a distinctive triple roof.

56. FULL COURT PRESS 5.12a ★★★ Bolts (optional TCU)
This intense line follows a relentless series of edges and is well-protected by bolts. The hardest move edges past the third bolt, but the continuity forces many climbers into a turnover. You'll likely want to stick-clip the first bolt.

57. BABY FIT 5.11c ★★ Gear to 1 inch (wires, TCUs)
The leftmost of three tricky routes ascends a shallow, mostly fixed corner through a patch of sandy, gray rock. The odd crux jogs left to a lone pin, then cuts back right on thin edges. Without a long sling or double ropes, you'll throw a fit over the exasperating rope drag.

58. BAT FLAKE 5.10a ★ Gear to 2.5 inches
The dirtiest section of the Catwalk Cliff is a stretch of flaky rock to the right of two tiers of small roofs. A filthy crack skirts the roof on the right, then finishes on a solid, right-leaning flake. Named for an unexpected encounter on the first ascent, **Bat Flake** almost never gets climbed.

59. SATAN'S AWAITING 5.11a ★★ Gear to 1.5 inches (small wires)
This route attacks the center of three cracks splitting small, double-tiered roofs. The most intimidating moves are simple, but the fiendish crux jams the final crack.

60. RISING STAR 5.10b ★★ Gear to 2.5 inches
A forgettable line pulls around the left side of the obvious, gray roofs. After clearing the second roof, jam a pleasant crack to the anchors.

61. WHITE DWARF 5.11b/c R ★★ Gear to 2 inches (small wires)
A dangerous open book starting on some frothy rock looms just left of **Rising Star.** The insecure crux protects scantily with bad R.P.s.

62. NIGHT SHIFT 5.11b ★★★ Gear to 2 inches (small wires)
An intricate seam splits the shallow corner left of **White Dwarf.** A crux lieback protects well, if you can hang out long enough to place the R.P.s. Tall climbers won't even notice the second crux – a long stretch between good holds.

63. GROUND ZERO 5.10d ★★★ Gear to 1.5 inches (small wires)
Once poorly-protected, R.P.s now eliminate any degree of seriousness from this technical corner. The funky crux comes low with a subtle blend of face holds and stems.

64. QUASAR 5.10a ★★★ Gear to 2.5 inches
This enjoyable crack rises above a blocky start on frothy rock. After soloing easy jugs, jam a charming sequence of locking jams to the anchor.

Photo: Bruce Adams

Catwalk Cliff – Center

62. NIGHT SHIFT 5.11b ★★★

63. GROUND ZERO 5.10d ★★★

64. QUASAR 5.10a ★★★

65. EROGENOUS ZONE 5.10c ★★

66. BATTLE OF THE BULGE 5.10a ★

67. BLOOD CLOT 5.10b ★★★★

68. CRACK-A-NO-GO 5.11b ★★★

69. CRUEL SISTER 5.10a ★★★★

70. CATALYST (a.k.a. CHILD ABUSE)
    5.12a/b ★★★★

71. TAXDOR 5.9 X ★

72. SOUTHERN CROSS 5.11a ★★★

65. EROGENOUS ZONE 5.10c ★★ Gear to 2 inches
A shallow inside corner above a square ledge lurks immediately left of **Quasar.** A titillating crux at the start submits to a seductive series of finishing jams.

66. BATTLE OF THE BULGE 5.10a ★ Gear to 4 inches
A few overgrown cracks capped by small roofs are beyond **Erogenous Zone.** A conspicuous offwidth splits the left side of this mediocrity. Rarely climbed, the only highlight pulls around a measly roof.

67. BLOOD CLOT 5.10b ★★★★ Gear to 3 inches (wires)
This classic, locking hand/finger crack is among the best routes on Smith basalt. Once the hardest route in the Gorge, **Blood Clot's** immense popularity has never wavered. After crux finger jams cruise past a bulge, the climbing eases quickly.

68. CRACK-A-NO-GO 5.11b ★★★ Gear to 3.5 inches (small wires)
For a few weeks in 1981, this finger crack stood atop Gorge free climbing. Bordered by easier cracks, it provides a good place to sample 5.11 with the security of a toprope. Once past a gnarly bulge at the start, a crux sequence of tip jams and edges lead to a moderate fist crack.

69. CRUEL SISTER 5.10a ★★★★ Gear to 3.5 inches
Without rival, **Cruel Sister** is the finest hand crack in the Gorge. For years, climbers came just to sample its charms. Set in a shallow corner, the crack widens gradually from thin-hand jams, through a locking section, to some fist jams on the final bulge.

70. CATALYST (a.k.a. CHILD ABUSE) 5.12a/b ★★★★ Bolts
The left column of Cruel Sister contains a brilliant sport route. Long a test piece on toprope, the climb was bolted, led and renamed after power drills came on the scene. Good shakes on square-cut edges break an onslaught of unique moves. The blank crux comes near the top, just when your power fades away.

71. TAXDOR 5.9 X ★ Gear to 4 inches
You can climb the left side of the **Catalyst** column by thrutching up a nasty, runout offwidth. Not surprisingly, no one ever bothers.

Beyond **Taxdor,** the attractive columns deteriorate into some dirty corners rising above a pile of rubbish. Despite appearances, several of these lines are worth climbing, and they offer the easiest routes on the West Columns. In a gardening effort of legendary proportions, Chuck Buzzard transformed this impossibly-overgrown jungle into a legitimate crag. Since almost no one climbs here, some of the vegetation has grown back in recent years.

72. SOUTHERN CROSS 5.11a ★★★ Gear to 2 inches (small wires)
Despite rave reviews after early ascents, this route drifted into obscurity; today, it usually sports a few bushes. Start left of **Taxdor,** and climb past a peg to fun moves in a well-protected corner.

73. HARVEST 5.11b ★★ Gear to 2.5 inches (small wires)
An obscure seam splits the column left of the **Southern Cross** dihedral. Start with the right of two cracks above a flat-faced pillar. An unlikely series of moves leads to a delicate crux just below the top.

74. GRIM TALES 5.11a ★ Gear to 2.5 inches (small wires)
This homely route is crammed tightly in a small corner left of **Harvest.** Although almost no one ever tries, the moves are better than they look. At the top, cut right to the **Cruel Sister** anchor.

75. PATENT LEATHER PUMP 5.10a ★ Gear to 3 inches
Diverging cracks mark this so-so route in an inside corner. After stems at the start, finish mainly up the left crack to an anchor.

76. OLD AND IN THE WAY   5.10c ★★   Gear to 2 inches
An engaging thin crack rises left of a corner with double cracks. A pumping start leads to a technical crux on some rough rock at mid-height.

77. FATHER MERCY   5.11b ★★   Gear to 1.5 inches (small wires)
Easily overlooked, this thin seam splits a flat, dark wall. Mercifully, the crux at the start protects easily with R.P.s.

78. CONVERSION EXCURSION   5.10a ★★   Gear to 3.5 inches
A dark dihedral plugged with two closely-spaced cracks splits the cliff line left of **Father Mercy**. A mediocre pitch jams the corner, then steps left to anchor bolts.

79. BEAN TIME   5.10d ★   Gear to 1.5 inches (wires)
A contrived corner rises just right of a menacing chimney. Ignoring the column to the left, jam and stem continuous moves to an anchor.

80. LAVA TUBE   5.7 X ★   Gear to 2 inches
Despite the grade, this obvious slot makes a poor choice for beginners. Bad protection and awkward squirming eliminates any reason to try.

81. BRAIN DEATH   5.11b R ★★   Gear to 4 inches (small wires)
A prominent, detached column split by a crack juts out from the left side of the Catwalk Cliff. Begin atop a massive block and boulder past an awkward crux to an easy wide crack. Unfortunately, you won't find satisfying placements when you need them most.

82. ON THE SPOT   5.9 ★   Gear to 3 inches
This passable crack jams the left side of the **Brain Death** column. An annoying direct line up a block-plugged wide crack protects poorly, but luckily you can move in from the right.

83. WASTED WORDS   5.10a ★   Gear to 4 inches
If you hate fist jams, expect a struggle on the short, sickle-shaped crack at the crux. Start with the rightmost of two closely-spaced cracks, then cut right past some blocks. Above a ledge, easy jams end at anchor bolts.

84. LOST SOULS   5.9 ★   Gear to 3 inches
The leftmost of parallel cracks jams awkwardly past the same loose blocks as **Wasted Words**, but finishes with an enjoyable face crack in a shallow corner. Move up and left to an anchor.

85. RELIGIOUS FERVOR   5.10a ★★   Gear to 4 inches
This obvious wide crack splits a left-facing corner. After a committing lieback at the start, moderate finger/hand jams finish.

86. SITTING DUCK   5.9 ★   Gear to 3 inches
A hand crack sporting a loose-looking block rises just left of **Religious Fervor**. Some awkward, dirty jams move cautiously past the block to a finish on unusually gnarly rock. You can contrive a 5.10a near the top by avoiding the crack to the right.

87. GREASY SPOON   5.10a ★★   Gear to 4 inches
A slender pillar capped with a touch of white rests in a corner below three cracks. The right line jams past a crux finger crack at the start, then climbs a simple wide section to the anchor.

88. DIRE WOLF   5.8 ★   Gear to 1.5 inches (wires)
This passable thin crack finger-jams a shallow inside corner directly above a small pillar. Step cautiously past a guillotine flake and cut left to bolts.

89. DELICATESSEN   5.8 ★   Gear to 4 inches
A low-angled crack branches off from the start of **Dire Wolf**. While no delicacy, you still might enjoy this short hand/fist crack. A massive bush once blocked the start, so the first-ascent party began with a desperate foot shuffle from the left.

90. FAST FOOD JUNKY 5.8 ★   Gear to 4 inches
This mediocre route climbs double wide cracks in a block-capped slot. Some starting jams up the
left crack lead to easy stemming below the roof. Cut left if you've had enough, or pull around to
right if you crave more.

91. PHALLIC SYMBOL 5.7 ★   Gear to 2.5 inches
A series of dirty, unaesthetic jams up double cracks lead past a slender block to anchor bolts. The
hardest moves come in the first few feet, climbing either side of a large block.

Photo: Bruce Adams

Catwalk Cliff – Left Side

70. CATALYST (a.k.a. CHILD ABUSE)
    5.12a/b ★★★★
71. TAXDOR 5.9 X ★
72. SOUTHERN CROSS 5.11a ★★★
73. HARVEST 5.11b ★★
74. GRIM TALES 5.11a ★
75. PATENT LEATHER PUMP 5.10a ★
76. OLD AND IN THE WAY 5.10c ★★
77. FATHER MERCY 5.11b ★★
78. CONVERSION EXCURSION 5.10a ★★
79. BEAN TIME 5.10d ★
80. LAVA TUBE 5.7 X ★

81. BRAIN DEATH 5.11b R ★★
82. ON THE SPOT 5.9 ★
83. WASTED WORDS 5.10a ★
84. LOST SOULS 5.9 ★
85. RELIGIOUS FERVOR 5.10a ★★
86. SITTING DUCK 5.9 ★
87. GREASY SPOON 5.10a ★★
88. DIRE WOLF 5.8 ★
89. DELICATESSEN 5.8 ★
90. FAST FOOD JUNKY 5.8 ★
91. PHALLIC SYMBOL 5.7 ★
92. CHIMNEY OF GHOULS 5.7 R ★

92. CHIMNEY OF GHOULS 5.7 R ★ Gear to 4 inches (small wires)
An ominous wide crack marking the end of the Cat Walk Cliff lurks around the corner left of **Phallic Symbol.** The stems and liebacks are fun, but you'll have trouble finding decent protection.

Star Wall

Just when it seems the fun is over, along comes the Star Wall. For years, these full-length columns contained the hardest routes in the entire Gorge. The shorter lines to the right aren't special, but the corners beyond are brilliant test pieces. A few unclimbed seams along the way will surely catch the attention of future Gorge hardmen.

93. OLD TROUBLE'S NUMBER SEVEN 5.10b ★ Gear to 2.5 inches
The Star Wall begins with an ugly section of dark rock sprouting bushes. About eight feet left of the biggest bush rises a respectable hand crack.

94. PINK ROADGRADER 5.10d ★ Gear to 1.5 inches (small wires)
This unlikely route begins just left of **Old Trouble's Number Seven.** After pulling around a blank crux at the start, bulldoze through some weeds to the top.

95. KNEEGOBEE 5.8 ★ Gear to 4 inches
A left-facing corner sits just right of a block-plugged wide crack. The moves look desperate, but stems to the left slash the grade.

96. LAST DAYS 5.10a ★★★ Gear to 2.5 inches
This left-facing corner, bordered by some hanging vines, lurks beyond four unclimbed (unrecorded?) cracks. A flurry of entertaining finger/hand jams on good rock ends at an anchor.

97. ST. PADDEE'S DAY 5.10a ★ Gear to 4 inches
An awesome display of greenery guards the base of this otherwise high-quality line. If you survive the sticker-bush massacre at the start, you'll relish the clean finishing crack.

98. TURNING POINT 5.10a ★★ Gear to 4 inches
Double wide cracks in a dark, ugly corner loom just left of a bush-choked dihedral. An awkward start is followed by some excellent finger jams above.

99. LETHAL DOSE 5.11a R ★★ Gear to 2 inches (small wires)
Gambling with this seam might give you a lethal dose. Tangle with some dirty rock and unsatisfying protection at the start, with a 5.10 finish as your reward.

100. MANTRA 5.10a ★★★ Gear to 3 inches
Don't let the mangy beginning scare you away from this delightful route. The charms of the finger/hand jams more than make up for the offensive start.

101. CRY OF THE GERBIL 5.12b ★★★ Bolts
John Rich named this arousing corner after his favorite pet. If they survive a delicate stemming move low, a crux face sequence above the sixth bolt stops most climbers in their tracks. Shaky pins once protected the moves, but today there are nothing but bolts.

102. DARK STAR 5.11d/12a ★★★ Gear to .75 inch (TCUs, wires)
Once Smith's hardest route, this attractive corner still gives climbers fits. Sticky rubber stripped the insecure smears at the crux of their original grade. After starting with 5.11 stemming, four fixed pegs protect the hardest moves near the top.

103. NEUTRON STAR 5.12a ★★★★ Gear to .75 inch
This exquisite face climb comes from the same era as **Dark Star.** Some strenuous edges past a bolt entering a flaring slot are the hardest moves, but the crux comes from the continuity of the climbing. Except for a couple od nuts at the start, the entire line sports fixed gear.

104. JONNY AND THE MELONHEADS   5.12b ★★★   Gear to 1 inch (small wires, TCUs)
Named in honor of the second-ascent team, this desperately shallow dihedral left of **Neutron Star**
never caught on. The crux pulls around a strenuous bulge, after fighting for satisfying nut
placements. The pin-protected moves above are easier, but you'll still encounter a few haunting
sections of holdless basalt.

105. MORNING STAR   5.10c ★★★★   Gear to 2.5 inches
During the late seventies, this alluring crack was the hardest route in the Gorge. After a one inch

Photo: Bruce Adams

Star Wall – Right Side

93. OLD TROUBLE'S NUMBER SEVEN
    5.10b ★
94. PINK ROADGRADER   5.10d ★
95. KNEEGOBEE   5.8 ★

96. LAST DAYS   5.10a ★★★
97. ST. PADDEE'S DAY   5.10a ★
98. TURNING POINT   5.10a ★★
99. LETHAL DOSE   5.11a R ★★

Photo: Bruce Adams

Star Wall – Left Side

98. TURNING POINT 5.10a ★★
99. LETHAL DOSE 5.11a R ★★
100. MANTRA 5.10a ★★★
101. CRY OF THE GERBIL 5.12b ★★★
102. DARK STAR 5.11d/12a ★★★
103. NEUTRON STAR 5.12a ★★★★

104. JONNY AND THE MELONHEADS
     5.12b ★★★
105. MORNING STAR 5.10c ★★★★
106. NIGHT CROSSING 5.11b ★★
107. FREON 5.10a ★

crack gets things going, unrelenting jams slowly build a healthy pump. The likeness of a climber sculpted into the stone at the base mystifies anyone walking by.

106. NIGHT CROSSING   5.11b ★★   Gear to 2.5 inches (small wires)
A face seam leading into a deep dihedral rises around the corner left of **Morning Star.** After an annoyingly hard blind-reach off an undercling, easy stems above a big ledge finish to the anchor.

107. FREON   5.10a ★   Gear to 4 inches
A conspicuous wide crack marks the end of the Star Wall. When first climbed, it was possibly the first 5.10 in the entire Gorge. Unfortunately, a fine grit clinging to the rock turns any ascent into a trying ordeal.

Jungleland

The final series of corners on the west side of the Gorge is the undeveloped Jungleland. A lack of clean lines and a horrific bushwack along the base keeps all but the most inquisitive climbers away. Surprisingly, some classic cracks rise above the jungle, justifying a visit. For about 200 feet beyond the Star Wall, the columns are short and broken – stacked one atop another. Ahead, you'll spot a prominent chimney that marks the beginning of Jungleland.

108. WHISPERS   5.10a ★★   Gear to 3.5 inches
A hand crack rises 15 feet right of Jungleland's first chimney. After scrambling up broken columns, jam dark rock to a finish pulling around a blocky section. To descend, traverse far left to the anchors atop **Masquerade.**

109. TREE ROUTE   5.9 ★   Gear to 3.5 inches
Triple cracks, starting off a short stack of columns, are around the corner and downhill from the initial chimney of Jungleland. A sickly tree grows just to the left. After climbing the cracks, cut left to some fun hand/fist jams.

110. HAND JIVE   5.9 ★   Gear to 3.5 inches
This forgotten line rises 40 feet left of the **Tree Route,** just beyond distinctive, parallel cracks. Solid jams lead past some blocks into a flare. After finishing up a slot, walk left to an anchor.

111. HERKY JERKY   5.9 ★   Gear to 4 inches
A distinctive, zigzagging wide crack splits a dark, flat face right of a massive column. Start to the right, then move left to the crux struggle.

112. JUDAS   5.10a ★   Gear to 3 inches
If you're counting on some fun climbing, this dirty hand crack will only betray you. Start slightly right of an unmistakable chimney and jam a left-leaning crack on ominous, dark rock.

113. BIG CHIMNEY   5.7 X ★★★   Gear to 2 inches (wires)
A towering pillar split by an alluring thin crack stands apart from the main cliff. Despite sparse protection, chimney enthusiasts love slithering up the narrow corridor behind this column.

114. MASQUERADE   5.12b R ★★★★   Gear to 1 inch (small wires, TCUs)
This stunning seam splits the river face of the **Big Chimney** column. It's worth hacking through the jungle if only to gaze at **Masquerade.** Brush-up on your gear-placing skills before considering an attempt, since you won't find any fixed protection. The crux comes near the start, fiddling with R.P.s, and pulling on make-believe holds.

115. BUSH DOCTOR   5.10b ★★★   Gear to 3 inches
This fun hand/finger crack is around the corner from an offwidth and is hidden from view about 30 feet beyond **Masquerade.** You'll have to hack your way to the base without ever getting a decent view, but you'll enjoy the climbing once you emerge from the foliage.

116. RAZOR BOY 5.10c ★★   Gear to 2.5 inches
The last route on West Columns requires the maximum amount of jungle travel to reach the
base. The climb sits just right of a prominent green pillar, but you won't catch a glimpse until
you're standing beneath it. A few razor jams at the start lead to a crux skirting a small, diagonal
roof.

Photo: Alan Watts

Jungleland

108. WHISPERS 5.10a ★★   112. JUDAS 5.10a ★
109. TREE ROUTE 5.9 ★   113. BIG CHIMNEY 5.7 X ★★★
110. HAND JIVE 5.9 ★   114. MASQUERADE 5.12b R ★★★★
111. HERKY JERKY 5.9 ★   115. BUSH DOCTOR 5.10b ★★★

EAST COLUMNS

Several isolated sections of columnar basalt are across the river from the West Columns. The rock compares favorably with the west-side lines, but the area contains far fewer climbs and almost no one visits. Despite the neglect, the East Columns offer some great routes that are unlike anything else in the Gorge. Since no one lives above, several climbs continue through the rimrock to the top. The dramatic change from smooth-sided jam cracks to strenuous face moves on edges and pockets adds spice to the longer routes. The standards don't come close to matching the west side, but the 5.10s and 5.11s will please anyone climbing at that level.

   The main reason why few climbers visit the East Columns has more to do with the access than the rock quality. During low-water conditions, you can hop boulders across the river below **Cruel Sister;** otherwise, the only approach involves a long hike.

So Low Wall

A cluster of pint-sized columns that is easily overlooked is just upstream from the Student Wall. The cracks are so short they barely qualify as routes, but many of them make excellent miniatures of the longer Gorge classics. For climbers unsure of their stamina, they serve as a good training ground for the real thing.

117. LITTLE WEENIE   5.7 ★   Gear to 3 inches
   The first route on the wall jams a laughably short crack just right of a small pillar. **Little Weenie** isn't very long or hard, so few climbers find it satisfying.

118. RUNT'S GRUNT   5.7 ★   Gear to 4 inches
   This short wide crack sits in the leftmost of several inside corners. After an awkward entrance move, simple liebacks and stems end quickly at an anchor.

119. SAWED OFF RUNT   5.8 ★★   Gear to 3 inches
   Parallel hand cracks jam opposite sides of a hanging column. The enjoyable left crack concludes after a fleeting series of locking jams.

120. PIPSQUEAK   5.8 ★★★   Gear to 3 inches
   The only thing disappointing about this sublime crack is that it ends so quickly. Bomber hand jams breeze the right side of a hanging column to anchor bolts.

121. LITTLE SQUIRT   5.9 ★★   Gear to 2.5 inches
   Some sinker finger jams highlight the face crack just left of an offwidth. Unfortunately, the route ends abruptly after only a quick spurt of pleasure.

122. DWARF'S DELIGHT   5.8 ★★★   Gear to 4 inches
   Tucked in a four-foot-wide slot are an offwidth and a thin crack. At first glance, the route looks like a nasty struggle, but it's actually a fun stemming exercise between both walls.

123. SHORT MAN'S COMPLEX   5.9 ★   Gear to 3.5 inches
   Diverging cracks lie around a sharp corner right from **Dwarf's Delight.** The left line jams awkwardly up a right-facing dihedral, then muscles past a bulge to anchor bolts.

124. STUNTED GROWTH   5.8 R ★★   Gear to 3 inches
   Ascend the rightmost of two diverging cracks via enjoyable hand jams up a heavily textured face. The fun ends when you cut left on face holds around an intimidating bulge.

125. NAPOLEON COMPLEX   5.10d ★★   Gear to 3 inches
   The desperate stems and tip jams starting this tight corner might be your Waterloo. After the crux, move far right to an anchor.

126. SHORT STUFF 5.10b ★ Gear to 2 inches
Parallel cracks rise above some blocks scattered at the base on the right side of the So Low Wall.
The locking finger jams up the left crack might be worth doing if they weren't choked with dirt.

127. PUNK KID 5.11c ★ TR
The last route on the So Low Wall follows an innocent-looking crack. If scrubbed, the grade
would drop; for now, the filthy flares are a real struggle.

So Low Wall

117. LITTLE WEENIE 5.7 ★
118. RUNT'S GRUNT 5.7 ★
119. SAWED OFF RUNT 5.8 ★★
120. PIPSQUEAK 5.8 ★★★
121. LITTLE SQUIRT 5.9 ★★
122. DWARF'S DELIGHT 5.8 ★★★

123. SHORT MAN'S COMPLEX 5.9 ★
124. STUNTED GROWTH 5.8 R ★★
125. NAPOLEON COMPLEX 5.10d ★★
126. SHORT STUFF 5.10b ★
127. PUNK KID 5.11c ★

Windfall Wall

An impressive stretch of columns towers just upstream from the So Low Wall, past the jungle. Known as the Windfall Wall, this seldom-visited crag offers the best routes on the East Columns. Unlike the usual Gorge climb, which ends atop the columnar basalt, these routes continue through the bulging rimrock to the top. A fixed anchor along the rim allows a two-rope rappel back down to the base. Even though the best approach crosses the river and hikes along a path from the south, I've described the routes moving upstream left to right

128. EMMAUS 5.10a ★★ Gear to 2.5 inches
A short finger/hand crack highlights the first route on the Windfall Wall. After scrambling up a staircase of broken pillars, cruise sharp jams in a left-facing corner. A fun bulge and hand shuffle right lead to a belay. If you can't muster the courage to rappel off the hair-raising anchor, climb junky blocks (5.7) to the top.

129. ZEALOT 5.12a ★★★ Gear to 1 inch (small wires, TCUs)
A short, perplexing seam is tucked in a shallow corner just right of Emmaus. Flaring jams, nebulous stems and strenuous nut placements make Zealot the hardest route on the East Columns. Above the corner, either rap off or climb steep junk to the top.

130. MIDNIGHT CREEPER 5.8 ★★ Gear to 3 inches
Far better than it looks, this block-plugged wide crack starts above a staircase of columns. You won't need to do a single offwidth move, thanks to a finger crack just inches to the left. From the top of a pillar, scramble past a bad anchor, then finish up creepy flakes.

130a. JEEPERS CREEPERS 5.8 X ★★ Gear to 3 inches
A higher-quality finish to Midnight Creeper cuts right across a blank face to an easy corner. Unfortunately, a fall on the hardest moves will break both your legs, as you will slam into the pillar below.

131. ACROSS THE WATER 5.9 ★★ Gear to 4 inches
The right side of the Midnight Creeper pillar offers a stemming problem between two wide cracks. You'll use a few fist jams, but good stems eliminate the need to plunge into the depths of the offwidth. Atop the pillar, either finish left, or see Jeepers Creepers.

132. MARGO'S MADNESS 5.10b ★★★ Gear to 3 inches
This gorgeous face crack splits the center of the column right of Across the Water. After an awkward entrance from either side, a memorable series of finger stacks and thin-hand jams quickly give way to a moderate flare. Either move left past a block-slung anchor or finish via Jeepers Creepers.

133. FOOL'S PLEASURE 5.10a ★★★ Gear to 4 inches
Widening slowly from finger slots at the start to fist jams near the top, this attractive crack plugs a right-facing corner bordering Margo's Madness. Move left atop the pillar, following one of two second-pitch options to the rim.

134. LAMA MOMMA 5.10b ★★★ Gear to 4 inches
A varied crack in a left-facing corner highlights this high-quality romp to the top of the cliff. Start with a scramble up broken columns, then hand/fist jam to a finger crack crux. Either cut right to a rappel anchor, or finish with a solid corner.

135. BABY WALKS 5.10a ★★★ Gear to 3.5 inches
Another enjoyable line follows a hand/fist crack just right of an off-width. Begin with a wandering traverse from the left, then race strenuous jams to an anchor. If you don't want to rappel off, attack a dangerously runout direct line on face holds (5.9).

136. WINDFALL 5.11b ★★★ Gear to 1 inch (small wires)
An attractive seam rises from the ground right of several moderate cracks. After blowing past the

Photo: Bruce Adams

Windfall Wall

128. EMMAUS   5.10a ★★
129. ZEALOT   5.12a ★★★
130. MIDNIGHT CREEPER   5.8 ★★
130a. JEEPERS CREEPERS   5.8 X ★★
131. ACROSS THE WATER   5.9 ★★
132. MARGO'S MADNESS   5.10b ★★★
133. FOOL'S PLEASURE   5.10a ★★★
134. LAMA MOMMA   5.10b ★★★

135. BABY WALKS   5.10a ★★★
136. WINDFALL   5.11b ★★★
137. HARD ATTACK   5.11a ★★★
138. THE SHEEPGATE   5.11c ★★
139. MISTER REACH   5.11b ★★★
140. BRIDGE OF SIGHS   5.10d ★★
141. GENOCIDE   5.10b ★★

crux flare at the start, you'll have little chance to catch your wind on the continuous moves above. Most climbers rap off, but a fun finish veers right on good holds to a pocketed, crack-split wall.

137. HARD ATTACK 5.11a ★★★ Gear to 2.5 inches (wires)
Closely-spaced cracks in an inside corner are just right of **Windfall**. Begin with good jams, then step left around a tricky roof to fun stemming between two seams. You can weasel over to anchors, but the actual route attacks a breathtaking crack on the rimrock.

138. THE SHEEPGATE 5.11c ★★ Gear to 2.5 inches (wires, TCUs)
This demanding route steps right around the **Hard Attack** roof, then tip jams a tough corner. The crux comes on a holdless face move above the first of three bolts on the rimrock.

139. MISTER REACH 5.11b ★★★ Gear to 1 inch (wires, TCUs)
If stemming is your cup of tea, then make a date with **Mister Reach**. A few fixed pins protect the muscle-pulling stems at the crux.

140. BRIDGE OF SIGHS 5.10d ★★ Gear to 2.5 inches
Two closely-spaced seams in a shallow corner are near the right end of the cliff. After jamming the cracks, exit right around a blank crux on some hidden holds. There's no anchor atop the columns, so veer up and right over intimidating bulges to easy climbing.

141. GENOCIDE 5.10b ★★ Gear to 3 inches
A dark face split by gnarly cracks marks the right boundary of the Windfall Wall. Just to the left lurks a mediocre, right-facing dihedral capped by a small roof. The corner succumbs to painful jams before joining **Bridge of Sighs** below the bulges.

Beyond the Windfall Wall, the basalt degenerates into a long series of blank bulges and corners. Since few cracks split this puny, 25-foot high section of rock, you'll find only one route even remotely worth roping up for.

142. DINK 5.8 ★ Gear to 3 inches
A short hand crack sits just left of an inside corner plugged with a guillotine flake. The jams are fun, but after thrashing past a bush you'll find no convenient way down.

Hand Job Wall
The first cliff of any consequence upstream from the Windfall Wall offers several cracks. Much like the west side, the routes end atop the columnar joints without venturing onto the blocky rimrock.

143. LOST AND FOUND 5.8 ★★ Gear to 3 inches
You'll pass under a leaning pillar as you walk upstream from some non-descript columns. A left-facing corner sporting finger locks between wide slots sits 25 feet beyond this pillar.

144. HUCKLEBERRY HOUND 5.7 ★★ Gear to 3 inches
A fleeting series of stems and hand jams polish off this shallow corner above a unique cave.

145. GAGGED AND BOUND 5.7 R ★ Gear to 3.5 inches
An obvious slot plugged by broken columns rises right of **Huckleberry Hound**. After a simple chimney, either risk getting stuck squeezing through a tight hole, or hand traverse left to anchors.

146. INTO WHITE 5.9 ★★ Gear to 1.5 inches (wires)
A few weeds grow in the first full-length corner right of a chimney. After some good jams, the crack peters out to face holds near the top. Traverse far right to rappel slings.

147. STRAWBERRY BLONDE 5.11c ★★ Gear to 1 inch (small wires, TCUs)
Stacked with hard moves, **Strawberry Blonde** snubs most attempts. Anyone using brute force on the delicate crux (protected by a fixed pin) gets slapped in the face. Start atop a leaning block, just right of the dirty seam.

148. DEMANDER CODY 5.9 ★★   Gear to 2 inches
Perhaps the most distinctive feature on the Hand Job Wall is a missing chunk of column that left a roof-capped chimney in its place. An intimidating sequence underclings left around the roof, then jams a shallow, lichen-covered corner.

149. MINES OF MORIA 5.7 R ★★   Gear (Friends to #2, Headlamp)
This claustrophobic chimney is the most unusual route in the entire Gorge. More of a spelunking

Photo: Bruce Adams

Hand Job Wall

143. LOST AND FOUND 5.8 ★★
144. HUCKLEBERRY HOUND 5.7 ★★
145. GAGGED AND BOUND 5.7 R ★
146. INTO WHITE 5.9 ★★
147. STRAWBERRY BLONDE 5.11c ★★
148. DEMANDER CODY 5.9 ★★
149. MINES OF MORIA 5.7 R ★★
150. CODY'S CORNER 5.8 ★★

151. MCKENZIE'S WAY 5.11b ★★
152. KILLER JISM 5.11b ★★
153. UGLY AS SIN 5.11a ★
154. HAND JOB 5.10b ★★★
155. ORIGINAL SIN 5.10c ★★★
156. BLITZKRIEG 5.9 ★
157. BLITZEN 5.10c ★

adventure than a rock climb, **Mines of Moria** enters a dark chimney behind a missing section of column. Squirm toward the light above, then follow another hidden chimney to the top.

150. CODY'S CORNER   5.8 ★★   Gear to 2.5 inches
Reach blindly to good jams out the right exit around the hanging column. Once safely past the roof, cut right to the finishing corner.

151. MCKENZIE'S WAY   5.11b ★★   Gear to 2 inches
A short crux followed by simple climbing, makes this tips crack a natural for anyone looking for a cheap 5.11. Begin with the starting crack of **Cody's Corner,** then shuffle right to thin jams.

152. KILLER JISM   5.11b ★★   Gear to 1 inch (small wires)
This nasty route follows an overgrown seam rising above a small, slanting block. The insecure moves at the crux are a bit hard to swallow.

153. UGLY AS SIN   5.11a ★   Gear to 2.5 inches (TCUs)
Unusually dirty, this ignored route jams an ugly, unforgiving corner above a six foot pillar.

154. HAND JOB   5.10b ★★★   Gear to 2.5 inches
The best route on the wall jams and stems between double cracks just right of a five foot chunk of basalt. After a tricky bouldering start, you'll savor the clean, well-protected moves above.

155. ORIGINAL SIN   5.10c ★★★   Gear to 2.5 inches
Strenuous finger stacks and thin-hand jams cap this long-standing test piece. You'll likely arrive at the crux just toasted enough to insure a struggle. Dirty rock in the starting corner detracts from the fun, but it shouldn't scare you away.

156. BLITZKRIEG   5.9 ★   Gear to 4 inches
After a single glance, most climbers pass on this zigzagging off-width. If you're looking for a tussle, stem double cracks low, then storm awkward moves past a few loose blocks.

157. BLITZEN   5.10c ★   Gear to 3.5 inches
A short, leaning crack borders **Blitzkrieg.** After scrambling atop a pillar, some annoying hand/fist jams give way to crux finger slots near the top.

Arrington Columns

A fourth-class descent chimney marks the right end of the Hand Job Wall. Beyond are dozens of short, jumbled columns ending at a ledge running along the entire cliff. With only a few exceptions, the routes are humdrum, so most climbers walk on by. Those who climb here usually forego the simple rimrock finishes, rappeling instead from anchor bolts on the ledge.

158. CRUNCH TIME   5.8 ★   Gear to 3 inches
The first line on the Arrington Columns jams a mediocre crack rising above the highest point on the hillside. A killer block guarding the final moves awaits some unlucky climber. Either rappel from anchor bolts, or follow a crack (5.5) to the top.

159. EXILED MAN   5.8 ★   Gear to 3 inches
A hand crack is crammed tightly next to **Crunch Time.** Unfortunately, after a few fun jams, you'll face a risky clash with a detached flake.

160. BROTHERS CHILD   5.10c ★★★   Gear to 2.5 inches
Unlike most routes on the Arrington Columns, this line offers two memorable pitches. Some climbers rappel after the starting corner, but the best section attacks the overhanging rimrock. Start just right of an eight-foot pillar.
1.   5.10b After some flaky rock at the start, fun jams end at an anchor.
2.   5.10c Muscle an intimidating crack over a bulge to big face holds. Walk off 100 feet downstream via the Hand Job Wall chimney.

161. CHIMNEY SWEEP   5.7 R ★★   Gear to 4 inches
Easy but poorly-protected stems between wide cracks lead to a ledge. Either rappel, or follow a simple (5.5) second pitch to the left.

162. MASTER LOONY   5.11a ★★★★   Gear to 2.5 inches
Unlike anything else in the Lower Gorge, this exceptional route shouldn't be missed. Anyone bored with straight-in cracks and stemming corners will thrill over the exciting jugs at the crux, which muscle around a bolted roof. The starting crack (5.10b) makes a fine affair in its own right, but the real fun begins above.

Photo: Bruce Adams

Arrington Columns

158. CRUNCH TIME   5.8 ★
159. EXILED MAN   5.8 ★
160. BROTHERS CHILD   5.10c ★★★
161. CHIMNEY SWEEP   5.7 R ★★
162. MASTER LOONY   5.11a ★★★★
163. LOONY TUNES   5.11b R ★★
164. TUNED OUT   5.9 R ★
165. STUFFED TURKEY   5.8 R ★

166. OFF TEMPO   5.10a ★★★
167. BANANA SPLIT   5.8 ★★
168. CHIMNEY FIRE   5.7 R ★
169. LUCKY GUY   5.10c ★★
170. COMMON CRIMINAL   5.8 ★★
171. BANNED FOR LIFE   5.10b ★
172. SHACKLES AND CHAINS   5.8 ★★
173. SLEEPING DOG   5.7 ★

163. LOONY TUNES   5.11b R ★★   Gear to 1.5 inches (small wires)
A blank, sparsely-protected corner looms just right of **Master Loony.** Sensible climbers stem off a block to the right at the crux, but loony purists sometimes ignore it completely (5.11c). Atop the crack, either finish to the rim, or cut left to rappel anchors.

164. TUNED OUT   5.9 R ★   Gear to 6 inches
This awkward, uninspiring slot squeezes past a detached block to a few fist jams. Above the crack, finish with a simple chimney.

The next several routes jam short cracks to a spacious ledge below the rimrock. Bolt anchors allow a quick descent, but you'll have three options if you go for the top. A chimney on the left and a ramp to the right are easy pointless scrambles. The only decent finish stems a steep, inside corner (5.7) between the other exits.

165. STUFFED TURKEY   5.8 R ★   Gear to 4 inches
Some stems between two wide cracks lead into a finishing chimney. Poor protection and dirty rock eliminates any good reason to try.

166. OFF TEMPO   5.10a ★★★   Gear to 5 inches
Offwidth lovers (are there any?) will enjoy this clean crack, which splits a flat face between two columns.

167. BANANA SPLIT   5.8 ★★   Gear to 4 inches
Clean, double cracks rise above a small, lichen-covered block. Some passable stems and liebacks end at anchor bolts.

168. CHIMNEY FIRE   5.7 R ★   Gear to 4 inches
Another mediocre stemming problem looms between two columns above a massive chunk of basalt. Begin with a scramble up the right side of the starting block.

169. LUCKY GUY   5.10c ★★   Gear to 2.5 inches
Some deceptively tricky jams master this lichen-covered corner that lies right of a square, 10-foot block.

170. COMMON CRIMINAL   5.8 ★★   Gear to 3.5 inches
An unmistakable pillar wedges in the upper section of a deep-set corner. After climbing into a slot, locking hand jams exit around the left side of the obstacle.

171. BANNED FOR LIFE   5.10b ★   Gear to 2.5 inches
A disappointing thin crack rises right of the hanging tooth on **Common Criminal.** After finessing past a loose block on finger jams, avoid a blank finish by veering left.

172. SHACKLES AND CHAINS   5.8 ★★   Gear to 3 inches
A quick hand crack splits the short corner above a sagebrush-capped ledge. Hexes work better than Friends in the angular slots.

173. SLEEPING DOG   5.7 ★   Gear to 4 inches
The last of several identical chimneys between widely-spaced columns isn't worth doing, but it protects well.

174. SLASHER   5.10c ★★   Gear to 3 inches
The overgrown corners along the right end of the Arrington Columns offer few options. The only eye-catching line finger jams to slings, then attacks a jumbled crack splitting the rimrock. The best climbing comes on the strenuous finish, but the start alone makes a good jaunt (5.10b).

Shakespeare Cliff

The final East Column crag offers some excellent, full-length cracks. Since the corners aren't especially steep, the cliff contains the best sub-5.10 routes in the entire Gorge. Several unclimbed (or at least unrecorded) routes still await ascents. The first routes start on the shorter left side of the wall.

175. LOVE STRUCK ROMEO 5.8 ★★ Gear to 3 inches
Behind a free-standing pillar rises a hand crack bordered by an off-width. When the going gets tough, you can pacify yourself by stemming right. Above the crack, simple moves lead to a final chimney.

176. BIG WOODY 5.9 ★★ Gear to 3 inches
Double cracks converge to an inverted spike to the right of a distinctive, balanced column. **Big Woody** skirts around the left side of the tooth, then jams a stiff hand crack to easy scrambling.

177. AS YOU LIKE IT 5.10b ★★★ Gear to 3 inches
This enjoyable crack in a left-facing corner should suit you just fine. Start off the right side of a flat block, then fly up locking hand slots to a finger jam crux. Finish with a crank around a rimrock bulge.

178. SORON 5.9 ★★ Gear to 4 inches
Double cracks split the left side of a massive, flat column. After some thrashy moves in the starting flare, jam and stem to a final pull over a steep bulge.

179. MUCH ADO ABOUT NOTHING 5.10d ★★★ Gear to 3 inches
Capped by an intimidating finger-crack roof, this exciting pitch starts just right of a flat-faced column. The original route ended prematurely at slings (5.9), but you won't want to miss the spectacular finish.

180. AZOG 5.9 ★★ Gear to 3 inches
This moderate line jams the third crack right of **Much Ado About Nothing**. Atop the shallow dihedral, avoid the ominous rimrock by sidestepping right to an anchor.

180a. MID SUMMERS NIGHT SCREAM 5.7 ★★ Gear to 3 inches
An alternate finish to **Azog** cuts left through the rimrock via jugs, then mantels to the bolts atop **Much Ado About Nothing.**

181. TWO GENTLEMEN'S PNEUMONIA 5.7 ★★ Gear to 4 inches
A massive chunk of basalt plugs a wide crack on the left side of a pillar. Easy moves lead past this block to a short jam crack ending at anchor bolts.

182. LUST'S LABOR'S COST 5.10b ★★★ Gear to 3 inches
Parallel cracks split the wall around the corner to the right of a block-plugged wide crack. Scramble up easy, fractured rock to a large ledge, then savor an enjoyable, tongue-twister of a finger crack on the left.

183. KING SMEAR 5.11a ★★ Gear to 3 inches
This tricky route tackles thin, cuticle-tearing jams in a smooth-sided corner.

Photo: Bruce Adams

Shakespeare Cliff

175. LOVE STRUCK ROMEO 5.8 ★★

176. BIG WOODY 5.9 ★★

177. AS YOU LIKE IT 5.10b ★★★

178. SORON 5.9 ★★

179. MUCH ADO ABOUT NOTHING
     5.10d ★★★

180. AZOG 5.9 ★★

180a. MID SUMMERS NIGHT SCREAM 5.7
     ★★

181. TWO GENTLEMEN'S PNEUMONIA
     5.7 ★★

182. LUST'S LABOR'S COST 5.10b ★★★

183. KING SMEAR 5.11a ★★

Jeff Ellington climbs the Lower Gorge's Cruel Sister (5.10a).

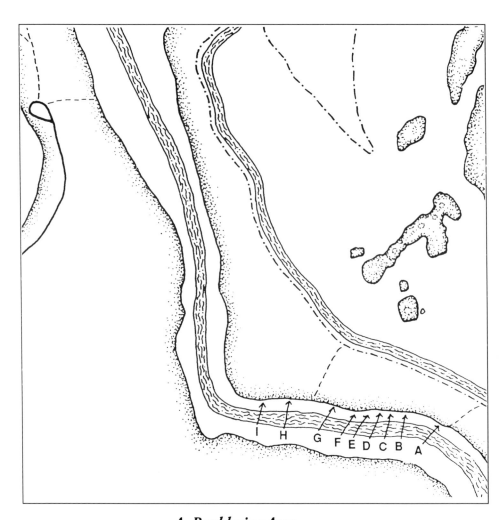

A. *Bouldering Area*
B. *Crowded House*
C. *First Pedestal*
D. *Middle Earth*
E. *Second Pedestal*
F. *Vatican Wall*
G. *Playing in Traffic Area*
H. *Ivory Coast*
I. *Red Columns*

THE UPPER GORGE

Smith Basalt Finally Entered the sport-climbing era with the recent development of the Upper Gorge. Located upstream from the traditional columns, along the northern bank of the Crooked River, these remote crags boast a phenomenal collection of modern test pieces. For the advanced climber, the area offers the best climbing in the entire Gorge, and one of the greatest concentrations of hard routes anywhere at Smith. Most of the lines are precarious stemming problems, technical faces or gorgeous arêtes; often you'll find a combination in a single pitch. Aside from this diversity, the routes of the Upper Gorge feature perfect rock and cerebral, crafty sequences.

But the quality of the climbing isn't what sets the Upper Gorge apart from Smith's other basalt. Instead, it's the open-armed embracing of the sport-climbing ethic. Except for a handful of easier lines, you won't need the typical Gorge rack of Friends and R.P.s here; bolts protect almost everything. A few climbs are difficult to work out on lead, since they usually received a top-rope wiring before being bolted. Fortunately, these are the exception, as the Upper Gorge is truly an area of convenience. Often, you can traverse along the top of the columnar basalt from anchor to anchor, and you can reach any route from above if you'd prefer toproping.

To some climbers, portions of the Upper Gorge may seem overdeveloped, as a bewildering number of bolts cover the best sections of cliff. But the lines are well-defined, and the density results more from the nature of the columnar basalt than an over-zealous compressing of routes. The area might nauseate a staunch traditionalist, but most climbers feel like a kid in a candy store, trying to decide which treat to sample next.

From the earliest days of Gorge climbing, explorers turned the bend and gazed upon a seemingly endless series of blank corners. A few rappel slings appeared atop some obvious cracks in the mid-seventies, possibly the result of Wayne Arrington's efforts. The first documented climb in the Upper Gorge waited until 1979, when Paul Landrum and Jim Davis pioneered **Land of the Lost** (5.10a) on the Second Pedestal. For climbers of that era, these hand cracks were the only possible lines, since everything else required bolts. During the boom years of the eighties, Gorge climbers explored the area, but no one relished the idea of agonizing hand drilling. Still, the legend quickly spread that the "5.12 Wall" held the future of Gorge climbing.

For nearly a decade after the first ascents on the First and Second Pedestals, absolutely nothing happened here. This changed with remarkable swiftness in 1989 as motivated climbers arrived with the necessary fire power. John Rich was the first to explore new lines, but the most credit goes to Tom Egan and Jeff Frizzell. During six frenzied months they tore the place apart, leaving two dozen routes in their wake, including Frizzell's **Hot Lava,** and Egan's **Controlled Hysteria** (both 5.13a). Hit hard with Gorge fever, the two did everything they could to add to the amenities short of hauling down a Coke machine. Aside from hacking paths through the thick brush and drilling hundreds of bolts, they left tennis cans buried in cairns at anchors on the rim. These cans contained information including the names and grades of every route below. Eventually Egan turned to the tuff, but Frizzell continued his onslaught of new routes, capped by **Big Tuna** (5.13b), **Cuban Slide** and **Feminazis** (5.13a)

Unlike the rest of the Gorge, these columns contain dozens of untapped options. Over the next decade, the number of lines surely will double before climbers exhaust the potential. Oddly, the place sees only limited traffic; on many busy weekends, it's completely deserted. For those who visit, this isolation adds greatly to the charm. The solitude might diminish as the word spreads, but I don't think overcrowding will be a problem.

You have three main options to approach the Upper Gorge. During low-water conditions, you can enter at the West Columns and step across the river below Cruel Sister. Two hundred yards of boulder-hopping leads upstream and around the corner to the end of the Red Columns. If you can't make the river crossing here, but still want to reach the Gorge through the park, take a right at the bridge below Picnic Lunch Wall and hike around the bend to the base of the Burma Road. After a half-mile walk along the canal, an indistinct trail branches off the auxiliary road below, leading into the Upper Gorge.

By far the easiest approach is from the south along the canal road. Nearby locals haven't always looked favorably on this entrance, so **please** keep a low profile. Repeated conflicts might force the closure of the entire Upper Gorge. Currently, you can use this access hassle-free, but things might change as the usage increases. If you're ever confronted, be polite and use another entrance.

To approach the Upper Gorge via the canal road, go east along N.E. Wilcox Avenue one-half mile beyond Crooked River Drive. Pull off the road, parking just before the small canal bridge. Hike over a massive bridge spanning the canyon, then take the leftmost of three roads at the fork. Don't walk along the canal. This move keeps you away from nearby houses. After a half mile, just after the view of the columns disappears, an indistinct trail steps left through the rubble into the canyon.

Note: The downstream cliffs (The Red Columns and Ivory Coast) are currently closed to climbing due to liability concerns of the property owners. Unfortunately, these crags contain the hardest routes in the entire area. Until the situation changes, please do not climb on this section of columns.

BOULDERING AREA

After you first enter the Upper Gorge, skirt along the base of a unique section of rimrock that ranges from 15 to 30 feet in height. Heavily-pocketed, and graced with a sandy landing, this small crag provides Smith's best basalt bouldering. Here, you'll find a pumping traverse and an excellent selection of boulder problems. The longest lines are too high for safe bouldering, but there are some top-rope anchors along the rim. The following two routes are at the far left end of the cliff:

1. KID'N PLAY 5.8 ★★ Bolts (optional gear to 2.5 inches)
   The easiest sport climb in the area starts with a simple crack, then steps right onto a fun, pocketed buttress.

2. CRANKING WITH KARI 5.10c ★★★ Bolts
   A steep, flat-faced buttress rises just to the left of **Kid'n Play**. The cranks between pockets make a great warm-up for the harder routes.

THE CROWDED HOUSE

Beyond the second of two free-standing pillars, a rough trail scrambles downhill from the bouldering area into the Upper Gorge. You'll first come to a cliff called the Crowded House, named in honor of the closely-spaced routes. The sport-climbing era first came to the Upper Gorge here, as the whir of a power drill shattered the stillness of a January morning. This crag contains an excellent selection of well-protected lines, making it the most popular choice for first time visitors. A rappel anchor atop the rim enables quick approaches from above if you don't want to lead anything.

3. PRUNING THE FAMILY TREE 5.10c ★★ Bolts
   The first bolted line tackles a column right of a hand crack. The hardest moves are on the mediocre lower section, but the upper buttress is a lot more fun.

4. SINK THE SUB 5.10a ★ Gear to 3 inches
   A forgettable hand crack rises immediately left of a bolted column. Start after a long traverse from the left and jam flaky rock to the rim.

5. DANCES WITH DOGS 5.11c ★★★ Bolts
   This deceptively difficult seam begins with a scramble up a staircased series of columns. The crux finesses side pulls and smears in a very shallow, left-facing corner.

Photo: Alan Watts

Crowded House

3. PRUNING THE FAMILY TREE   5.10c
★★
4. SINK THE SUB   5.10a ★
5. DANCES WITH DOGS   5.11c ★★★
6. BLIND DOGS NEED BONES TOO
5.10d ★★★

7. HIEROGLYPHICS   5.11d ★★★★
8. CELIBATE WIVES   5.12a ★★★
9. ANIMATION   5.11c ★★
10. MOJOMATIC   5.12a/b ★★★★
11. INTEGRATED IMAGING   5.12a ★★★
12. CHIENNE NO MORE   5.12a ★★★

6. BLIND DOGS NEED BONES TOO   5.10d ★★★   Bolts
Dubbed an "American classic" by the leader of the first-ascent team, this enjoyable route makes a good warm-up. While repeats called it something short of a masterpiece, you'll appreciate the well-protected sequence of stems, jams and face moves.

7. HIEROGLYPHICS   5.11d ★★★★   Bolts
This classic line follows a seam splitting a flat buttress. You'll encounter a few tough-to-decipher cruxes, but the escalating pump near the top will give you more trouble than any single move.

8. CELIBATE WIVES   5.12a ★★★   Bolts
Another demanding route that features relentless moves up a gentle inside corner. The technical crux hits at the fourth bolt, but the climbing remains strenuous to the anchor.

9. ANIMATION   5.11c ★★   Bolts
This double-seamed corner rises above a distinctive, swooping ramp. Although not up to the standards of its neighbors, the vigorous stems tempt many climbers.

10. MOJOMATIC   5.12a/b ★★★★   Bolts
An undisputed Gorge classic, this arête shouldn't be missed. An energetic series of slaps and pinches up the edge leads to a delicate crux near the top. If, after clipping the anchors, you're still aching for more, try toproping the climb using only the arête (5.12c).

11. INTEGRATED IMAGING   5.12a ★★★   Bolts
Although not as attractive as the routes to the right, this demanding face is better than it looks. Start behind a massive sagebrush, and finesse a series of artsy moves on awkwardly angled holds.

12. CHIENNE NO MORE   5.12a ★★★   Bolts
Insecure palming highlights this prominent, right-facing corner. You won't quit bitching about the desperate moves until you clear the crux bulge midway up.

13. EASY FOR SOME   5.11a/b ★★   Bolts
A bolt line with a one-move crux is tucked in a corner just left of a square-cut column,. You'll either romp or get stomped, depending upon whether you can make a reach to a hidden hold.

THE FIRST PEDESTAL AREA

A prominent squeeze chimney marks the boundary between the Crowded House and the First Pedestal Area. Here, you'll find a few moderate, but uninspiring cracks, and the bolted columns of the **Three Stooges**.

14. JOHN-A-THON   5.8   TR
A tasteless ordeal slithers up a dirty squeeze chimney. All things considered, there isn't a worse route on Smith basalt.

15. PREDATOR   5.12+ ?   Project
An overhanging buttress rises between a menacing chimney and a hand crack. Since every move goes free on toprope, someone will eventually drill the bolts.

16. BANNED FOR LIFE   5.10b ★   Gear to 4 inches
An obvious crack splits the column just left of a fearsome chimney. After a flaky start, some good jams give way to an awkward slot near the top.

17. CURLY   5.11d ★★★   Bolts
The first of the **Three Stooges** attacks a bolted column sandwiched between two jam cracks. Tough side pulls at the crux give way to a pumpy finish.

18. SQUEEZE PLAY   5.10b ★★   Gear to 2.5 inches
This dihedral rises above a 30-foot column. Begin by jamming the right side of the pillar to a ledge, then mix stems and finger locks to the top.

19. MOE 5.11b/c ★★ Bolts
Stooge number two begins on the right side of a short column, then veers left to a bolted arête.
After moderate climbing, throw a "moe" (nyuck, nyuck) at the top.

First Pedestal

13. EASY FOR SOME 5.11a/b ★★
14. JOHN-A-THON 5.8
15. PREDATOR 5.12+ ?
16. BANNED FOR LIFE 5.10b ★
17. CURLY 5.11d ★★★
18. SQUEEZE PLAY 5.10b ★★

19. MOE 5.11b/c ★★
20. LARRY 5.12a/b ★★★
21. P.W. 5.9 ★★
22. BACK HANDED SLAP 5.8 ★★
23. FIRST PEDESTAL CRACK 5.10a ★

20. LARRY 5.12a/b ★★★ Bolts
The final stooge starts with a lackluster crack then steps left to a ledge. The relentless finish face climbs an attractive buttress.

21. P.W. 5.9 ★★ Gear to 2.5 inches
Midway along the First Pedestal Area are three short cracks, rising above two twenty foot columns. The center crack follows locking jams, with optional stems to an off-width. Begin with some tricky, vegetated moves to the left.

22. BACK HANDED SLAP 5.8 ★★ Gear to 3 inches
The leftmost of the three cracks looming above a short stack of columns involves some enjoyable hand jams. Begin with a strenuous sequence past a bush.

23. FIRST PEDESTAL CRACK 5.10a ★ Gear to 3.5 inches
An obvious crack splits the face of the free-standing First Pedestal. The rock improves greatly after a dirty start, but few climbers bother.

MIDDLE EARTH

A series of high-quality test pieces extends for about 150 feet between the First and Second Pedestals. You can reach any of the anchors by rappeling from bolts atop the rimrock.

24. MISSING IN ACTION 5.10a ★★ Gear to 3 inches
This right-leaning hand crack is tucked in a corner of gray rock left of the First Pedestal.

25. GET THAT FEELING 5.11d ★★★ Bolts
Insecure and continuous stems keep you absorbed from the moment you clip the first bolt. Begin with a few jams leading into the double-seamed corner.

26. NATURAL ART 5.11c ★★★ Bolts
Among the better routes of its grade, **Natural Art** is a fine introduction to the subtle art of Gorge climbing. Artsy, well-protected stems between widely-spaced seams loosens your muscles for the more difficult routes.

27. PROJECT 5.12 ?
An undone, river-rounded seam rises around the corner and left of **Natural Art.** All the moves go, and someone likely will have succeeded by the time this book goes to press.

28. UP COUNTRY 5.12a ★★★ Bolts
Despite a dirty-looking start, this memorable arête makes an excellent choice. Fun jugs near the base give way to increasingly crafty moves, broken by good shakes.

29. UNIQUE MONIQUE 5.12a ★★★ Bolts
Two precarious cruxes guard the inside corner just left of **Up Country.** The best moves come on the upper face, muscling past an overhang.

30. NAXIS 5.10b ★★ Bolts
The easiest bolted route on Middle Earth makes a fine warm-up for nearby desperates. Moderate but sustained stems, jams and edges follow closely-spaced cracks through a finishing slot.

31. GAPERS ON A TANGENT 5.12a/b ★★★ Bolts
A triangular roof caps this diverse, shallow corner. The hardest section tames some baffling stems and face holds on the lower wall. After a good shake, shift gears and storm a strenuous crack on finger stacks.

32. HOT LAVA 5.13a ★★★ Bolts
An unrelenting series of puzzling, balancey moves made this orange-streaked wall the first 5.13 in the Gorge. After figuring out the scorching cruxes, you'll need good endurance to link them together. Most climbers work the moves beforehand on toprope, since the bolts are far apart.

33. TOMB OF LOVE 5.11d ★★★ Bolts
A captivating route sits around the corner and left of **Hot Lava.** A flurry of stems leads to a tricky crux past a blank section near the top. Finish with an energetic pull over a steep bulge to anchor bolts.

34. FEMINAZIS 5.13a ★★★★ Bolts
This overhanging edge ranks with the Upper Gorge's most impressive lines. The difficulties mount until a desperate crux hits at three-quarters height. Fighting a pump, slap past rounded holds to an anchor.

35. BUSHWACKER 5.11d ★★ Gear to 1 inch (small wires, TCUs)
An obscure stemming problem between double seams rises immediately left of a sweeping arête. Despite some challenging moves, no one ever bothers because there aren't any bolts.

Photo: Alan Watts

Middle Earth

23. FIRST PEDESTAL CRACK 5.10a ★
24. MISSING IN ACTION 5.10a ★★
25. GET THAT FEELING 5.11d ★★★
26. NATURAL ART 5.11c ★★★
27. PROJECT 5.12 ?
28. UP COUNTRY 5.12a ★★★
29. UNIQUE MONIQUE 5.12a ★★★

30. NAXIS 5.10b ★★
31. GAPERS ON A TANGENT 5.12a/b ★★★
32. HOT LAVA 5.13a ★★★
33. TOMB OF LOVE 5.11d ★★★
34. FEMINAZIS 5.13a ★★★★
35. BUSHWACKER 5.11d ★★

Middle Earth – Left Side

34. FEMINAZIS   5.13a ★★★★
35. BUSHWACKER   5.11d ★★
36. BLAME IT ON RIO   5.12b ★★★
37. PERUVIAN SKIES   5.12d ★★★★

38. PROJECT   5.13– ?
39. PROJECT   5.12+ ?
40. E-TYPE JAG   5.11a ★★★★

36. BLAME IT ON RIO 5.12b ★★★ Bolts
A real delight, this quality route offers a day-and-night mixture of insecure stems and sheer thuggery. The lower wall contains the hardest moves, but the most memorable moment comes when you pull around a big roof, feet swinging wildly in space. A pocketed second pitch (5.10b) finishes to the top of the rimrock.

37. PERUVIAN SKIES 5.12d ★★★★ Bolts
Like its neighbor to the right, **Peruvian Skies** combines delicate smears/edges in a vertical corner with powerful lock-offs above. The hardest move comes low, but everyone fails (with pumped forearms) when weaving through the final overhang.

38. PROJECT 5.13–?
Immediately left of **Peruvian Skies** are two unfinished dihedrals. The right corner will rank among the hardest stemming problems in the Gorge.

39. PROJECT 5.12+?
The left of two unfinished corners will soon contain another techno-thriller.

40. E-TYPE JAG 5.11a ★★★★ Bolts
Unlike anything else in the Gorge, this bucket arête capped by a roof is one of Smith's best 5.11s. The first bolt protects a mantel onto a pedestal; unclipping it eliminates any rope drag.

SECOND PEDESTAL AREA

Resembling its counterpart upstream, the Second Pedestal Area contains three mediocre routes. You won't find any bolts here, so don't forget your rack.

41. PROJECT 5.11?
This crack, with its sandy stems at the start, sits a few feet left of E-Type Jag. After a few tips jams, a moderate hand crack finishes.

42. SECOND PEDESTAL CRACK 5.10a ★★ Gear to 4 inches
Undercut by a roof, this attractive crack splits the face of the Second Pedestal. Although sandy at the start, you'll enjoy the finishing hand/fist crack.

43. LAND OF THE LOST 5.10a ★★★ Gear to 3 inches
A hand crack splitting a flat face rises above a block just left of the Second Pedestal. Look for a perfect oval hole on the right wall, just above the starting ledge.

THE VATICAN WALL

After a non-stop onslaught of bolted routes, the wall left of the Second Pedestal is almost completely untouched. This will inevitably change over the next few years, but for now there are only two options.

44. THE SIGN OF THE PRIEST 5.10b ★★ Bolts
Among the easiest sport climbs in the area, this bolted line makes a decent warm-up. Start with jumbled face climbing, then step right to a finishing dihedral.

45. PROJECT 5.11+?
A corner with a face-climbing start rises just left of The Sign of the Priest. It'll likely be bolted by the time you visit.

Photo: Alan Watts

Second Pedestal and Vatican Wall

40. E-TYPE JAG   5.11a ★★★★
41. PROJECT   5.11 ?
42. SECOND PEDESTAL CRACK   5.10a ★★

43. LAND OF THE LOST   5.10a ★★★
44. THE SIGN OF THE PRIEST   5.10b ★★
45. PROJECT   5.11+ ?

PLAYING IN TRAFFIC AREA

The last section of columns before a gully rises above a row of juniper trees and snags. It offers only a few routes now, but someday it'll be packed with sport climbs.

46. JUST DO IT   5.10a ★★★   Gear to 3 inches
This enjoyable crack, hidden by two juniper trees lurks in the midst of blank corners. After starting up the right side of a short pillar, widening jams in a shallow dihedral end at an anchor.

47. PLAYING IN TRAFFIC   5.12b/c ★★★★   Bolts
A wonderful arête rises midway between two snags, about 60 feet left of **Just Do It.** Begin on some polished rock, then frolic through an enjoyable series of pumping moves. A complex crux near the top will mow you down if you're not careful.

48. SPELLBOUND 5.11c ★★ Gear to 3.5 inches
An inside corner borders the left side of the **Playing in Traffic** column. Three bolts protect the hardest climbing at the start, but you'll need to bring gear for the finger/hand crack finish.

49. VIRTUAL BEACH 5.11a ★ Bolts
Easier and dirtier than it looks, this box corner needs some traffic to brush the sand away.

50. PROJECT 5.11+ ?
The column left of **Virtual Beach** will soon sport an entertaining route capped by a dyno to an unmistakable hueco.

51. THE SEAP 5.10b ★★ Bolts
This atypical jug-haul hides behind a snag just before the columns disappear. Unfortunately, it seaps when the canal runs; it's either dirty or wet, depending on the season.

Photo: Alan Watts

Playing in Traffic Area

46. JUST DO IT 5.10a ★★★
47. PLAYING IN TRAFFIC 5.12b/c ★★★★
48. SPELLBOUND 5.11c ★★

49. VIRTUAL BEACH 5.11a ★
50. PROJECT 5.11+ ?
51. THE SEAP 5.10b ★★

IVORY COAST/REDCOLUMNS

The top-notch routes of the Ivory Coast and Red Columns are separated from the rest of the Upper Gorge by a gully. Dubbed the 5.12 Wall in the mid-eighties, these cliffs lived up to their original billing. The Ivory Coast stretches from the right side of the cliff to a bolted column called The Urge; the Red Columns rise beyond. To reach anchors atop any route on this crag, rappel from a variety of bolts on the rim.

Instead of hacking through the jungle down the entire Upper Gorge, a better approach hikes down a prominent gully just to the right of the cliff. To find this ravine, hike a quarter-mile beyond the normal entrance off the canal road to a trail that branches to the left.

Note: This entire area is currently closed to climbing, due to liability concerns of the owners. Please climb elsewhere until the situation changes.

52. SHRIMPTON'S SHRINE 5.12a ★★ TR
Easy to pass by, this obscure toprope problem isn't worth setting a rope on. Look for an indistinct right-facing corner distinguished by a couple of elongated pockets.

53. ORPHAN'S CRUEL 5.12b ★★★ Bolts
This shallow inside corner deserves more attention than it receives. Don't let a little flaky rock turn you off – the moves are invigorating, sustained and never boring.

54. CHILLIN' IN THE PENZO 5.12b/c ★★★ Bolts
This varied line rises two corners left of **Orphan's Cruel**. After starting to the right, wander up pockets on the left, then cut back right to buckets before the stemming crux.

55. PINK PRIMITIVE 5.11b ★★★ Bolts
This excellent warm-up tackles the left side of a prominent edge. You'll take in a little of everything, from face moves and stems to finger jams. Finish with an enjoyable romp up the arête to the right.

56. THE FUGITIVE 5.11d ★★ Bolts
A shallow inside corner splits a section of dirty gray rock just right of a stemming box. After a crux start on creaky holds, the climbing improves, as stems and face holds lead past a small roof to an anchor.

57. WARDANCE 5.12a ★★★ Bolts
This attractive box corner is an excellent stemming exercise. Your forearms might feel fresh, but your worn-out legs will be quivering on the final moves.

58. BIG TUNA 5.13b ★★★★ Bolts
Without rival, this impressive column is the hardest route on Smith basalt. A bewildering array of delicate, bouldery moves just keep coming. The difficulties slowly ease above the technical crux at the fourth bolt, but you'll likely be too pumped to notice.

59. STEAMING CAFE FLIRTS 5.12b/c ★★★ Bolts
A vicious stemming problem in a tight inside corner sits immediately left of the **Big Tuna** column. A bizarre series of technical moves will tax your problem-solving abilities. The bolts are far enough apart that some climbers prefer a toprope.

60. CONTROLLED HYSTERIA 5.13a ★★★★ Bolts
This desperate seam storms a frenzied series of insecure stems and face moves. The climbing eases after a relentless onslaught of cruxes in the first half of the route.

61. SLACK MACKEREL 5.12b ★★★ Bolts
A right-facing dihedral is tucked just right of a sharp arête. Although tightly crammed with **Controlled Hysteria** near the top, the demanding liebacks and stems are highly recommended.

Photo: Alan Watts

Ivory Coast

52. SHRIMPTON'S SHRINE 5.12a ★★
53. ORPHAN'S CRUEL 5.12b ★★★
54. CHILLIN' IN THE PENZO 5.12b/c ★★★

55. PINK PRIMITIVE 5.11b ★★★
56. THE FUGUTIVE 5.11d ★★
57. WARDANCE 5.12a ★★★

Photo: Alan Watts

Ivory Coast (on page 280)

57. WARDANCE   5.12a ★★★
58. BIG TUNA   5.13b ★★★★
59. STEAMING CAFE FLIRTS   5.12b/c ★★★
60. CONTROLLED HYSTERIA   5.13a
    ★★★★
61. SLACK MACKEREL   5.12b ★★★
62. SAVAGE TRUTH   5.13 ?

63. NEW BREED LEADER   5.12b ★★★★
64. PEACH NAILS   5.12b ★★★★
65. CUBAN SLIDE   5.13a ★★★
66. THE URGE   5.12c/d ★★★★
67. COLORSPLASH   5.10b ★★★
68. SPECIAL EFFECTS   5.11d ★★★

Photo: Alan Watts

Red Columns

69. YELLOW FIN   5.12a/b ★★★
70. BANGSTICK   5.11b ★★★
71. SHARK-INFESTED WATERS   5.12b
    ★★★★
72. PROJECT   5.12+ ?
73. THE BIG KILL   5.12a ★★★
74. SCREAMS AND WHISPERS   5.12b ★★★

75. BRAZILIAN SKIES   5.12b/c ★★★★
76. RED LILY Q   5.12b ★★★
77. PERSUASION   5.12a ★★★
78. PROJECT   5.12 ?
79. SLAY THE DRAGON   5.12c ★★★
80. RAINBOW'S END   5.11c ★★
81. ALMOST SOMETHING   5.10b ★★

62. SAVAGE TRUTH 5.13 ? Project
    This sharp arête is perhaps the most attractive line in the entire Upper Gorge. Despite a barrage of attempts, no one has linked the incessant series of intricate moves.

63. NEW BREED LEADER 5.12b ★★★★ Bolts
    A striking inside corner, marked by an odd slot at the first bolt, looms left of **Savage Truth**. After mastering consistently technical stems, finish with pumping face holds.

64. PEACH NAILS 5.12b ★★★★ Bolts
    Set in a shallow corner, this unrelenting line makes a fine choice. The hardest moves aren't far off the ground, but you'll be fighting the entire way to the anchor.

65. CUBAN SLIDE 5.13a ★★★ Bolts
    Smith's hardest stemming problem rises just right of an obvious, flat-faced column. Stacked with hard moves from bottom to top, you could (and will) fall off almost anywhere.

66. THE URGE 5.12c/d ★★★★ Bolts
    This gorgeous column is a fine change of pace from the typical Gorge stemming corner. A delightful series of baffling boulder problems, split by good shakes, don't ease up until the anchor. Bolts safely protect the moves, but expect a sporting mantel onto a ledge past the fourth bolt.

67. COLORSPLASH 5.10b ★★★ Gear to 3 inches
    An appealing finger/hand crack splits the yellow face left of **The Urge**. Few climbers experience the naturally protected jams, since no one ever brings a rack into the Upper Gorge.

68. SPECIAL EFFECTS 5.11d ★★★ Bolts
    This tricky line stands just left of **Colorsplash**. Although easier than the nearby sport routes, it'll surprise anyone expecting a stroll. The difficulties begin at the fourth bolt and continue unabated through a new, improved finish.

69. YELLOW FIN 5.12a/b ★★★ Bolts
    Stems, arête moves and a finishing mantel around a small roof highlight this quality route. The hardest section pulls into an inside corner after cutting left around a roof formed by a missing section of column.

70. BANGSTICK 5.11b ★★★ Bolts
    This box corner sits just right of a bolted column. A lively series of stems and palming moves lead to fun pockets below the anchor.

71. SHARK-INFESTED WATERS 5.12b ★★★★ Bolts
    Consistently difficult, this alluring column ranks among the best climbs in the Upper Gorge. Expect some desperate moments puzzling over how to clip the bolts. The biting crux comes at the top, with a strenuous face move over a bulge.

72. PROJECT 5.12+ ?
    The corner immediately left of **Shark-Infested Waters** will someday contain a challenging stemming problem. Every move goes free except for one horrendous section.

73. THE BIG KILL 5.12a ★★★ Bolts
    The moves on this typical Gorge stemming corner are crafty, but not unlike other nearby lines.

74. SCREAMS AND WHISPERS 5.12b ★★★ Bolts
    The third corner left of **Shark-Infested Waters** face climbs to a swooping wave and ends at an anchor.

75. BRAZILIAN SKIES 5.12b/c ★★★★ Bolts
    This stemming nightmare lurks between double seams in a box corner. If you love stemming, you'll thrill over this mind-numbing battle. Otherwise, walk on by.

76. RED LILY Q   5.12b ★★★   Bolts

The first corner left of **Brazilian Skies** offers another bolted test piece. Persistent, artsy moves lead past a one-finger pocket at a bulge, easing gradually near the top.

77. PERSUASION   5.12a ★★★   Bolts

This compelling, shallow corner starts above a small, white-capped slab. If you stick a throw to a sloper, you'll be through the crux, but the thought-provoking moves never really let up. Expect a tough clip just before the crux.

78. PROJECT   5.12 ?

A right-facing corner rises just right of **Slay the Dragon**. A toprope effort uncovered a reasonable sequence, but it never got bolted.

79. SLAY THE DRAGON   5.12c ★★★   Bolts

This challenging route follows the last attractive seam in the Upper Gorge. The hardest move stems past a boulder problem at the second bolt. The climbing eases briefly, but many gallant efforts end near the top at a blind face move.

80. RAINBOW'S END   5.11c ★★   Bolts

This technical line rises around the corner left of **Slay The Dragon**. If you can force yourself to stay right, expect some tricky moves. Unfortunately, the holds lead off-route to the left.

81. ALMOST SOMETHING   5.10b ★★   Bolts

The only easy sport route on the Red Columns is a reasonable but ungainly warm-up. Begin by liebacking a pillar, then master a short crux in a shallow, bolt-studded corner.

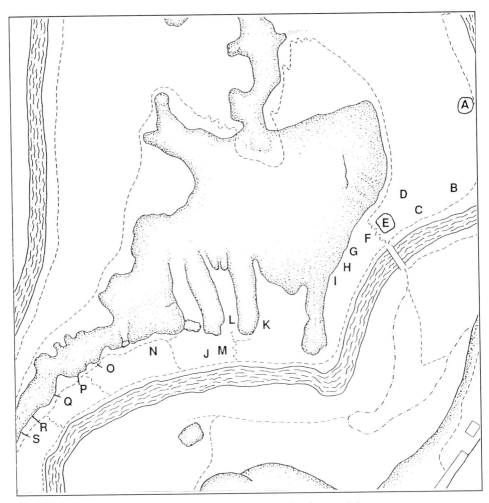

A. Red Wall Boulders

B. Practice Boulder

C. The Cave

D. Circus Boulder

E. Picnic Lunch Wall Boulders

F. Mantel Block/Dinosaur Boulder

G. Leaning Slab

H. K&B Slab

I. Puke-a-Lot Traverse

J. The Pharaoh

K. Slack Jaw Traverse

L. Lysurgic Roof

M. Where Boneheads Dare

N. Morning Glory Wall Traverse

O. Tator Tots Direct

P. Moonshine Face

Q. Overhanging Face

R. Testament Slab Traverse

S. Combination Blocks Traverse

BOULDERING

LONG BEFORE THE AGE of lycra and sticky rubber, the most impressive exploits at Smith quietly took place on a scattering of boulders below today's sport crags. During the early 80s, a day at Smith often meant a day on the boulders, since there weren't many bolted faces. This forgotten era set the stage for the emergence of Smith sport climbing. It was on a collection of puny boulders that locals first gained the strength and confidence to leave the security of jam cracks. Soon the arena shifted; they left the boulders behind, and brought their newly-acquired skills to the steep faces and arêtes. Today, blinded by the brilliant sport routes, most climbers aren't even aware of Smith's well-developed bouldering scene.

I feel that if only climbers knew what was here, Smith bouldering might enjoy a resurgence. For this reason, I'm including this section in this guide. Admittedly, today's boulder problems don't come close to matching the depth or quality of Smith's lead climbs. But several lines have historical significance, and the problems help build the explosive power necessary for the hardest routes. Typical of Smith tuff, the rock varies from perfect stone to corn flakes; fortunately, the harder problems are flawlessly solid.

Grading boulder problems is far more ambiguous than rating lead climbs. It's always easier to grade a long series of moves than a single, extreme crank. I considered using no grading scale at all, but since everyone enjoys placing a number on their accomplishments, I've created a Smith Rock system. It's subject to the same flaws as any other scale, but it avoids the need to rate Smith problems relative to bouldering elsewhere. Each problem receives a grade from S1 to S5, with liberal use of minuses and pluses. S1s might rate from 5.9 to 5.10, while the S5s will push even today's top climbers. Below I've listed examples of each grade at Smith:

S1 **Moonshine Hand Traverse**
S2 **The Overhanging Flake**
S3 **Total Eclipse**
S4 **Combination Traverse**, round trip
S5 **Cave Traverse** with **Jones Exit**

The Smith bouldering scale has nothing to do with the B grades first used by John Gill, nor the V system used at Hueco Tanks. I've not calibrated my system to match these. In using a scale specific to Smith Rock, I'm ranking problems only in comparison with each other, without inviting debate over whether a problem is B2 or V7.

The grades I've given aren't iron-clad and are based on an estimate of the difficulty for an average-sized climber. I've based the grades purely on my memory and personal biases, so they won't always be consistent – or accurate for that matter. I look at the S-system only as a starting point – with time, the grades should more accurately reflect reality. Along with the difficulty grade, I've employed the same zero-through-four-star quality system used on Smith lead climbs.

You can find each problem by referring to the photos and sketches I've included. A brief narrative highlights every boulder, but I've not bothered with written descriptions for each problem. After all, how much can you say about a single dynamic move? Still, I'll let you know when a problem is dangerously long, loose, or plagued with a bad landing. The lines listed here aren't even close to a complete selection of Smith bouldering. In particular, I've ignored dozens of contrived variations (often ranking among the hardest at Smith) so I won't have to describe what is and isn't a legal hold.

I haven't included dozens of other rocks offering good bouldering. You'll find worthwhile problems at the Aggro Gully, the Southern Tip, the West Side Area, Easy's Playhouse, the Old Climber's Camp and below the Marsupial Crags. There's also excellent basalt bouldering at the entrance to the Upper Gorge (See Chapter 14) and a recently discovered area below the bivouac area.

PICNIC LUNCH BOULDERS

You'll find some enjoyable climbing on the boulders strewn below Picnic Lunch Wall. The short approach, and isolation from the more-travelled areas makes them worth visiting.

River Boulder

This big, crumbly boulder sits along the trail nearest the bridge. If you want to hike out under your own power, don't slip off near the top.

1. THE NOSE   S2 ★★★   Rounded arête on the right.
   a. S2+ Do the start without the right side pull.
   b. S3– Begin slightly left, reaching to a pocket.
   c. S3– Start five feet left, and traverse right along a seam.
2. LOOSE LUCY   S2+ ★   Dangerous.
3. BLACK DIKE   S2 ★★   Scary.
4. KENT'S BIG DAY   S1+ ★   Loose.
5. LEFT CRACK   S2– ★★   Right-leaning seam.

Trail Block

The small, slabish blob above the bridge contains a bewildering assortment of contrived problems. The staircase ruins the landing below the lines on the left.

6. TRAIL WALKING   S1– ★★   Uncontrived face on the right.
7. OBLONG LUNGE   S2+ ★★   Throw from the oblong pocket up and left to a jug.
8. LEACH LUNGE   S3– ★★   Pull up, and throw right to a jug.
9. ORIGINAL ROUTE   S1+ ★★★   Uncontrived edges on the left.

Roof Boulder

A clean block with a distinctive roof on its downhill face sits directly above the River Boulder.

10. THIN EXCUSE   S2– ★   Ugly thin crack on right wall – bad landing.
11. ORIGINAL ROUTE   S1+ ★★★   Jugs on the arête.
12. ADAMS ROOF   S2– ★★★   Uncontrived over the roof.
    a. S3– Pull over the roof, but use no jugs to the right.
13. LEAP OF FAITH   S2+ ★★   Jump from a boulder to holds at the lip.
14. TRAVERSE   S2+ ★★★   This pumping round-trip around a corner is a great workout.

Cave Man Boulder

Undercut by a cave, this boulder sits at the second switchback above the bridge.

15. RIGHT SIDE   S1+ ★   One move.
16. STONE AGE   S2– ★★   From a good jug, climb straight up.
17. MR. SLATE   S2 ★★   Cut right or left to a sloper.
18. LEFT EDGE   S2– ★★

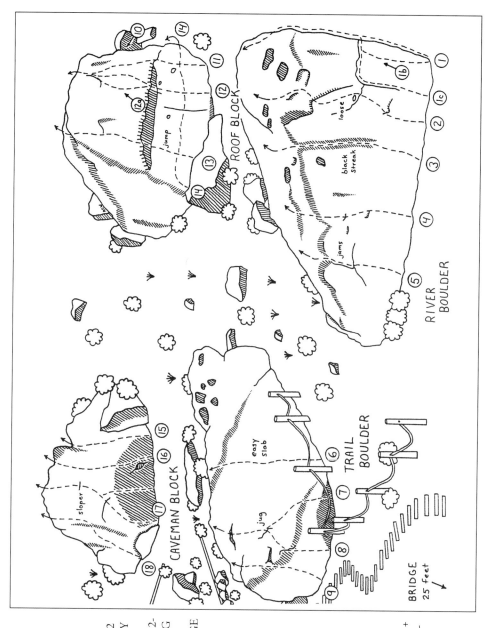

Picnic Lunch
Wall Boulders

1. THE NOSE S2
2. LOOSE LUCY S2+
3. BLACK DIKE S2
4. KENT'S BIG DAY S1+
5. LEFT CRACK S2-
6. TRAIL WALKING S1-
7. OBLONG LUNGE S2+
8. LEACH LUNGE S3-
9. ORIGINAL ROUTE S1+
10. THIN EXCUSE S2-
11. ORIGINAL ROUTE S1+
12. ADAMS ROOF S2-
13. LEAP OF FAITH S2+
14. TRAVERSE S2+
15. RIGHT SIDE S1+
16. STONE AGE S2-
17. MR. SLATE S2
18. LEFT EDGE S2-

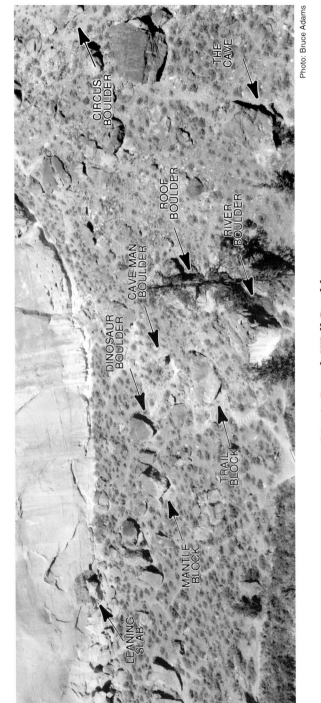

Photo: Bruce Adams

Picnic Lunch Wall Boulders

Dinosaur Boulder

A pointed slab sits left of the trail. There is a rounded mantel (# 19 S3– ★) on its downhill side.

Mantel Block

This blob rests off the trail to the left, just beyond the Dinosaur Boulder. Undercut by an overhang, it delights the rare breed of climber who loves mantels. You can crank over the lip just about anywhere, but the most distinctive problems are as follows:

20. MANTEL PIECE   S2+ ★★   Rounded arête on the right.
21. CENTER MANTEL   S3– ★★   Start with a good right hold.
22. ORIGINAL MANTEL   S2– ★★★   Pull past circular jugs on the left.
23. LIP TRAVERSE   S3 ★★   Move left to right, with the Mantel Piece finish.

Circus Boulder

This small block lurks uphill to the right of the Roof Boulder. It has a steep downhill face.

24. CIRCUS LUNGE   S2– ★★★★   Dyno from jugs to a big knob.
25. CENTER ROUTE   S2 ★★
26. BIG TOP   S2 ★★   Thin flakes on the right.

The Cave

Without rival, The Cave offers the most difficult boulder problems at Smith. To approach, turn right at the bridge and hike 100 feet along the trail.

27. ORIGINAL EXIT   S2– ★★★   Spring from the ground to the lip.
  a.   S2+   Leave the ground statically.
28. JONES PROBLEM   S4 ★★★   Exit The Cave from left to right.
29. LEFT EXIT   S2+ ★★   Jump from the ground, a la the **Original Exit.**
  a.   S3   Leave the ground statically.
30. CAVE TRAVERSE   S4– ★★★   Traverse inner wall from right to left.
  a.   S4   Add the left exit.
  b.   S5   Add the Jones exit.

Practice Boulder

A massive boulder comes next in line beyond the Cave. The routes are long enough that you'll get hurt if you fall near the top. Popular with classes, these routes are easily toproped.

31. DRILL TEAM   S1+ ★★★   Fun bulge (5.9) on left with good holds.
32. FIRST TIMER   S1 ★★   Awkward jugs (5.8) in the center.
33. PRACTICE SLAB   S1– ★★   Wander up the right slab (5.7).
34. FAKING IT   S1– ★★   Quick crank on the right.

Photos: Bruce Adams

The Cave

27. ORIGINAL EXIT   S2- ★★★
28. JONES PROBLEM   S4 ★★★

29. LEFT EXIT   S2+ ★★
30. CAVE TRAVERSE   S4– ★★★

Practice Boulder

31. DRILL TEAM   S1+ ★★★
32. FIRST TIMER   S1 ★★

33. PRACTICE SLAB   S1- ★★
34. FAKING IT   S1- ★★

Picnic Lunch Wall Base

A few worthwhile problems stretch along the base of Picnic Lunch Wall. These lines are popular since they're near the parking lot and stay dry in a downpour.

Leaning Slab

An unmistakable slab, leaning away from the base of the wall, is perched below **Snack Crack.** The overhanging river face is marked by an intimidating crack (#35, S1–, ★★) with a fatal landing. The hidden slab contains several moderate friction problems (#36, S1– to S1+, ★★), more akin to the Glacier Point Apron than the tuff of Smith Rock.

K + B Slab

Marked by K+B etched into the rock, this distinctive, crack-split flake balances against the base of Picnic Lunch Wall.

37. HAND TRAVERSE S1 ★★ Move either direction.
38. FINGER CRACK S2 ★★★ Uncontrived.
    a. S3– Climb the crack strictly (statically S3).
    b. S3+ Fingers and feet in crack.
39. SICK LITTLE SEAM S3– ★ Fingers in seam, feet anywhere.

Puke–A–Lot Wall Traverse

If it's raining hard and you really want to do some bouldering, the best choice is this traverse (#40, ★★) along the base of Picnic Lunch Wall. Done in its entirety, the traverse rates at S3–, with an awkward crux off a small boulder at the far right end. Most climbers bypass this hard move, dropping the grade to S2+.

RED WALL BOULDERS

Several boulders studded with high quality problems are below Red Wall. To reach the area, turn right at the bridge and follow the trail past the Practice Boulder to the rocks on the left.

Red Clot Rock

This boulder, with several problems on perfect rock sits nearest the trail.

41. JUG ROUTE S1+ ★★★★ Fun cranks between jugs.
    a. One-handed S4 Easy if you can power through a one-arm pull-up – impossible if you can't.
    b. S2 Start sitting down.
42. RED CLOT S2+ ★★★★ Classic.
    a. S3– From the first of two buckets on the **Jug Route,** power left and finish with Red Clot.
43. LEFT ROUTE S2 ★★
44. BACKSIDE PROBLEM S2– ★★

Simple Simon

Easy jugs (#45, S1–, ★★) lead past a bulge on the boulder immediately left of Red Clot Rock.

The Blob/Red Hare Rock

Two closely–spaced boulders are behind Red Clot Rock. The right block contains a few simple problems, while the more appealing Red Hare Rock sits to the left.

46. FAT SLOB   S1+ ★★

47. BLOBULAR   S1 ★★   Easy groove on The Blob.

48. QUICK TICK   S2 ★★★   A fun mantel on the left side. Don't use a small boulder.

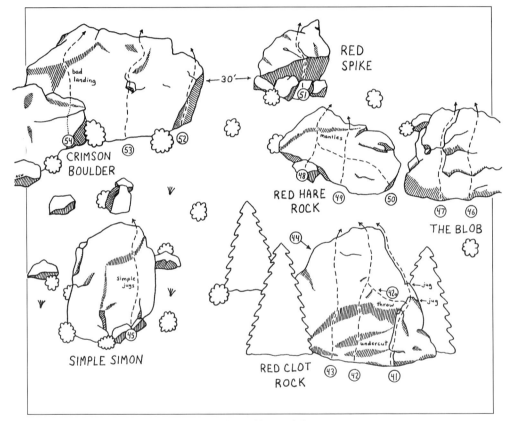

Red Wall Boulders

41. JUG ROUTE   S1+ ★★★★
42. RED CLOT   S2+ ★★★★
43. LEFT ROUTE   S2 ★★
44. BACKSIDE PROBLEM   S2– ★★
45. SIMPLE SIMON   S1– ★★
46. FAT SLOB   S1+ ★★
47. BLOBULAR   S1 ★★

48. QUICK TICK   S2 ★★★
49. CENTER MANTEL   S2+ ★★★
50. TRAVERSE   S2+ ★★★
51. RED SPIKE   S1 ★★
52. RIGHT EDGE   S3– ★★
53. CENTER ROUTE   S2+ ★★★
54. ADAMS ROUTE   S2 ★★

49. CENTER MANTEL S2+ ★★★

50. TRAVERSE S2+ ★★★ Move right to left on pockets, finishing with **Quick Tick.**

Red Spike
Lieback a short flake (#51, S1, ★★) on the distinctive, pointed block above Red Hare Rock.

Crimson Boulder
This impressive reddish boulder sits uphill to the left of the other problems in the area.

52. RIGHT EDGE S3– ★★

53. CENTER ROUTE S2+ ★★★

54. ADAMS ROUTE S2 ★★ Good holds on the left, with a very bad landing.

MORNING GLORY WALL AREA
Several forgotten boulder problems are near Morning Glory Wall. Despite their convenience, most of them receive only limited attention.

The Pharoah
After walking around the base of Shiprock, you'll come to this appealing, squarish boulder with a distinctive pocket.

55. RIGHT ARETE S2– ★★

56. POCKET ROUTE S2 ★★★★ A Smith Rock classic.
   a. S3 Don't use the obvious pocket.

57. LEFT ARETE S3– ★★★

Miscellaneous Problems
58. WHERE BONEHEADS DARE (S2+) ★★ A narrow gully is just past the third boardwalk beyond Shiprock. An intimidating boulder looms uphill on the left side of the gully. Begin with a hard sequence on the uphill side of the face, then finish with scary jugs.

59. SLACK JAW TRAVERSE S2+ ★★★ This long traverse moves uphill along the base of the Shipwreck Wall. The crux comes quickly, with a tough move skirting a rounded bulge.

60. LYSERGIC ROOF S2 ★ A cave, split by an obvious roof crack lurks low in the Aggro Gully. A poor man's **Separate Reality,** hand jams to a crux pull around the lip.

61. MORNING GLORY WALL TRAVERSE S2 ★★★ A popular warm-up traverse cuts along the base of the Zebra Area. The traverse typically begins at the **Zebra Seam** and continues across the wall, ending after a tough sequence just left of **Lion's Jaw.** You can continue much further, ending well past the Peanut.

Morning Glory Wall Boulders

DIHEDRALS & CHRISTIAN BROTHERS

You'll find some excellent bouldering amid the most heavily developed sport crags at Smith. These problems are the most popular in the park, since they make good warm-ups for the bolted routes.

Tator Tots Direct

This impressive line was the most significant problem of the late 70s. I've listed only the uncontrived ways to crank the overhang, ignoring several extreme variants (S4 to S4+) since they're hard to describe. Unfortunately, the park service unwittingly destroyed the landing when they laid their wooden staircase.

62. ROOF BYPASS S2 ★★   Edges on the right; terrible landing.

63. ORIGINAL LINE S2+ ★★★★   Start right and move left over the roof.

64. DIRECT ROUTE S4– ★★★★   Begin directly below the roof.

Dihedrals Traverses

65. TOTAL ECLIPSE S3 ★★★★   This long traverse cuts across the heart of the Dihedrals. Start

below **Take a Powder** or **Chain Reaction** and move in either direction. The entire traverse offers a great work-out, but several no-hands rests make it little harder than its individual sections. I've listed the best portions below:

a. SUNSHINE TRAVERSE S3– ★★★ The wall right of **Sunshine**.

b. LAST WALTZ TRAVERSE S3– ★★★ The long section between **Moonshine** and **Sunshine**.

c. MOONSHINE TRAVERSE S3– ★★★★ The wall from **Moonshine** around the corner to **Chain Reaction**.

Moonshine Face

The pocketed face on the left wall of Moonshine Dihedral contains several classic problems and dozens of contrived variations. A flat landing allows you to throw yourself at these lines with wild abandon. Below, I've listed only the least contrived boulder problems.

66. RIGHT POCKETS S3– ★★★ Once extremely difficult, these one-finger pockets somehow grew into two-fingers slots.

67. CENTER POCKETS S3– ★★★ Move right or left.

68. ORIGINAL POCKETS S2+ ★★★ Start just right of the finger crack.

69. MOONSHINE HAND TRAVERSE S1+ ★★★★ Classic finger crack.
    a. S1 Avoid the crux start by climbing jugs to the left.
    b. S3– Climb the vertical portion of the crack one-handed.

70. NASTY SEAM S3 ★★ Keep your fingers in the seam left of the finger crack.

Overhanging Flake

The classic overhanging flake below Boy Prophet contains the most-climbed boulder problem at Smith.

71. REGULAR ROUTE S2 ★★★★ Classic pocket pulling.

72. LEFT ARETE S3 ★★★ Rough landing.

73. TESTAMENT SLAB TRAVERSE S1 ★★★ An easy warm-up traverse cuts either direction across the wall between **The Beard** and **Old Testament.**

Combination Blocks Traverse

This often-tried endurance problem is the best traverse at Smith. Rarely completed, the **Combination Block Traverse** was among the better by-products of the early-80s bouldering frenzy. Several "direct" problems join the traverse from various places.

74. COMBINATION BLOCKS TRAVERSE S3+ ★★★★ Slightly harder left to right.
    a. Round trip S4– Move left to right, touching a foot to the dirt, then reverse.

75. BUTT SCRAPING TRAVERSE S4– ★★ Move left to right, barely off the deck.
    a. Circle Game S4 Do the low traverse, then complete the loop by moving left on the regular line.

76. DIRECT STARTS ★★
    a. S2+ Start below the right lip of the roof.
    b. S3– Reach between a pocket and edge.
    c. S3– Awkward seam.
    d. S3 Right route, with high-step.

Photos: Bruce Adams

Moonshine Face

65c. MOONSHINE TRAVERSE portion of
    TOTAL ECLIPSE S3 ★★★★
66. RIGHT POCKETS S3- ★★★
67. CENTER POCKETS S3- ★★★

68. ORIGINAL POCKETS S2+ ★★★
69. MOONSHINE HAND TRAVERSE S1+
    ★★★★
70. NASTY SEAM S3 ★★★

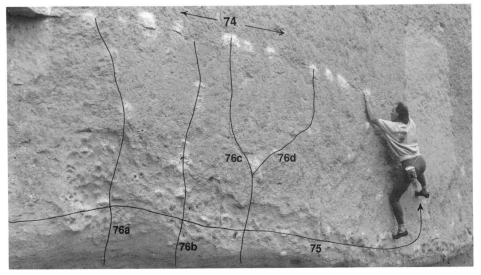

Combination Blocks Traverse

74. COMBINATION BLOCKS TRAVERSE
    S3+ ★★★★

75. BUTT SCRAPING TRAVERSE S4- ★★
76. DIRECT STARTS ★★

FIRST ASCENT
INFORMATION

This appendix contains first-ascent information on every route in the book, except for boulder problems. Keeping track of "who-did-what-when" is a difficult task; when you add **how** they did it to the equation, it becomes even more tricky. Despite my best efforts, this section is subject to more errors than any other part of the book. I've used a variety of designations to define "what was done when" in the history of the route. The following definitions will help you decipher the codes:

PREP: Preparation: This give credit to the person who first cleaned and/or bolted a route. They may have worked out some portions of the route free, but they didn't do enough to earn credit for the first ascent.

F.A.: First Ascent: The first person to climb a route, whether aid or free. There is a fine line between preparation and a first ascent. To qualify as a first ascent on a sport climb, all sections must go free and a substantial portion of the preparation must have been completed.

F.F.A.: First Free Ascent: This indicates the first free ascent of a route previously climbed either on aid, or with a hand on the rope. If the same person who did the first ascent also freed the route, I've used only the F.A. designation.

F.R.A.: First Recorded Ascent: These routes likely were climbed earlier, but no record exists about who actually did them.

F.R.F.A.: First Recorded Free Ascent.

YY: Yo-Yo: These routes were first led after leaving the rope through high points after falls.

TR: Toprope: First climbed using a toprope.

LEAD: The first lead of a route previously climbed free on toprope.

SOLO: The first ascent was done alone, but utilized ropes and protection devices.

F.S.: Free Solo: These first ascents were done without a rope.

PICNIC LUNCH WALL AREA

1. SCORPIO 5.8 X F.A. Curt Haire, Ray Stewart, April 1977
1a. I LOST MY LUNCH 5.9 X F.A. Mark Cartier, Jim Anglin, October 19, 1980
2. FOOL'S OVERTURE 5.9 R ★ F.A. Mike Smelsar, Dana Horton, fall 1977)
3. HIGHWAY 97 5.12c ★★★ F.A. first two pitches, Brooke Sandahl, winter 1989; F.A. upper pitch, TR, Brooke Sandahl, 1990
4. LA SIESTA 5.11d ★★★ F.A. Brents Hawks, winter 1989
5. SPARTACUS 5.12a ★★ F.A. Ed Barry, Tom Herbert, Mark Chapman, fall 1987
6. APPIAN WAY 5.12a ★★ F.A. Ed Barry, Tom Herbert, Mark Chapman, fall 1987
7. NO PICNIC 5.10c R ★ F.A. Jim Anglin, Mike Hartley, July 3, 1981
7a. FARMERS VARIATION 5.10a X F.A. Craig Benesch, Doug Kozlik, fall 1981
8. TEDDY BEAR'S PICNIC 5.10b ★★ F.A. Mark Whalan, June 1990
9. FREE LUNCH 5.10a R ★ F.A. upper three pitches (via **Unfinished Symphony**), Jeff Thomas, Steve Moore, April 1972; F.F.A. last two pitches (via **Unfinished Symphony**) Dean Fry, Larry Kemp, May 6, 1972; F.A. first two pitches, Dan Foote, Mike Smelsar, Brian Holcomb, fall 1976; F.F.A. entire route, Jeff Thomas, Willis Krause, February 12, 1977

10. UNFINISHED SYMPHONY 5.12b ★★ F.A. Kim Schmitz, Dean Caldwell, summer 1965; F.F.A. first pitch, Alan Watts, May 14, 1982
11. COLESLAW AND CHEMICALS 5.12d ★★ F.A. Tedd Thompson, fall 1988; F.F.A. Darius Azin, fall 1988
12. PUBIC LUAU 5.11d/12a ★★ F.A. Brooke Sandahl, spring 1986
13. PUBIC LUAU DIRECT 5.12b ★★ F.A. TR, Brooke Sandahl, spring 1986
14. PROJECT 5.14a ? F.A. Darius Azin, fall 1988; F.F.A. uncompleted
15. ZORTEX THRUX A4 F.A. Scott Davis, early 80s
16. MIDNIGHT SNACK 5.12b/c ★★ F.A. Alan Watts, May 26, 1982
17. SNACK CRACK 5.13b ★★ F.A. Alan Watts, April 1988
18. SOFT SHOE BALLET 5.10a A4 X ★ F.A. Bob McGown, Bill Antel, Jeff Alzner, Bruce Birchell, November 1978
19. PROJECT 5.15 ? Prep: Scott Franklin, 1989
20. PICNIC LUNCH WALL 5.9 A3+ R ★ F.A. Tom Bauman, Kim Schmitz, October 21-22, 1969
21. BUBBA'S IN BONDAGE 5.7 A3 ★ F.A. first pitch, Alan Lester, Chuck Wheeler, winter 1982; F.A. second pitch, Jim Anglin, spring 1983
22. SUICIDAL TENDENCIES 5.11d ★ F.A. Kurt Smith, spring 1988
23. TOUCH 5.11c ★★ F.A. Kurt Smith, spring 1988
24. JOURNEY TO IXTLAN 5.10b A5 X F.A. first two pitches, Bob McGown, Jeff Alzner, March 1979; F.A. upper pitches, Bob McGown, Mark Simpson, summer 1981
25. EAST CHIMNEY 5.7 X F.A. Jim Ramsey, Jerry Ramsey, 1959.
26. WEST CHIMNEY 5.7 X F.A. Ross Petrie, Dave Pearson, 1946
27. CITY DUMP 5.7 R F.A. Steve Lyford, Jack Callahan, Jeff Thomas, March 31, 1974
28. VANISHING UNCERTAINTY 5.9 ★ R F.A. Andy Embick, Ted Schuck, 1972; F.F.A. Jeff Thomas, Steve Lyford, March 31, 1974
29. WASTE LAND 5.8 R F.A. Jeff Thomas, Steve Lyford, Jack Callahan, March 31, 1974

THE WOODEN SHIPS/THE GULLIES

1. PROJECT 5.13 ? Prep: Unknown
2. MOTHER'S MILK 5.12d ★★ F.A. Jay Greene, Gary Rall, May 21, 1991
3. WALKING WHILE INTOXICATED 5.10b ★★ F.A. Tom Heins, Tom Egan, December 7, 1990
4. FLIGHT OF THE PATRIOT SCUD BLASTER 5.11b ★★ F.A. Tom Heins, Tom Egan, February, 1991
5. PURPLE ACES 5.11b/c ★★ F.A. Jeff Frizzell, December 2, 1990
6. MORE SANDY THAN KEVIN 5.10d/11a ★★ F.A. Tom Heins, December 1, 1990
7. LIQUID JADE 5.12a/b ★★★ F.A. Tom Egan, Tom Heins, December 6, 1990
8. BLUE LIGHT SPECIAL 5.11a ★★★ F.A. Tom Egan, December 1990
9. TIME TO POWER 5.12c ★★★ F.A. TR, Eric Johnson, 1990, F.F.A. John Collins, spring 1992
10. SHIPWRECK 5.9 R F.A. Dean Fry, Terri Raider, January 3, 1973
11. GHOST RIDER 5.12b ★ F.A. Martin Grullich, fall 1987
12. HIGHWAY TO HELL 5.12a ★★ F.A. Martin Grullich, fall 1987
13. VILLAIN 5.13d ★★★ F.A. Geoff Weigand, spring 1990
14. WHITE WEDDING 5.13d/14a ★★★ F.A. Michael Keiss, fall 1987; F.F.A. Jean Baptiste Tribout, June 1988
15. BADMAN 5.13d/14a ★★★ F.A. Alan Watts, August 1990; F.F.A. Jean Baptiste Tribout, January 1991
16. PROJECT 5.13+ ? F.A. uncompleted
17. AGGRO MONKEY 5.13b ★★★ Prep: Martin Gulich; F.A. TR, Sean Olmstead, spring 1988; F.F.A. Martin Atkinson, May 1988
18. SCENE OF THE CRIME 5.13b/c ★★★ F.A. Sean Olmstead, spring 1990; F.F.A. Jean Baptiste Tribout, spring 1990
19. CRIME WAVE 5.13c ★★★ F.A. Tom Herbert, October 1991
20. THE QUICKENING 5.12d ★★ F.A. Kevin Lawlor, October 1990
21. PROJECT 5.13c ? F.A. Sean Olmstead, November 1990; F.F.A. uncompleted
22. SPEWING 5.12d ★★ F.A. Colin Lantz, February 22, 1991
23. PROJECT 5.12 ? Prep: Kent Benesch, 1989; F.A. uncompleted
24. CAUSTIC 5.12b/c ★ F.A. Jim Hall, spring 1991

25. SEASONAL EFFECTIVENESS DISORDER   5.10a ★★★   F.A. Pete Keane, February 1991
26. SKINNY SWEATY MAN   5.11a ★★   F.A. Pete Keane, Tom Heins, February 1991
27. CRANKENSTEIN   5.11a ★★   F.A. Tom Heins, Pete Keane, February 1991
28. THE BURL MASTER   5.13 ?   Prep: Kent Benesch, 1989
29. MONKEY BOY   5.12c ★★   F.A. Sean Olmstead, fall 1989
30. UP FOR GRABS   5.11d ★★★   F.A. Sean Olmstead, August 1988
31. NO NUKES   5.10b ★   F.A. Avary Tichner, 1981
32. TOXIC   5.11b ★★★★   F.A. Colin Lantz, Greg Robinson, fall 1987
33. TOXIC TOPROPE   5.12a/b ★★   F.A. TR, Darius Azin, spring 1990
34. FEET OF CLAY   5.12b ★★★   F.A. Adam Grosowsky, fall 1989
35. POWER   5.13b ★★★   F.A. Brooke Sandahl, YY, spring 1989
36. SOLAR   5.9 ★★   F.A. upper pitch, via No Doz, Dean Fry, Russ Bunker, February 24, 1973; F.F.A. Jeff Thomas, Steve Lyford, March 11, 1977
37. NO DOZ   5.9 A4 X   F.A. Dean Fry, Russ Bunker, February 24, 1973
38. TIME'S UP   5.13a/b ★★★   F.A. Dan Goodwin, fall 1987; F.F.A. Geoff Weigand, spring 1988
39. SLIT YOUR WRIST   5.13b ★★★   F.A. Geoff Weigand, spring 1988
40. PROJECT   5.13d ?   Prep: Kent Benesch, spring 1990
41. SKELETON SURFER   5.11b ★★   F.A. James Fredericks, Ted Otto, summer 1989
42. THE BLADE   5.12a ★★★   F.A. Tedd Thompson, Darius Azin, fall 1987
43. CHICKEN McNUGGETS   5.10b ★★★   F.A. Tom Heins, Pete Keane, March 1, 1991
44. COCAINE CRACK   5.11b ★★   F.A. Bob McGown, Doug Bower, July 1979; F.F.A. Alan Watts, Kent Benesch, November 13, 1981
45. VOMIT LAUNCH   5.11b ★★★★   F.A. Kent Benesch, spring 1987
46. FREEBASE   5.12a ★★★★   F.A. Dan Goodwin, fall 1987
47. POWDER UP THE NOSE   5.10d ★★★   F.A. Marc Dube, fall 1987
48. SHAKE 'N FLAKE   5.11b ★★   F.A. Tedd Thompson, fall 1987
49. RABID   5.12b ★★   F.A. Rick Lince, fall 1987
50. BOUND IN BOGOTA   5.10d ★★   F.A. Tom Egan, December 1990
51. PITCH IT HERE   5.10d ★   F.A. Tom Heins, August 1990
52. DOUBLE EDGED SWORD   5.10c ★   F.A. Tom Heins, August 1990
53. DESMOND'S TUTU   5.10b R ★   F.A. Tom Heins, November 1990

MORNING GLORY WALL

1. STAND AND DELIVER   5.12c ★★   F.A. Adam Grosowsky, fall 1988
2. BEND OVER AND RECEIVE   5.13a ★★   F.A. Adam Grosowsky, spring 1989; F.F.A. Geoff Weigand, September 1989
3. PROJECT   5.14 ?   F.A. Jason Karn, spring 1991
4. PROJECT   5.13 ?   Prep: Tom Egan, 1990
5. BONGO FURY   5.13a ★★★   F.A. Jeff Frizzell, June 1991
6. QUEST TO FIRE   5.12a R ★★★   F.A. John Collins, spring 1991
7. HIPPO'S ON ICE   5.10a ★   F.A. Cecil Colley, Gary Gallagher, Tim Olson, winter 1990
8. PROJECT   5.12- ?   Prep: Tim Olson, winter 1990
9. GIMME SHELTER   5.11d R ★★   F.A. Kent Benesch, 1984
10. EXILE ON MAIN STREET   5.11a ★★★   F.A. Kent Benesch, 1984
11. OXYGEN   5.13a/b ★★★   F.A. Darius Azin, October 1987
12. JAM MASTER J   5.13d ★★★   Prep: Darius Azin, 1988; F.A. Jerry Moffatt, November 1988
13. DA KINE CORNER   5.12b/c ★★★★   F.A. Brooke Sandahl, spring 1987
14. WHITE HEAT   5.13c/d ★★★★   F.A. Alan Watts, April 1988
15. KINGS OF RAP   5.12d ★★★★   F.A. Brooke Sandahl, spring 1987
16. WASTE CASE   5.13b ★★★★   F.A. Alan Watts, April 1988
17. VICIOUS FISH   5.13c/d ★★★★   F.A. Alan Watts, March 1988
18. CHURNING IN THE WAKE   5.13a ★★★★   F.A. Sean Olmstead, March 1987
18a. CHURNING SKY   5.13a ★★★★   F.A. Craig Smith, spring 1987
18b. CHURNING IN THE OZONE   5.13b ★★★★   F.A. Geoff Weigand, fall 1988
19. SIGN OF THE TIMES   5.12d ★   F.A. Dan Goodwin, fall 1987

20. TACO CHIPS   5.12d ★★★   F.A. Jean Marc Troussier, November 1986
21. SLUM TIME   5.10a   F.A. Bob McGown, 1980
22. PROJECT   5.12 ?   Prep: Jordan Mills, 1988
23. OVERBOARD   5.11c (5.11a/b lower part) ★★★   F.A. Martin Grullich, spring 1987
24. MAGIC LIGHT   5.12b (5.11a lower part) ★★   F.A. Martin Grullich, spring 1987
25. ENERGY CRISIS   5.12b ★★★   F.A. Martin Grullich, spring 1987
26. SKETCH PAD   5.12d ★★★   F.A. Martin Grullich, F.F.A. Geoff Weigand, fall 1988
27. MANE LINE   5.13a ★★   F.A. Alan Watts, winter 1989
28. LION'S CHAIR   5.11a R ★★★   F.A. first two pitches, Phil Dean, Steve Heim, 1968; F.A. upper pitches, Phil Dean, George Selfridge, 1968; F.F.A. second and fourth pitches, Bob McGown, Jeff Thomas, April 16-17, 1977; F.F.A. entire route, Jeff Thomas, Ted Johnson, June 5, 1977
29. PROJECT   5.13+ ?   Prep. Alan Watts, 1988
30. DANDY LINE   5.12d ★★   F.A. Dan Goodwin, fall 1987; F.F.A. Alan Watts, January 1988
31. ZEBRA SEAM   5.11d R ★★★   F.A. Bob Martin, Ray Snyder, 1970; F.F.A. TR, Alan Watts, August 29, 1981; F.F.A. lead Steve Byrne, 1984
32. ZEBRA DIRECT   5.11a ★★★ F.A. Alan Watts, Bill Ramsey, May 26, 1979
33. GUMBY   5.10b ★★★   F.A. Alan Watts, Brooke Sandahl, spring 1987
34. ZEBRA   5.10a ★★★   F.A. via **Zebra Seam**, Bob Martin, Ray Snyder, 1970; F.F.A. via potholes, Dean Fry, Jeff Thomas, January 14, 1973
34a. ZION   5.9 ★★★   F.A. Jeff Thomas, Chris Mannix, April 24, 1977
35. LIGHT ON THE PATH   5.9 ★★   F.A. Alan Quine, winter 1988
36. CAT SCAN   5.11a ★   F.A. Chris Snyder, summer 1989
37. IN HINDS WAY   5.9   F.A. Chuck Buzzard, Jerry Radant, 1984
38. CHOSS IN AMERICA   5.12c ★★★   F.A. Duane Raleigh, fall 1988
39. ONE TIME TRICK   5.11a ★   F.A. YY, Alan Lester, 1982
40. LION'S JAW   5.8 ★★★   F.A. Tom Bauman, Bob Bauman, 1967
40a. LION'S JAW CHIMNEY   5.7   F.A. unknown
41. TAMMY BAKKER'S FACE   5.10c ★★   F.A. Mike Mahoney, 1988
42. POPISM   5.11b R ★★   F.R.A. Alan Watts, summer 1989
43. POP GOES THE NUBBIN   5.10a ★★   F.A. Jeff Thomas, Chris Jones, October 22, 1978
44. PEANUT BRITTLE   5.8 R ★★   F.A. Jeff Thomas, Chet Sutterlin, March 18, 1977
45. HOP ON POP   5.8 ★★★   F.A. Alan Watts, JoAnn Miller-Watts, fall 1989
46. FRIDAY'S JINX   5.7 R ★★   F.A. Dean and Paul Fry, March 10, 1973
46a. SUNDAY'S JINX   5.7   F.A. Pat Carr, 1977
47. CRACK OF INFINITY   5.10b ★★★   F.A. second pitch, Bob Grundy, April 7, 1974; F.A. third pitch, Bob McGown, Mike Smelsar, 1976; F.F.A. entire route, Jeff Thomas, Chet Sutterlin, March 19, 1977
47a. INFINITY VARIATION   5.10a ★★   F.A. Bill McKinney, Avary Tichner, 1978
48. CALAMITY JAM   5.10c ★★★   F.A. Jeff Thomas, Mike Smelsar, March 13, 1977
48a. CATASTROPHIC CRACK   5.12A R ★★   F.A. Alan Watts, March 10, 1983
48b. SANDBAG   5.10c R ★   F.A. Alan Watts, summer 1987
49. PACK ANIMAL   5.8 R ★★★   F.A. via direct start, Tom Rogers, Jeff Elphinston, 1972; F.F.A. Jeff Thomas, Jack Callahan, April 7, 1974
49a. PACK ANIMAL DIRECT   5.10b ★★★★   F.A. Tom Rogers, Jeff Elphinston, 1972; F.F.A. Jeff Thomas, Chet Sutterlin, March 18, 1977
49b. SUNDANCER   5.10a ★   F.A. Tim Olson, Tony Bishop, Cecil Colley, January 28, 1989
50. HEADLESS HORSEMAN   5.10d ★★★   F.A. Doug Phillips, summer 1987; F.F.A. Greg Phillips, summer 1987
51. EQUUS   5.11b ★★   F.A. Alan Watts, August 1987
52. FOURTH HORSEMAN   5.7 R ★   F.R.A. Jim Ramsey, Bruce Hahn, 1964
53. THIRD HORSEMAN   5.10b R ★   F.R.A. Jim Ramsey, Bruce Hahn, 1964, F.F.A. unknown
54. SECOND HORSEMAN   5.6 R ★   F.R.A. Jim Ramsey, Bruce Hahn, 1964
55. FIRST HORSEMAN   5.7 R ★   F.R.A. Jim Ramsey, Bruce Hahn, 1964
56. RIDERLESS HORSE   5.7 X   F.R.A. Alan Watts, 1985
57. NORTH SLAB CRACK   5.3 X ★★   F.A. unknown

58. HOW LOW CAN YOU GO? 5.6 ★★★ F.A. TR, unknown; F.A. lead, Alan Watts, JoAnn Miller-Watts, June 1, 1991
59. SHAMU 5.9 ★★★ F.A. Alan Watts, JoAnn Miller-Watts, June 1, 1991
60. LOW BLOW 5.10b ★ F.A. TR, Alan Watts, June 1, 1991
61. FLOAT LIKE A BUTTERFLY 5.10b ★★★★ F.A. TR, Alan Watts, June 1, 1991
62. ROPE-DE-DOPE CRACK 5.8 ★★ F.A. unknown
63. STING LIKE A BEE 5.10b/C ★★★ F.R.A. TR, Alan Watts, 1980

THE DIHEDRALS

1. LICHEN IT 5.7 ★★★ F.A. Alan Watts, JoAnn Miller-Watts, October 17, 1989
2. RIGHT SLAB CRACK 5.5 ★★ F.A. unknown
3. EASY READER 5.6 ★★★ F.A. Alan Watts, JoAnn Miller-Watts, summer 1989
4. LEFT SLAB CRACK 5.4 ★★ F.A. unknown
5. GINGER SNAP 5.8 ★★★ F.A. Alan Watts, JoAnn Miller-Watts, summer 1989
6. CINNAMON SLAB 5.6 ★★★ F.A. F.S. Bob Bauman, mid-60s
7. CINNAMON TOAST 5.7 R ★ F.A. Jeff Thomas, Chet Sutterlin, Tim Carpenter, Roseann Lehman, March 19, 1977
8. KARATE CRACK 5.10a ★★★ F.A. Dean Caldwell, Byron Babcock, fall 1966; F.F.A. Dean Fry, Steve Lyford, October 7, 1973
9. PEAPOD CAVE 5.10a ★★ F.A. Dean Caldwell, Byron Babcock, fall 1966; F.F.A. Dean Fry, Steve Lyford, October 7, 1973
10. SLOW BURN 5.11d R ★★★ F.A. Alan Watts, April 2, 1983
11. CROSSFIRE 5.12a/b R ★★★★ F.A. Alan Watts, May 1, 1984
12. POWER DIVE 5.12a R ★★★★ F.A. Alan Watts, April 14, 1984
13. KAROT TOTS 5.11b ★★★★ F.A. Dave Jensen, George Cummings, 1970; F.F.A. Alan Watts, Mark Cartier, October 4, 1980
14. FIRING LINE 5.12b ★★★ F.A. Alan Watts, March 24, 1984
15. KARATE WALL (a.k.a. POWERLINE) 5.12b ★★★★ F.A. Alan Watts, May 26, 1984
16. LOW PROFILE 5.12b/c R ★★★★ F.A. Alan Watts, April 18, 1984
17. LATEST RAGE 5.12b ★★★★ F.A. Alan Watts, February 18, 1984
18. WATTS TOTS 5.12b ★★★★ F.A. Alan Watts, February 11, 1983
18a. MEGA WATTS 5.13b ★★★ F.A. Alan Watts, 1989
18b. KILO WATTS 5.12b ★★★ F.A. Alan Watts, summer 1987
19. TRIVIAL PURSUIT 5.10d R ★★ F.A. Alan Watts, November 10, 1983
20. TATOR TOTS 5.10a R ★★ F.A. Jeff Thomas, Mike Smelsar, February 26, 1977
21. LATIN LOVER 5.12a ★★★ F.A. Jean Marc Troussier, October 1986
22. PEEPSHOW 5.12a/b ★★ F.A. Alan Watts, September 1988
23. UPPER CEILING 5.7 R ★ F.A. Dean Caldwell, Jim Kindler 1966
23a. SISTINE VARIATION 5.8 ★ F.A. Jeff Thomas, Dean Fry, November 4, 1972
24. LESTER TOTS 5.10b R ★ F.A. Alan Watts, Chris Grover, March 3, 1983
25. ALMOST NOTHING 5.11d R ★★ F.A. Jean Marc Troussier, October 1986
26. TAKE A POWDER 5.12a ★★★ F.A. Alan Watts, August 1987
27. POWDER IN THE EYES 5.12c ★★★ F.A. Jean Marc Troussier, October 1986
28. PROJECT 5.13d F.A. Alan Watts, December 1989; F.F.A. uncompleted
29. SUNSHINE DIHEDRAL 5.11d ★★★★ F.A. first pitch, Tom Bauman, late 60s; F.A. entire route, Tom Rogers, Dan Muir, Jack Barrar. F.F.A. TR, Chris Jones, July 6, 1979. F.F.A. lead, Alan Watts, Alan Lester, July 18, 1981
30. FRENCH CONNECTION 5.13b ★★★★ F.A. Alan Watts, fall 1984; F.F.A. Jean Baptiste Tribout, October 1988)
31. TO BOLT OR NOT TO BE 5.14a ★★★★ F.A. TR, Alan Watts, fall 1984; F.F.A. Jean Baptiste Tribout, November 7, 1986)
32. LAST WALTZ 5.12c ★★★★ F.A. Alan Watts, October 8, 1983
32a. LAST WALTZ DIRECT 5.12c X ★★★ F.A. Alan Watts, February 1985
33. MOONDANCE 5.11c ★★★ F.A. Alan Watts, Chris Grover, January 28, 1984
34. WEDDING DAY 5.10b ★★★ F.A. Graeme Aimeer, Grant Davidson, 1984

35.   THE FLAT EARTH   5.12a/b ★   F.A. Eric Horst, May 1991
36.   MOONSHINE DIHEDRAL   5.9 ★★★★   F.A. first pitch, Dave Jensen, Bob Pierce, 1963; F.A. entire route, unknown; F.F.A. Dean Fry, Jeff Thomas, November 4, 1972
36a. MOONSHINE VARIATION   5.10b X ★★★
37.   HEINOUS CLING   5.12c ★★★★   F.A. lower part, Alan Watts, April 25, 1983; F.A. upper part, Alan Watts, March 22, 1984; F.F.A. entire pitch, Alan Watts, April 29, 1984
38.   DARKNESS AT NOON   5.13a ★★★★   F.A. lower part, Alan Watts, March 17, 1984; F.F.A. upper portion, May 26, 1984; F.F.A. entire route, Alan Watts, March 9, 1985
39.   CHAIN REACTION   5.12c ★★★★   F.A. Alan Watts, February 26, 1983
40.   PROJECT   5.13?   Prep. Alan Watts, December 1990
41.   RATTLESNAKE CHIMNEY   5.6 ★   F.A. George Cummings, John Hall, May 1963
42.   ANCYLOSTOMA   5.9 ★★   F.A. Brian Baker, 1988
43.   BOOKWORM   5.7 ★★★   F.R.A. Dave Jensen, 1970
43a. VARIATION   5.7 ★★   F.R.A. Dave Jensen, 1970
44.   BUNNY FACE   5.7 ★★★   F.A. first pitch, Jeff Thomas, Ken Currens, March 26, 1977; F.A. entire route, JoAnn Miller, Alan Watts, August 1987
45.   METHUSELAH'S COLUMN   5.10a R ★   F.A. Dean Fry, Paul Fry, March 10, 1973
46.   RABBIT STEW   5.7 ★★   F.A. unknown
47.   LYCOPODOPHYTA   5.7 ★★   F.A. Dean Fry, Jeff Thomas, December 17, 1972
48.   HELIUM WOMAN   5.9 ★★   F.A. Kevin Pogue, Jay Goodwin, April 1990
49.   CAPTAIN XENOLITH   5.10a ★★   F.A. Kevin Pogue, Jay Goodwin, March 20, 1991
50.   DETERIORATA   5.8 ★   F.A. Jeff Thomas, Steve Lyford, March 3, 1974
51.   GO DOG GO   5.12c ★★★   F.A. Alan Watts, September 1988
52.   VISION   5.12b ★★   F.A. Colin Lantz, spring 1988)

THE CHRISTIAN BROTHERS – EAST

1.   DEEP SPLASH   5.11d ★★   F.A. Tom Egan, April 1991
2.   RAWHIDE   5.11d ★★★   F.A. Brooke Sandahl, winter 1988
3.   SMOOTH BOY   5.13b ★★★   F.A. Erik Johnson, winter 1990; F.F.A. Jean Baptiste Tribout, January 1991
4.   CHOKE ON THIS   5.12d ★★★   F.A. Kent Benesch, January 1988
5.   DREAMIN'   5.12A R ★★★★   F.A. Brooke Sandahl, February 1988
6.   BOY PROPHET   5.12b R ★★★★   F.A. Alan Watts, April 22, 1984
7.   RUDE BOYS   5.13c ★★★★   F.A. Alan Watts, hang, February 1985; F.F.A. Jean Baptiste Tribout, October 1986
8.   RUDE FEMMES   5.13c/d ★★★★   F.A. Alan Watts, October 21, 1988
9.   SCARFACE   5.14a ★★★★   F.A. Scott Franklin, April 1988
10. AIR TO SPARE   5.9 A4+ X ★   F.A. Jim Anglin, Tom Blust, February 28, 1981
11. PROJECT   5.15?   Prep. Scott Franklin, Darius Azin, 1989
12. SHOES OF THE FISHERMAN   5.11b ★★   F.A. Jeff Thomas, Ralph Moore, March 31, 1975; F.F.A. Jeff Thomas, April 24, 1977
12a. TOES OF THE FISHERMAN   5.13b   F.A. Alan Watts, March 10, 1984; F.F.A. uncompleted
13. WARTLEY'S REVENGE   5.11b ★★★★   F.A. Tom Rogers, Wayne Haack, Ken Jern, 1972; F.F.A. Jeff Thomas, Chris Jones, November 4, 1978
14. THE RIGHT SIDE OF THE BEARD   5.7 ★★★   Tom Bauman, Jan Newman, October 13, 1968
15. RISK SHY   5.12a ★★★ X   F.A. F.S. Alan Watts, November 14, 1984
16. THE LEFT SIDE OF THE BEARD   5.6 ★★★   F.A. Tom Bauman, Jan Newman, October 13, 1968
17. THE CLAM   5.11b ★   F.A. Doug Phillips, spring 1989; F.R.F.A. Alan Watts, May 1989
18. GOLGOTHA   5.11b ★★★   F.A. Alan Watts, Mel Johnson, June 20, 1981
18a. TEMPTATION   5.10a ★★   F.A. Alan Watts, Wayne Kamara, March 17, 1981
19. BARBECUE THE POPE   5.10b ★★★   F.A. Brooke Sandahl, January 1987
20. NEW TESTAMENT   5.10a ★★★   F.A. unknown, F.F.A. Dean Fry, Larry Kemp, February 18, 1973
21. REVELATIONS   5.9 ★★★   F.A. Tim Carpenter, John Tyreman, 1975
22. IRREVERENCE   5.10a ★★★   F.R.A. TR, Jeff Thomas, late 70s; F.A. lead, Alan Watts, JoAnn Miller-Watts, August 1988
23. NIGHTINGALE'S ON VACATION   5.10b ★★   F.A. Alan Watts, Amy Bruzzano, JoAnn Miller-Watts, July 6 1990

24. OLD TESTAMENT 5.7 ★★ F.R.A. Jack Barrar, Wayne Arrington, 1973
25. HEATHEN'S HIGHWAY 5.10a ★★ F.A. Jim Anglin, Mike Hartley, October 28, 1979
26. GOTHIC CATHEDRAL 5.8 R F.A. Bob Bauman, Ken Jern, mid-sixties
26a. ISLAND IN THE SKY 5.8 X F.A. Mike Steele, John Steele, 1981
27. LAST GASP 5.9 X F.A. Tom Rogers, Clay Cox, 1972
27a. SAFETY VALVE 5.7 R F.A. unknown
28. PROJECT 5.13 ? Prep: Kent Benesch, 1989
29. PRIVATE TRUST 5.11c R ★★★ F.A. Alan Watts, January 27, 1984
30. CHARLIE'S CHIMNEY 5.6 X ★★★ F.A. Dean Caldwell, Val Kiefer, 1967
31. OVERNIGHT SENSATION 5.11a ★★★ F.A. Brooke Sandahl, winter 1987
32. TINKER TOY 5.9 ★★★ X F.A. Jeff Thomas, Alan Watts, Bill Ramsey, February 19, 1978
33. DOUBLE TROUBLE 5.10b ★★ F.A. Tom Heins, spring 1990
34. BOWLING ALLEY 5.5 ★★ F.A. Dean Caldwell, Val Kiefer, 1967
35. DOUBLE STAIN 5.13a/b ★★★ F.A. Dave Jensen, 1969; F.F.A. Alan Watts, May 22, 1984
36. BUM RUSH THE SHOW 5.13b ★★★ F.A. Brooke Sandahl, March 31, 1991
37. TOYS IN THE ATTIC 5.9 ★★ F.A. Bill Ramsey, Chris Jones, July 19, 1979
37a. CHILD'S PLAY 5.10c ★★ F.A. Alan Watts, Bruce Birchell, July 5, 1980
38. HESITATION BLUES 5.10b ★★★ F.A. Alan Watts, Kent Benesch, August 23, 1980
39. BLUE BALLS 5.10b ★★ X F.A. F.S. Alan Watts, summer 1985
39. ATTIC ANTICS 5.11b ★★ F.A. Alan Watts, June 10, 1982
40. RING OF FIRE 5.11D ★★★ F.A. Brooke Sandahl, June 1988
41. TOY BLOCKS 5.10a ★★ F.A. Jeff Thomas, Shari Kearney, May 28, 1977
41a. SELF PRESERVATION VARIATION 5.10a ★★★ F.A. Mike Hartley, Jim Anglin, August 25, 1979
42. DANCER 5.7 ★★★ F.A. Tim Carpenter, John Tyreman, 1976
42a. DANCER CONTINUATION 5.8 ★ F.A. Jeff Thomas, Ken Stroud, February 14, 1976
43. JETE 5.8 ★★★ F.A. Alan Watts, JoAnn Miller-Watts, August 1988

SMITH ROCK GROUP

1. THE ASTERISK 5.7 X ★ F.A. Jim Ramsey, Jerry Ramsey, 1961
2. SKY RIDGE 5.8 R ★★ F.A. via Sky Dive, Dave Jensen, George Cummings, 1968; F.A. upper pitch, Steve Lyford, Scott Schmidt, 1973
2a. SKY RIDGE VARIATION 5.8 R ★ F.A. Jeff Thomas, Tim Carpenter, Ed Beacham, August 1972
2b. SKY DIVE 5.10c ★★★ F.A. Dave Jensen, George Cummings, 1968; F.F.A. Tom Blust, Spurge Cochran, February 1981
3. SKY WAYS 5.10a R F.A. Jeff Thomas, Doug Phillips, Scott Hansen, May 11, 1974; F.F.A. Mark Cartier, Jim Anglin, fall 1981)
4. BY WAYS 5.8 R F.A. Jean Yves Poublan, Walt Allegar, July 4, 1980
5. SKY CHIMNEY 5.7 ★★ F.A. Dave Jensen, George Cummings, fall 1969; F.F.A. Doug Phillips, Jack Callahan, winter 1974)
5a. SKY CHIMNEY VARIATION 5.7 R F.A. unknown
6. WHITE SATIN 5.9 ★★★ F.A. Jeff Thomas, Doug Phillips, March 11, 1974
7. GRETTIR'S SAGA 5.10a ★★ F.A. Mike Steele, 1982
8. BLACK VELCRO 5.9 ★ R F.A. lower three pitches, Bob Johnson, Doug Phillips, 1975; F.A. entire route, Jeff Thomas, Mark Cartier, August 19, 1978
9. SNIBBLE TOWER 5.9 A1 R F.A. Jon Marshall, John Haek, 1969; F.F.A. via variation, Alan Kearney, Shari Kearney, 1976
10. CONDOR 5.10c ★★ F.A. Jim Anglin, John Rich, 1986
11. LIVIN' LARGE 5.13 ? Prep. Brooke Sandahl, spring 1991
12. 100% BEEF 5.13 ? Prep. Brooke Sandahl, spring 1991
13. SMITH SUMMIT – EAST WALL 5.8 X F.A. Dean Fry, Wayne Arrington, May 27, 1973; F.F.A. Jeff Thomas, Steve Lyford, February 23, 1974
14. CARABID 5.6 R ★★ F.A. Chet Sutterlin, Bob Bury, 1977
15. DRILL 'EM AND FILL 'EM 5.10a ★★ F.A. Mike Puddy, Alan Watts, summer 1987
16. PHOENIX 5.10a ★★★★ F.A. Ken Currens, winter 1976
17. LICENSE TO BOLT 5.11b ★★★ F.A. Brooke Sandahl, spring 1987

18. FRED ON AIR   5.10d ★★★   F.A. TR, Brooke Sandahl, Alan Watts, 1987; F.A. lead, Rick Lince, 1987
19. FLAKE CHIMNEY   5.6 R   F.A. unknown
20. VULTURE RIDGE   5.6 X   F.R.A., F.S. Alan Watts, spring 1991
21. YODERIFIC   5.11d ★★   F.A. Jim Yoder, 1988
22. KUNZA KORNER   5.10c ★★★★   F.A. Ralph Moore, 1976; F.F.A. Alan Watts, Jeanne Kunza, June 9, 1980
23. WAVE OF BLISS   5.11d X ★★★   F.A. Brooke Sandahl, spring 1984
24. YODER EATERS   5.10d   F.A. Jim Yoder, spring 1990
25. PROJECT   5.12 ?   Prep. Jim Yoder, spring 1990
26. CRUMBLE PIE   5.9 R ★   F.A. Jim Yoder, spring 1990
27. SKYLIGHT   5.10c ★★   F.A. Jeff Thomas, Chris Jones, July 1979; F.F.A. Jeff Thomas, Bill Ramsey, July 18, 1979
28. BITS AND PIECES   5.7 X ★   F.A. Brian Holcomb, Dan Foote, Don Johnson, April 1977
28a. BITS OF FECES   5.8 R   F.A. Pat Carr, 1982
29. STAGEFRIGHT   5.12a ★★   F.A. Alan Watts, April 16, 1983
30. TEARS OF RAGE   5.12b ★★   F.A. Alan Watts, April 16, 1983
31. NO BRAIN, NO PAIN   5.10d R ★★   F.A. Jeff Thomas, Bill Ramsey, July 19, 1979; F.F.A. Alan Watts, Alan Lester, April 25, 1981
32. NO PAIN, NO GAIN   5.11c ★★   F.A. Alan Watts, Alan Lester, August 17, 1981
33. ZIGZAG   5.8 ★   F.A. unknown, 1970s
34. CULL'S IN SPACE   5.10c ★★★   F.A. Jim Anglin, Mike Hartley, 1980
35. FLOUNDER CORNER   5.2 ★   F.A. unknown
36. HOOK, LINE AND SINKER   5.7 ★   F.A. Pat Carr, Alan Watts, 1977
37. SUNSET BOULEVARD   5.8 ★   F.A. Bob Marshall, Wayne Haack, 1972
38. SUNSET SLAB   5.9 ★★★★   F.A. Dan Carlson, Paul Fry, July 1989
39. SMITH SUMMIT – WEST   F.A. Charles Dotter, Tony Bates, Jeff Dotter, Marcia Bilbao, June 1967
40. NORTHWEST CORNER   5.2 ★★   F.R.A. Jim Ramsey, Jack Watts, 1960
41. SHAFT   5.10b ★★   F.A. Steve Lyford, 1974
42. SOUTH FACE   5.0 A1 ★★   F.A. Nick Dodge, Jay Barton, 1963
43. THE PLATFORM   5.1 R ★   F.R.A. Jim Ramsey, Jack Watts 1960

WEST SIDE CRAGS

1. INSIDE CORNER   5.10c ★★   F.A. Jim Ramsey, Jerry Ramsey 1961; F.F.A. Jim Ramsey, Bruce Hahn, August 1961
2. PROJECT   5.13 ?   F.A. aid line, Alan Campbell, 1970s; F.F.A. uncompleted
3. CHRISTIAN BROTHERS TRAVERSE   5.7 X ★   F.A. The Priest, Kim Schmitz, Eugene Dod, Alan Amos, April 5, 1964; F.A. The Monk, Bill Cummins, Jon Marshall, Ted Davis, Ken Wallen, 1964; F.A. The Pope, unknown; F.A. The Friar (south side), Ted Davis, Bill Cummins, Juli Beall, 1965; F.A. The Abbot, Jon Marshall, Gerald Bjorkman, April 5, 1964
4. ABBOT GULLY   5.5 A2 X   F.A. Ted Davis, Jon Marshall, March 1964
4a. NORTHEAST ARETE   5.6 X   F.A. Kim Schmitz, 1964
5. ROOTS OF MADNESS   5.11a ★ R   F.A. Chuck Buzzard, 1986
6. HOT MONKEY LOVE   5.11a ★★   F.A. Mike Pajunas, Jon Sprecher, Jim Davis, April 28, 1991
7. FALLEN ANGEL   5.10c R ★★   F.A. Mike Smelsar, Nancy Baker, October 1978
8. MODERN ZOMBIE   5.10d ★★★   F.A. Mike Pajunas, June 8, 1991
9. MIDRIFF BULGE   5.10a ★★   F.A. Jeff Thomas, Mike Smelsar, February, 1977
10. MANIC NIRVANA   5.10c ★   F.A. Mike Pajunas, Jon Sprecher, May 18, 1991
11. MONK CHIMNEY   5.7   F.A. Kim Schmitz, Eugene Dod, December 1967
12. THE SNAKE   5.9 R ★★   F.A. Jeff Thomas, Tim Carpenter, May 26, 1974
12a. VENOM   5.10b ★★   F.A. unknown
12b. REPTILE   5.8 R ★   F.A. unknown
13. THE GOLDEN ROAD   5.11b ★★   F.A. Kent Benesch, Tom Blust, August 1981
14. SPLIT IMAGE   5.12c/d ★★★★   F.A. Alan Watts, March 3, 1984
15. MADE IN THE SHADE   5.12c ★★★   F.A. Jandy Cox, Steve Zeke, spring, 1989; F.F.A. Alan Watts, John Rich, September 30, 1989
16. CLING ON   5.9 ★★★   F.A. Jeff Thomas, Doug Phillips, Greg Phillips, July 7, 1974

17. A DESPERATE MAN   5.9 ★★   F.A. Doug Phillips, 1986
18. HEMP LIBERATION   5.10d ★★   F.A. John Collins, summer 1990
19. LORDS OF KARMA   5.12c ★★★   F.A. John Collins, March 1991
20. STRUNG OUT   5.9 ★   F.A. Jeff Thomas, Doug Phillips, Greg Phillips, July 7, 1974
21. STRUCK OUT   5.6 X   F.A. unknown
22. PROJECT   5.13 ?   Prep. unknown
23. HEAVEN CAN WAIT   5.7 R ★   F.A. Kent Benesch, Chris Haunold, August 1979
24. ANGEL FLIGHT BUTTRESS   5.8 R ★★   F.A. Mike Smelsar, Dick Morse, October 1978
25. FOLLIES OF YOUTH (a.k.a. HIGH SAGE)   5.9 R ★   F.A. Mike Smelsar, Mark Cartier, October 1978
26. COMMON HOUSEHOLD FLY   5.5 ★   F.A. unknown
27. ARACHNID BOOGIE   5.9 ★   F.A. unknown
28. TARANTULA   5.11d ★   F.A. Alan Watts, July 12, 1981
29. SPIDERMAN   5.7 ★★★★   F.A. Steve Strauch, Danny Gates, 1969
29a. SQUASHED SPIDER   5.7 ★★ X   F.A. Mike Smelsar, 1978
29b. SPIDERMAN VARIATION   5.7 ★★★   F.A. unknown
30. WIDOW MAKER   5.9 ★★★ R   F.A. Dan Foote, 1976
31. BEST LEFT TO OBSCURITY   5.10a R   F.A. Mike Hartley, Jim Anglin, 1981
32. EXPLOSIVE ENERGY CHILD   5.10d R ★★★   F.A. Mike Smelsar, Bob McGown, fall 1976; F.F.A. Mike Smelsar, John Tyreman, spring 1977
32a. MORE OR LESTER   5.10c ★★   F.A. TR, Alan Lester, 1981
33. OUT OF HARM'S WAY   5.8 ★★★   F.A. Paul Fry, 1988
34. IN HARM'S WAY   5.7 ★★★   F.A. Bob Johnson, Doug Phillips, September, 1975
35. LITTLE FEAT   5.10b ★★   F.A. Mike Hartley, Jim Anglin, June 16, 1980
36. CORNERSTONE   5.11d ★★   F.A. Chuck Buzzard, 1986
36a. CORNERSTONE VARIATION   5.10a ★★   F.A. Chuck Buzzard, 1986
37. DEATH TAKES A HOLIDAY   5.12a ★★★   F.A. Tom Blust, 1988
38. PROJECT   5.11/12 ?   Prep. unknown, 1991
39. DOCTOR DOOM   5.9 R ★★   F.A. Jeff Thomas, Steve Lyford, Tim Miller, Tom Minderhout, April 20, 1974
40. WHAT'S UP DOC?   5.11 ? ★★   F.A. unknown, 1991
41. NECROMANCER   5.8 ★   F.A unknown
42. CAPTAIN FINGERS   5.10a R ★   F.A. Craig Benesch, Kent Benesch, fall 1980
43. WESTERN CHIMNEY   5.5 R ★★★   F.A. George Cummings, Roger Peyton, April 1963
44. CHUCK'S SMELLY CRACK   5.10b R ★   F.A. Chuck Buzzard, 1986
45. PALO VERDE   5.6 A3 ★★   F.A. Jim Anglin, Mike Hartley, January 1, 1981
46. PETROGLYPH CRACK   5.7 ★   F.A. unknown
47. COWS IN AGONY   5.11a/b ★★   F.A. Tom Feldmann, Mike Paulson, spring 1989
48. CLIFF DWELLING CRACK   5.8 ★★ R   F.A. unknown
49. JUNIPER FACE   5.11d ★★   F.A. unknown
50. CHIMNEY DE CHELLY   5.10a R ★★   F.A. Jeff Thomas, Ken Currens, March 25, 1977
51. DESOLATION ROW   5.11a ★★   F.A. Alan Watts, Pat Carr, June 27, 1981
52. SHADOW OF DOUBT   5.12a ★★★   F.A. Greg Collum, Matt Kerns, 1988
53. REASON TO BE   5.10d ★★★   F.A. Greg Collum, Matt Kerns, 1988
54. TALE OF TWO SHITTIES   5.10a ★★★   F.A. first two pitches, Monty Mayko, Bruce Casey, December 4, 1977; F.F.A. entire route, Jeff Thomas, Chris Jones, Mike Hartley, September 30, 1978
55. SUNDOWN   5.9 ★★★   F.A. Alan Kearney, Shari Kearney, November 1978
56. DOWN'S SYNDROME   5.10a R ★★   F.A. Chuck Buzzard, winter 1980
57. MINAS MORGUL   5.11d ★★   F.A. Wayne Arrington, 1972; F.F.A. Alan Watts, May 3, 1981
58. BAD MOON RISING   5.11a ★★★   F.A. Jerry Messinger, June 1989
59. MOONS OF PLUTO   5.10d ★★★★   F.A. Frank Cornelius, 1984
60. SCREAMING YELLOW ZONKERS   5.10b ★★★★   F.A. Kent Benesch, Alan Watts, 1982
61. COSMOS   5.10a ★★★   F.A. Mike Pajunas, Jon Sprecher, Gary Rall, June 9, 1989
62. TREZLAR   5.10a ★★★★   F.A. Tom Rogers, Clay Cox, Bob Johnson, 1972; F.F.A. Jeff Thomas, Jim Davis, April 3, 1976

63. FOUR Fs   5.8   F.A. Mike Barbitta, fall 1985
64. LICHEN PERSUASION   5.7   F.A Jon Sprecher, Pat Carr, fall 1978
65. RED SCARE   5.10b ★★   F.A. Mike Pajunas, Jon Sprecher, June 1, 1989
66. WE BE TOYS   5.10a ★   F.A. Mike Pajunas, Jon Sprecher, June 2, 1989
67. LITTLE WICKED THING   5.10a ★   F.A. Mike Pajunas, Jon Sprecher, June 2, 1989
68. BOP TILL YOU DROP   5.11a ★★★   F.A. Bruce Casey, 1988
69. MATTHEW 7:24   5.10b ★★   F.A. Tom Heins, 1990
70. AGGRO BUMBLY   5.10d ★★★   F.A. unknown

MONKEY FACE AREA

1. SLOW TRAIN   5.7 ★   F.A. Tim Carpenter, 1984
2. DIAMONDS AND RUST   5.8 R   F.A. Mark Cartier, Mike Smelsar, winter 1979
3. PERPETUAL MOTION   5.9 ★   F.A. Mike Hartley, John Rich, 1980
4. DOLF'S DIHEDRAL   5.8 ★★   F.A. Bill Ramsey, Mary Ellen Dolf, spring 1980)
5. POTENTIAL ENERGY   5.10b R ★★   F.A. via direct start, Alan Lester, Chuck Wheeler, fall 1980; F.F.A. via regular start, Alan Watts, John Barbella, July 28, 1981
6. FLEX YOUR HEAD   5.11c ★★   F.A. Alan Lester, Chuck Wheeler, fall 1980; F.F.A. Jim Davis, 1988
7. PROJECT   5.12 ?   Prep. Jim Davis, 1989
8. KING KONG   5.9 R ★★   F.A. Scott Arighi, Jim Neiland, 1967; F.F.A. Steve Strauch, Danny Gates, 1970
8a. KING KONG DIRECT   5.10a R ★   F.A. Alan Watts, Bill Ramsey, July 27, 1978
9. GODZILLA   5.8 ★   F.A. Tom Bauman, Nov. 26, 1966, F.F.A. Steve Strauch, Dan Gates, 1970
10. SMAUG   5.10b ★ R   F.A. second pitch, Tom Rogers, Al Balmforth, 1970; F.A. entire route, Jeff Thomas, Avary Tichner, September 2, 1978)
11. BLOW COCOA   5.11c ★   F.A. Kent Benesch, summer 1989
12. MONKEY FARCE   5.10b R ★★   F.A. Jeff Thomas, Mike Smelsar, April 2, 1977
13. WEST FACE VARIATION   5.8 ★★★   F.A. Tom Bauman, Bob Ashworth, September 11, 1965; F.F.A. Tom Bauman, Bob Ashworth, April 9, 1967
13a. VARIATION   5.8 ★★★   F.A. unknown
13b. VARIATION   5.7 X ★★   F.A. unknown
13c. VARIATION   5.9 R ★★   F.A. unknown
13d. VARIATION   5.8 X ★   F.A. Bill Ramsey, Alan Watts, August 26, 1978
14. DRUG NASTY (a.k.a. DEAN'S DREAM)   5.11c ★   F.A. Dean Hart, 1987
15. MOVING IN STEREO   5.11d ★★★   F.A. Kent Benesch, 1986
16. ASTRO MONKEY (a.k.a. SOUTHWEST CORNER)   5.11d ★★★   F.A. first four pitches, Tom Bauman, 1970; F.A. upper two pitches, via **Monkey Space**, Bob McGown, 1978; F.F.A. second pitch, Mike Seeley, 1972; F.F.A. third and fourth pitches, Jeff Thomas, Mike Smelsar, April 3, 1977; F.F.A. upper pitches, Chris Jones, Bill Ramsey, April 21, 1979; F.F.A. first pitch, Alan Watts, Tom Blust, June 18, 1980; F.F.A. entire route, Alan Watts, Chris Grover, July 21, 1983)
16a. VARIATION   5.7 ★ X   F.A. unknown
16b. VARIATION   5.7 ★★
16c. VARIATION   5.11A ★★★   F.A. unknown; F.F.A. Alan Watts, John Barbella, July 27, 1981
17. POSE DOWN   5.12c ★★★   F.A. Kent Benesch, summer 1989
17a. VARIATION   5.12a/b A0 ★★★
18. WEST FACE   5.12a A1 ★★★★   F.A. Dean Caldwell, Byron Babcock, Bill Lentsch, 1962; F.F.A. final pitch, Chris Jones, Bill Ramsey, April 21, 1979; F.F.A. first pitch, with aid start, Alan Watts, July 26, 1981; F.F.A. third pitch, Alan Watts, summer 1985
19. SHEER TRICKERY   5.12b ★★★   F.A. Ron Kauk, Wolfgang Gullich, Alan Watts, June 1989
19a. PROJECT   5.13+ ?   Prep. Alan Watts, June 1989
20. PROJECT   5.12 ?   Prep. Robert Rogoz, fall 1989
21. THE BACKBONE   5.13a ★★★★   F.A. second pitch, Alan Watts, 1987; F.F.A. third pitch, Alan Watts, summer 1985; F.F.A. entire route, Ron Kauk, June 1989
22. NORTHWEST PASSAGE   5.12a A0 (or 5.12b) ★★★★   F.A. second pitch, Tom Bauman, Bob Ashworth, 1968; F.A. entire route, Jeff Thomas, Steve Moore, April 28, 1973; F.F.A. second pitch, Alan Watts, November 3, 1981; F.F.A. entire route, with aid start, Hidetaka Suzuki, 1985;
23. NORTH FACE   5.12a ★★★★   F.A. via bolt line, Dean Caldwell, Jim Kindler, December 1967; F.A.

regular route, Tom Bauman, Bob Ashworth, March 28, 1968; F.F.A. (with aiding the bolt line) Alan Lester, 1983; F.F.A. regular line, Alan Watts, summer 1985
23a. ORIGINAL START A1 F.A. Dean Caldwell, Jim Kindler, December 1967
24. SPANK THE MONKEY 5.12a R ★★★★ F.A. Alan Watts, summer 1985
25. EAST FACE 5.13c/d ★★★★ F.A. Kim Schmitz, Gerald Bjorkman, summer 1964; F.F.A. final pitch, with toprope, Alan Watts August 21, 1983 F.F.A. to first anchor, Alan Watts, September 24, 1983; F.F.A. upper portion, YY, Alan Watts, August 25, 1984; F.F.A. entire first pitch, YY, Alan Watts, August 31, 1985
26. JUST DO IT 5.14c ★★★★ Prep. Alan Watts, June 1989; F.F..A. entire route, Jean Baptiste Tribout, April 6, 1992
26a. JUST DO IT (lower part) 5.13c ★★★★ Prep. Alan Watts, June 1989; F.A. Jean Baptiste Tribout, April 1992
27. MEGALITHIC 5.12d ★★★★ F.A. Brooke Sandahl, fall 1990
28. RISING EXPECTATIONS 5.11d ★★★★ F.A unknown; F.F.A. Chris Jones, Alan Watts, September 13, 1979
29. PIONEER ROUTE 5.7 A1 ★★★★ F.A. Dave Bohn, Jim Fraser, Vivian Staender, January 1, 1960; F.F.A. Panic Point, unknown
29a. YOUNG PIONEERS 5.12d ★★★ F.A. Alan Watts, August 1985
30. CLOSE SHAVE 5.12c R ★★★ F.A. Alan Watts, August 1985
31. BOHN STREET–WEST FACE CAVE 5.12a R ★ F.A. Dave Jensen, Bob Martin, January 1963; F.F.A. Alan Watts, July 15, 1983
31a. ORIGINAL FINISH A2
32. MONKEY SPACE 5.11b ★★★★ F.A. Bob McGown, 1978; F.F.A., Chris Jones, Bill Ramsey, April 21, 1979
33. CHICKEN LITTLE 5.6 ★ F.A. Mike Smelsar, Tom Easthope, August 1978)
34. MR. TOAD'S WILD RIDE 5.9 R ★ F.A. Mike Smelsar, Tom Easthope, August 1978
35. GREAT EXPECTATIONS 5.7 ★★ F.A. Paul Fry, Jeff Thomas, March 6, 1977
36. FUNGUS ROOF 5.10c X F.A. Mike Barbitta
37. SCABIES 5.8 X F.A. Mike Smelsar, John Tyreman, 1978
38. HAWKLINE MONSTER 5.10a R ★ F.A. Chuck Buzzard, solo, 1980
39. NEW WORLD 5.8 R ★ F.A. Mike Smelsar, Nancy Baker, March 1979

RED WALL AREA
1. TITANIUM JAG 5.10b ★★ F.A. Tim Olson, Greg Lyon, Cecil Colley, March 25, 1989
2. BILL'S FLAKE 5.10a ★★ F.A. Bill Ramsey, Alan Watts, August 17, 1978
3. FINGER PUPPET 5.10a ★★ F.A. Jim Boucher, May 1988
4. PHANTASMAGORIA 5.10b ★ F.A. Tim Olson, Cecil Colley, November 13, 1989
5. POP ART 5.10c ★ F.A. Eric Horst, May 1991
6. DANCES WITH CLAMS 5.10a ★★ F.A. Tom Heins, Pete Keane, April 1991
7. PAPER TIGER 5.10a ★★ F.A. upper pitches via Super Slab, Jeff Thomas, Mark Cartier, August 27, 1978; F.A. entire route, Mike Hartley, Jim Anglin, December 15, 1979
7a. KARL MARX VARIATION 5.10a R F.A. Mike Barbitta, 1988
8. SUPER SLAB 5.6 ★★★★ F.A. Danny Gates, 1969; F.F.A. Danny Gates, Neal Olsen, 1970
8a. VARIATION 5.6 X ★★★★ F.A. unknown
9. PANAMA EXPRESS 5.9 ★★ F.A. Jim Anglin, Mike Hartley, January 2, 1980
10. PANAMA RED 5.8 R ★★ F.A. Mike Smelsar, Mark Cartier, 1979
11. AMPHETAMINE GRIP 5.7 R ★★★ F.A. Danny Gates, Steve Strauch, 1970
11a. GRIPPED 5.9 ★ F.A. unknown
12. RED ROVER 5.7 R ★★ F.A. Dana Horton, circa 1980
13. IRON CURTAIN 5.9 R ★★ F.A. Jeff Thomas, Chris Mannix, April 24, 1977
14. HELTER SKELTER 5.10c R ★★ F.A. first pitch, Jeff Thomas, John Rakovsky, May 8, 1977; F.A. entire route via variation, Mike Smelsar, Ed Newville, spring 1978
14a. VARIATION 5.8 F.A. Mike Smelsar, Mark Cartier, spring 1978
14b. IF SIX WERE NINE 5.10b ★★ F.A. Bruce Birchell, June 1979
15. RIDE THE LIGHTNING 5.11b ★★★ F.A. Kent Benesch, Tom Blust, Doug Phillips, 1987
16. CHAIRMAN MAO'S LITTLE RED BOOK 5.11a ★★★ F.A. unknown, F.F.A. Jeff Thomas, Chris Jones, Alan Watts, July 21, 1979
17. FINGERS OF FATE 5.10d ★★★ F.A. Mike Hartley, Jim Anglin, June 30, 1979; F.F.A. Alan Lester, fall 1979

18. SOLE SURVIVOR 5.11b ★★★ F.A. Kurt Smith, spring 1988
19. GONE WITH THE FLAKE 5.9 ★ F.A. Jeff Thomas, Roger Robinson, December 15, 1974
20. HO CHI MINH TRAIL 5.7 A3 R F.A. Wayne Haack, Steve Strauch, 1969
21. SHANGHAI 5.10A X ★ F.A. Bill Ramsey, Alan Watts, July 17, 1978
22. CARTOON DEFICIENCY 5.10c ★ F.A. Mike Pajunas, 1989
23. LET'S FACE IT 5.10b ★★★ F.A. TR, Mike Smelsar, 1979; F.F.A. Tom Egan, Mike Paulson, October 1988
24. PEKING 5.8 ★★ F.A. Tom Bauman, Osa Thatcher, May 5, 1969
25. MOSCOW 5.6 ★★★ F.A Pat Callis, Mickey Schurr, 1965
25a. MONGOLIANS 5.10b R ★★ F.A. Jeff Thomas, Chris Jones, October 1, 1978
26. HAVANA 5.6 ★ F.A. unknown
27. METAMORPHIC MANEUVERS 5.9 R ★ F.A. Mike Barbitta, Hunt, October 1984
28. I ALMOST DIED 5.11A ★★★ F.A. Avary Tichner, August 1978; F.F.A. Jeff Thomas, Ken Currens, October 28, 1978
29. RED RYDER 5.8 R ★★ F.A. Wayne Haack, Steve Thompson, 1975
29a. FLEX 5.9 ★★★ F.A. unknown
30. THE YOUNG AND THE RESTLESS 5.9 R ★ F.A. Dan Foote, Mike Smelsar, September 1976
30a. THE YOUNG AND THE WORTHLESS 5.7 X F.A. Cheri Richardson, Alan Lester, summer 1979
31. PROJECT 5.12 ? Prep. Brooke Sandahl, 1990
32. BUGGING OUT 5.12d ★★★ F.A. Brooke Sandahl, 1990; F.F.A. Scott Franklin, 1990)
33. BOYS IN THE HOOD 5.11d ★★★★ F.A. Brooke Sandahl, 1989
33a. ADAM SPLITTER 5.12c ★★ F.A. TR, Adam Grosowsky, 1990
34. BIG BOSS MAN 5.12a ★★★ F.A. Brooke Sandahl, 1989
35. STRAIGHT OUT OF MADRAS 5.12c ★★★ F.A. Brooke Sandahl, 1990; F.F.A. Scott Franklin, 1991

MONUMENT AND STAENDER RIDGE

1. DEFINITELY CAJUN 5.12a ★★★ F.A. Jeff Frizzell, Tom Egan, December 29, 1989
2. PLEASURE PRINCIPLE 5.10d ★★ F.A. Tom Egan, Jeff Frizzell, December 29, 1989
3. LONDON TOWER 5.10a R F.A. Dean Fry, Russ Bunker, April 14, 1974
4. DEAD BABY BUBBAS 5.10a ★ F.A. Alan Lester, 1982
5. NORTHWEST RIDGE 3rd Class ★ F.A. unknown
5a. CHOCKSTONE CHIMNEY 4th class ★ F.A. Jim Ramsey, Jerry Ramsey, 1959
6. HOWL 5.12a R ★★ F.A. Greg Collum, Matt Kerns, Jim Yoder, 1988
7. VICTORY OF THE PROLETARIAN PEOPLE'S AMBITION ARETE 5.7 X F.A. Brian Holcomb, Steve Martin, spring 1980
8. BRUCE'S TRAVERSE 5.7 X ★ F.A. Bruce Hahn, Jim Ramsey, 1963
9. A LITTLE SEDUCTION 5.12a ★★★ F.A. Tom Egan, spring 1990
10. THE NORTH RIDGE 4th Class ★★ F.A. unknown
10a. NORTH RIDGE DIRECT 5.2 ★★★ F.A. unknown
11. ABRAXAS 5.10d A0 R ★ F.A. lower pitches, Steve Strauch, Wayne Haack, 1969; F.A. complete route, Steve Strauch, Danny Gates, 1969; F.F.A. fourth pitch, Wayne Arrington, Ken Currens, 1977; F.F.A. second pitch, Mark Cartier, Mark Jonas, 1981
12. SANDS OF TIME 5.7 A4 R F.A. F.S. Todd Rentchler, fall 1977
13. SOUTHEAST FACE 5.7 A3 X F.A. Ted Davis, Willy Zeigler, June 1966
14. PROJECT 5.12 ? Prep. Tom Egan, 1989
15. OSA THATCHER'S NEEDLE 5.7 X F.A. Bob Martin, Eugene Dod, 1961
16. BIRD DUNG CHIMNEY 5.4 X F.A. unknown
17. DECEPTION CRACK 5.10a ★ F.A. Bruce Burling, Frank Jager, 1970; F.F.A. Jeff Thomas, Ted Johnson, June 4, 1977
18. BRAIN SALAD SURGERY 5.11a ★★★ F.A. Jeff Thomas, March 28, 1976
19. STREET WALKER 5.6 F.A. Jeff Thomas, Cindy Jones, December 7, 1974
20. JUNIPER GULLY 5.6 A1 X F.A. Dean Caldwell, Byron Babcock, 1960
21. LIBERTY BELL CHIMNEY 5.5 X ★ F.A. Jack Janacek, J. Harrower, 1954
22. THE EAR 5.7 R ★ F.A. Tom Rogers, 1969
22a. VARIATION 5.4 F.A. unknown
23. THE PRODUCT 5.13a ★★★★ F.A. aid seam, Tom Bauman, Bob Ashworth, March 24, 1969; F.F.A. entire route, Tom Egan, 1990

24. PROJECT 5.13 ? Prep. Jeff Frizzell, 1990
25. JAMBOREE 5.8 ★★ (F.A. unknown)
26. RIB TRAVERSE 5.6 X ★★★ F.A. unknown
27. INSTANT REPLAY 5.6 ★★★ F.A. Tom Rogers, Steve Wilson, 1969
28. PARKING LOT CRACK 5.8 ★★ F.A. F.S. Bob Bauman, mid- 60s
29. PROJECT 5.12 ? Prep. Tom Egan, Jeff Frizzell, 1990
30. MUNCHKIN LAND 5.7 ★★ F.A. unknown
31. LOLLYPOP LEAGUE 5.5 ★★★★ F.A. unknown
32. ORANGE PLANET 5.12 ? F.A. uncompleted
33. OUT OF CONTROL 5.10c ★★ F.A. Jeff Thomas, Mike Smelsar, May 14, 1977; F.F.A. Paul Landrum, Ken Currens, 1978.
34. FREE SPIRIT 5.8 ★★ F.A. Jeff Thomas, Scott Hansen, April 28, 1974
35. SCOOP ROUTE 5.4 X ★ F.A. Vivian and Gil Staender, 1955
36. MIDNIGHT RIDER 5.10a R ★ F.A unknown; F.F.A. Jeff Thomas, Mike Smelsar, May 14, 1977
37. NORTH SIDE 5.5 ★★★ F.A. Dave Pearson, Ross Petrie, 1946
38. D.A.R. CRACK 5.10a ★★ F.A. Tom Rogers, John Sanborn, Don Johnson, 1970; F.F.A. Jeff Thomas, Scott Hansen, April 28, 1974
39. SUNJAMMER 5.10b ★★★ F.A. TR, Del Young, Mead Hargis, summer 1971; F.F.A. Del Young 1972
40. SOUTH FACE 5.6 X ★ F.A. unknown
41. CHOPPER 5.8 ★★★ F.A. TR, Del Young, Dave Jensen, summer 1971; F.F.A Del Young, 1972
42. SLOPPER 5.9 ★ F.A. Del Young, 1972
43. NORTH RAMP 4th class ★★ F.A. unknown
43a. VARIATION 5.0 ★★ F.A. unknown
43b. SILLY CRACK 5.8 ★★ F.A. unknown
44. EASY STREET 5.7 R ★ F.A. unknown
45. THRASHER 5.8 A2 ★ F.A. Jeff Thomas, Scott Hansen, April 28, 1974
46. LIMESTONE CHIMNEY 5.2 ★★ F.R.A. Vivian and Gil Staender, 1955
46a. VARIATION 5.6 ★ F.A. unknown
47. JUNIPER SNAG 5.6 R ★★ F.A. Jim Ramsey, Clinton DeShazer, 1961
48. EAST CHIMNEY 5.4 X ★★★ F.A. Bruce Hahn, Jim Ramsey, 1963
49. SKID ROW 5.7 ★ F.A. Jeff Thomas, Charly Brown, November 3, 1974
50. LOST FOX 5.9 ★★★ F.A. Steve Lyford, Bob Johnson, 1973
51. BUMP AND GRIND 5.9 ★★ F.A. Ray Smutek, Iain Lynn, 1969; F.F.A. unknown
52. DELIVERANCE 5.9 ★ F.A. TR, Tom Rogers, 1970
53. DIRECT NORTHWEST CRACK 5.4 ★★ F.A. Jim Ramsey, Jerry Ramsey, 1958
54. LIEBACK FLAKE 5.4 ★ F.A. Miles and Dorothy Paul, 1970)
55. PRUNE FACE 5.7 ★★ F.A. unknown
56. LOWER WEST CHIMNEY 5.7 R ★ F.A. Vivian and Gil Staender, 1956
57. SOUTH BUTTRESS 5.3 X ★★★ F.A. Vivian and Gil Staender, 1956
58. PEANUTS 5.8 ★★ F.A. unknown
59. DEFECATION CRACK 5.7 ★★ F.A unknown
59a. NUT CASE 5.8 ★★ F.A. unknown
60. EAST SIDE CHIMNEY 5.4 ★ F.A. unknown
61. DESIDERATA 5.9 ★★★ F.A. unknown; F.F.A. Jeff Thomas, Jim Eliot, March 6, 1974
62. NORTH CHIMNEY 5.1 ★★ F.R.A. Dave Pearson, Ross Petrie, 1946
63. NORTHWEST CORNER 5.3 ★★ F.A. Jim Ramsey, Clinton DeShazer, 1961
63a. WEST LEDGES 5.1 ★ F.A. unknown
64. FALLING ROCK ZONE 5.6 R F.A. unknown
65. SMUT 5.12c/d ★★★ F.A. Dave Jensen, 1960; F.F.A. Alan Watts, January 4, 1981
66. AFFLICTION 5.6 A4 R ★ F.A. unknown
67. NORTH LEDGE 5.6 R ★ F.A. unknown
68. SOUTH BOWL 5.5 X F.A. Jim Ramsey, Ken Bierly, 1964
69. ROTTEN CRACK 5.8 X F.A Vivian and Gil Staender, 1956; F.F.A. Kim Schmitz, mid-60s
70. FRICTION ARETE 5.4 X F.A. Jim Rixon, Kim Schmitz, 1965

71. ORANGE PEEL 5.6 X F.A. unknown
72. LEMON PEEL 5.8 X ★ F.A. unknown
73. BROWN COW 5.6 X F.A. unknown
74. COW PIE 5.6 X F.A. unknown

THE MARSUPIAL CRAGS

1. HEATSTROKE 5.10b ★★ F.A. Eric Freden, Charles Arnett, June 1986
2. THIN AIR 5.9 ★★★ F.A. unknown; F.F.A. first pitch, Larry and Susan Kemp, August 1971; F.A. second pitch, Eric Freden, Paul Underwood, May 1987
3. CATTY CORNER 5.8 ★ F.A. Doug Phillips, Bob Johnson, 1974
4. CRAZIES 5.7 ★★ F.A. Ed Beacham, 1972; F.F.A. unknown
5. DESERT SOLITAIRE 5.9 X ★ F.A. Jeff Thomas, Keith Edwards, Dean Fry, November 25, 1972
6. ROUND RIVER 5.4 ★★★ F.A. unknown
6a. ROUND RIVER DIRECT 5.8 X F.A. Jeff Thomas, October 26, 1974
7. CATFIGHT CRACKS 5.9 R F.A. first pitch, Tom Rogers, Jack Barrar, 1969; F.F.A. Dean Fry, Jeff Thomas, September 30, 1972
8. C.L. CONCERTO 5.9 A4 R F.A. Dean Fry, Jack Barrar, September 13-14, 1972
9. SANTIAM HIGHWAY LEDGES 5.10a ★ F.A. Bill Cummins, J. Marshall, Jim Neiland, 1969; F.F.A. Jeff Thomas, Brian Holcomb, October 5, 1984
10. GREEN GULLY 5.6 ★ F.A. Jon Marshall, Carol Anderson, September 1967
11. WHITECLOUD 5.7 R ★★ F.A. Tom Rogers, Jack Barrar, April 10, 1971; F.F.A. Tom Rogers, Wayne Arrington, early 70s
12. THE THUMB 5.7 ★★ F.A. Ted Davis, Bill Cummins, Sue Davis, Willy Ziger, 1964
13. THE GREAT ROOF 5.6 A3 ★★★ F.A. Steve Heim, Jim Nieland, 1967
14. PIN BENDER 5.8 A2 ★ F.A. Dean Fry, Russ Bunker, February 17, 1973
15. PROJECT 5.12 ? Prep. Jeff Frizzell, summer 1990
16. WEST FACE 5.5 X ★★★ F.A. unknown
17. WEST GULLY 5.10c ★★★ F.A. Ted Davis, Jon Marshall, 1963; F.F.A. Alan Watts, 1981
17a. VARIATION 5.7 ★★ F.A. Jeff Thomas, Guy Keene, November 2, 1974
18. SOUTH BUTTRESS 5.5 X ★★★★ F.A. Bruce Watson, Brian Watson, Charles Cunningham, 1970
19. CAVE ROUTE 5.6 X ★★★★ F.A. to the base of summit horn, Jim and Jerry Ramsey, 1960; F.A. to summit, Ted Davis, Jon Marshall, 1963
20. DIAGONAL CRACK 5.4 X ★ F.A. Jim Ramsey, Jerry Ramsey, 1960
21. DOGFIGHT CRACK 5.8 R F.A. Jeff Thomas, Doug Phillips, November 16, 1974
22. OPOSSUM NOTCH 5.0 ★ F.A. Ted Davis, Don Chattin, 1963
23. MINI HALF DOME 5.8 R ★★ F.A. unknown
24. EYE SORE 5.12a F.A. unknown
25. DELIRIUM TREMENS 5.10a ★★★★ F.A. Dave Jensen, 1970; F.F.A. Del Young, summer 1972
26. BLURRED VISION 5.12a ★★ F.A. Tom Egan, Jeff Frizzell, January 1989
27. WALLABY 5.9 ★ F.A. Kim Schmitz, Alan Amos, Jon Marshall, 1963; F.F.A. Alan Lester, Alan Watts, January 30, 1982
28. NORTH LEDGES TRAVERSE 5.6 X F.A. Kim Schmitz, Alan Amos, Jon Marshall, 1963
29. SOUTH FACE 5.6 X F.A. Eugene Dod, Gerald Bjorkman, 1964
30. JOEY – SOUTHWEST SIDE 5.4 X F.A. Jim Ramsey, Jerry Ramsey, 1961
31. SOLSTICE SLAB 5.8 ★ F.A. Eric Freden, Brian Baird, June 1983
32. LOST HARDWARE ROUTE 5.6 R ★ F.A. unknown; F.F.A. Tom Rogers, Jack Barrar, M. Youngblood, John Sanborn, 1970
33. OVER THE HILL 5.7 R ★★★ F.A. Jeff Thomas, Bill Thomas, Brian Holcomb, May 22, 1983
34. THE FAR SIDE 5.9 ★★ F.A. Jeff Thomas, Brian Holcomb, September 6, 1984
35. DISAPPEARING TOWER 5.7 ★ F.A. unknown
36. POCKET HOLD ROUTE 5.3 X ★★★ F.A. unknown
37. DEVIL IN DISGUISE A1 ★★ F.A. unknown
38. GUNSIGHT ROCK 5.1 ★ F.A. Geodetic Survey Team, 1940s
39. SPIRAL 5.1 X ★★★ F.A. Johnny Bissell, summer 1935
39a. DIRECT VARIATION 5.5 R ★ F.A. Jim Ramsey, Bruce Hahn, 1963

39b. SOUTH SPIRAL   5.3 X ★   F.A. unknown
40. SOUTH FACE   5.3 X ★   F.A. John Ohrenschall, C. Richards, 1957
41. LEANING BRAVE   5.7 X   F.A. Dave Jensen, Jim Benham, 1963
42. PAPOOSE, SOUTHEAST RIDGE   5.1 X   F.A. Bruce Hahn, Jim Ramsey, 1963
43. LITTLE BIG HORN   5.3 X   F.A. unknown
44. LITTLE FINGER   5.6 ★★★   F.A. unknown
45. INDEX FINGER   5.4   F.A. unknown
46. TILTED SLAB   5.3 X   F.A. E.J. Zimmerman, Charlie Zimmerman, 1952
47. SOUTH CHIMNEY   5.7 R ★   F.A. Ross Petrie, Dave Wagstaff, Bill Van Atta, March 1949

BASALT RIMROCK
1.   SOFT ASYLUM   5.12b ★★★   F.A. Jeff Frizzell, September 2, 1991
2.   FLICKER FLASH   5.10a ★   F.A. Alan Watts, 1984
3.   FLASH IN THE PAN   5.11a/b ★   F.A. TR, Alan Watts, 1984
4.   LIGHTNING   5.11a ★   F.A. TR, Alan Watts, 1984
5.   RAMBO ROOF   5.12b ★★★   F.A. TR, Brooke Sandahl, spring 1986
6.   PROJECT   5.12+ ?   Prep. Jeff Frizzell, Fall 1991
7.   GREENHOUSE   5.8 X ★   F.A. unknown
8.   JERSEY SHORE   5.7 ★★   F.A. unknown
8a. VARIATION   5.8 R ★   F.A. unknown
9.   LEAN CUISINE   5.6 ★★   F.A. unknown
10. LITTLE WONDER   5.10b ★★   F.A. unknown
11. THUMPER   5.8 ★★   F.A. unknown
12. BLOCK HEAD   5.7 ★   F.A. unknown
13. MEAT GRINDER   5.8 ★★   F.A. Wayne Arrington, mid-70s
14. DOUBLE TIME   5.7 ★   F.A. unknown
15. DEVIL'S DELIGHT   5.9 R ★   F.A. unknown
16. SWAN SONG   5.10b ★★   F.A. unknown
17. BIG BAD WOLF   5.10c X ★   F.A. unknown
18. JIMINY CRICKET   5.8 ★★   F.A. unknown
19. PHANTOM   5.10a ★   F.A. unknown
20. HANDYMAN   5.7 ★★★   F.A. unknown
21. SWEET SPOT   5.10c ★★   F.A. unknown
22. PUMPKIN PATCH   5.5 ★★   F.A. unknown
23. WHO PUDDING   5.8 R ★★   F.A. unknown
24. WHO HASH   5.8 R ★★   F.A. unknown
25. PLAYING WITH FIRE   5.7 ★★   F.A. unknown
26. BURN BABY BURN   5.10a ★★★   F.A. unknown
27. FIRESTARTER   5.10d ★★   F.A. unknown
28. LIFEGUARD   5.7 R ★★   F.A. unknown
29. IF I RAN THE CIRCUS   5.10b ★★★   F.A. unknown
29a. RUNAWAY BUNNY   5.11d ★★   F.A. TR Alan Watts,, 1984
30. WOMAN IN THE MEADOW   5.11a ★★   F.A. Chip Brejc, Jeff Frizzell, July 1991
31. THE HEATHEN   5.13?   Prep. Jeff Frizzell, July 1991
32. PROJECT   5.12?   F.A. TR, Jeff Frizzell, July 1991
33. HANG IT LOOSE   5.10b R ★★   F.A. Wayne Arrington, mid-70s
34. JUNGLE FEVER   5.11b/c ★★   F.A. Jeff Frizzell, July 1991
35. TORRID ZONE   5.12a ★★★   F.A. Jeff Frizzell, July 1991
36. HAVANA SMACK   5.13 ?   Prep. Jeff Frizzell, July 1991
37. THE FOUR NYMPHS   5.12a/b ★★   F.A. Chip Brejc, Jeff Frizzell, July 1991
38. SIDEWALK CAFE   5.11c ★★   F.A. Chip Brejc, Jeff Frizzell, July 1991
39. SPRING BREAK   5.5 ★★   F.A. unknown
40. FLUNKED OUT   5.6 ★★   F.A. unknown
41. CRAM SESSION   5.8 ★   F.A. unknown
42. FIST FIGHT   5.8 ★★   F.A. unknown

43. FRAT JERKS   5.8 ★★   F.A. unknown
44. BON FIRE   5.8 ★★   F.A. unknown
45. PASSING GRADE   5.9 ★★★   F.A. unknown
46. PUPPET MASTER   5.11a ★★★   F.A. TR, unknown
47. POP QUIZ   5.11c ★★   F.A. unknown; F.F.A. Ted Johnson, Catherine Freer, early 80s
48. FIGHT SONG   5.10a ★★★   F.A. unknown
49. EMBRYONIC   5.11d ★★★   F.A. Jeff Frizzell, Susan Price, September 1, 1991
50. DRILLING ZONA   5.11c ★★★★   F.A. Jeff Frizzell, August 5, 1991
50a. PROJECT   5.13 ?   Prep., Jeff Frizzell, summer 1991
51. CLASS DISMISSED   5.12a ★★   F.A. Alan Lester, 1983
52. FIRST AID   5.8 A1 ★★   F.A. Mike Volk, 1984
53. CARDIAC FIB   5.10c ★★   F.A. Chuck Buzzard, 1983
54. CARDIAC KID   5.8 ★★   F.A. unknown
55. THE LIVING END   5.10b ★★   F.A. unknown
56. CHEAT SHEET   5.11a ★★   F.A. Chuck Buzzard, fall 1984
57. SCHOOL'S OUT   5.7 ★★   F.A. unknown
58. PROM NIGHT   5.7 ★★★   F.A. unknown
59. DOOR KNOB PEOPLE   5.7 ★★   F.A. unknown
59a. SLAM DANCE   5.8 ★   F.A. unknown
60. RAGE   5.7 ★★   F.A. unknown
61. DUNCE CAP   5.8 R ★★   F.A. unknown
62. BAD MANNERS   5.7 ★★ F.A. unknown
62a. CHARM SCHOOL   5.7 ★★ F.A. unknown
63. PANIC SEIZURE   5.11b ★   F.A. Alan Watts, summer 1985
64. LITTLE BLACK SAMBO   5.9 X ★★   F.A. unknown
65. GLOBAL MOTION   5.10b ★★★   F.A. unknown
66. HOMECOMING QUEEN   5.7 ★★   F.A. unknown
67. SILLY BOY   5.10b ★★★   F.A. unknown
68. HEART THROB   5.7 ★★★   F.A. unknown
68a. DANCING HEARTS   5.10b ★★   F.A. unknown
69. DEAD WEEK   5.8 ★★   F.A. unknown
70. THESEUS   5.10c ★★★   F.A. Del Young, 1971
71. LITTLE BO PEEP   5.10c ★★★   F.A. unknown
72. DEEP SLEEP   5.8 ★★★   F.A. unknown
73. THE VIRGIN SLAYER   5.9 ★★★   F.A. unknown
74. LABYRINTH   5.10b ★★★   F.A. unknown
75. MINOTAUR   5.10d ★★   F.A. Del Young, 1971
76. BIG MAN ON CAMPUS   5.9 ★★★   F.A. unknown
77. ASTRO BUNNY   5.10b/c TR ★★   F.A. unknown
78. BLOCK PARTY   5.10b TR ★★   F.A. unknown
79. SPLASH   5.10c ★★   F.A. unknown
80. AVANT GARDE   5.11a ★★   F.A. unknown

LOWER GORGE
1. LITTLE ORPHAN JAMMIES   5.10d ★★   F.A.Chuck Buzzard, Jerry Randant, January, 1984
2. SQUEAL AND PEAL   5.11c ★★   F. A. Chuck Buzzard, July 1984; F.F.A. Alan Watts, August 7, 1984
3. CRETIN'S RETREAT (a.k.a. CRETIN'S REVENGE)   5.10c ★★   F.A. to old anchor, Stu Stuller, Pete Pollard, 1981; F.A. entire route, Chuck Buzzard, 1983
4. ORIFACE   5.10b ★★★   F.A. Chuck Buzzard, Jerry Radant, January 1984
5. THE FERRET'S DEAD   5.9 ★★   F.A. Chuck Buzzard, John Rich, April 1984
6. COX ROCKS   5.8 ★   F.A. Wayne Arrington, 1974
7. THREE FINGERED HACK   5.10c ★★   F.A. Tom Blust, Doug Phillips, 1981
8. HACK ATTACK   5.12b ?   F.A. TR, Chuck Buzzard, 1985; F.F.A. uncompleted
9. VULTURE CREST   5.9 ★   F.A. unknown
10. TERROR BONNE   5.10a R ★   F.A. Chuck Buzzard, Jeff Turner, 1984

11. PHYSICAL ABUSE 5.10a ★★ F.A. Wayne Arrington, 1974
12. BYRNE'S REVENGE 5.11b R ★★ F.A. Chuck Buzzard, fall 1985
13. MAD MAN 5.8 ★ F.A. Wayne Arrington, Bob Ashworth, April 1973
14. WILDFIRE 5.10b ★★★★ F.A. Paul Landrum, Ken Currens, March 1975
15. LA VIE DANSANE 5.11d R ★★ F.A. Chuck Buzzard, fall 1985
16. CRIME WAVE 5.11b ★★★ F.A. Alan Lester, 1983
17. GRUFF 5.10a ★★★ F.A. Ken Currens, Paul Landrum, March 1975
18. RIM JOB 5.10b ★★★ F.A. Jim Davis, Chris Grover, 1979
19. IRON CROSS 5.11b ★★ F.A. Alan Watts, Mike Puddy, October 6, 1983
20. NEUTRAL ZONE 5.11a ★★ F.A. Alan Watts, Mike Puddy, October 5, 1983
21. BADFINGER 5.10b ★★★★ F.A. Todd Rentchler, Terri Schulz, June 1975
22. SOFT TOUCH 5.10d ★ F.A. Alan Watts, Kent Benesch, October 28, 1983
23. ORGAN GRINDER 5.10a ★ F.A. Jeff Thomas, Paul Fry, August 1975
24. ON THE ROAD 5.11a ★★★★ F.A., Chris Grover, Jim Davis, 1980
25. EDGE OF THE ROAD 5.12c TR ★★★ F.A., TR, Alan Watts, March 31, 1984
26. TITUS 5.9 ★ F.A. Wayne Arrington, 1973
27. SPLIT DECISION 5.12a ★★★ F.A. Alan Watts, April 2, 1984
28. PURE PALM 5.11a ★★★★ F.A. Alan Watts, April 2, 1984
29. CORNERCOPIA 5.10b ★★★ F.A. Steve Byrne, Sean Olmstead, 1983
30. TEACHERS IN SPACE 5.11d ★★ F.A. John Rich, 1986
31. BOLD LINE 5.10c ★★ F.A. Chuck Buzzard, Graeme Aimeer, June 1983
31a. PASS OVER 5.10c ★★ F.A. Chuck Buzzard, June 1983
32. RESUSCITATION 5.12b/c ★★★ F.A. John Rich, October 1988
33. PROJECT 5.12 ? F.A. on aid, John Rich, 1988; F.F.A. uncompleted
34. WHITE TRASH 5.12a ★★★★ F.A. John Rich, September, 1988
35. LION OF JUDAH 5.11d ★★★ F.A., TR, Chuck Buzzard, August 1984; F.A. lead, John Rich, 1989
35a. JUDAH DIRECT 5.12a TR ★★ F.A. TR, Alan Watts, August 19, 1984
36. CRY OF THE POOR 5.11a ★★★★ F.A. Chuck Buzzard, March 1984
37. JUST SAY YES 5.12a ★★★ F.A. TR, direct line, Alan Watts, September 15, 1984; F.A. regular route, John Rich, October 1988
38. OUT OF DARKNESS 5.11a ★★★ F.A. Chuck Buzzard, Pete Pollard, May 1984
39. TRY TO BE HIP 5.12a ★★★★ F.A. John Rich, October 1988
40. JESSIE'S LINE 5.11b/c R ★★ F.A. Chuck Buzzard, Alan Watts, June 1984
41. COME TO THE QUIET 5.10d ★★ F.A. Chuck Buzzard, Jerry Radant, 1982
42. ON EAGLES WINGS 5.11c X ★ F.A., TR, Chuck Buzzard, 1984; F.F.A. Alan Watts, August 13, 1984
43. SEAM OF DREAMS 5.11b ★★ F.A Chuck Buzzard, Steve Byrne, July 1984
44. FLUTTER BY 5.11b ★ F.A. Chuck Buzzard, August 1984
45. SEND YOUR CLONE 5.10c R ★ F.A. Chuck Buzzard, Steve Byrne, August 1983
46. BOLDERDASH 5.10a ★ F.A Chuck Buzzard, August 1983
47. PROMETHEUS 5.10c ★★★ F.A. Ken Curren, Paul Landrum, March 1975
48. NORTHERN LIGHTS 5.11d ★★★ F.A. Alan Watts, October 1, 1983
49. LAST CHANCE 5.10c ★★★★ F.A. Chris Grover, Jim Davis, 1980
50. STRIKE FORCE 5.12a R ★★ F.A. Alan Watts, October 5, 1983
51. SILENT HOLOCAUST 5.11c ★★ F.A. Chuck Buzzard, September 1983; F.F.A. Alan Watts, September 27, 1983
52. DIMINISHING RETURNS 5.10c ★★ F.A. Chuck Buzzard, October 1983
53. SPIRITUAL WARFARE 5.11a ★★★ F.A. Chuck Buzzard, Jerry Radant, October 1983
54. THE PEARL 5.11b ★★★★ F.A. Chuck Buzzard, Jerry Radant, October 1983
55. NUCLEAR 5.11d ★★★ F.A. John Rich, October 1987
56. FULL COURT PRESS 5.12a ★★★ F.A. John Rich, July 1988
57. BABY FIT 5.11c ★★ F.A. John Rich, Mike Puddy, June 1988
58. BAT FLAKE 5.10a ★ F.A. Sean Olmstead, Steve Byrne, 1982
59. SATAN'S AWAITING 5.11a ★★ F.A. Steve Byrne, Sean Olmstead, 1983
60. RISING STAR 5.10b ★★ F.A. Kent Benesch, Alan Watts, October 18, 1980

61. WHITE DWARF   5.11b/c R ★★   F.A. Alan Watts, Chris Grover, October 1, 1983
62. NIGHT SHIFT   5.11b ★★★   F.A. Alan Watts, September 27, 1983
63. GROUND ZERO   5.10d ★★★   F.A. Alan Watts, May 1, 1982
64. QUASAR   5.10a ★★★   F.A. Alan Watts, Alan Lester, October 11, 1980
65. EROGENOUS ZONE   5.10c ★★   F.A. Kent Benesch, Alan Watts, May 1, 1982
66. BATTLE OF THE BULGE   5.10a ★   F.A. Jeff Thomas, Del Young, Talbot Bielfielt, February 1976
67. BLOOD CLOT   5.10b ★★★★   F.A. Jeff Thomas, Jack Callahan, January 1975
68. CRACK-A-NO-GO   5.11b ★★★   F.A. TR, Chris Jones, Bill Soule, 1978; F.F.A. TR, Alan Watts, March 18, 1980; F.F.A. lead, Alan Watts, June 28, 1981
69. CRUEL SISTER   5.10a ★★★★   F.A. Mike Seeley, Wayne Arrington, October 1974
70. CATALYST (a.k.a. CHILD ABUSE)   5.12a/b ★★★★   F.A. TR, Alan Watts, November 1, 1981; F.A. lead, Jeff Frizzell, Tom Egan, December 1988
71. TAXDOR   5.9 X ★   F.A. Wayne Arrington, 1973
72. SOUTHERN CROSS   5.11a ★★★   F.A. Pat Carr, Craig Benesch, 1983
73. HARVEST   5.11b ★★   F.A. Chuck Buzzard, Steve Mrazek, June 1984
74. GRIM TALES   5.11a ★   F.A. Chuck Buzzard, Jerry Radant, August 1984
75. PATENT LEATHER PUMP   5.10a ★   F.A. Chuck Buzzard, June 1984
76. OLD AND IN THE WAY   5.10c ★★   F.A Chuck Buzzard, Jerry Radant, Jeff Frank, June 1984
77. FATHER MERCY   5.11b ★★   F.A. Chuck Buzzard, Jeff Frank, July 1984
78. CONVERSION EXCURSION   5.10a ★★   F.A. Chuck Buzzard, Jeff Turner, August 1984
79. BEAN TIME   5.10d ★   F.A. Chuck Buzzard, Jerry Radant, August 1984
80. LAVA TUBE   5.7 X ★   F.A. Chuck Buzzard, August 1984
81. BRAIN DEATH   5.11b R ★★   F.A. Chuck Buzzard, TR, August 8, 1984; F.F.A. Alan Watts, Mike Puddy, August 8, 1984
82. ON THE SPOT   5.9 ★   F.A. unknown
83. WASTED WORDS   5.10a ★   F.A. unknown
84. LOST SOULS   5.9 ★   F.A. unknown
85. RELIGIOUS FERVOR   5.10a ★★   F.A. unknown
86. SITTING DUCK   5.9 ★   F.A. unknown
87. GREASY SPOON   5.10a ★★   F.A. Ralph Moore, 1976
88. DIRE WOLF   5.8 ★   F.A unknown
89. DELICATESSEN   5.8 ★   F.A. Tim Carpenter, Doug Phillips, 1976
90. FAST FOOD JUNKY   5.8 ★   F.A. Ralph Moore, 1976
91. PHALLIC SYMBOL   5.7 ★   F.A. unknown
92. CHIMNEY OF GHOULS   5.7 R ★   F.A unknown
93. OLD TROUBLE'S NUMBER SEVEN   5.10b ★   F.A. Steve Mrazek, Chuck Buzzard, September 1984
94. PINK ROADGRADER   5.10d ★   F.A. Chuck Buzzard, Steve Marazek, September 1984
95. KNEEGOBEE   5.8 ★   F.A. Chuck Buzzard, Steve Mrazek, September 1984
96. LAST DAYS   5.10a ★★★   F.A Chuck Buzzard, March 1984
97. ST. PADDEE'S DAY   5.10a ★   F.A. Chuck Buzzard, March 1984
98. TURNING POINT   5.10a ★★   F.A. Chuck Buzzard, Eve Dearborn, March 1983
99. LETHAL DOSE   5.11a R ★★   F.A. Alan Watts, Sean Olmstead, September 30, 1983
100. MANTRA   5.10a ★★★   F.A. Paul Landrum, John Zeneroski, March 1975
101. CRY OF THE GERBIL   5.12b ★★★   F.A. John Rich, 1986
102. DARK STAR   5.11d/12a ★★★   F.A. Alan Watts, Bill Ramsey, July 14, 1981
103. NEUTRON STAR   5.12a ★★★★   F.A. Alan Watts, November 1, 1981
104. JONNY AND THE MELONHEADS   5.12b ★★★   F.A. Alan Watts, July 20, 1984
105. MORNING STAR   5.10c ★★★★   F.A. Paul Landrum, Ken Currens, March 1975
106. NIGHT CROSSING   5.11b ★★   F.A. Alan Watts, April 3, 1984
107. FREON   5.10a ★   F.A. Jeff Thomas, May 1974
108. WHISPERS   5.10a ★★   F.A. Alan Watts, Todd Brubanno, 1984
109. TREE ROUTE   5.9 ★   F.A. unknown
110. HAND JIVE   5.9 ★   F.A. Wayne Arrington, 1974
111. HERKY JERKY   5.9 ★   F.A. Wayne Arrington, December 1974

112. JUDAS   5.10a ★   F.A Chuck Buzzard, 1984
113. BIG CHIMNEY   5.7 X ★★★   F.A. Wayne Arrington 1974
114. MASQUERADE   5.12b R ★★★★   F.A. Alan Watts, Brooke Sandahl, May 8, 1984
115. BUSH DOCTOR   5.10b ★★★   F.A. Brooke Sandahl, Alan Watts, April 13, 1984
116. RAZOR BOY   5.10c ★★   F.A. Brooke Sandahl, Alan Watts, April 3, 1984
117. LITTLE WEENIE   5.7 ★   F.A. unknown
118. RUNT'S GRUNT   5.7 ★   F.A. unknown
119. SAWED OFF RUNT   5.8 ★★   F.A. unknown
120. PIPSQUEAK   5.8 ★★★   F.A. unknown
121. LITTLE SQUIRT   5.9 ★★   F.A. unknown
122. DWARF'S DELIGHT   5.8 ★★★   F.A. unknown
123. SHORT MAN'S COMPLEX   5.9 ★   F.A. unknown
124. STUNTED GROWTH   5.8 R ★★   F.A. unknown
125. NAPOLEON COMPLEX   5.10d ★★   F.A. TR, Alan Watts, August 1991
126. SHORT STUFF   5.10b ★   F.A. TR, Alan Watts, August 1991
127. PUNK KID   5.11c TR ★   F.A. TR, Alan Watts, August 1991
128. EMMAUS   5.10a ★★   F.A. unknown
129. ZEALOT   5.12a ★★★   F.A. Chuck Buzzard, 1985
130. MIDNIGHT CREEPER   5.8 ★★   F.A. Jeff Thomas, Cindy Jones, March 1976
130a. JEEPERS CREEPERS   5.8 X ★★   F.A. Jeff Thomas, Doug Phillips, mid-70s
131. ACROSS THE WATER   5.9 ★★   F.A. Jeff Thomas, Bob Grundy, 1974
132. MARGO'S MADNESS   5.10b ★★★   F.R.A. Chuck Buzzard, Jerry Radant, January 1984
133. FOOL'S PLEASURE   5.10a ★★★   F.R.A. Chuck Buzzard, Jeff Turner, November 1983
134. LAMA MOMMA   5.10b ★★★   F.R.A. Chuck Buzzard, Jeff Turner, December 1984
135. BABY WALKS   5.10a ★★★   F.R.A. first pitch, Chuck Buzzard, March 1982; F.R.A. entire route, Jerry Radant, Chuck Buzzard, January 1984
136. WINDFALL   5.11b ★★★   F.A. Chuck Buzzard, Jerry Radant, March 1984
137. HARD ATTACK   5.11a ★★★   F.A. Chuck Buzzard, March 1984
138. THE SHEEPGATE   5.11c ★★   F.A. unknown
139. MISTER REACH   5.11b ★★★   F.A. John Rich, Chuck Buzzard, 1985
140. BRIDGE OF SIGHS   5.10d ★★   F.A. Chuck Buzzard, January 1984
141. GENOCIDE   5.10b ★★   F.A. Chuck Buzzard, November 1983
142. DINK   5.8 ★   F.A. unknown
143. LOST AND FOUND   5.8 ★★   F.A. unknown
144. HUCKLEBERRY HOUND   5.7 ★★   F.A. unknown
145. GAGGED AND BOUND   5.7 R ★   F.A. unknown
146. INTO WHITE   5.9 ★★   F.R.A. Chuck Buzzard, November 1983
147. STRAWBERRY BLONDE   5.11C ★★   F.A. Steve Mrazek, September 1985
148. DEMANDER CODY   5.9 ★★   F.R.A. Chuck Buzzard, Jerry Radant, March 1982
149. MINES OF MORIA   5.7 R ★★   F.A. Wayne Arrington, 1975
150. CODY'S CORNER   5.8 ★★   F.R.A. Chuck Buzzard, Jerry Radant, March 1982
151. MCKENZIE'S WAY   5.11b ★★   F.A. Chuck Buzzard, Jerry Radant, April 1984
152. KILLER JISM   5.11b ★★   F.A. Steve Mrazek, Chuck Buzzard, August 1985
153. UGLY AS SIN   5.11a ★   F.A. Chuck Buzzard, Jerry Radant, 1984
154. HAND JOB   5.10b ★★★   F.A. Wayne Arrington, Tom Bauman, 1975
155. ORIGINAL SIN   5.10c ★★★   F.A. Jeff Thomas, March 1976
156. BLITZKRIEG   5.9 ★   F.A. Jeff Thomas, Bob Grundy, May 1974
157. BLITZEN   5.10c ★   F.A. unknown
158. CRUNCH TIME   5.8 ★   F.A. unknown
159. EXILED MAN   5.8 ★   F.A. unknown
160. BROTHERS CHILD   5.10c ★★★   F.A. Chuck Buzzard, December 1984
161. CHIMNEY SWEEP   5.7 R ★★   F.A. unknown
162. MASTER LOONY   5.11a ★★★★   F.A. Chuck Buzzard, Jerry Radant, December 1984
163. LOONY TUNES   5.11b R ★★   F.A. Chuck Buzzard, 1985

164. TUNED OUT 5.9 R ★ F.A. unknown
165. STUFFED TURKEY 5.8 R ★ F.A. unknown
166. OFF TEMPO 5.10a ★★★ F.A. unknown
167. BANANA SPLIT 5.8 ★★ F.A. unknown
168. CHIMNEY FIRE 5.7 R ★ F.A. unknown
169. LUCKY GUY 5.10c ★★ F.A. unknown
170. COMMON CRIMINAL 5.8 ★★ F.A. unknown
171. BANNED FOR LIFE 5.10b ★ F.A. unknown
172. SHACKLES AND CHAINS 5.8 ★★ F.A. unknown
173. SLEEPING DOG 5.7 ★ F.A. unknown
174. SLASHER 5.10c ★★ F.A. unknown
175. LOVE STRUCK ROMEO 5.8 ★★ F.A. unknown
176. BIG WOODY 5.9 ★★ F.A. Steve Mrazek, John Long, July 1984
177. AS YOU LIKE IT 5.10b ★★★ F.A. Tom Rogers, 1973/74
178. SORON 5.9 ★★ F.A. Wayne Arrington, 1973
179. MUCH ADO ABOUT NOTHING 5.10d ★★★ F.A. to first anchors, Wayne Arrington, 1973; F.A. entire route, Chuck Buzzard, 1982
180. AZOG 5.9 ★★ F.A. Wayne Arrington, 1974
180a. MID SUMMERS NIGHT SCREAM 5.7 ★★ F.A. Jerry Radant, Chuck Buzzard, 1982
181. TWO GENTLEMEN'S PNEUMONIA 5.7 ★★ F.R.A. Chuck Buzzard, Paddee Buzzard, 1983
182. LUST'S LABOR'S COST 5.10b ★★★ F.A. Chuck Buzzard, February 1984
183. KING SMEAR 5.11a ★★ F.A. Chuck Buzzard, February 1984

UPPER GORGE
1. KID'N PLAY 5.8 ★★ F.A. Kari and John McDaniel, July 1991
2. CRANKING WITH KARI 5.10c ★★★ F.A. John and Kari McDaniel, July 1991
3. PRUNING THE FAMILY TREE 5.10c ★★ F.A. Jeff Frizzell, February 16, 1992
4. SINK THE SUB 5.10A ★ F.A. John Fup, summer 1990
5. DANCES WITH DOGS 5.11c ★★★ F.A. Cyndee and John McDaniel, July 1991
6. BLIND DOGS NEED BONES TOO 5.10d ★★★ F.A. Mark Larisch, Tom Egan, Jeff Frizzell, March 1989
7. HIEROGLYPHICS 5.11d ★★★★ F.A. Tom Egan, Jeff Frizzell, March 1989
8. CELIBATE WIVES 5.12a ★★★ F.A. Jeff Frizzell, Tom Egan, February 1989
9. ANIMATION 5.11c ★★ F.A. Tom Egan, Jeff Frizzell, February 1989
10. MOJOMATIC 5.12a/b ★★★★ F.A. Jeff Frizzell, Tom Egan, March 1989
11. INTEGRATED IMAGING 5.12a ★★★ F.A. Tom Egan, Jeff Frizzell, March 1989
12. CHIENNE NO MORE 5.12a ★★★ F.A. TR, Jeff Frizzell, 1990; F.A. lead, John and Cyndee McDaniel, July 1991
13. EASY FOR SOME 5.11a/b ★★ F.A. John and Cyndee McDaniel, July 1991
14. JOHN-A-THON 5.8 F.A. TR, John McDaniel, July 1991
15. PREDATOR 5.12+ ? F.A. TR, John McDaniel, July 1991; F.F.A. uncompleted
16. BANNED FOR LIFE 5.10b ★ F.R.A. Pete Chamus, Tedd Whitson, fall 1990
17. CURLY 5.11d ★★★ F.A. Jeff Frizzell, February 1, 1992
18. SQUEEZE PLAY 5.10b ★★ F.R.A. Pete Chamus, Tedd Whitson, fall 1990
19. MOE 5.11b/c ★★ F.A. Jeff Frizzell, February 9, 1992
20. LARRY 5.12a/b ★★★ F.A. Jeff Frizzell, February 13, 1992
21. P.W. 5.9 ★★ F.A. TR, Roy Presswood, summer 1990
22. BACK HANDED SLAP 5.8 ★★ F.R.A. Pete Chamus, Tedd Whitson, fall 1990
23. FIRST PEDESTAL CRACK 5.10a ★ F.R.A. Pete Chamus, Tedd Whitson, fall 1990
24. MISSING IN ACTION 5.10a ★★ F.A. unknown
25. GET THAT FEELING 5.11d ★★★ F.A. John Rich, Tom Egan, 1990
26. NATURAL ART 5.11c ★★★ F.A. Tom Egan, 1990
27. PROJECT 5.12 ? F.A. TR, Tom Egan, 1991; F.F.A. uncompleted
28. UP COUNTRY 5.12a ★★★ F.A. Tom Egan, Jeff Frizzell, November 3, 1990
29. UNIQUE MONIQUE 5.12a ★★★ F.A. Jeff Frizzell, Alan Watts, March 16, 1991
30. NAXIS 5.10b ★★ F.A. Jeff Frizzell, February 1991

31. GAPERS ON A TANGENT 5.12a/b ★★★ F.A. Jeff Frizzell, Tom Egan, November 28, 1990
32. HOT LAVA 5.13a ★★★ F.A. Jeff Frizzell, May 1989
33. TOMB OF LOVE 5.11d ★★★ F.A. Jeff Frizzell, February 1991
34. FEMINAZIS 5.13a ★★★★ F.A. Jeff Frizzell, March 8, 1992
35. BUSHWACKER 5.11d ★★ F.A. John Rich, 1990
36. BLAME IT ON RIO 5.12b ★★★ F.A. John Rich, 1990
37. PERUVIAN SKIES 5.12d ★★★★ F.A. Jeff Frizzell, August 15, 1991
38. PROJECT 5.13–? Prep. Jeff Frizzell, spring 1991
39. PROJECT 5.12+? F.A., TR, Jeff Frizzell, spring 1991
40. E-TYPE JAG 5.11a ★★★★ F.A. Jeff Frizzell, November 23, 1991
41. PROJECT 5.11? Prep. John Fup, March 1992)
42. SECOND PEDESTAL CRACK 5.10a ★★ F.A. unknown
43. LAND OF THE LOST 5.10a ★★★ F.A. Paul Landrum, Jim Davis, 1979
44. THE SIGN OF THE PRIEST 5.10b ★★ F.A. John and Cyndee McDaniel, March 1992
45. PROJECT 5.11+? Prep. John McDaniel, March 1992
46. JUST DO IT 5.10a ★★★ F.A. Tom Egan, Jeff Frizzell, April 1989
47. PLAYING IN TRAFFIC 5.12b/c ★★★★ F.A. Tom Egan, October 1989
48. SPELLBOUND 5.11c ★★ F.A. Tom Egan, Mark Larisch, March 1989
49. VIRTUAL BEACH 5.11a ★ F.A. John and Cyndee McDaniel, February 1992
50. PROJECT 5.11+? F.A. Jeff Frizzell, John McDaniel, March 1992, F.F.A. uncompleted
51. THE SEAP 5.10b ★★ F.A. Jeff Frizzell, February 17, 1992
52. SHRIMPTON'S SHRINE 5.12a ★★ F.A. TR, Jeff Shrimpton, Jeff Frizzell, 1990
53. ORPHAN'S CRUEL 5.12b ★★★ F.A. Jeff Frizzell, July 1989
54. CHILLIN' IN THE PENZO 5.12b/c ★★★ F.A. Jeff Frizzell, March 19, 1992
55. PINK PRIMITIVE 5.11b ★★★ F.A. Jeff Frizzell, Tom Egan, November 8, 1990
56. THE FUGUTIVE 5.11d ★★ F.A. Jeff Frizzell, March 16, 1992
57. WARDANCE 5.12a ★★★ F.A. Tom Egan, April 1989
58. BIG TUNA 5.13b ★★★★ F.A. Jeff Frizzell, November 15, 1990
59. STEAMING CAFE FLIRTS 5.12b/c ★★★ F.A. Jeff Frizzell, March 1989
60. CONTROLLED HYSTERIA 5.13a ★★★★ F.A. Tom Egan, August 1989
61. SLACK MACKEREL 5.12b ★★★ F.A. Jeff Frizzell, March 1989
62. SAVAGE TRUTH 5.13? F.A. Tom Egan 1990, F.F.A. uncompleted
63. NEW BREED LEADER 5.12b ★★★★ F.A. Jeff Frizzell, March 1989
64. PEACH NAILS 5.12b ★★★★ F.A. Jeff Frizzell, November 1990
65. CUBAN SLIDE 5.13a ★★★ F.A. Jeff Frizzell, spring 1991
66. THE URGE 5.12c/d ★★★★ F.A. Jeff Frizzell, July 1989
67. COLORSPLASH 5.10b ★★★ F.A. Tom Egan, March 1989
68. SPECIAL EFFECTS 5.11d ★★★ F.A. to old anchor, Tom Egan and Mark Larisch, April 1989. F.A. to new anchor, Jeff Frizzell, March 26, 1992
69. YELLOW FIN 5.12a/b ★★★ F.A. Jeff Frizzell, March 26, 1992
70. BANGSTICK 5.11b ★★★ F.A. Jeff Frizzell, March 26, 1992
71. SHARK-INFESTED WATERS 5.12b ★★★★ F.A. Tom Egan, October 1, 1989
72. PROJECT 5.12+? F.A. TR, Tom Egan, fall 1990, F.F.A uncompleted
73. THE BIG KILL 5.12a ★★★ F.A. Jeff Frizzell, March 14, 1992
74. SCREAMS AND WHISPERS 5.12b ★★★ F.A. TR, Jeff Frizzell, 1990
75. BRAZILIAN SKIES 5.12b/c ★★★★ F.A. Tom Egan, July 1989
76. RED LILY Q 5.12b ★★★ F.A. Jeff Frizzell, March 1992
77. PERSUASION 5.12a ★★★ F.A. Tom Egan, June 1989
78. PROJECT 5.12? F.A. TR, Tom Egan, summer 1989, F.F.A. uncompleted
79. SLAY THE DRAGON 5.12c ★★★ F.A. Tom Egan, May 1989
80. RAINBOW'S END 5.11c ★★ F.A. Tom Egan, May 1989
81. ALMOST SOMETHING 5.10b ★★ F.A. Tom Egan, September 1989

ROUTES BY RATING

4th Class, 5.0

- [ ] Chockstone Chimney 4th Class ★ (182)
- [ ] North Ramp 4th Class ★★ (191)
- [ ] North Ridge, The 4th Class ★★ (183)
- [ ] Opossum Notch 5.0 ★ (206)
- [ ] South Face 5.0 A1 ★★ (128)

5.1

- [ ] Gunsight Rock ★ (209)
- [ ] North Chimney ★★ (195)
- [ ] Papoose, Southeast Ridge X (211)
- [ ] Platform, The R ★ (128)
- [ ] Spiral X ★★★ (210)
- [ ] West Ledges ★ (195)

5.2

- [ ] Flounder Corner ★ (127)
- [ ] Limestone Chimney ★★ (191)
- [ ] North Ridge Direct ★★★ (183)
- [ ] Northwest Corner ★★ (128)

5.3

- [ ] Little Big Horn X (211)
- [ ] North Slab Crack X ★★ (84)
- [ ] Northwest Corner ★★ (195)
- [ ] Pocket Hold Route X ★★★ (208)
- [ ] South Buttress X ★★★ (193)
- [ ] South Face X ★ (211)
- [ ] South Spiral X ★ (211)
- [ ] Tilted Slab X (212)

5.4

- [ ] Bird Dung Chimney X (185)
- [ ] Diagonal Crack X ★ (206)
- [ ] Direct Northwest Crack ★★ (193)
- [ ] East Side Chimney ★ (195)
- [ ] Easy Chimney X ★★★ (193)
- [ ] Friction Arete X (197)
- [ ] Index Finger X ★ (212)
- [ ] Joey – Southwest Side X (208)
- [ ] Left Slab Crack ★★ (88)
- [ ] Lieback Flake ★ (193)
- [ ] Round River ★★★ (201)
- [ ] Scoop Route X ★ (189)

5.5

- [ ] Bowling Alley ★★ (114)
- [ ] Common Household Fly ★ (139)
- [ ] Liberty Bell Chimney X ★ (185)
- [ ] Lollypop League X ★★★★ (188)
- [ ] North Side ★★★ (189)
- [ ] Pumpkin Patch ★★ (220)
- [ ] Right Slab Crack ★★ (88)
- [ ] South Bowl X (197)
- [ ] South Buttress X ★★★★ (206)
- [ ] Spring Break ★★ (224)
- [ ] West Face X ★★★ (205)
- [ ] Western Chimney R ★★★ (143)
- [ ] Abbot Gully A2 X (134)

5.6

- [ ] Affliction R ★ (195)
- [ ] Brown Cow X (197)
- [ ] Carabid R (121)
- [ ] Cave Route X ★★★★ (206)
- [ ] Charlie's Chimney x ★★★ (112)
- [ ] Chicken Little ★ (165)
- [ ] Cinnamon Slab ★★★ (88)
- [ ] Cow Pie X (197)
- [ ] Doctor Doom Variation (143)
- [ ] Easy Reader ★★★ (88)
- [ ] Falling Rock Zone R (195)
- [ ] Flake Chimney R (122)
- [ ] Flunked Out ★★ (224)
- [ ] Great Roof, The A3 ★★★ (203)
- [ ] Green Gully ★ (203)
- [ ] Havana ★ (175)
- [ ] How Low Can You Go? ★★★ (84)
- [ ] Instant Replay ★★★ (188)
- [ ] Juniper Gully 5.6 A1 X ★ (185)
- [ ] Juniper Snag R ★★ (191)
- [ ] Lean Cuisine ★★ (217)
- [ ] Left Side Of The Beard, The ★★★ (109)
- [ ] Little Finger X ★★★ (212)
- [ ] Lost Hardware Route R ★ (208)
- [ ] Moscow ★★★ (175)
- [ ] North Ledge R ★ (195)
- [ ] North Ledges Traverse X (207)
- [ ] Northeast Arete X (134)
- [ ] Orange Peel X (197)
- [ ] Palo Verde A3 ★★ (143)
- [ ] Rattlesnake Chimney ★ (98)
- [ ] Rib Traverse X ★★★ (187)
- [ ] Second Horseman R ★ (83)
- [ ] South Face X ★ (189)
- [ ] Street Walker (185)
- [ ] Struck Out X (137)
- [ ] Super Slab ★★★★ (170)
- [ ] Vulture Ridge X (123)

5.7

- [ ] Amphetamine Grip R ★★★ (172)
- [ ] Asterisk, The X ★ (117)
- [ ] Bad Manners ★★ (229)
- [ ] Big Chimney X ★★★ (252)
- [ ] Bits and Pieces X ★ (126)
- [ ] Block Head ★ (217)
- [ ] Bookworm ★★★ (98)
- [ ] Bruce's Traverse X ★ (183)
- [ ] Bunny Face ★★★ (98)
- [ ] Charm School ★★ (229)
- [ ] Chimney Fire R ★ (262)
- [ ] Chimney of Ghouls R ★ (249)
- [ ] Chimney Sweep R ★★ (261)
- [ ] Christian Brothers Traverse X ★ (133)
- [ ] Cinnamon Toast R ★ (88)
- [ ] City Dump R (47)
- [ ] Crazies ★★ (200)
- [ ] Dancer ★★★ (115)
- [ ] Defecation Crack ★★ (195)
- [ ] Disappearing Tower X ★ (208)
- [ ] Door Knob People ★★ (229)
- [ ] Double Time ★ (217)
- [ ] Ear, The R ★ (187)
- [ ] East Chimney X (45)
- [ ] Easy Street R ★ (191)
- [ ] First Horseman R ★ (83)
- [ ] Fourth Horseman R ★ (83)
- [ ] Friday's Jinx R ★★ (80)
- [ ] Gagged and Bound R ★ (258)
- [ ] Great Expectations ★★ (165)
- [ ] Handyman ★★★ (220)
- [ ] Heart Throb ★★★ (229)
- [ ] Heaven Can Wait R ★ (137)
- [ ] Ho Chi Minh Trail A3 R (174)
- [ ] Homecoming Queen ★★ (229)
- [ ] Hook, Line And Sinker ★ (127)
- [ ] Huckleberry Hound ★★ (258)
- [ ] In Harm's Way ★★★ (142)
- [ ] Jersey Shore ★★ (217)
- [ ] Lava Tube X ★ (247)
- [ ] Leaning Brave X (211)
- [ ] Lichen It ★★★ (88)
- [ ] Lichen Persuasion (148)
- [ ] Lifeguard R ★★ (220)
- [ ] Lion's Jaw Chimney (78)
- [ ] Little Weenie ★ (254)
- [ ] Lower West Chimney R ★ (193)
- [ ] Lycopodophyta ★★ (98)
- [ ] Mid Summer's Night Scream ★★ (263)
- [ ] Mines of Moria R ★★ (259)
- [ ] Monk Chimney (135)
- [ ] Munchkin Land ★★ (188)
- [ ] Old Testament ★★ (110)
- [ ] Osa Thatcher's Needle X (185)
- [ ] Out Of Harm's Way ★★★ (142)
- [ ] Over the Hill R ★★★ (208)

5.7

- ☐ Petroglyph Crack ★ (144)
- ☐ Phallic Symbol ★ (248)
- ☐ Pioneer Route A1 ★★★★ (162)
- ☐ Playing with Fire ★★ (220)
- ☐ Prom Night ★★★ (229)
- ☐ Prune Face ★★ (193)
- ☐ Rabbit Stew ★★ (98)
- ☐ Rage ★★ (229)
- ☐ Red Rover R ★★ (172)
- ☐ Riderless Horse X (83)
- ☐ Right Side Of The Beard ★★★ (109)
- ☐ Runt's Grunt ★ (254)
- ☐ Safety Valve R (112)
- ☐ Sands of Time A4 R (184)
- ☐ School's Out ★★ (228)
- ☐ Skid Row ★ (193)
- ☐ Sky Chimney ★★ (118)
- ☐ Sky Chimney Variation R (118)
- ☐ Sleeping Dog ★ (262)
- ☐ Slow Train ★ (153)
- ☐ South Chimney R ★ (212)
- ☐ South Face X (207)
- ☐ Southeast Face A3 X (184)
- ☐ Spiderman ★★★★ (139)
- ☐ Spiderman Variation ★★★ (139)
- ☐ Squashed Spider X ★★ (139)
- ☐ Sunday's Jinx (80)
- ☐ Thumb, The ★★ (203)
- ☐ Two Gentlemen's Pneumonia ★★ (263)
- ☐ Upper Ceiling R ★ (95)
- ☐ Victory of the Proletarian People's Ambition Arete X (183)
- ☐ West Chimney X (46)
- ☐ Whitecloud R ★★ (203)
- ☐ Young and the Worthless, The X (177)
- ☐ Bubba's In Bondage 5.7 A3 ★ (45)

5.8

- ☐ Angel Flight Buttress R ★★ (137)
- ☐ Back Handed Slap ★★ (272)
- ☐ Banana Split ★★ (262)
- ☐ Bits of Feces R (126)
- ☐ Bon Fire ★★ (224)
- ☐ By Ways R (118)
- ☐ Cardiac Kid ★★ (227)
- ☐ Catty Corner ★ (200)
- ☐ Chopper ★★★ (191)
- ☐ Cliff Dwelling Crack ★★ (144)
- ☐ Cody's Corner ★★ (260)
- ☐ Common Criminal ★★ (262)
- ☐ Cox Rocks ★ (235)
- ☐ Cram Session ★ (224)
- ☐ Crunch Time ★ (260)
- ☐ Dancer Continuation ★ (115)
- ☐ Dead Week ★★ (230)
- ☐ Deep Sleep ★★★ (230)
- ☐ Delicatessen ★ (247)
- ☐ Deteriorata ★ (100)
- ☐ Diamonds and Rust R (153)
- ☐ Dink ★ (258)
- ☐ Dire Wolf ★ (247)
- ☐ Dogfight Crack R (206)
- ☐ Dolf's Dihedral ★★ (153)
- ☐ Dunce Cap R ★★ (229)
- ☐ Dwarf's Delight ★★★ (254)
- ☐ Exiled Man ★ (260)
- ☐ Fast Food Junky ★ (248)
- ☐ First Aid A1 ★★ (227)
- ☐ Fish Fight ★★ (224)
- ☐ Four Fs (148)
- ☐ Frat Jerks ★★ (224)
- ☐ Free Spirit ★★ (189)
- ☐ Ginger Snap ★★★ (88)
- ☐ Godzilla ★ (155)
- ☐ Gothic Cathedral R (112)
- ☐ Greenhouse X ★ (217)
- ☐ Hop On Pop ★★★ (80)
- ☐ Island In The Sky X (112)
- ☐ Jamboree ★★ (187)
- ☐ Jeepers Creepers X ★★ (256)
- ☐ Jete ★★★ (115)
- ☐ Jiminy Cricket ★★ (220)
- ☐ John-A-Thon TR (270)
- ☐ Kid'n Play ★★ (268)
- ☐ Kneegobee ★ (249)
- ☐ Lemon Peel X ★ (197)
- ☐ Lion's Jaw ★★★ (78)
- ☐ Lost and Found ★★ (258)
- ☐ Love Struck Romeo ★★ (263)
- ☐ Mad Man ★ (237)
- ☐ Meat Grinder ★★ (217)
- ☐ Midnight Creeper ★★ (256)
- ☐ Mini Half Dome R ★★ (207)
- ☐ Necromancer ★ (143)
- ☐ New World R ★ (166)
- ☐ Nut Case ★★ (195)
- ☐ Pack Animal R ★★★ (83)
- ☐ Panama Red R ★★ (172)

5.8

- [ ] Parking Lot Crack ★★ (188)
- [ ] Peanut Brittle R ★★ (80)
- [ ] Peanuts ★★ (193)
- [ ] Peking ★★ (175)
- [ ] Pin Bender A2 ★ (204)
- [ ] Pipsqueak ★★★ (254)
- [ ] Red Ryder R ★★ (177)
- [ ] Reptile R ★ (135)
- [ ] Rope-De-Dope Crack ★★ (84)
- [ ] Rotten Crack X (197)
- [ ] Round River Direct X (201)
- [ ] Sawed Off Runt ★★ (254)
- [ ] Scabies X (165)
- [ ] Scorpio X (39)
- [ ] Shackles and Chains ★★ (262)
- [ ] Shamu ★★★ (84)
- [ ] Silly Crack ★★ (191)
- [ ] Sistine Variation ★ (95)
- [ ] Sky Ridge R ★★ (117)
- [ ] Sky Ridge Variation R ★ (117)
- [ ] Slam Dance ★ (228)
- [ ] Solstice Slab ★ (208)
- [ ] South Summit – East Wall X (121)
- [ ] Stuffed Turkey R ★ (262)
- [ ] Stunted Growth R ★★ (254)
- [ ] Sunset Boulevard ★ (127)
- [ ] Thrasher A2 ★ (191)
- [ ] Thumper ★★ (217)
- [ ] Wasteland R (47)
- [ ] West Face Variation ★★★ (155)
- [ ] Who Hash R ★★ (220)
- [ ] Who Pudding R ★★ (220)
- [ ] Zigzag ★ (127)

5.9

- [ ] A Desperate Man ★★ (137)
- [ ] Across the Water ★★ (256)
- [ ] Air To Spare A4+ X ★ (106)
- [ ] Ancylostoma ★★ (98)
- [ ] Arachnid Boogie ★ (139)
- [ ] Azog ★★ (263)
- [ ] Big Man on Campus ★★★ (230)
- [ ] Big Woody ★★ (263)
- [ ] Black Velcro R ★ (118)
- [ ] Blitzkrieg ★ (260)
- [ ] Bump and Grind ★★ (193)
- [ ] C.L. Concerto A4 R (202)
- [ ] Catfight Cracks R (201)
- [ ] Cling On ★★★ (136)
- [ ] Crumble Pie R ★ (124)
- [ ] Deliverance ★ (193)
- [ ] Demander Cody ★★ (259)
- [ ] Desert Solitaire X ★ (200)
- [ ] Desiderata ★★★ (195)
- [ ] Devil's Delight R ★ (217)
- [ ] Doctor Doom R ★★ (143)
- [ ] Far Side, The R ★★ (208)
- [ ] Ferret's Dead, The ★★ (235)
- [ ] Flex ★★★ (177)
- [ ] Follies Of Youth R ★ (138)
- [ ] Fool's Overture R ★ (39)
- [ ] Gone with the Flake ★ (174)
- [ ] Gripped ★ (172)
- [ ] Hand Jive ★ (252)
- [ ] Helium Woman ★★ (98)
- [ ] Herky Jerky ★ (252)
- [ ] I Lost My Lunch X (39)
- [ ] In Hinds Way (78)
- [ ] Into White ★★ (258)
- [ ] Iron Curtain R ★★ (172)
- [ ] King Kong R ★★ (153)
- [ ] Last Gasp X (112)
- [ ] Light On The Path ★★★ (78)
- [ ] Little Black Sambo X ★★ (229)
- [ ] Little Squirt ★★ (254)
- [ ] Lost Fox ★★★ (193)
- [ ] Lost Souls ★ (247)
- [ ] Metamorphic Maneuvers R ★ (177)
- [ ] Moonshine Dihedral ★★★★ (97)
- [ ] Mr. Toad's Wild Ride R ★ (165)
- [ ] No Doz A4 X (61)
- [ ] On the Spot ★ (247)
- [ ] P.W. ★★ (272)
- [ ] Panama Express ★★ (172)
- [ ] Passing Grade ★★★ (224)
- [ ] Perpetual Motion ★ (153)
- [ ] Picnic Lunch Wall A3+ R ★ (45)
- [ ] Revelations ★★★ (110)
- [ ] Shipwreck R (52)
- [ ] Short Man's Complex ★ (254)
- [ ] Sitting Duck ★ (247)
- [ ] Slopper ★ (191)
- [ ] Snake, The R ★★ (135)
- [ ] Snibble Tower A1 R (119)
- [ ] Solar ★★ (61)
- [ ] Soron ★★ (263)
- [ ] Strung Out ★ (137)
- [ ] Sundown ★★★ (144)
- [ ] Sunset Slab ★★★★ (127)

5.9

- [ ] Taxdor X ★ (246)
- [ ] Thin Air ★★★ (199)
- [ ] Tinker Toy X ★★★ (112)
- [ ] Titus ★ (240)
- [ ] Toys In The Attic ★★ (114)
- [ ] Tree Route ★ (252)
- [ ] Tuned Out R ★ (262)
- [ ] Vanishing Uncertainty R ★ (47)
- [ ] Virgin Slayer, The ★★★ (230)
- [ ] Vulture Crest ★ (235)
- [ ] Wallaby ★ (207)
- [ ] White Satin ★★★ (118)
- [ ] Widow Maker R ★★★ (139)
- [ ] Young and the Restless, The R ★ (177)
- [ ] Zion ★★★ (78)

5.10a

- [ ] Baby Walks ★★★ (256)
- [ ] Bat Flake ★ (244)
- [ ] Battle of the Bulge ★ (246)
- [ ] Best Left To Obscurity R (142)
- [ ] Bill's Flake ★★ (169)
- [ ] Bolderdash ★ (242)
- [ ] Burn Baby Burn ★★★ (220)
- [ ] Captain Fingers R ★ (143)
- [ ] Captain Xenolith ★★ (100)
- [ ] Chimney De Chelly R ★★ (144)
- [ ] Conversion Excursion ★★ (247)
- [ ] Cornerstone Variation ★★ (142)
- [ ] Cosmos ★★★ (148)
- [ ] Cruel Sister ★★★★ (246)
- [ ] D.A.R. Crack ★★ (189)
- [ ] Dances with Clams ★★ (169)
- [ ] Dead Baby Bubbas ★ (182)
- [ ] Deception Crack ★ (185)
- [ ] Delirium Tremens ★★★★ (207)
- [ ] Down's Syndrome R ★★ (144)
- [ ] Drill 'Em And Fill 'Em ★★ (121)
- [ ] Emmaus ★★ (256)
- [ ] Farmers Variation X (41)
- [ ] Fight Song ★★★ (225)
- [ ] Finger Puppet ★★ (169)
- [ ] First Pedestal Crack ★ (272)
- [ ] Flicker Flash ★ (216)
- [ ] Fool's Pleasure ★★★ (256)
- [ ] Free Lunch R ★ (42)
- [ ] Freon ★ (252)
- [ ] Greasy Spoon ★★ (247)
- [ ] Grettir's Saga X (118)
- [ ] Gruff ★★★ (237)
- [ ] Hawkline Monster R ★ (166)
- [ ] Heathen's Highway ★★ (110)
- [ ] Hippo's On Ice ★ (70)
- [ ] Infinity Variation ★★★ (80)
- [ ] Irreverance ★★★ (110)
- [ ] Judas ★ (252)
- [ ] Just Do It ★★★ (276)
- [ ] Karate Crack ★★★ (88)
- [ ] Karl Marx Variation R (170)
- [ ] King Kong Direct R ★ (155)
- [ ] Land of the Lost ★★★ (275)
- [ ] Last Days ★★★ (249)
- [ ] Little Wicked Thing ★ (149)
- [ ] London Tower R (182)
- [ ] Mantra ★★★ (249)
- [ ] Methuselah's Column R ★ (98)
- [ ] Midnight Rider R ★ (189)
- [ ] Midriff Bulge ★★ (135)
- [ ] Missing in Action ★★ (272)
- [ ] New Testament ★★★ (110)
- [ ] Off Tempo ★★★ (262)
- [ ] Organ Grinder ★ (237)
- [ ] Paper Tiger ★★ (169)
- [ ] Patent Leather Pump ★ (246)
- [ ] Peapod Cave ★★ (88)
- [ ] Phantom ★ (220)
- [ ] Phoenix ★★★★ (121)
- [ ] Physical Abuse ★★ (235)
- [ ] Pop Goes The Nubbin ★★ (80)
- [ ] Quasar ★★★ (244)
- [ ] Religious Fervor ★★ (247)
- [ ] Santiam Highway Ledges ★ (203)
- [ ] Second Pedestal Crack ★★ (275)
- [ ] Self Preservation Variation ★★★ (114)
- [ ] Shanghai X ★ (174)
- [ ] Sink the Sub ★ (268)
- [ ] Sky Ways R (118)
- [ ] Slum Time (73)
- [ ] Soft Shoe Ballet A4 X ★ (44)
- [ ] St. Paddee's Day ★ (249)
- [ ] Sundancer ★ (83)
- [ ] Tale of Two Shitties ★★★ (144)
- [ ] Temptation ★★ (110)
- [ ] Terror Bonne R ★ (235)
- [ ] Toy Blocks ★★ (114)
- [ ] Trezlar ★★★★ (148)
- [ ] Turning Point ★★ (249)
- [ ] Wasted Words ★ (247)
- [ ] We Be Toys ★ (149)
- [ ] Whispers ★★ (252)
- [ ] Zebra ★★★ (78)

5.10b

- [ ] Almost Something ★★ (283)
- [ ] As You Like It ★★★ (263)
- [ ] Badfinger ★★★★ (237)
- [ ] Banned for Life ★ (262, 270)
- [ ] Barbecue The Pope ★★★ (110)
- [ ] Block Party ★★ (230)
- [ ] Blood Clot ★★★★ (246)
- [ ] Blue Balls ★★ (114)
- [ ] Bush Doctor ★★★ (252)
- [ ] Chicken McNuggets ★★★ (63)
- [ ] Chuck's Smelly Crack R ★ (143)
- [ ] Colorsplash ★★★ (282)
- [ ] Cornercopia ★★★ (240)
- [ ] Crack Of Infinity ★★★ (80)
- [ ] Dancing Hearts ★★ (230)
- [ ] Desmond's Tutu R ★ (64)
- [ ] Double Trouble ★★ (112)
- [ ] Float Like A Butterfly TR ★★★★ (84)
- [ ] Genocide ★★ (258)
- [ ] Global Motion ★★★ (229)
- [ ] Gumby ★★★ (74)
- [ ] Hand Job ★★★ (260)
- [ ] Hang It Loose R ★★ (222)
- [ ] Heatstroke ★★ (199)
- [ ] Hesitation Blues ★★★ (114)
- [ ] If I Ran The Circus ★★★ (222)
- [ ] If Six Were Nine ★★ (172)
- [ ] Journey To Ixtlan A5 X (45)
- [ ] Labyrinth ★★★ (230)
- [ ] Lama Momma ★★★ (256)
- [ ] Lester Tots R ★ (95)
- [ ] Let's Face It ★★★ (175)
- [ ] Little Feat ★★ (142)
- [ ] Little Wonder ★★ (217)
- [ ] Living End, The ★★ (227)
- [ ] Low Blow TR ★ (84)
- [ ] Lust's Labor's Cost ★★★ (263)
- [ ] Margo's Madness ★★★ (256)
- [ ] Matthew (7:24 ★★ (149)
- [ ] Mongolians R ★★ (175)
- [ ] Monkey Farce R ★★ (155)
- [ ] Moonshine Variation X ★★★ (97)
- [ ] Naxis ★★ (272)
- [ ] Nightingale's On Vacation ★★ (110)
- [ ] No Nukes ★ (59)
- [ ] Old Trouble's Number Seven ★ (249)
- [ ] Oriface ★★★ (235)
- [ ] Pack Animal Direct ★★★★ (83)
- [ ] Phantasmagoria ★ (169)
- [ ] Potential Energy R ★★ (153)
- [ ] Red Scare ★★ (148)
- [ ] Rim Job ★★★ (237)
- [ ] Rising Start ★★ (244)
- [ ] Screaming Yellow Zonkers ★★★★ (148)
- [ ] Seap, The ★★ (277)
- [ ] Shaft ★★ (128)
- [ ] Short Stuff ★ (255)
- [ ] Sign of the Priest, The ★★ (275)
- [ ] Silly Boy ★★★ (229)
- [ ] Smaug R ★ (155)
- [ ] Squeeze Play ★★ (270)
- [ ] Sunjammer ★★★ (189)
- [ ] Swan Song ★★ (217)
- [ ] Teddy Bear's Picnic ★★ (41)
- [ ] Third Horseman R ★ (83)
- [ ] Titanium Jag ★★ (169)
- [ ] Venom ★★ (135)
- [ ] Walking While Intoxicated ★★ (50)
- [ ] Wedding Day ★★★ (97)
- [ ] Wildfire ★★★★ (237)

5.10c

- [ ] Astro Bunny ★★ (230)
- [ ] Big Bad Wolf X TR ★ (220)
- [ ] Blitzen ★ (260)
- [ ] Bold Line ★★ (240)
- [ ] Brothers Child ★★★ (260)
- [ ] Calamity Jam ★★★ (80)
- [ ] Cardiac Fib ★★ (227)
- [ ] Cartoon Deficiency ★ (174)
- [ ] Child's Play ★★ (114)
- [ ] Condor ★★ (121)
- [ ] Cranking with Kari ★★★ (268)
- [ ] Cretin's Retreat (a.k.a. Cretin's Revenge) ★★ (235)
- [ ] Cull's In Space ★★★ (127)
- [ ] Diminishing Returns ★★ (244)
- [ ] Double Edged Sword R ★ (64)
- [ ] Erogenous Zone ★★ (246)
- [ ] Fallen Angel R ★★ (135)
- [ ] Fungus Roof X (165)
- [ ] Helter Skelter R ★★ (172)
- [ ] Inside Corner ★★ (131)
- [ ] Kunza Korner ★★★★ (123)
- [ ] Last Chance ★★★★ (242)
- [ ] Little Bo Peep ★★★ (230)
- [ ] Lucky Guy ★★ (262)
- [ ] Manic Nirvana ★ (135)

5.10c

- ☐ More Or Lester TR ★★ (142)
- ☐ Morning Star ★★★★ (250)
- ☐ No Picnic R ★ (41)
- ☐ Old and in the Way ★★ (247)
- ☐ Original Sin ★★★ (260)
- ☐ Out of Control ★★ (189)
- ☐ Pass Over ★★ (240)
- ☐ Pop Art ★ (169)
- ☐ Prometheus ★★★ (242)
- ☐ Pruning the Family Tree ★★ (268)
- ☐ Razor Boy ★★ (253)
- ☐ Sandbag R ★ (81)
- ☐ Send Your Clone R ★ (242)
- ☐ Sky Dive ★★★ (118)
- ☐ Skylight ★★ (126)
- ☐ Slasher ★★ (262)
- ☐ Splash ★★ (230)
- ☐ Sting Like A Bee TR ★★★ (84)
- ☐ Sweet Spot ★★ (220)
- ☐ Tammy Baker's Face ★★ (79)
- ☐ Theseus ★★ (230)
- ☐ Three Fingered Hack ★★ (235)
- ☐ West Gully ★★★ (205)

5.10d

- ☐ Aggro Bumbly ★★★ (149)
- ☐ Bean Time ★ (247)
- ☐ Blind Dogs Need Bones Too ★★★ (270)
- ☐ Bridge of Sighs ★★ (258)
- ☐ Come to the Quiet ★★ (242)
- ☐ Explosive Energy Child R ★★★ (142)
- ☐ Fingers of Fate ★★★ (174)
- ☐ Firestarter ★★ (220)
- ☐ Fred On Air ★★★ (122)
- ☐ Ground Zero ★★★ (244)
- ☐ Headless Horseman ★★★ (83)
- ☐ Hemp Liberation ★★ (137)
- ☐ Little Orphan Jammies ★★ (235)
- ☐ Minotaur ★★ (230)
- ☐ Modern Zombie ★★★ (135)
- ☐ Moons of Pluto ★★★★ (148)
- ☐ Much Ado About Nothing ★★★ (263)
- ☐ Napoleon Complex ★★ (254)
- ☐ No Brain, No Pain R ★ (126)
- ☐ Pink Roadgrader ★ (249)
- ☐ Pitch It Here ★ (64)
- ☐ Pleasure Principle ★★ (181)
- ☐ Powder Up The Nose ★★★ (64)
- ☐ Reason To Be ★★★ (144)
- ☐ Soft Touch ★ (237)
- ☐ Trivial Pursuit R ★★ (92)
- ☐ Yoder Eaters (123)

5.11a

- ☐ Avant Garde ★★ (230)
- ☐ Bad Moon Rising ★★★ (148)
- ☐ Blue Light Special ★★★ (50)
- ☐ Bop Till You Drop ★★★ (149)
- ☐ Bound In Bogota ★★ (64)
- ☐ Brain Salad Surgery ★★★ (185)
- ☐ Cat Scan ★ (78)
- ☐ Chairman Mao's Little Red Book ★★★ (174)
- ☐ Cheat Sheet ★★ (228)
- ☐ Crankenstein ★★ (57)
- ☐ Cry of the Poor ★★★★ (240)
- ☐ Desolation Row ★★ (144)
- ☐ E-Type Jag ★★★★ (275)
- ☐ Exile On Main Street ★★★ (70)
- ☐ Grim Tales ★ (246)
- ☐ Hard Attack ★★★ (258)
- ☐ Hot Monkey Love ★★ (135)
- ☐ I Almost Died ★★★ (177)
- ☐ King Smear ★★ (263)
- ☐ Lethal Dose R ★★ (249)
- ☐ Lightning TR ★ (216)
- ☐ Lion's Chair R ★★★ (74)
- ☐ Master Loony ★★★★ (261)
- ☐ More Sandy Than Kevin ★★ (50)
- ☐ Neutral Zone ★★ (237)
- ☐ On the Road ★★★★ (238)
- ☐ One Time Trick ★ (78)
- ☐ Out of Darkness ★★★ (241)
- ☐ Overnight Sensation ★★★ (112)
- ☐ Puppet Master TR ★★★ (224)
- ☐ Pure Palm ★★★★ (240)
- ☐ Roots Of Madness R ★ (134)
- ☐ Satan's Awaiting ★★ (244)
- ☐ Skinny Sweaty Man ★★ (57)
- ☐ Southern Cross ★★★ (246)
- ☐ Spiritual Warfare ★★★ (244)
- ☐ Ugly As Sin ★ (260)
- ☐ Virtual Beach ★ (277)
- ☐ What's Up Doc? ★★ (143)
- ☐ Woman in the Meadow ★★ (222)
- ☐ Zebra Direct ★★★ (74)

5.11b

- [ ] Attic Antics ★★ (114)
- [ ] Bangstick ★★★ (282)
- [ ] Brain Death R ★★ (247)
- [ ] Bryne's Revenge R ★★ (237)
- [ ] Clam, The ★ (109)
- [ ] Cocaine Crack ★★ (63)
- [ ] Cows in Agony ★★ (144)
- [ ] Crack-A-No-Go ★★★ (246)
- [ ] Crime Wave ★★★ (237)
- [ ] Easy For Some ★★ (270)
- [ ] Equus ★★ (83)
- [ ] Father Mercy ★★ (247)
- [ ] Flash in the Pan TR ★ (216)
- [ ] Flight Of The Patriot Scud Blaster ★★ (50)
- [ ] Flutter By ★ (242)
- [ ] Golden Road, The ★★ (135)
- [ ] Golgotha R ★★★ (110)
- [ ] Harvest ★★ (246)
- [ ] Iron Cross ★★ (237)
- [ ] Jungle Fever ★★ (222)
- [ ] Karot Tots ★★★★ (89)
- [ ] Killer Jism ★★ (260)
- [ ] License To Bolt ★★★ (121)
- [ ] Loony Tunes R ★★ (262)
- [ ] McKenzie's Way ★★ (260)
- [ ] Mister Reach ★★★ (258)
- [ ] Monkey Space ★★★★ (165)
- [ ] Night Crossing ★★ (252)
- [ ] Night Shift ★★★ (244)
- [ ] Panic Seizure ★ (229)
- [ ] Pearl, The ★★★★ (244)
- [ ] Pink Primitive ★★★ (278)
- [ ] Popism R ★★ (80)
- [ ] Ride the Lightning ★★★ (174)
- [ ] Seam of Dreams ★★ (242)
- [ ] Shake 'n Flake ★★ (64)
- [ ] Shoes Of The Fisherman ★★ (109)
- [ ] Skeleton Surfer ★★ (61)
- [ ] Sole Survivor ★★★ (174)
- [ ] Toxic ★★★★ (59)
- [ ] Vomit Launch ★★★★ (63)
- [ ] Wartley's Revenge ★★★★ (109)
- [ ] Windfall ★★★ (256)

5.11c

- [ ] Animation ★★ (270)
- [ ] Baby Fit ★★ (244)
- [ ] Blow Cocoa ★ (155)
- [ ] Dances with Dogs ★★★ (268)
- [ ] Drilling Zona ★★★★ (226)
- [ ] Drug Nasty (a.k.a. Dean's Dream) ★★ (157)
- [ ] Flex Your Head ★★ (153)
- [ ] Jessie's Line R ★★ (242)
- [ ] Moe ★★ (271)
- [ ] Moondance ★★★ (97)
- [ ] Natural Art ★★★ (272)
- [ ] No Pain, No Gain ★★ (127)
- [ ] On Eagles Wings X ★★ (242)
- [ ] Overboard ★★★ (73)
- [ ] Pop Quiz ★★ (224)
- [ ] Private Trust R ★★★ (112)
- [ ] Punk Kid TR ★ (255)
- [ ] Purple Aces ★★ (51)
- [ ] Rainbow's End ★★ (283)
- [ ] Sheepgate, The ★★ (258)
- [ ] Sidewalk Cafe ★★ (222)
- [ ] Silent Holocaust ★★ (243)
- [ ] Spellbound ★★ (277)
- [ ] Squeal and Peal ★★ (235)
- [ ] Strawberry Blonde ★★ (258)
- [ ] Touch ★★ (45)
- [ ] White Dwarf R ★★ (244)

5.11d

- [ ] Almost Nothing R ★★ (95)
- [ ] Astro Monkey (a.k.a. Southwest Corner) ★★★ (157)
- [ ] Boys in the Hood ★★★★ (178)
- [ ] Bushwacker ★★ (273)
- [ ] Cornerstone ★★ (142)
- [ ] Curly ★★★ (270)
- [ ] Deep Splash ★★ (106)
- [ ] Embryonic ★★★ (225)
- [ ] Fugutive, The ★★ (278)
- [ ] Get That Feeling ★★★ (272)
- [ ] Gimme Shelter R ★★ (70)
- [ ] Hieroglyphics ★★★★ (270)
- [ ] Juniper Face ★★ (144)
- [ ] La Vie Dansane R ★★ (237)
- [ ] Lion of Judah ★★★ (240)
- [ ] Minas Morgul ★★ (144)
- [ ] Moving in Stereo ★★★ (157)
- [ ] Northern Lights ★★★ (242)
- [ ] Nuclear ★★★ (244)

5.11d

- [ ] Rawhide ★★★ (106)
- [ ] Ring Of Fire ★★★ (114)
- [ ] Rising Expectations ★★★★ (162)
- [ ] Runaway Bunny ★★ (222)
- [ ] Slow Burn R ★★★ (88)
- [ ] Special Effects ★★★ (282)
- [ ] Suicidal Tendencies ★ (45)
- [ ] Sunshine Dihedral ★★★★ (95)
- [ ] Tarantula ★ (139)
- [ ] Teachers in Space ★★ (240)
- [ ] Tomb of Love ★★★ (273)
- [ ] Up For Grabs ★★★ (58)
- [ ] Wave Of Bliss X ★★★ (123)
- [ ] Yoderific ★★ (123)
- [ ] Zebra Seam ★★★ (74)

5.12a

- [ ] A Little Seduction ★★★ (183)
- [ ] Appian Way ★★ (41)
- [ ] Big Boss Man ★★★ (178)
- [ ] Big Kill, The ★★★ (282)
- [ ] Blade, The ★★★ (62)
- [ ] Blurred Vision ★★ (207)
- [ ] Bohn Street – West Face Cave R ★ (162)
- [ ] Catastrophic Crack R ★★ (81)
- [ ] Celibate Wives ★★★ (270)
- [ ] Chienne No More ★★★ (270)
- [ ] Class Dismissed ★★ (227)
- [ ] Dark Star ★★★ (249)
- [ ] Death Takes A Holiday ★★★ (142)
- [ ] Definitely Cajun ★★★ (181)
- [ ] Dreamin' R ★★★★ (106)
- [ ] Eye Sore (207)
- [ ] Freebase ★★★★ (64)
- [ ] Full Court Press ★★★ (244)
- [ ] Highway To Hell ★★ (53)
- [ ] Howl R ★★ (183)
- [ ] Integrated Imaging ★★★ (270)
- [ ] Judah Direct TR ★★ (240)
- [ ] Just Say Yes` ★★★ (241)
- [ ] Latin Lover ★★★ (92)
- [ ] Neutron Star ★★★★ (249)
- [ ] North Face ★★★★ (160)
- [ ] Northwest Passage A0 ★★★★ (160)
- [ ] Persuasion ★★★ (283)
- [ ] Power Dive R ★★★★ (89)
- [ ] Pubic Luau ★★ (44)
- [ ] Quest To Fire R ★★★ (69)
- [ ] Risk Shy X ★★★ (109)
- [ ] Seasonal Effectiveness Disorder ★★★ (57)
- [ ] Shadow of Doubt ★★★ (144)
- [ ] Shrimpton's Shrine TR ★★ (278)
- [ ] Spank the Monkey R ★★★★ (160)
- [ ] Spartacus ★★ (41)
- [ ] Split Decision ★★★ (240)
- [ ] Stagefright ★★ (126)
- [ ] Strike Force R ★★ (242)
- [ ] Take A Powder ★★★ (95)
- [ ] Torrid Zone ★★★ (222)
- [ ] Try to be Hip ★★★★ (242)
- [ ] Unique Monique ★★★ (272)
- [ ] Up Country ★★★ (272)
- [ ] Wardance ★★★ (278)
- [ ] West Face A1 ★★★★ (159)
- [ ] White Trash ★★★★ (240)
- [ ] Zealot ★★★ (256)

5.12b

- [ ] Blame It On Rio ★★★ (275)
- [ ] Boy Prophet R ★★★★ (106)
- [ ] Catalyst (a.k.a. Child Abuse) ★★★★ (246)
- [ ] Crossfire R ★★★★ (88)
- [ ] Cry of the Gerbil ★★★ (249)
- [ ] Energy Crisis ★★★ (74)
- [ ] Feet Of Clay ★★★ (61)
- [ ] Firing Line ★★★ (92)
- [ ] Flat Earth, The ★ (97)
- [ ] Four Nymphs, The ★★ (222)
- [ ] Gapers on a Tangent ★★★ (272)
- [ ] Ghost Rider ★ (53)
- [ ] Hack Attack (235)
- [ ] Jonny and the Melonheads ★★★ (250)
- [ ] Karate Wall ★★★★ (92)
- [ ] Kilo Watts TR ★★★ (92)
- [ ] Larry ★★★ (272)
- [ ] Latest Rage ★★★★ (92)
- [ ] Liquid Jade ★★★ (50)
- [ ] Magic Light ★★ (73)
- [ ] Masquerade R ★★★★ (252)
- [ ] Mojomatic ★★★★ (270)
- [ ] New Breed Leader ★★★★ (282)
- [ ] Orphan's Cruel ★★★ (278)
- [ ] Peach Nails ★★★★ (282)
- [ ] Peepshow ★★ (92)

5.12b

- ☐ Pubic Luau Direct TR ★★ (44)
- ☐ Rabid ★★ (64)
- ☐ Rambo Roof TR ★★★ (216)
- ☐ Red Lily Q ★★★ (283)
- ☐ Screams and Whispers ★★★ (282)
- ☐ Shark-Infested Waters ★★★★ (282)
- ☐ Sheer Trickery ★★★ (159)
- ☐ Slack Mackerel ★★★ (278)
- ☐ Soft Asylum ★★★ (216)
- ☐ Tears of Rage ★★ (126)
- ☐ Toxic Toprope TR ★★ (59)
- ☐ Unfinished Symphony ★★ (43)
- ☐ Vision ★★ (100)
- ☐ Watts Tots ★★★★ (92)
- ☐ Yellow Fin ★★★ (282)

5.12c

- ☐ Adam Splitter TR ★★ (178)
- ☐ Brazilian Skies ★★★★ (282)
- ☐ Caustic ★ (55)
- ☐ Chain Reaction ★★★ (98)
- ☐ Chillin' in the Penzo ★★★ (278)
- ☐ Choss In America ★★★ (78)
- ☐ Close Shave R ★★★ (162)
- ☐ Da Kine Corner ★★★★ (70)
- ☐ Edge of the Road TR ★★★ (238)
- ☐ Go Dog Go ★★★ (100)
- ☐ Heinous Cling ★★★★ (97)
- ☐ Highway 97 ★★★ (41)
- ☐ La Siesta ★★★ (41)
- ☐ Last Waltz ★★★★ (97)
- ☐ Last Waltz Direct X ★★★ (97)
- ☐ Lords Of Karma ★★★ (137)
- ☐ Low Profile R ★★★★ (92)
- ☐ Made In The Shade ★★★ (136)
- ☐ Midnight Snack ★★ (44)
- ☐ Monkey Boy ★★ (58)
- ☐ Orange Planet (189)
- ☐ Playing in Traffic ★★★★ (276)
- ☐ Pose Down ★★★ (159)
- ☐ Powder In The Eyes ★★★ (95)
- ☐ Resuscitation ★★★ (240)
- ☐ Slay the Dragon ★★★ (283)
- ☐ Stand And Deliver ★★ (67)
- ☐ Steaming Cafe Flirts ★★★ (278)
- ☐ Straight Out of Madras ★★★ (178)
- ☐ Time To Power ★★★ (50)

5.12d

- ☐ Bugging Out ★★★ (178)
- ☐ Choke On This ★★★ (106)
- ☐ Coleslaw and Chemicals ★★ (44)
- ☐ Dandy Line ★★ (74)
- ☐ Kings Of Rap ★★★★ (70)
- ☐ Megalithic ★★★★ (162)
- ☐ Mother's Milk ★★ (50)
- ☐ Peruvian Skies ★★★★ (275)
- ☐ Predator (270)
- ☐ Quickening, The ★★ (53)
- ☐ Sign Of The Times ★ (73)
- ☐ Sketch Pad ★★★ (74)
- ☐ Smut ★★★ (195)
- ☐ Spewing ★★ (54)
- ☐ Split Image ★★★★ (135)
- ☐ Taco Chips ★★★ (73)
- ☐ Urge, The ★★★★ (282)
- ☐ Young Pioneers ★★★ (162)

5.13a

- ☐ Backbone, The ★★★★ (159)
- ☐ Bend Over And Receive ★★ (67)
- ☐ Bongo Fury ★★★ (69)
- ☐ Churning In The Wake ★★★★ (73)
- ☐ Churning Sky ★★★★ (73)
- ☐ Controlled Hysteria ★★★★ (278)
- ☐ Cuban Slide ★★★ (282)
- ☐ Darkness At Noon ★★★★ (97)
- ☐ Feminazis ★★★★ (273)
- ☐ Hot Lava ★★★ (272)
- ☐ Mane Line ★★ (74)
- ☐ Product, The ★★★★ (187)

5.13b

- ☐ Aggro Monkey ★★★ (53)
- ☐ Big Tuna ★★★★ (278)
- ☐ Bum Rush The Show ★★★ (114)
- ☐ Double Stain ★★★ (114)
- ☐ French Connection ★★★ (95)
- ☐ Mega Watts TR ★★★★ (92)
- ☐ Mega Watts TR ★★★ (92)
- ☐ Oxygen ★★★ (70)
- ☐ Power ★★★ (61)
- ☐ Slip Your Wrist ★★★ (61)
- ☐ Smooth Boy ★★★ (106)
- ☐ Snack Crack ★★ (44)
- ☐ Time's Up ★★★ (61)
- ☐ Toes Of The Fisherman (109)
- ☐ Waste Case ★★★★ (71)

5.13

- ☐ 100% Beef (121)
- ☐ Havana Smack (222)
- ☐ Heathen, The (222)
- ☐ Livin' Large (121)
- ☐ Savage Truth (282)
- ☐ Burl Master, The (57)

5.13c

- ☐ Crime Wave ★★★ (53)
- ☐ Just Do It (lower part) ★★★★ (162)
- ☐ Rude Boys ★★★★ (106)
- ☐ Scene Of The Crime ★★★ (53)

5.13d

- ☐ East Face ★★★★ (160)
- ☐ Jam Master J ★★★ (70)
- ☐ Vicious Fish ★★★★ (73)
- ☐ Villain ★★★ (53)
- ☐ White Heat ★★★★ (70)

5.14

- ☐ Badman 5.14a ★★★ (53)
- ☐ Scarface 5.14a ★★★★ (106)
- ☐ To Bolt Or Not To Be 5.14a ★★★★ (95)
- ☐ White Wedding 5.14a ★★★ (53)
- ☐ Just Do It 5.14c ★★★★ (162)

INDEX

Access: It's everybody's concern

the **ACCESS FUND**

THE **ACCESS FUND,** a national, non-profit climbers organization, is working to keep you climbing. The Access Fund helps preserve access and protect the environment by providing funds for land acquisitions and climber support facilities, financing scientific studies, publishing educational materials promoting low-impact climbing, and providing start-up money, legal counsel and other resources to local climbers' coalitions.

Climbers can help preserve access by being responsible users of climbing areas. Here are some practical ways to support climbing:

- COMMIT YOURSELF TO "LEAVING NO TRACE." Pick up litter around campgrounds and the crags. Let your actions inspire others.

- DISPOSE OF HUMAN WASTE PROPERLY. Use toilets whenever possible. If none are available, choose a spot at least 50 meters from any water source. Dig a hole 6 inches (15 cm) deep, and bury your waste in it. *Always pack out toilet paper* in a "Zip-Lock"-type bag.

- UTILIZE EXISTING TRAILS. Avoid cutting switchbacks and trampling vegetation.

- USE DISCRETION WHEN PLACING BOLTS AND OTHER "FIXED" PROTECTION. Camouflage all anchors with rock-colored paint. Use chains for rappel stations, or leave rock-colored webbing.

- RESPECT RESTRICTIONS THAT PROTECT NATURAL RESOURCES AND CULTURAL ARTIFACTS . Appropriate restrictions can include prohibition of climbing around Indian rock art, pioneer inscriptions, and on certain formations during raptor nesting season. Power drills are illegal in wilderness areas. *Never chisel or sculpt holds in rock on public lands, uless it is expressly allowed* – no other practice so seriously threatens our sport.

- PARK IN DESIGNATED AREAS, not in undevelpoed, vegetated areas. Carpool to the crags!

- MAINTAIN A LOW PROFILE. Other people have the same right to undisturbed enjoyment of natural areas as do you.

- RESPECT PRIVATE PROPERTY. Don't trespass in order to climb.

- JOIN OR FORM A GROUP TO DEAL WITH ACCESS ISSUES IN YOUR AREA. Consider clean-ups, trail building or maintenance, or other "goodwill" projects.

- JOIN THE ACCESS FUND. To become a member, *simply make a donation (tax-deductible) of any amount.* Only by working together can we preserve the diverse American climbing experience.

The Access Fund. Preserving America's diverse climbing resources.
The Access Fund • P.O. Box 17010 • Boulder, CO 80308